RECENT ISSUES IN INTERNATIONAL MONETARY ECONOMICS

Studies in Monetary Economics

Editors

KARL BRUNNER
STANLEY FISCHER

Associate Editors

RUDIGER DORNBUSCH
PIETER KORTEWEG
THOMAS MAYER

Volume 2

NORTH-HOLLAND PUBLISHING COMPANY – AMSTERDAM · NEW YORK · OXFORD

Recent Issues in International Monetary Economics

THIRD PARIS-DAUPHINE CONFERENCE ON
MONEY AND INTERNATIONAL MONETARY PROBLEMS
MARCH 28–30, 1974

Edited by

E. CLAASSEN and P. SALIN
Université Paris-IX-Dauphine

1976

NORTH-HOLLAND PUBLISHING COMPANY – AMSTERDAM · NEW YORK · OXFORD

ISBN North-Holland for this series 0 7204 0560 2
ISBN North-Holland for this volume 0 7204 0382 0
ISBN American Elsevier for this volume 0 444 11023 2

Publishers

NORTH-HOLLAND PUBLISHING COMPANY-AMSTERDAM
NORTH-HOLLAND PUBLISHING COMPANY, LTD.-OXFORD

Sole distributors for the U.S.A. and Canada

AMERICAN ELSEVIER PUBLISHING COMPANY, INC.
52 VANDERBILT AVENUE
NEW YORK, N.Y. 10017

Library of Congress Cataloging in Publication Data

Paris–Dauphine Conference on Money and International Monetary Problems, 3d, 1974
Recent issues in international monetary economics

(Studies in monetary economics, v. 2)
Includes index

(1) International finance (2) Balance of payments (3) Foreign exchange problem (I) Claassen, Emil Maria, 1934– (II) Salin, Pascal (III) Title

HG3881.P294 1974 332.4'5 75-44183
ISBN 0-444-11023-2 (American Elsevier)

PRINTED IN THE NETHERLANDS

INTRODUCTION TO THE SERIES

This new series will publish books of interest to students and researchers working in the fields of macroeconomics, monetary theory and policy, banking and the operation of financial markets. It is intended that works of empirical emphasis will be included in the series along with theoretical contributions. Publications will include research monographs and the proceedings of significant conferences. The editors welcome submissions of manuscripts for inclusion in the series.

LIST OF PARTICIPANTS

SVEN W. ARNDT, Crown College, University of California, Santa Cruz
ANTHONY B. ATKINSON, O.E.C.D., Paris
EMIL-MARIA CLAASSEN, Université Paris-IX-Dauphine, Paris
RUDIGER DORNBUSCH, College of Arts and Science, University of Rochester, Rochester
WILLIAM H. BRANSON, Woodrow Wilson School of Public and International Affairs, Princeton University, Princeton
JEAN-CLAUDE CHOURAQUI, Division des Etudes Monétaires de l'O.C.D.E., Paris
MICHAEL CONNOLLY, College of Business Administration, University of Florida, Gainesville
MICHELE FRATIANNI, Centre d'Etudes Economiques, Université Catholique de Louvain, Louvain
JACOB A. FRENKEL, University of Chicago, Chicago
MILTON FRIEDMAN, University of Chicago, Chicago
HELMUT FRISCH, Institut für Volkswirtschaftlehre, Technische Hochschule, Vienna
JACQUES L'HUILLIER, Faculté des Sciences Economiques et Sociales, Université de Genève, Geneva
HARRY G. JOHNSON, London School of Economics, London
RONALD JONES, London School of Economics, London
PETER B. KENEN, International Finance Section, Princeton University, Princeton
SERGE-CHRISTOPHE KOLM, CEPREMAP, Paris
JURGEN KROMPHARDT, Fachbereich Wirtschaftswissenschaften, Justus Liebig Universität, Giessen
MICHAEL KUCZYNSKI, Pembroke College, Cambridge
DAVID LAIDLER, University of Manchester, Manchester
ASSAR LINDBECK, Institute for International Economic Studies, University of Stockholm, Stockholm
FRIEDRICH LUTZ, University of Zurich, Zurich
FRITZ MACHLUP, International Finance Section, Princeton University, Princeton
STEPHEN MARRIS, O.E.C.D., Paris
JACQUES MELITZ, Ministère de l'Economie et des Finances, Paris
ALLAN H. MELTZER, Graduate School of Industrial Administration, Carnegie-Mellon University, Pittsburgh
MARCUS MILLER, Bank of England, London
ROBERT A. MUNDELL, University of Waterloo, Waterloo
BERNARD MUNIER, U.E.R. Expérimental et Pluridisciplinaire de Luminy, Marseille
JOHAN MYHRMAN, Institute for International Economic Studies, University of Stockholm, Stockholm
A.R. NOBAY, University of Southampton, Southampton
LARS NYBERG, Institute for International Economic Studies, University of Stockholm, Stockholm
MICHAEL PARKIN, University of Manchester, Manchester
JOHN PATTISON, O.E.C.D., Paris
DANIEL PILISI, Université Paris-IX-Dauphine, Paris
STEPHEN PORTER, O.E.C.D., Paris
HUBERT PREVOT, Ministère de l'Economie et des Finances, Paris
R. PRISSERT, Centre de Formation de la Profession Bancaire, Nice

JACQUES RUEFF, Académie Française, Paris
PASCAL SALIN, Université Paris-IX-Dauphine, Paris
WOLFGANG STUTZEL, Institut für Geld- und Kreditwesen, Universität des Saarlandes, Saarbrücken
ALEXANDER SWOBODA, Institut Universitaire de Hautes Etudes Internationales, Geneva
DEAN TAYLOR, College of Business Administration, University of Florida, Gainesville
JUAN URRUTIA, Facultad de Ciencas Economicas, Bilbao
STAFFAN VIOTTI, Institute for International Economic Studies, University of Stockholm, Stockholm
JEAN WEILLER, Université Paris-I-Panthéon-Sorbonne, Paris
MANFRED WILLMS, Wirtschafts- und Sozialwissenschaftliche Fakultät, Christian Albrechts Universität, Kiel
FRANCIS WOEHRLING, Commission des Communautés Européennes, Brussels

PREFACE

We are happy to present the second publication of the Paris–Dauphine Conference on Money and International Monetary Problems which took place for the third time at the University of Paris–Dauphine on March 28th to 30th, 1974. The first publication, under the title *Stabilization Policies in Interdependent Economies* and equally produced by North-Holland (1972), was the outcome of the First Paris–Dauphine Conference on Money and International Monetary Problems in March, 1971.

During the last years monetary theory applied to the international economy progressed rapidly as the reader will notice in the first three parts of the book concerned, respectively, with the *Monetary Approach to the Balance of Payments*, the *Portfolio Approach to the Balance of Payments*, and the *Optimum Level of Reserves*. However, facts changed rapidly too and, in particular, the last two parts, on *International Aspects of Inflation* and *Floating Exchange Rates*, take account of them.

This volume of a conference proceedings has two rather unusual features. On the one hand, it is characterized by a series of surveys on four fields in international monetary economics and by a summary statement on recent experiences and the future outlook of floating exchange rates. Under this aspect the book represents a helpful introduction to the most recent developments in international monetary economics. On the other hand, it gathers a great number of most distinguished academic economists of Europe and the United States and the lively discussion among them has been summed up at the end of each paper.

The Third Paris–Dauphine Conference has been made possible by the generous financial help of the Centre National de la Recherche Scientifique to whom we and all participants of the Conference are extremely thankful.

EMIL-MARIA CLAASSEN
PASCAL SALIN

CONTENTS

PART I

The Monetary Approach to the Balance of Payments

Chapter 1.1

MONETARY APPROACHES TO BALANCE-OF-PAYMENTS THEORY*

Alexander K. SWOBODA

Monetary approaches to the balance of payments have recently returned to fashion and to the center stage of controversy in international monetary economics. Some, not to say much, confusion often surrounds the issues at stake. In that context, clarity is not helped by the setting up and triumphant demolition of various straw-men by participants in the debate nor by some of the more unsubtle claims made for "the" theory in the heat of controversy or in the process of attempting to corner part of the market for economic science and revealed truth.

The remarks that follow attempt to offer a more dispassionate view of the rationale for, and methods of analysis used by monetary approaches to balance-of-payments and adjustment theory. One central theme of the argument is that a diversity of theorizing can be characterized as embodying the essential ingredients of a monetary approach but that the way in which these ingredients are combined with each other and with other strands of analysis is sufficiently varied to suggest that there is no such thing as "the" monetary theory of the balance of payments, or, at least, that such portmanteau label can be stuck on a wide variety of bottles. These, however, have some features in common and this paper tries to identify the major ones.

The first section of the paper defines the sense in which the balance of payments is an essentially monetary phenomenon. That does not mean, of course, that theories of the balance of payments need to be monetary; the essential ingredients of monetary theories of payments imbalances are summarized in the second section in terms, mainly, of comparative statics. The

*This paper, or draft, represents a "last-minute" attempt at presenting some general remarks on "the" monetary approach to the balance of payments at the request of the conference's organizers. It includes material developed in connection with a research project on "National Economic Policy and the International Monetary System" at The Graduate Institute of International Studies under a grant from the Ford Foundation, and with the author's lectures on international monetary economics at both the Institute and London School of Economics.

next section is a brief reminder of the fact that international monetary economics is usually not concerned with an analysis of the balance of payments in isolation only but also with its relation with other variables, say, internal balance, the implication being that most models of the adjustment process incorporate non-monetary features as well. Moreover, the *process* of international adjustment is a dynamic one that can be analyzed in terms of comparative statics only in special circumstances; various methods for capturing disequilibrium phenomena such as the balance of payments per unit of time, employment and relative price effects, etc., in a manner that is consistent with a monetary approach are listed in section 4. A simple illustration of some of the main issues this raises is offered in the next section. Some of the approaches that fall under the general heading monetary carry a "monetarist" flavour reminiscent of, but different from, similar strands in general monetary theory and policy analysis; brief remarks on this topic are offered in section 6.

This paper refers only casually and in passing to the abundant literature on money and the balance of payments that has accumulated over the past twenty or thirty years; nor are its many antecedents in earlier writings traced. It thus does not constitute a survey of the literature but, at best, a framework for such a survey.

1. The Monetary Approach to the Balance of Payments

It is necessary to define what one means by the balance of payments before discussing any particular approach to it; more precisely, it is necessary to define what one means by a surplus or deficit in that balance. This is not the place to retrace the many controversies surrounding that concept and the particular meanings attached to it in measures proposed by the IMF (official compensatory financing), Meade, Nurkse, or the U.S. Department of Commerce. The nature of a fixed exchange-rate system suggests that the proper definition is the rate of change in the international reserves of a country, the latter being defined as those assets that are held by the monetary authorities in order to stabilize the exchange rate in the event of an ex ante private excess demand or supply of foreign exchange. Analytically, this concept of the balance of payments is applicable to either an individual or a nation or any other economic unit. The balance of payments of an individual is the variation in his cash account, that is, by definition, the excess of receipts over payments on current plus capital account, exclusive of cash transactions. In the international context, the analogue to the cash account is the international reserve account since variations in the latter reflect the excess of receipts over payments on current plus capital account of the resident public of one country with residents of the rest of the world.

What constitutes cash or money within a given economy is an issue of considerable analytical and empirical difficulty. In the present context and for the case of an individual, the crucial feature of money is that it can immediately be exchanged for goods and other assets at a given price because the same circulating medium is accepted throughout the country. In the international context, it is the intervention of the foreign-exchange stabilization agency that makes it possible to exchange domestic money for foreign goods or assets at a given price. In the first case, there is only one commodity called money; in the second, exchange-stabilization operations endow the total of various national monies linked by fixed rates with the properties of a Hicksian composite commodity. The implications of this proposition will be considered in a later section.

The balance of payments having been *defined* as the rate of change of international reserves (statistically, as the "official settlements" measure of payments imbalances), and this being analogous to the change in the cash or monetary account of an individual, the sense in which the balance of payments is of necessity an essentially monetary phenomenon should immediately be apparent. Consider the balance sheet of the consolidated monetary sector of an open economy:

Assets	Liabilities
D	M
R	

M stands for the stock of money, R for international reserves, D for all other assets net of all other liabilities of the consolidated banking system (monetary authorities plus all other issuers of money). For simplicity and verbal convenience call D the domestic assets of the banking system, which it will indeed be if only the central bank holds foreign assets in the form of international reserves. The balance-sheet identity, $R = M - D$, can be differentiated with respect to time yielding,

$$\mathrm{d}R/\mathrm{d}t = \mathrm{d}M/\mathrm{d}t - \mathrm{d}D/\mathrm{d}t. \tag{1}$$

Since $\mathrm{d}R/\mathrm{d}t$ is nothing else but the balance of payments and is identically equal to the difference between the rate of change of the money stock and the rate of domestic credit creation it is obvious that the balance of payments is a monetary phenomenon. I would, and will to some extent, argue that explicit and systematic recognition of this simple truism goes a long way towards pointing to correct solutions to important policy and theoretical problems.

Still, arguing that the balance of payments is a monetary phenomenon does not, in itself, imply that all approaches to the balance of payments must, of necessity, be monetary. Consider an economy where the only objects of exchange are goods and money (there is no market for other capital assets). Then, the following statement about the balance of payments, B,

$$B/P = Y - E, \tag{2}$$

where Y is real national income, E is real total expenditure of residents, both being defined ex post and as rates of flow per unit of time, and P is the price level, is just as much of a correct identity as (1). Correct theorizing about Y and E (the absorption approach) should, in this simple case, produce exactly the same result as correct theorizing about D and M.[1] But it is sometimes all too easy to make mistakes when one neglects to focus attention on the monetary nature of the balance of payments as expressed in identity (1), if only as a check on the logical consistency of one's theory, particularly in the theory of policy. For $\mathrm{d}M/\mathrm{d}t$ expression (1) can be re-written as

$$\mathrm{d}M/\mathrm{d}t = \mathrm{d}R/\mathrm{d}t + \mathrm{d}D/\mathrm{d}t, \tag{3}$$

and equilibrium in a stationary open economy cannot obtain as long as (3) is not equal to zero which, with zero rate of expansion of the domestic assets of the monetary sector, requires a zero balance of payments. But this is a topic for balance-of-payments *theory*, the subject of the next section, rather than of balance-of-payments identities, the subject of the present one.

2. The Monetary Approach to Balance-of-Payments Theory

Although there is no such thing as "the" monetary theory of the balance of payments, one can recognize some common features that characterize what we may call monetary approaches to balance-of-payments theory. These approaches recognize the fundamental importance of identity (1) above and attempt, through varied means, to turn it into a theory. To do so they characteristically postulate a stable demand for money function, a stable supply of money function, and define a number of relationships (equalities) that must hold in equilibrium. The bare bones of such a theory for a stationary economy will incorporate, among others, the following types of equation:

[1]This point is explicitly recognized and further discussed in Mundell (1968, ch. 10, pp. 150–151).

$$M_d = f(.\,.\,.\,.\,.), \tag{4}$$

$$M_s = g(D + R), \quad g' > 0, \tag{5}$$

$$B \equiv dR/dt, \tag{6}$$

$$M_d = M_s. \tag{7}$$

Equation (4) states that the demand for money is a stable function of a number of variables, say, income, the rate of interest, etc. Equation (5) specifies the money supply process: the money supply is a stable and increasing function of the stock of international reserves and domestic assets of the banking system; in the simplest model, D is treated as an exogenous variable, though it need not be. Equation (6) defines the balance of payments. Equation (7) specifies the equilibrium condition of the model.

What can such a simple (and incomplete) model teach us? Not much, in one sense, and quite a lot in another. If we are dealing with a stationary economy the arguments of the money demand function cannot be changing in equilibrium. In equilibrium, therefore, the demand for money is given; since, in equilibrium, it must be equal to the supply of money, the latter cannot be changing. Hence, for a given value of D, R cannot be changing, and therefore equilibrium requires that the balance of payments be zero. This means that in terms of the comparative statics analysis of full equilibrium positions, the question "what is the effect of an exogenous policy or autonomous disturbance on the balance of payments" is either senseless or can be given a very simple answer: zero.[2]

Three (inter-related) implications of this characterization of monetary approaches to balance-of-payments theory are worth noting at this stage. First, unless continuously rekindled (usually by growth in the arguments entering the demand for money function or continuous changes in D in a stationary economy – the latter being, however, incompatible with a fixed stock of reserves in the world economy in the long run), balance-of-payments disequilibria must, of necessity, be of a transitory nature. This is, of course, the conclusion that Johnson reaches in his celebrated 1958 "Towards a General Theory of the Balance of Payments",[3] and is but a reflection of the working of the automatic specie–flow mechanism. Second, the monetary approach to

[2]In addition, if it is possible to postulate that a zero balance of payments is compatible, other things equal, with one level of the money stock only – a postulate that can be derived from most theories of the *small* open economy – the money stock becomes a fully endogenous variable in equilibrium and, in equilibrium again, monetary policy only affects the stock of reserves. See, for instance, Swoboda (1973a).

[3]See Johnson (1968, pp. 153–168).

balance-of-payments theory does *not* tell us what the balance of payments is at any single point of time. It tells us what the stock of reserves must be in the final equilibrium, and hence whether it has increased or decreased over the adjustment period, given the initial stock. It thus predicts that, over that period, surpluses must have exceeded deficits (or vice-versa) to cumulate into an increase (decrease) in the stock of reserves. Third, the monetary approach, in its simplest form, is a theory about the long run, in that it makes predictions as to the outcome of disturbances *after* full adjustment has taken place.

The above discussion is in full accord with Michael Mussa's excellent characterization of what he calls "the monetary approach to the balance of payments". In his view, three main features define this approach. It emphasizes the fact that the balance of payments, defined as the official settlements account is an essentially monetary phenomenon, uses the demand for money and the money supply process as tools to organize thought concerning the balance of payments, and concentrates on the longer-run consequences of policy changes for the balance of payments.[4] As Mussa emphasizes, this does emphatically *not* mean that real factors do not affect the balance of payments (or vice-versa) but simply that, to do so they must of necessity affect the demand and supply of money.

3. A Monetary Approach to What?

The first concern of a monetary approach, as defined above, is, of course, to provide an explanation of the balance of payments. However, as remarked previously, it actually provides, in its simplest version, an explanation of the equilibrium distribution of money *stocks* and hence, given domestic assets of national banking systems, of the equilibrium distribution of reserve *stocks* in the world economy. Balance-of-payments *flows* occur in disequilibrium only and their analysis is the object of the next section.

Practitioners of the approach do not limit the focus of their attention to the balance of payments alone. It also provides a framework that seems natural for the analysis of a number of phenomena that, in the context of an open economy, appear to be essentially monetary in nature. Among these, the analysis of devaluation and of inflation figure prominently. Devaluation is seen as an essentially monetary phenomenon since it consists in changing the rate at which the authorities stand ready to buy and sell international reserves against domestic cash balances; it can be analyzed as a tax on cash balances held in

[4]See Mussa (1973, pp. 7–21).

domestic currency, a form of debasement of the currency as classical writers were wont to recognize. Inflation (or a variation in the general price level) is essentially monetary since it is defined as a steady rise in the price of goods in terms of money. In an international context inflation must be discussed at two levels: that of the determination of the world price level and that of the connection between the world and national price levels.

In addition, international monetary economics has long been concerned with a number of problems of which the balance of payments is only part. Prominent among those are problems of macroeconomic policy in the open economy, neatly, though not entirely accurately, summarized in the analysis of conflicts between internal and external balance. It is obvious that an equilibrium analysis limited to stock equilibrium in the money market of the type outlined above is inadequate to deal with that type of problem. A monetary approach, however, can contribute to the elucidation of such questions, if only because it helps define the long-run equilibrium towards which the economy tends. The basic tool of analysis, however, is general equilibrium analysis (even if only of the limited macroeconomic type) including some definition of disequilibrium states. The contribution of the monetary approach is three-fold: it helps define the long run, emphasizes the monetary nature of payments adjustment, and characterizes payments imbalances as *disequilibrium* phenomena, the subject to which the next section is addressed.

4. Payments Adjustment: Comparative Statics, Stability and Dynamics

The balance of payments is a flow per unit of time which, according to a monetary approach, is equal to zero in equilibrium in a stationary economy. From a policy point of view, however, the rate of flow per unit of time and, hence, the chronological time span needed for equilibrium to be restored is of crucial importance. This section discusses the respective roles of three main methodological tools of economic theory – comparative static, stability, and dynamic analysis – in explaining the process of international payments adjustment.

The theory of payments adjustment is concerned with the following question: supposing that equilibrium in an open economy is lost, how is equilibrium regained? The answer given by economic theory comes in three parts: comparative statics tells us what the final effect of a disturbance (or policy) will be by comparing the final with the initial equilibrium after full adjustment has taken place; stability analysis tells whether the final equilibrium, under some dynamic postulate, is likely to be reached; dynamic analysis is concerned with determining the *process* of adjustment itself. Each of these methods plays a crucial, though often misspecified, role in various approaches to balance-of-payments theory and, more generally, to the theory of adjustment in open economics.

A monetary approach was described in terms of comparative statics in section 2 above. The main conclusions that can be derived from the approach, under the assumptions of perfectly fixed exchange rates, stationary economies (including stationary expectations), and stability, can be listed briefly. (1) An increase in domestic credit in any one national economy results in an increase in the world money stock and hence an increase in world money income. (2) Such an increase will decrease the stock of reserves of the country initiating the change in inverse proportion to its size and, hence, increase the stock of reserves of the rest of the world; in the limit where the ratio of the size of the country to that of the rest of the world tends to zero – the small country assumption – the money supply of the initiating country does not change in equilibrium which implies that the stock loss of reserves is equal to the domestic assets increase. (3) A change in real variables, say, an exogenous change in the terms of trade due to a change in tastes, productivity, or commercial policy, will affect the balance of payments in so far as it affects the demand for money relative to the supply forthcoming from domestic sources, a cumulative surplus in the balance of payments emerging if the demand increases relative to the supply, and vice-versa for a deficit. (4) In general, the comparative statics of a monetary approach assert that the nominal supply of money in an open economy is an endogenous variable in equilibrium through the balance-of-payments adjustment process that establishes the equilibrium distribution of the world money supply.[5]

These conclusions are valid only if the system under analysis is stable. Typically, two conditions turn out to be crucial or necessary, though not always sufficient, in stability analysis of monetary models of the balance of payments: there must be a direct relationship between the balance of payments and the rate of change of the money supply and an increase in the money stock must, other things equal, deteriorate the balance of payments.[6] The first of these is usually incorporated in the analysis as one of the dynamic postulates under

[5]Thus, in a monetary approach, the equilibrium distribution of *specie* (reserves) is replaced by the equilibrium distribution of *money stocks*. The two statements are equivalent (a) if specie is the circulating medium or (b) if the ratio of reserves to money stock is kept constant. In any event, once the distribution of money stocks *and* of national stocks of other than international reserve assets are known the distribution of foreign-exchange reserve stocks is also known.

[6]Swoboda (1972a, 1973a).

which stability is examined, the second usually turns out to be an explicit or implicit necessary condition for stability.

Stability analysis plays a very important role in adjustment theory, a role that extends beyond simply checking whether comparative statics analysis is justified in the first place. For it gives a first glimpse into the economics of adjustment *processes* and is intimately bound with the issue of the automaticity of international adjustment. That automaticity coupled with a statement of the conditions under which money is neutral – to be interpreted as not affecting real variables in equilibrium – is what allows us to develop and have confidence in the powerful results of the barter theory of international trade. Stability of the payments adjustment process is usually sufficient to insure neutrality of money in most models of the *small* open economy under fixed exchange rates, of whatever ilk, since, for these models, given real behaviour function, a unique level of the money stock is compatible with payments equilibrium.[7] For a large open economy, or for the world economy as a whole, neutrality of money obtains under basically the same conditions (essentially price and wage flexibility and absence of distribution effects) as in the analysis of the closed economy.

Though full-equilibrium comparative static methods and stability analysis can achieve powerful results and insights in adjustment theory, they fail to capture several characteristics of the adjustment process that are theoretically relevant and of crucial interest to the policy-maker. These characteristics include the balance of payments at any point in time, output and employment effects, relative price effects (between imports and exports – the terms of trade, traded and non-traded goods, capital and labor, etc.), sectoral production shifts in the transition from disequilibrium to equilibrium, the behaviour of the structure of the balance of payments, and the determinants of the actual speed of adjustment, to cite but a few. Ideally, these effects should all be captured simultaneously in a full non-tatonnement disequilibrium model of simultaneous adjustment in all of the economy's relevant markets. Given existing analytical knowledge and tools, such a model is not feasible or interpretable at present. Much of the history of adjustment theory can be viewed as an attempt to find the strategic simplifying assumptions needed to gain some insight into these disequilibrium effects without specifying a full general disequilibrium model, or to reduce the latter to manageable proportions.

A number of such assumptions have been used by practitioners of a monetary approach to the balance of payments – by which, I mean mainly

[7]See footnote 2, above.

those who would recognize that the balance of payments must of necessity be equal to zero in a stationary economy and in the absence of a steady rate of change of the domestic assets of the consolidated banking system. These assumptions vary depending on the problem at hand and take on specific forms that differ from author to author. Six principal types can, however, be identified.

(1) Comparative equilibrium dynamics. This type of analysis has been used extensively by Mundell and later Johnson to analyze the relationship between growth, inflation, the *rate* of domestic credit expansion and the change of reserves per unit of time.[8] Since we are dealing with non-stationary economies, the balance of payments need not be zero in equilibrium. The latter is characterized by the equality of actual and anticipated *rates of change* (of prices and incomes) rather than of levels, and by the equality of both stock and flow demand and supply of money. The balance of payments is simply equal to the difference between the rate of growth of the demand for money and the rate of growth of the supply provided by domestic sources. In addition, goods markets are continuously cleared in the sense that production is exogenously determined and the world rate of inflation is that which equates the growth of the world demand for money with the growth of the world supply of money; hence, as there are only money and goods in the model (or the securities market is allowed to clear), the goods market is in (inflationary) equilibrium. The path of adjustment from one dynamic equilibrium to another is not specified in detail, though Mundell does show what the required interest-rate and real-balance stock adjustments are.

(2) Impact and long-run effects. After a disturbance, the payments adjustment mechanism will restore long-run equilibrium. It is sometimes convenient to define the impact effect of a disturbance as its impact on relevant variables before adjustment through the balance of payments has begun, that is, at the initial stock of reserves and money. The advantage of this procedure is that it defines the initial state of disequilibrium which, whatever specific adjustment mechanism is postulated, will then have to be eliminated. It also allows one to capture the disequilibrium value of the balance of payments, the level of income, relative prices, and so on, at one specific point of the adjustment process. For instance, the impact effect of a devaluation is seen, on certain assumptions, as a reduction in real cash balances given the stock of nominal balances which produces a reduction of desired expenditure, the effect of

[8]See, in particular, Mundell (1968, ch. 9; 1971, ch. 15), and Johnson (1973). See also Komiya (1969).

which on the terms of trade and the relative price of traded and non-traded goods can be analyzed in a manner analogous to that used in the theory of international transfers.[9] The definition of impact effects, however, requires exact specification of what markets are allowed to clear and what behaviour functions are satisfied at the point of impact. Various alternative specifications have been proposed, some of which are listed below.

(3) Quasi-equilibrium points. Quasi-equilibrium points as defined by Mundell and this writer are characterized by the fact that the public's behaviour functions are satisfied in all markets, even though there might be a payments disequilibrium through the systematic intervention of government authorities.[10] For instance, in the context of an *IS–LM* model suitably modified to take the openness of a small economy into account, a quasi-equilibrium may be defined as a situation in which the money supply is being kept constant over time by the monetary authorities through neutralization operations at a level that implies a payments disequilibrium. This, in a sense, is an impact effect that is made to last through the neutralization operation. The goods market clears in that desired aggregate expenditure (absorption plus the balance of trade) is equal to income produced and the stock demand for money and securities is equal to the supply. There is, however, a flow excess private supply of securities matched by a flow private excess demand for foreign exchange; these are, however, instantaneously satisfied by the authorities who prevent at every moment of time these disequilibria from affecting the goods and money markets by absorbing the flow excess supply of securities at the existing rate of interest through their neutralization operations and supplying the foreign exchange at the existing rate of exchange through their exchange stabilization operations.[11] This type of analysis makes it possible to capture a disequilibrium situation with equilibrium methods; it makes it possible, for instance, to say something definite and logically consistent on the effects of a temporary increase in the money supply (which we know is untenable in the long run if only because reserve stocks are finite) on the level of income, prices, the interest rate, the structure of the balance of payments, and the rate of deficit or surplus per unit of time.

(4) Stock-adjustment models. Comparative dynamic equilibrium models give us a view of payments imbalances that is of an essentially equilibrium

[9]This is of course one of the standard procedures used by Dornbusch in his work on devaluation. See, for instance, Dornbusch (1973a, 1973b).

[10]See Swoboda (1972b), and also Mundell (1961).

[11]See Swoboda (1972b, p. 169, footnote 9).

nature; impact effect analysis captures one point of the adjustment process, long-run analysis the end point of that process; quasi-equilibrium analysis yields conclusions about disequilibria when automatic adjustment processes are prevented from operating by the action of monetary authorities. None of these captures the full adjustment process. Stock-adjustment methods of analysis, pioneered by Prais, advocated by Mundell and Johnson, and extensively developed by Dornbusch represent one way of tracing out the full path of adjustment to an initial disequilibrium.[12] The natural breeding ground of such methods is one where money and goods are the only objects of exchange, a stock disequilibrium in the money market having as a counterpart an adjustment of expenditure on goods relative to income. On the assumptions that goods markets clear (in the sense that ex ante expenditure plans are always realized), i.e., that there is continuous and instantaneous flow equilibrium but that stock disequilibria in the money market are not necessarily adjusted to instantaneously, it is possible to trace out the full path of adjustment once the speed of adjustment of desired flows to stock disequilibria is known. This makes it possible to specify the behaviour of the money supply, the balance of payments and the price level at every point of time in an otherwise frictionless world (goods arbitrage is assumed to be instantaneous). An archetype of such an adjustment model for a single small open economy is presented in the next section as it illustrates, in simple fashion, several of the issues discussed so far. Note, finally, that the comparative equilibrium dynamics models described in subsection (1) above can be interpreted as special cases of the stock-adjustment class of models, namely, models where continuous and instantaneous equality between the stock demand and supply for money is maintained through a speed of adjustment that tends towards infinity.

(5) Other adjustment mechanisms. Obviously stock-adjustment mechanisms are not the only ones that can be envisaged. In particular, once assets other than money are introduced the stock-adjustment method of analysis loses some of its simplicity and, hence, some of its appeal. Among the many alternatives, only one, proposed by Michael Mussa, will be mentioned here. In Mussa's analysis, which assumes capital immobility but national securities markets, changes in the rate of interest rather than discrepancies between actual and desired cash balances determine the relationship between income and domestic expenditure and hence the balance of trade and payments at any point of time.[13] Instantaneous short-run equilibrium is defined by flow equilib-

[12]See Prais (1961), Mundell (1968, ch. 8; 1971), Johnson (1973), and, among others, Dornbusch (1973a, 1973b).

[13]See Mussa (1973, section III).

rium in the goods market and stock equilibrium in the asset market, the latter being achieved through variations in the rate of interest. This does not imply, however, that the balance of payments is in equilibrium since income and expenditure are equal only in the long run. In the short run where they are not the payments disequilibrium implies a change in the money supply which, in turn, continuously changes the rate of interest, the balance of payments at any point of time being determined by the instantaneous equilibrium conditions mentioned above. Mussa's analysis is thus very similar to that of quasi-equilibrium points, the difference being that, no neutralization policies being assumed, adjustment is allowed to take place on a path each point of which corresponds to the quasi-equilibrium point associated with a particular but continuously changing money stock.

(6) Non-clearing markets. All the methods mentioned above represent ways of analyzing disequilibrium phenomena. In one sense, the simplest way of representing disequilibrium is to assume that some market does not clear. This is, of course, the simplest justification for the assumption of a rigid money wage and/or money illusion in the labour market as a tool of analysis of unemployment in Keynesian theory: we recognize that, basically, unemployment is a disequilibrium phenomenon but the difficulty of modelling it formally as such suggests the short-cut of postulating some type of rigidity or irrationality that enables us to analyze it with the help of comparative-statics, equilibrium, methods. This same device can be used in the analysis of adjustment in an open economy. For instance, postulating a rigid money wage, or immobility of some factor as between sectors, makes it possible to derive conclusions as to the employment effects of the monetary process of international adjustment. One crucial implicit assumption of this type of analysis is that the long run relevant to completion of the payments adjustment process is shorter than the long run over which the market that is assumed not to clear in the analysis will, eventually, clear.

All six of these methods of analysis are theoretically correct, logically consistent, though not necessarily empirically relevant, ways of capturing selected features of the adjustment process. In addition, however, the literature is replete with theoretically incorrect attempts to achieve similar results. Prominent among these is the so-called elasticities approach to adjustment and devaluation at least in its more naive standard versions. Besides sometimes confusing rather hopelessly stability and comparative statics issues, that approach commits one cardinal sin in terms of the foregoing discussion. It fails to recognize that asking the question "what is the effect of a devaluation on the balance of trade (or payments)" defined as a flow per unit of time cannot have any other answer than zero in full equilibrium; and, as a corollary, it entirely fails to specify the nature of the disequilibrium state under which the question may have a meaning. This is not to deny that some such specification, for which the results of that approach would hold, can be found; in fact, Kemp and Dornbusch, among others, have provided such a specification.[14] It requires so many special assumptions as to be near to senseless, assumptions that would most probably be deemed absurd by proponents of the elasticities approach. Neither is it to deny that changes in relative prices, and hence some elasticities, may play an important role in the adjustment process; all that is claimed is that the latter must first be specified in logically consistent fashion.

5. A Simple Illustration

To illustrate the fairly abstract and general discussion so far, consider, as an example, a very simple model of the expenditure-flow mechanism of adjustment. That model, though exceedingly simple, does bring out some of the essential features of a monetary approach to balance-of-payments theory and of the role of comparative statics, stability, and dynamic (of the stock-adjustment variety) analysis. It is also my favourite introduction to automatic adjustment mechanisms and to the theories of devaluation and imported inflation.

Assume a small country (or region) which produces and consumes a good that is also produced and consumed abroad and whose foreign-currency price is fixed in the international market. Given the exchange rate, the domestic money price of goods is also given: goods arbitrage is instantaneous and perfect. Assume no capital movements; goods and money are the only objects of exchange. Production (national income) is given and remains at full employment. Expenditure (or absorption in Alexander's terminology) is a direct function of the level of income and of the stock of real balances. Algebraically,

$$B = \bar{Y} - A, \tag{8}$$

$$A = A(\bar{Y}, M/P^*), \tag{9}$$

$$B = (1/P^*)\,\mathrm{d}R/\mathrm{d}t = (1/P^*)\,\mathrm{d}M/\mathrm{d}t, \tag{10}$$

where symbols are defined as before ($A = E$), and P^* is the exogenously given price level.

[14]See Kemp (1964, pp. 235–236).

Equation (8) states that the balance of payments in real terms is equal to the fixed level of real income, $\bar{Y}$, minus absorption. Equation (9) specifies the expenditure function. Equation (10) states that the balance of payments in real terms is equal to the rate of change of reserves (in real terms) and that the latter is itself equal to the rate of change of real money balances. This last simplification, which can easily be relaxed, is appropriate, at a given exchange rate, (a) in a world where gold, or the foreign currency, is the circulating medium, or (b) in which the authorities keep the domestic assets of the banking system constant.[15]

The *comparative statics* of this model are not difficult to establish once it is recognized that the economy cannot be in equilibrium unless $\mathrm{d}M/\mathrm{d}t = 0$. Equations (8)–(10) immediately suggest that, given P^* and $\bar{Y}$, equilibrium obtains at that stock of real balances for which absorption is equal to income. An exogenous increase in the price level or Humean cut in the money supply leads to a decrease in absorption relative to income and hence a payments surplus. "Money flows over the exchanges" until the previous equilibrium is re-established. These points are illustrated in figure 1.

Suppose that initial equilibrium at E is disturbed by a cut in the supply of money that lowers the stock of real balances to $(M/P^*)_1$. This tax on cash balances reduces absorption relative to income by CD, the balance-of-

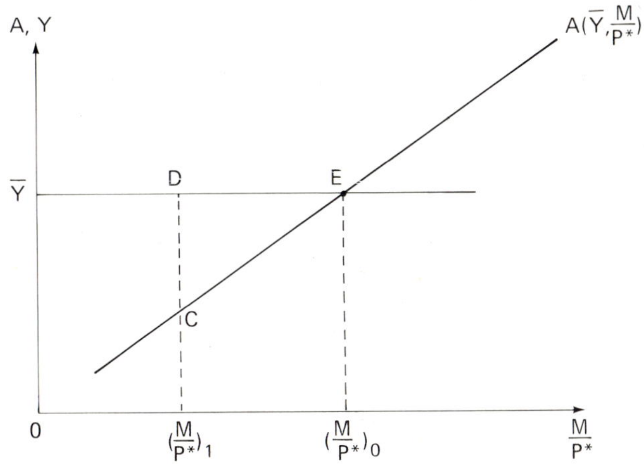

FIGURE 1

[15]Were the monetary authorities to maintain a fixed ratio of foreign reserves to the money stock, equation (10) would be rewritten as $(1/P^*)\mathrm{d}M/\mathrm{d}t = mB$, where m is the reciprocal of the ratio of foreign reserves to the money stock.

payments surplus. Equilibrium will be restored when the cumulated surplus has returned the stock of real balances to $(M/P^*)_0$, and payments equilibrium again obtains. Intuitively, stability of this adjustment process requires simply a positive functional dependence of absorption on the stock of real balances and a positive association of payments surpluses with rates of change of the stock of nominal balances. We only know, however, that the system will tend to move from a disequilibrium at $(M/P^*)_1$ to equilibrium at E – and the cumulated surplus this implies – but not how long this will take nor what the rate of flow of reserves will be at every point of the process.

To get a more precise view of the adjustment *process*, and a more formal statement of stability conditions, requires a more specific formulation of the expenditure function. This is provided by

$$A = Y + \alpha(M_s/P^* - M_d/P^*). \tag{11}$$

Equation (11), a specific version of (9), states that expenditure depends on income and the discrepancy between actual (M_s/P^*) and desired (M_d/P^*) real cash balances. When that discrepancy is equal to zero all income is spent; when it is not the economy adjusts expenditure relative to income in order to bring actual stocks of cash assets in line with desired stocks. An excess of cash balances is gotten rid of by spending in excess of income, and vice-versa. The coefficient of adjustment has the dimension 1/time to make equation (11) dimensionally consistent and indicates how rapidly stock adjustment is taking place. In a closed economy we would postulate that money income (prices with full employment) adjusts to the difference between expenditure and income; in a small open economy under fixed exchange rates it is the stock of nominal balances that adjusts.

To complete the formal analysis it is convenient to specify the desired stock of real balances as being proportional to income or expenditure, the motivation behind this specification being the usual transactions motive.[16] Assume that the desired stock of real cash balances is a constant fraction, k, of income, $\bar{Y}$. (Assuming instead that it is a constant proportion of A would only complicate the algebra slightly without affecting qualitative results in this simple case.) The solution for $M(t)$ can then be derived as follows:

$$\dot{M}/P = B = \bar{Y} - A = -\alpha(M/P^*) + \alpha k\bar{Y}, \tag{12}$$

$$\dot{M} + \alpha M = \alpha k\bar{Y}P = \alpha M^*, \tag{13}$$

[16]It could be argued that assuming the stock of real balances to be a function of income versus expenditure reflects a view of money as factor of production, and as medium of exchange in transactions, respectively. It can also be shown that equation (11) can be derived from an intertemporal maximization model on a number of simplifying assumptions. See, inter alia, Dornbusch's dissertation on this point.

$$M(t) = C\,e^{-\alpha t} + M^*, \tag{14}$$

$$M(t) = [M_0 - M^*]e^{-\alpha t} + M^*, \tag{15}$$

where $M^* = k\bar{Y}P^*$ denotes the equilibrium stock of nominal balances.

The adjustment process, depicted by equation (15), is stable if $M(t)$ converges to its equilibrium value M^* as $t \to \infty$, i.e., if $\alpha > 0$. In other words, stability requires simply that expenditure rise when there is an excess stock supply of cash balances. The adjustment process, represented by equation (15), is depicted in figure 2.

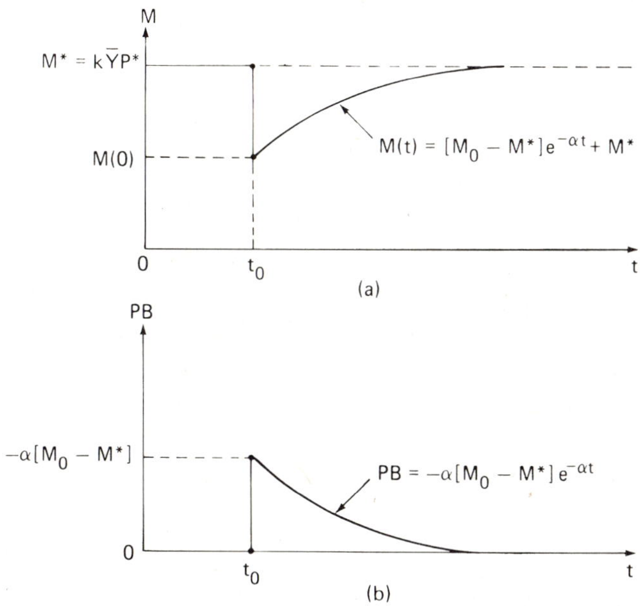

FIGURE 2

Figure 2a shows the path of the money supply, figure 2b that of the balance of payments in nominal terms, the one being, of course, the mirror image of the other. Given an initial disturbance, say an exogenous decrease in the money stock from its initial steady state level M^* to M_0, the economy adjusts by cutting expenditure, this cut generating a payments surplus that eventually restores the equilibrium money stock M^*. The magnitude of the initial surplus depends directly on the magnitude of the initial disturbance and on the speed of adjustment α. Through time the surplus progressively declines to zero as the discrepancy between actual and desired stocks diminishes.

In spite of its simplicity, this model puts into sharp relief several features of the monetary process of adjustment under fixed exchange rates that were discussed in previous sections of this paper:

(1) Given reasonable behaviour parameters, stability ("automaticity") of the monetary process of adjustment under fixed exchange rates is insured and money is neutral in equilibrium. Two features of the model are crucial in generating this result: the link between excess cash balances and the balance of payments (provided by $\alpha > 0$) and the link between the latter and the money supply [equation (10)].

(2) This automaticity implies that a payments deficit or surplus is transitory in nature.

(3) The automaticity of the adjustment mechanism can be broken if money does not matter for real behaviour ($\alpha = 0$) or if some mechanism prevents payments imbalances from affecting the money stock (e.g., neutralization policy, open-market purchases or sales of goods in the simple model).

(4) This model of adjustment is equally applicable to an individual economic unit or region in a single currency area or to a small country under fixed exchange rates (through the Hicksian composite commodity feature of all monies under fixed rates mentioned above). From a theoretical point of view, this implies that many problems of international adjustment under fixed rates can be studied in a manner similar to distributional problems within a single monetary economy. In fact, the model proposed above is very similar in spirit to that used by Archibald and Lipsey in their discussion of Patinkin's work.[17]

(5) This simple model can be used as a first approach to devaluation and imported inflation considered as "essentially" monetary phenomena. Devaluation is treated as an exogenous cut in real cash balances brought about not by a cut in nominal balances but by a rise in the domestic price level since $P^* = eP^*_f$, where e is the price of foreign in terms of domestic currency and P^*_f is the given foreign price level, under the assumption of goods market arbitrage. The adjustment process is exactly that described above though care must be taken to specify the impact effects on the money supply of the devaluation gain of the

[17]Archibald and Lipsey (1958).

monetary authorities on the existing stock of reserves. Similarly, imported inflation can be assimilated to an exogenous rise in the foreign price level, P_f^*.

(6) The very simplicity of the model suggests extensions that may be useful. For instance, introduce non-traded goods in addition to traded ones into the model. The domestic price level can then diverge from the foreign one during the adjustment period. To capture its evolution over time, however, requires careful specification as to which markets clear instantaneously and which do not and as to the exact dynamic postulates that are assumed. Similar remarks apply to variations in employment and the terms of trade and to the introduction of securities, expectation functions and two-country models, to mention but a few relevant extensions.

6. Monetary and Monetarist Approaches

Some practitioners of a monetary approach to the balance of payments have been dubbed "monetarists", sometimes in praise, sometimes in deprecation. Though it may be useful heuristically to distinguish among various shades and hues of monetarism in the approach to international monetary theory and policy, the categories one can define are less personal than analytical and practical, the same individual indulging in various types of theorizing depending on the purpose at hand.

Of all the characteristics that may be associated with various grades of monetarism, two might be emphasized in the present context: emphasis on the relevance of "long-run" equilibrium results and a conviction that monetary impulses are the crucial variable to focus on when dealing with a number of problems and policy issues. Thus in monetarist analysis in an international context, the equilibrium distribution of reserves, or the equilibrium rate of change of reserves in a dynamic equilibrium context, are emphasized as relevant to policy and are usually determined by fairly simple specifications of money supply processes and of the demand for money. Moreover, in analyzing problems such as the balance of payments, inflation, devaluation, and the determination of equilibrium exchange rates, monetary impulses are assumed to dominate "real" factors, often by postulating that the latter are determined exogenously with respect to the analysis at hand. Note, however, that the mechanism of transmission postulated in simple analysis of the open-economy monetarist variety is quite different from that envisaged by closed-economy "monetarists". Consider, for instance, inflation. In a closed-economy context the rate of monetary expansion is the exogenous variable (or impulse); in the open-economy context, prices rise abroad, squeeze real cash balances at home, and then the money supply expands.

The more monetarist version of monetary approaches to adjustment is useful in a number of contexts on analytical, empirical, and policy levels.

At an analytical level, equilibrium monetary models, of the stationary or dynamic kind, help focus on a number of broad issues that would be too difficult to analyze fully in full disequilibrium models as, for instance, the determinants of the overall rate of inflation in the world economy under fixed exchange rates. No one would deny that inflation rates can, and do, to some extent, differ in the short run; but, in a rapidly inflating world, factors such as differential productivity growth in traded and non-traded goods are dominated by general monetary impulses and the equilibrium models help capture a basic aspect of inflationary reality. To take another example, the possibility of postulating an equilibrium distribution of the world money stock (viewed as a Hicksian commodity) makes it possible to analyze financial interconnections among countries in a simple and intuitively appealing way. It is, to my knowledge, the only method of analyzing, for instance, Eurodollar creation which treats the reserve base of the Eurodollar system as an endogenous variable.[18] And it might not be that irrelevant to a short chronological run when capital mobility is considered. Other problems of course require disequilibrium methods.

At an empirical level, the distinction between equilibrium and disequilibrium models has an important bearing on the proper econometric method to be used. If the long run of monetarist theory occurs in a short lapse of chronological time, then ordinary methods of estimation are appropriate. For some phenomena there is evidence that this is approximately the case. For others, recourse to disequilibrium methods of estimation and specification of disequilibrium adjustment models is the appropriate way of confronting theory with empirical evidence.[19]

At a policy level, the relevance of monetarist prescriptions depends in part on how long the long run is. This is largely an empirical question. However, emphasis on the long run is also warranted by the insistence on the transitional nature of many of the real effects of monetary impulses. There are two justifications for this insistence on the relevance of equilibrium models for economic policy. The first, and in my view quite objectionable one, is that the short run does not matter. The second is that grievous policy mistakes are

[18]See Swoboda (1973b, pp. 149–168).

[19]Disequilibrium methods are emphasized in the project on "International Monetary Theory and Policy" directed at the London School of Economics by H. G. Johnson under a grant from the British Social Science Research Council, and at the Geneva project mentioned in the liminary footnote.

likely to be made through concentration on the short and at the expense of the long run; there are laws of economics that cannot be ignored. And with that view, I cannot but agree.

References

Archibald, G. C. and R. G. Lipsey, 1958, Monetary and value theory: A critique of Lange and Patinkin, Review of Economic Studies 26, pp. 1–22.

Claassen, E. and P. Salin, eds., 1972, Stabilization policies in interdependent economies (North-Holland, Amsterdam).

Connolly, M. B. and A. K. Swoboda, eds., 1973, International trade and money (Allen & Unwin, London).

Dornbusch, R., 1973a, Currency depreciation, hoarding and relative prices, Journal of Political Economy 81, pp. 893–915.

Dornbusch, R., 1973b, Devaluation, money, and nontraded goods, American Economic Review 68, no. 5, pp. 871–880.

Dornbusch, R., 1973c, A note on exchange rates in a popular model of international trade, mimeo.

Johnson, H. G., 1968, International trade and economic growth (Allen & Unwin, London).

Johnson, H. G., 1973, The monetary approach to balance of payments theory, in: Connolly–Swoboda (1973).

Kemp, M., 1964, The pure theory of international trade (Prentice-Hall, Englewood Cliffs).

Komiya, R., 1969, Economic growth and the balance of payments: A monetary approach, Journal of Political Economy 77, pp. 153–170.

Mundell, R. A., 1961, The international disequilibrium system, Kyklos 14, pp. 154–172. Reprinted in: Mundell (1968).

Mundell, R. A., 1968, International economics (Macmillan, New York).

Mundell, R. A., 1971, Monetary theory: Inflation, interest, and growth in the world economy (Goodyear, Pacific Palisades).

Mussa, M., 1973, Tariffs and the balance of payments: A monetary approach, Discussion Paper 73–13 (Department of Economics, University of Rochester).

Prais, S. J., 1961, Some mathematical notes on the quantity theory of money in an open economy, IMF Staff Papers 8, pp. 212–226.

Swoboda, A. K., 1972a, On limited information and the assignment problem, in: Claassen–Salin (1972).

Swoboda, A. K., 1972b, Equilibrium, quasi-equilibrium, and macroeconomic policy under fixed exchange rates, Quarterly Journal of Economics 86, pp. 162–171.

Swoboda, A. K., 1973a, Monetary policy under fixed exchange rates: Effectiveness, the speed of adjustment and proper use, Economica 40, no. 158, pp. 136–154.

Swoboda, A. K., 1973b, Eurodollars and the world money supply: Implications and control, in: A. K. Swoboda, ed., Europe and the evolution of the international monetary system (Institut Universitaire de Hautes Etudes Internationales/Sijthoff, Geneva/Leiden).

Chapter 1.2

SUMMARY OF THE DISCUSSION ON SWOBODA

Fritz MACHLUP, *Chairman*

Rudiger Dornbusch mentioned that in models where money is the only asset, it is possible to have a real balance effect but not a wealth effect. Equation (2) in the paper of Alexander Swoboda can be considered as a reduced form of a model with a non-traded asset. Thus, the government can determine the rate of interest and, thereby, expenditures. Equation (2) is thus compatible with a very Keynesian view of the transmission mechanism. If bonds were traded, there would be problems since the stock of reserves would be endogenous at some point of time.

Alexander Swoboda answered *Marcus Miller* that it is possible to reduce some problems to the only consideration of the demand for and supply of money, as it is the case of the problem of the balance of payments. Obviously there are arguments in the demand for money function and one may want to explain these arguments.

He also agreed with Rudiger Dornbusch that if domestic and foreign bonds are added to the model, things become more difficult; however, the official settlements balance of payments, i.e., the rate of change of reserves will still be equal – in a reduced form sense – to the difference between the rate of monetary expansion and the rate of expansion of assets other than foreign exchange reserves in the central bank balance sheet.

Agreeing that he had not specified in detail whether there was a disequilibrium type of real balance effect, or a wealth effect or any other sort of effect, he also underlined that this does not really matter in a one-good, one-asset model. These things certainly matter in other sorts of models including assets other than money. One could say that, in contrast to monetary approaches, monetarist approaches focus on long-run equilibrium phenomena and the dominance of monetary impulses. In the long run one has not to worry about adjustment and it would be wrong to accuse monetarists of misspecifying adjustment. They only assume that adjustment has taken place or is taking place rapidly or they do so for some bits of analysis which would be too difficult otherwise.

Jacob Frenkel re-emphasized Alexander Swoboda's statement. In his opinion the monetary approach has more to say than just care about long-run equilibrium situations. If one wants to know what happens to money, he must look at money. If one wants to know whether the balance of payments is an equilibrium story, a short-run story, a long-run story, he cannot escape the point that there is an excess flow demand for money which is exactly the channel through which the balance of payments operates. This is a true statement, almost a truism. What we have to explain is what determines this excess flow demand, whether it is in equilibrium, in long-run or short-run equilibrium, and there is certainly no necessity to call a zero balance of payments an equilibrium, contrarily to the widely held opinion inherited from mercantilists.

Rudiger Dornbusch agreed with these views, but he also pointed out that there are people who believe that harvest failures are responsible for inflation or balance of payments problems, so that it is important to look whether monetary irregularities are caused by real facts which would appear as arguments of the demand for money or by the authorities. The real debate is not mainly about the fact that money is related to the problems of inflation and the balance of payments but about the empirical evidence of the origin of monetary impulses.

William Branson explained that, when breaking the balance of payments into several items – current account, capital account, reserves, one ought to get the same result when studying the sum of the two first ones and when studying the third one. The monetary approach implies looking at the excess demand for money, which is called the balance of payments. But, as Rudiger Dornbusch underlined, one can ask which are the arguments in the demand for money function. And these arguments might be the same in the excess demand for commodities function and the excess demand for securities. Thus, the monetary approach does add to what was already known by looking at the two first items in the balance of payments. Therefore, what can we gain by just saying "the balance of payments is essentially a monetary phenomenon" and then taking the monetary approach?

Jacob Frenkel answered that it is just quite more natural and simpler to look at the monetary item than at all kinds of goods. This choice also has a policy implication, since you often hear that, in order to "improve" the balance of payments, you must favour exports and cut imports, for instance by subsidizing exports and imposing tariffs on imports; and we know that the only thing to do is to affect the excess flow demand for money.

For *Harry Johnson* too the policy aspect of the problem is important and he recalled all the debates which took place in the United States – and in other countries as well – attributing the balance of payments deficit to causes as foreign aid, overseas military spending or private investment, and arguments according to which balance-of-payments problems could be cured by cutting foreign military expenditures or some other sorts of expenditures. The eminent economists who gave such advices forgot the monetary side of the analysis. Certainly real analysis seems to be something you can hold in your hand and you can always think of exports increasing or imports decreasing. The real problem is to see the connection between these activities and what happens to other expenditures in the general equilibrium context. That is why monetary – and not necessarily monetarist – approaches are important: they do not worry about how much is spent on such or such item, but are concerned with general equilibrium. Now, the role attributed to money – i.e., monetarist versus non-monetarist approaches – is a matter of taste or of particular problems.

Rudiger Dornbusch declared he did not feel himself far from William Branson's position. In fact, the adjustment process can work primarily through the trade account or the capital account. The monetary approach really is a short-cut to find out what should be the answer.

Wolfgang Stützel expressed the belief that balance-of-payments problems have something to do with the fact that there are different currencies in the world, so that a country has a surplus when others desire its currency. Is not the monetary approach applicable to a one-currency world? This approach explains regional problems not international problems. Should there not be a demand for money function for each different currency?

Alexander Swoboda answered that fixing the exchange rate means creating a one-currency world, if the fixing is believed and effective, so that the total of the world money supply can be treated as a Hicksian composite good, without relative price changes between the composing currencies. In fact, the distribution of the sub-goods is very important, but the distribution of these different currencies within the total called the world money supply under fixed exchange rates will be resolved by the interaction of the demand for any particular currency and the supply of it. But the supply of any particular currency has two components, that which is produced domestically and that which is produced by the private economic agents themselves through trade with other countries and which is satisfied by the exchange stabilization interventions of the central banks, which translate the excess demands for any particular type of money into a reserve flow and hence an increase in the money supply, unless they carry out neutralization policies. Thus the approach does deal with a world of several paper currencies. But it also tells that one might not succeed in fixing the exchange rate, because if one does certain things one runs out of reserves or eats up the reserves.

About the Branson–Frenkel–Dornbusch exchange *Alexander Swoboda* said that we ought to stop talking about monetary approaches or the monetary approach to the balance of payments, since it is a totally redundant thing. The only reason why there is so much discussion about it is the mistakes made by practitioners of other approaches, for it is very easy to do bad mistakes when trying to redress a balance of payments if one forgets that the balance of payments is essentially a monetary phenomenon. We ought to kill the monetary approach and just talk about correct and incorrect approaches to the balance of payments.

Chapter 2.1

ADJUSTMENT MECHANISMS AND THE MONETARY APPROACH TO THE BALANCE OF PAYMENTS: A DOCTRINAL PERSPECTIVE

Jacob A. FRENKEL*

> *"The intellectual standard of this world-wide discussion had been inferior to that of the polemics on related matters between the classical economists in the early part of the 19th century. . . . Consequently, old mistakes were made over and over again, and much effort was wasted in rediscovering truths long familiar."*
>
> IVERSEN (1935, p. 259)

1. Introduction

The above quote from Carl Iversen written in the mid-thirties seems also appropriate today – forty years later – when a revival of the monetary approach to the balance of payments is taking place.

This paper explores what earlier generations of economists have said about what is known now as the monetary approach to the balance of payments.

The monetary approach to the balance of payments can be summarized by the proposition that the balance of payments is essentially a monetary phenomenon. The "balance of payments" refers to items that are "below the line", that is, to the "money account". In general, the approach emphasizes the role of the budget constraints and views the various accounts of the balance of payments as the "window" through which the various excess flow demands and supplies are cleared. Accordingly, surpluses in the trade account or in the capital account reflect excess flow supply of goods or of securities, respectively, and a surplus in the money account reflects an excess flow demand for money. Consequently, in analyzing the rate of change of international reserves (the money account), the monetary approach focuses on

*I am indebted to Rudiger Dornbusch for comments and suggestions. In revising the paper I have benefited from useful suggestions of Ronald Jones, Fritz Machlup, Jorge Marquez-Ruarte, Don McCloskey and Jacques Melitz. Given the doctrinal nature of the present paper I hasten to add that responsibility is mine alone.

the determinants of the excess flow demand for money.[1] Clearly, a consistent use of the budget constraint implies that the money account can be analyzed in terms of the determinants of all of the other accounts. As is usual, the balance of payments is analyzed as the sum of the balances on current and on the capital accounts. The monetary approach, however, recommends an analysis in terms of the direct behavioral relationships, that is, in terms of the excess flow demand for money.[2] Since the money account is determined by the excess flow demand for money, it is clear why it is viewed as a monetary phenomenon.[3]

The sum of the deficit in the capital account and the surplus in the money account measures the rate at which assets are being accumulated. This rate must be equal to the excess of income over expenditures on goods and services – the surplus in the current account. The absorption approach emphasizes the relationship between expenditures and income and thereby emphasizes the rate of accumulation or decumulation of assets (securities plus money). The monetary approach emphasizes a sub-set of the spectrum of assets – the rate of change in the monetary stock. The two main reasons for emphasizing this sub-set of assets are that (i) the monetary authorities, pegging the rate of exchange, are interested in the rate of change of the stock of international reserves, and (ii) monetary policy determines directly the rate of change of the domestic source component of the monetary base and thereby the flow supply of money. The assumption that the rate of hoarding is determined by a set of variables that are independent of the rate of change of the domestic source component of the monetary base implies that the money account of the balance of payments is influenced directly by monetary policy.

Accumulation or decumulation of assets depends on the relationship between expenditures and income and does *not* depend on the *composition* of expenditures either between exportables and importables or between commodities that, given the price structure, are tradables and non-tradables. Consequently, the monetary approach to the balance of payments (as well as the absorption approach) place less emphasis on the role of *relative* prices (which affect the composition of expenditures). On the other hand the general price *level* which determines the real value of nominal assets is emphasized along with other aggregate quantities that are relevant for macro-economic analysis.[4]

[1]For lucid summaries of the basic features of the monetary approach, see Johnson (1972) and Mussa (1976).

[2]For an analysis along these lines, see Frenkel (1971).

[3]The interrelationships among the various approaches that are implied by a consistent use of the budget constraint are analyzed in Johnson (1958) and Mundell (1968).

[4]Rudiger Dornbusch has forcefully emphasized these issues in a series of papers; see for example Dornbusch (1973, 1976a, 1976b). See also Mundell (1971).

Much of the current analysis of the adjustment mechanism emphasizes the role of relative prices either of exportables in terms of importables or of non-traded in terms of traded goods. It is typically alleged that these are the mechanisms envisaged by the classics. These, however, are not the central mechanisms that are emphasized by the monetary approach. The purpose of this paper is to argue that (i) the monetary approach was the dominant approach throughout the last two centuries, and (ii) it is inaccurate to describe the classical and the neoclassical adjustment mechanism as being based on changes in relative prices. In fact, many of these writers argued explicitly that one should de-emphasize the role of relative prices in the adjustment mechanism.

The outline of the paper is as follows: Sections 2 and 3 contain a simple model of the natural distribution of wealth and the adjustment mechanism. Section 4 discusses banking policies and section 5 contains some concluding remarks.

2. A Simple Model of the Natural Distribution of Wealth

Assume a fully employed stationary economy. The stationary state can be characterized by two equilibrium conditions: (1) The existing stocks of assets are held in the desired proportions – stock equilibrium, and (2) savings are zero so that income equals expenditures, that is, the supply of goods equals the demand for goods – flow equilibrium.

It is assumed that there are two assets, namely, equities and real cash balances. The desired ratio (l) of real cash balances (m) to the real value of equities is assumed to depend on the rate of interest (r),

$$m = l(r)y/r = \psi(r)y; \qquad \partial l/\partial r < 0, \quad \partial\psi/\partial r < 0; \qquad \psi(r) \equiv l(r)/r, \tag{1}$$

where y is the given number of permanent income streams (as determined by full employment), and y/r is the equity value of the claims on these streams. The real value of assets (a) is

$$a = m + y/r. \tag{2}$$

When portfolio equilibrium obtains, we can substitute (1) into (2) to yield

$$a = [1 + l(r)]y/r = \theta(r)y; \qquad \theta(r) \equiv [1 + l(r)]/r; \qquad \partial\theta/\partial r < 0, \tag{3}$$

and thus resulting in the reduced form

$$a = a(y, r); \qquad \partial a/\partial y > 0, \quad \partial a/\partial r < 0. \tag{3'}$$

Savings are viewed as the means by which desired assets are attained. It is assumed that individuals have a desired level of assets $\tilde{a}$ and that the rate of saving depends positively on the discrepancy between the desired and the actual levels,

$$S = F(\tilde{a} - a); \qquad \partial F/\partial(\tilde{a} - a) > 0, \quad F(0) = 0. \tag{4}$$

For simplicity it is assumed that the desired level of assets is constant (although the analysis would be unaffected if it were assumed that $\tilde{a}$ is an increasing function of the rate of interest). Thus,

$$S = G(a) = S(y, r); \qquad \partial G/\partial a < 0, \quad \partial S/\partial y < 0, \quad \partial S/\partial r > 0. \tag{5}$$

This saving function is a reduced form in the sense of embodying the assumption that portfolio equilibrium obtains. In the stationary state, the desired size of the portfolio is attained, savings are zero and income equals expenditures.

In describing the equilibrium of the world economy, it is assumed that there is free and frictionless trade in both securities (equities) and goods. It is also assumed that domestic and foreign equities are perfect substitutes in the portfolios of assets. Consequently, at each point of time the rates of return on domestic and foreign securities must be equalized as must the money price of goods in terms of each currency (the purchasing power parity). By an appropriate choice of units, the exchange rate is chosen to be unity.

Before proceeding with the analysis it is noteworthy that purchasing power parity and the equality of rates of return on securities due to international arbitrage are in the spirit of the classical and the neoclassical schools. Mill's description of the determination of the terms of trade is emphasizing the fact that:

> "By the fall, however, of cloth in England, cloth will fall in Germany also ... By the rise of linen in Germany, linen must rise in England also." [Mill (1874, Essay I)]

This was later formulated by Whewell (1856) as the "principle of international prices". Similarly, Wicksell emphasized that:

> "[t]here could not possibly exist different prices of the same commodity on both sides of the frontier ..., difference of prices in the two countries, [w]ould be theoretically impossible and practically confined between very narrow limits." [Wicksell (1918, p. 405)]

The "law of one price" is guaranteed by competition as was emphasized by Laughlin:

> "[t]he action of the international markets, with telegraphic quotations from every part of the world, precludes the supposition that gold prices

> could in general remain on a higher level in one country than another (cost of carriage apart), even for a brief time, because, in order to gain the profits merchants would seize the opportunity to send goods to the markets where prices are high." [Laughlin (1903, p. 369)]

Hawtrey, who interprets Ricardo's mechanism of adjustment as relying on the failure of arbitrage, argues that this mechanism could not prevail at modern times, and was in fact obsolete in Ricardo's time:

> "[t]he revolutionary changes in the means of communication . . . have unified markets to such a degree that . . . [t]here is practically, a single world market and a single world price . . . It was fallacious to explain the adjustment wholly in terms of the price level. There was even at that time [Ricardo's time], an approximation to a world price." [Hawtrey (1932, p. 144)]

On the whole, the reliance on the failure of arbitrage is probably a misinterpretation of the classical doctrine [Viner (1937, p. 317)].

Similarly, the concept of a unified world capital market and the role of capital mobility were an integral part of the classical school. Statements as "capital is becoming more and more cosmopolitan" [Mill (1893, book III, ch. XVII)], and "a cosmopolitan loan fund exists which runs everywhere as it is wanted, and as the rate of interest tempts it" [Bagehot (1880)] were common.

In fact, securities are in a "continual course of transition from places where the rate of interest is high to places where it is low" [Fullerton (1845, p. 149)].

Consequently, in what follows it is assumed that world markets are unified. Given the world's nominal supply of cash balances and the number of permanent income streams, long-run equilibrium is attained when in *each* country savings are zero and the actual stocks of assets are held at the desired proportions. Associated with this equilibrium there is a *unique* distribution of these assets between the two countries.

The number of permanent income streams in the world is assumed to be given by $\bar{y}$,

$$\bar{y} = y + y^*, \tag{6}$$

where y^* denotes the number of income streams owned by the rest of the world. Thus, at the stationary state we have

$$S(y, r) = 0, \tag{7}$$

and

$$S^*(y^*, r) = S^*(\bar{y} - y, r) = 0, \tag{8}$$

where an (*) denotes variables and functions relating to the foreign country.

The stationary state of the world is depicted in figure 1. The two loci in panel I describe combinations of rates of interest and numbers of domestically owned permanent income streams for which the domestic and the foreign rates of savings are zero [equations (7) and (8), respectively].[5] Long-run equilibrium is attained at point Q where the rate of interest is r_0 and the domestic ownership of permanent income streams is y_0. The foreign ownership of permanent income streams is $y_0^* = \bar{y} - y_0$. Given the equilibrium distribution of ownership of income streams, the real value of world's cash balances is determined in panel II which shows the world's liquidity preference schedule. In analogy to equation (1), the foreign demand for real cash balances is

$$m^* = \psi^*(r)y^*, \tag{9}$$

and thus the equilibrium world liquidity preference is

$$m + m^* = \bar{m} = [(1 - \lambda_0^*)\psi + \lambda_0^*\psi^*]\bar{y}, \tag{10}$$

where

$$\lambda_0^* = y_0^*/\bar{y}.$$

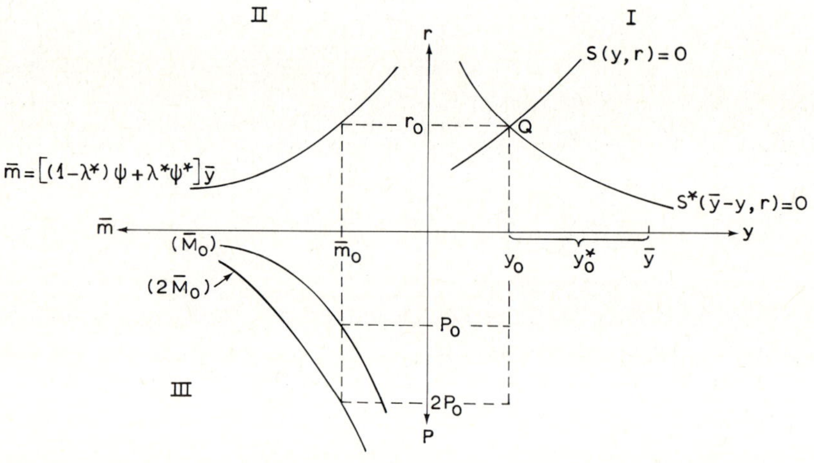

FIGURE 1

[5]For the sake of simplicity the role of the investment function is de-emphasized in the present analysis. It could be introduced by drawing investment schedules in the (y, r) space. At the stationary state the capital stock that is located in each country is such that the rate of net investment is zero. These stationary capital stocks determine the number of the world permanent income streams. For an explicit incorporation of the investment function, see Frenkel and Rodriguez (1975).

Since the equilibrium rate of interest is r_0, world holdings of real cash balances are $\bar{m}_0$. Panel III describes the determination of the world price level P. Given the world nominal money stock $\bar{M}_0$, the world real stock $\bar{m} = \bar{M}/P$ is related to the price level by a rectangular hyperbola in panel III. Thus, the equilibrium price level which is associated with $\bar{M}_0$ is P_0.

Consider now a once and for all doubling of the world nominal money stock. In terms of figure 1 this change is described by the second rectangular hyperbola in panel III corresponding to $2\bar{M}_0$. Since the system is homogeneous of degree zero in the nominal money stock and the price level, it is clear that the real variables are not affected in the new long-run equilibrium and thus the price level rises equiproportionally to $2P_0$. An important feature which is emphasized by figure 1 is that the relevant variable for the equilibrium of the long run is the *world* money stock. Therefore, it is unnecessary to specify the location from which the increased stock originates. The specification of the source of the increased money stock is, however, crucial for the analysis of the adjustment mechanism which is dealt with in the next section.

Since in equilibrium each country holds the desired stock of assets and those are held in the desired proportions, it follows that the unique distribution of world ownership of permanent income streams is associated with a unique distribution of holdings of cash balances. This distribution is illustrated in figure 2 which is drawn for the equilibrium ownership of permanent income streams. Panels I and III show the simultaneous long-run stock and flow equilibria in both countries, panel II shows that the rates of interest are equalized, and the angle γ in panel IV describes the unique equilibrium

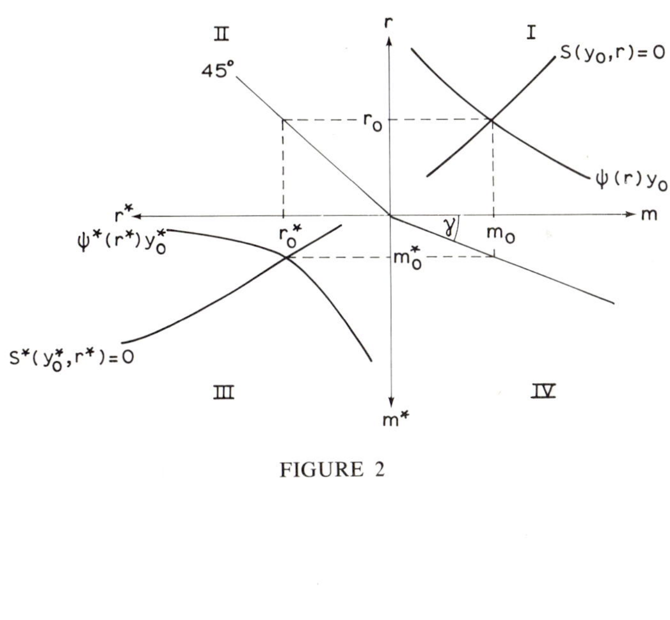

FIGURE 2

distribution of real cash balances. Since commodity prices are equalized by arbitrage (and the exchange rate is unity), γ also describes the distribution of nominal cash balances.

The natural distribution hypothesis is among the central propositions of the classical doctrine. It appeared in print more than 250 years ago in an impressive pamphlet by Gervaise:

> "A nation cannot retain more than its natural proportion of what is in the world and the balance of trade must run against it." [Gervaise (1720, p. 12)]

The natural distribution was regarded as almost a law of nature:

> "All water, wherever it communicates, remains always at a level. Ask naturalists the reason; they tell you, that were it to be raised in any one place, the superior gravity of that part not being balanced must depress it." [Hume (1752, pp. 62–64)]

The mechanism which assures this unique distribution is competition and arbitrage as stated by Ricardo:

> "Gold and silver having been chosen for the general medium of circulation, they are, by the competition of commerce, distributed in such proportions amongst the different countries of the world as to accommodate themselves to the natural traffic." [Ricardo (1821, p. 123)]

The explicit recognition of the neutrality of money from the world standpoint was provided by Mill:

> "A newly acquired stock of money would diffuse itself over all countries [until] money had diffused itself so equally that prices had risen in the same ratio in all countries, so that the alteration of price would be for all practical purposes ineffective." [Mill (1893, book III, pp. 194–195)]

The important implication of the natural distribution hypothesis is that under a fixed exchange rate the supply of money to any one country is endogenous. The channel through which this endogeneity is effected is the balance of payments. Consequently, the credit policy of the banking system is linked directly to the balance of payments, and the adjustment mechanism can not be properly analyzed without focusing on monetary policy and the resultant excess flow demand or supply of money.

3. The Adjustment Mechanism

The foregoing analysis emphasized that in the long run the natural distribution is unaffected by monetary changes, irrespective of their origin. It follows therefore that during the transition period a country whose money stock has risen beyond the "natural share", will have to run deficits in its balance of payments since this is the only way by which the initial distribution can be restored. Therefore, one of the basic principles of the classics is the notion that there can be no deficit unless there is an excess supply of money:

> "when the balance of trade runs . . . against a nation, we may conclude its denominator exceeds its natural proportion." [Gervaise (1720, p. 15)]

Similarly, Ricardo's statement to this effect is:

> "The temptation to export money in exchange for goods, or what is termed an unfavourable balance of trade, never arises but from a redundant currency." [Ricardo (1846, p. 267)]

The international mobility of capital and the condition for portfolio equilibrium play an important role in the transmission mechanism. Consider again an equilibrium which is disturbed by a doubling of the world money supply originating in the home country. At the initial equilibrium rate of interest and prices, both the value of the home country's assets and the ratio of money to equities exceed the desired quantities. Instantaneous short-run stock equilibrium requires that assets be held in the desired ratio and thus that the home country raise instantaneously its net creditor position by exchanging with the rest of the world part of the increased money stock for securities. Since at the initial prices and rate of interest there is excess world demand for securities and excess world supply of money, the rate of interest declines and the price level rises. Such a mechanism is described by Mill. A once and for all rise in the money stock:

> "would create a sudden fall in the rate of interest, which would probably send a great part of the twenty millions of gold out of the country as capital. . . . All prices would rise greatly." [Mill (1893, book III, pp. 195–196)]

The change in price level and the rate of interest is determined by the condition for instantaneous flow equilibrium according to which world income must equal world expenditures. Since domestic asset holdings exceed the desired level, expenditures will exceed income. Prices and the rate of interest will have to change in order that the value of foreign assets decline to a level which induces an excess of foreign income over expenditures just equal to the excess of domestic expenditures over income. Since along the path towards the new stationary state the home country decumulates assets, it must run a current account deficit.[6]

The determinants of the changes in prices and the rate of interest along the path can be best illustrated by analyzing the effects of an international transfer. Consider a once and for all change in the distribution of assets from the foreign towards the domestic country. The receiving country will instantaneously arrive at the desired composition of assets by exchanging some of the transferred assets for others; this takes place independently of the asset composition of the transfer. Consequently instantaneous portfolio equilibrium is attained when the home country holds more securities and more cash balances. The higher holdings of domestic assets and the lower holdings of foreign assets lowers home savings and raises foreign savings. Thus, both savings schedules in panel I of figure 1 are shifted to the left. The instantaneous equilibrium requires that world income equals world expenditures or equivalently, that world savings are zero,

$$S(y, r) + S^*(\bar{y} - y, r) = 0. \tag{11}$$

Since the transfer induces larger holdings of domestic securities, the rate of interest will rise or fall depending on the extent of the relative shifts of the savings schedules. Similarly, since the transfer reduces the ratio $\lambda^*(= y^*/\bar{y})$, the world liquidity preference schedule will rise or fall depending on whether $\psi \gtreqless \psi^*$. The relationship between the world rate of interest and the distribution of ownership of income streams can be ascertained from the flow equilibrium (11),

$$\frac{\mathrm{d}r}{\mathrm{d}y} = \left(\frac{\partial S^*}{\partial a^*}\,\theta^*(r) - \frac{\partial S}{\partial a}\,\theta(r)\right) \Big/ \left(\frac{\partial S}{\partial a}\frac{\partial \theta}{\partial r}\,y + \frac{\partial S^*}{\partial a^*}\frac{\partial \theta^*}{\partial r}\,y^*\right). \tag{12}$$

Equation (12) clarifies that the effects of the transfer depend on (i) the domestic and foreign marginal propensity to save and (ii) the domestic and foreign liquidity preference functions (which determine θ and θ^*). Clearly, as is usual in the analysis of the transfer problem, when these behavioral relationships are the same the transfer will have no effect on the rate of interest and on the price

[6]An algebraic formulation of the exact path is complicated due to the fact that along the path there are both adjustments that occur through time and adjustments that occur instantaneously in attaining a continuous portfolio balance. In view of these technical difficulties, previous treatments of the transition have resorted to a more simplified framework. It was either assumed that the home country is small and thus faces given world prices and rate of interest [Frenkel and Rodriguez (1975)] or that the country is large but that some of the assets are non-tradables [Dornbusch (1976a, 1976b)].

level. Generally, the fact that the model contains assets in addition to goods multiplies the number of the transfer criteria [Mussa (1971)]. The role of the velocities of circulation and the multiplicity of the transfer criteria were clearly recognized by Viner:

> "Adjustment to a disturbance will depend on the velocities of money in the two areas as well as on the manner in which the demand for different classes of commodities behave as the amounts of money are varied." [Viner (1937, p. 369)]

Similarly, the relationship between the world rate of interest and the distribution of ownership of income streams can be described in terms of elasticities as

$$\frac{\hat{r}}{\hat{y}}=\frac{(1-\lambda^*)\varepsilon^*-\lambda^*\varepsilon}{\lambda^*(\varepsilon\eta+\varepsilon^*\eta^*)}, \tag{12'}$$

where (ˆ) denotes a proportional change (e.g., $\hat{r}=\mathrm{d}r/r$), and where

$$\varepsilon=\frac{\partial S}{\partial a}\frac{a}{S}<0,$$

the elasticity of the saving rate with respect to assets,

$$\eta=\frac{\partial \theta}{\partial r}\frac{r}{\theta}<0,$$

the elasticity of the ratio a/y with respect to the rate of interest. ε^* and η^* are the corresponding elasticities of the foreign country. Equation (12′) clarifies the role of the relative size of the countries. Indeed, Robertson (1931) analyzes the transfer problem in terms of the relative size of the countries.[7]

To study the influence of the size of the countries consider the special case in which both countries have identical elasticities so that $\varepsilon=\varepsilon^*$ and $\eta=\eta^*$. In this case equation (12′) becomes

$$\frac{\hat{r}}{\hat{y}}=\frac{(y/y^*)-1}{2\eta}\gtrless 0 \quad \text{as} \quad y\lesseqgtr y^*. \tag{12''}$$

In this special case the world liquidity preference is independent of the distribution of assets and therefore the price level and the rate of interest must

[7]"The degree of burden depends primarily not on the *absolute* movement of gross income in Germany but upon their *relative* movements in the two countries . . . the amount of money in 'America' is likely to be large as compared with that in 'Germany', the proportionate rise in gross incomes in 'America' will, in fact, be small as compared with the proportionate fall in gross incomes in 'Germany'." [Robertson (1931, pp. 175–176)]

move in the same direction along the path of adjustment. Figure 3 illustrates this special case. Panel I describes the locus of short-run equilibria along which world income equals world expenditures, panel II describes the world liquidity preference, and panel IV describes the price level associated with alternative short-run equilibrium distribution of income streams.

So far the only price variable playing a role in the adjustment process has been the *price level* – the price of a composite good. Clearly, a meaningful definition of such a composite good requires that relative prices are unchanged. If much of the adjustment mechanism can be described in terms of transitory divergences between expenditures and income aimed at correcting asset positions, then indeed changes in relative prices should not be overemphasized. Relative prices will change as a result of different marginal spending propensities. Since there is no presumption of differences in these propensities, it seems that changes in relative prices should not be treated as the core of the adjustment process.

The question whether the adjustment mechanism operates through changes in relative prices (movements along demand curves) or through direct shifts of the demand due to changes in expenditures relative to income has been a major issue of debate. The accepted view, however, is that:

> "From Hume on, there was general agreement that some or all types of disturbances in international balance would result in changes in the terms of trade, and that these changes would contribute to the restoration of equilibrium." [Viner (1937, p. 319)]

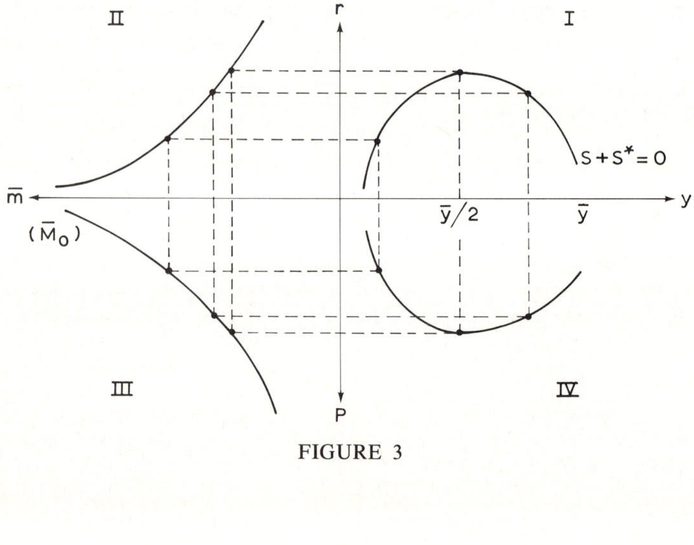

FIGURE 3

There exist, however, evidence which casts some doubt on Viner's unequivocal evaluation of the role that relative prices played in the classical doctrine.

One of the very first writers to emphasize the role of divergences between expenditures and income without mentioning relative prices is Gervaise. A rise in the monetary stock raises expenditures and induces a deficit. The process continues until the excess stock is diffused, and simultaneously, once the stock is reduced to its equilibrium level, expenditures and income coincide:

> "If a nation adds to its denominator . . . [t]he rich . . . consume more labour [goods] than before; . . . so that there enters in that nation, more labour than goes out of it . . . [The deficit] is paid in gold and silver until the denominator be lessen'd, in proportion to other nations; which also, and at the same time, proportions the number of the poor [production] to that of rich [consumption]." [Gervaise (1720, p. 7)]

If the balance of payments is viewed as a monetary phenomenon it is reasonable to apply the general principles of adjustment to monetary changes. This approach was adopted in the early 1730's by one of the originators of the theory of adjustment to monetary changes:

> "The increase in money will bring about an increase in expenditure . . . states which have acquired a considerable abundance of money ordinarily import many things from neighboring countries where money is scarce." [Cantillon (1755, pp. 263–267)]

Even Hume and Mill who are usually quoted as the main proponents of the relative price theory have made statements to the contrary. Hume in "*Of the jealousy of trade*" (1758) writes:

> "The inhabitants, having become opulents and skillful, desire to have every commodity in the utmost perception; . . . they make large importations from every foreign country." [Hume (1752, pp. 79–80)]

Similarly, Oswald in a private correspondence with Hume on the 1752 draft of "*Of the balance of trade*" commented on the apparent de-emphasis of the direct expenditure effects and suggested that:

> "The increased quantity of money . . . might, and certainly would, be sent to purchase . . . from foreign countries . . ." [Hume (1752, pp. 190–192)]

Hume recognized the validity of this point, and in reply he argued (1752, pp. 197–199): "Here, then is the flowing out of money already begun." On the other hand, Hume's statements concerning the changes in prices raise some questions whether his price adjustment assumes failure of arbitrage.[8]

Among Mill's statements on the basis of which he has been interpreted as supporting the relative price theory of adjustment is:

> "The natural effect [of a rise in the money stock] would be a rise in prices. This would check exports and encourage imports." [Mill (1893, book III, p. 194)]

Such statements were later criticized by Bastable who argued that:

> "having larger money incomes will purchase more at the same prices and thus bring about the necessary excess of imports over exports." [Bastable (1889)]

However, it is quite possible that Mill's concepts of "cheapness" and "dearness" do not mean necessarily actual price changes since he argued explicitly that:

> "I say this being well aware that the article would be actually at the same very price ... in England and in other countries. The cheapness however of the article is not measured solely by the money price, but by the price compared with money incomes of the consumers." [Mill (1893, book III, p. 187)]

Similarly:

[8]Consider, for example, Hume's famous paragraph (1752, p. 62) "Suppose four-fifths of all the money in Great Britain to be annihilated in one night, ... must not the price of *all* labour and commodities rise in proportion." (Italics added.) Recently, Samuelson (1971) provided an attempt to interpret Hume without reliance on the failure of arbitrage. It is of interest to note that some writers have accused Hume of plagiarism; Marx claims that Hume must have known Vanderlint's work while Hayek claims that he must have seen Cantillon's work [Sekine (1973, p. 274)]. Viner is aware of the possible lack of originality but finds no evidence that Hume saw Cantillon's work [Viner (1937, p. 74)]. Moreover, Viner suggests that Hume introduced a new mechanism of adjustment in the form of changes in the rate of exchange [Viner (1937, p. 84)]. However, even this mechanism was developed before Hume [Gervaise (1720, p. 13)]. Nicholson went further in ridiculing the notion that the general price level will have to change, arguing that "the notion that a new export can be obtained continuously only by an operation on the general level of prices of one country and the rest of the world is suggestive of the primeval simplicity in which roast pig can be obtained by a continuous series of conflagration" [Nicholson (1897, p. 289)]. The notion that prices are determined in the world market rather than in each country separately is also emphasized by Whale (1937) and by Laughlin who argues that "in truth, the value of gold is an affair of a world demand and a world supply" [Laughlin (1903, p. 370)]. The implication that prices, wages and rates of interest are closely linked together internationally has been verified empirically in studies on the operation of the gold standard [Triffin (1964), McCloskey and Zecher (1976)].

> "the English public, having more money, will have a greater power of purchasing foreign commodities . . . there will be an increase of imports; and by this, and the check to exportation, the equilibrium of imports and exports will be restored." [Mill (1893, book III, p. 187)][9]

Strong statements to the effect that the adjustment process is dominated by changes in expenditures relative to income rather than by changes in relative prices were also made by Nicholson (1897, ch. 26, p. 12), Wicksell (1918, p. 405), Bersciani-Turroni (1932, pp. 91–94), Ohlin (1929), Hawtrey (1927, p. 145) and many others. This is not to say, however, that the relative price approach did not exist but rather that the adjustment theory which is based on the relationship between expenditures and income was widely accepted and might have been the dominating view.[10]

4. Banking Policies

The immediate implication of viewing the balance of payments as a monetary phenomenon is that as long as the exchange rate is fixed and the domestic currency is convertible into gold, monetary policy which takes the form of credit creation has a direct bearing on the balance of payments.[11] This strong link has been recognized throughout the developments of balance of payments theory. Again Gervaise is among the first to emphasize this link:

> "Increase in credit will act on that nation as if it had drawn an equal sum from a gold or silver mine, and will preserve but its proportion of that increase." [Gervaise (1720, p. 9)]

[9]Viner (1937, pp. 200–201) is aware of this statement but he decides (with some reservations) that such passages are exceptions. It is not clear that Viner's evaluation on this matter is warranted.

[10]For a further discussion on the doctrinal origins of the alternative approaches see Haberler (1936), Iversen (1935) and Ohlin (1933). The debate between the two approaches probably culminated in the discussion between Ohlin and Keynes on the German reparation problem. In this discussion Keynes (1929) supported the relative price approach. By now it seems to be received that Keynes' arguments were inferior to those of Ohlin (1929). See also discussions by Rueff (1929) and Machlup (1964, part 5). Hawtrey even goes further in applying the principles of the monetary approach to a wider range of questions. For example, the channel through which a tariff affects the balance of payments is not through a simple relative price effect but rather through raising the demand for money "protective tariff does raise the price level . . . it accordingly requires an increased monetary circulation, and if the monetary system is such that that cannot be provided without the importation of gold, gold will be imported" [Hawtrey (1932, p. 244)]. For recent generalizations along these lines, see Johnson (1976) and Mussa (1976).

[11]In his comments on an earlier draft of this paper, Jacques Melitz pointed out that some of the classical controversies on the role of credit took place under the presumption of inconvertibility.

Thus, the money supply is completely endogenous and credit policy is eventually reflected only in changes in the composition of assets of the central bank. In fact, a "safe" way to lose reserves is a policy of credit expansion:

> "What pity Lycuzgus did not think of paper-credit when he wanted to banish gold and silver from Sparta!" [Hume (1752, p. 70)]

Similar descriptions can also be found in Mill (1874, book III, pp. 195–196).

The clearest and most consistent advocate of directing credit policy towards the balance of payments is Hawtrey:

> "A monetary disturbance of the balance of payments is caused by a maladjustment of credit, and is corrected by a suitable regulation of credit." [Hawtrey (1926, p. 53)]

There is no doubt what is the cause and what is the effect, and there is no doubt that the counterparts to the money account of the balance of payments are *all* of the other accounts rather than only the trade account:

> "An expansion of credit *causes* an unfavourable balance of payments . . . the change in the balance is no more than a symptom. And of course the balance that is in question is always the balance of *payments*, not the balance of trade in the narrower sense of the difference between exports and imports of material commodities." [Hawtrey (1927, p. 75) – italics in original]

Similar statements were made by Machlup in 1928:

> "If Schact, in the name of fighting an 'inflation' induced by foreign loans, promotes domestic credit creation, and thus tries to fight foreign-induced expansion by home-induced expansion, only one outcome can be expected: . . . there will soon be difficulties in paying for the increased imports since people will demand from the central bank the foreign exchange the inflow of which warded off as supposedly superfluous addition to reserves." [Machlup (1964, p. 410)]

Since the world as a whole is a closed system, the balance of payments reflects monetary policies in the various countries. Consequently it is not determined solely by the domestic rate of credit creation but rather by the domestic rate relatively to that in the rest of the world:

> "One lets credit expand a little faster than the others and loses gold; another lags behind and receives gold." [Hawtrey (1927, p. 110)]

The basic truism that the world is a closed system that is composed of interdependent countries implies that an individual central bank in the world system has no more power than a single member bank of a national system. This simple fact and its policy implications were widely recognized and accepted even by those who after the appearance of the *General Theory* became the most prominent Keynesians [Harrod (1933, p. 118) and Robinson (1935)]. Keynes himself, in his pre-*General Theory* era, forcefully emphasized the mutual interdependence of the various central banks:

> "One or two Central Banks acting alone would not, unless they were very preponderant in size, be able to change the weather or direct the storm – anymore than a single member bank can control the behaviour of a national system. If a single Central Bank lags behind in a boom it will be overwhelmed by excess reserve-resources, and if it steps in a depression it will have its reserve-resources quickly drawn from it.... each bank is necessarily governed by the *average* policy of the banks as a whole." [Keynes (1930, pp. 281–286) – italics in original][12]

This statement is extremely similar to the earlier quote from Hawtrey. A considerable change in Keynes' views must have occurred so as to result later in a bitter and lengthy debate with Hawtrey [see correspondence in Keynes (1973) and Hicks (1969)].

5. Concluding Remarks

The purpose of this paper was to provide some evidence in support of the claim that throughout the last two centuries the monetary approach to the balance of payments was widespread and in fact might have been the dominating approach. The overwhelming emphasis on the monetary aspects of the balance of payments and the implied policy implications were drastically changed with the Keynesian revolution. The classical theory was ridiculed as the Keynesian employment theory and a mechanical use of the foreign trade multipliers came to the forefront.[13] This significant shift of emphasis is reflected in most of the current textbook analyses of balance of payments theories.

[12]Although Keynes emphasized the symmetry and interdependence among the various central banks, he considered the Bank of England as the "conductor of the International Orchestra" [Keynes (1930, p. 307)]. Keynes' evaluation of the role of the Bank of England is criticized by McCloskey and Zecher (1976).

[13]The mechanical use of the foreign trade multipliers that is so popular in many of the textbooks does not characterize the originators of the theory. In his classic book on the foreign trade multiplier Machlup (1943) discusses explicitly the monetary consequences of the various changes by tracing out in detail the operation of the monetary mechanism on the balance sheet of the consolidated banking system. In fact the monetary aspects are analyzed in the first chapter of his book under the title "Prerequisites". These monetary mechanisms, however, were typically ignored by later users of the theory.

Although it is beyond the scope of this paper to trace out in detail the effect of the Keynesian revolution on the evolution of balance of payments theories, it is interesting to note one of the evaluations made by Sir Hubert Henderson:[14]

> "Nothing has done more in my opinion to lead modern economists astray than the practice which Lord Keynes brought into fashion in the 1930's of reasoning on the hypothesis of a 'closed economy'... It is paradoxical that British economists should have led this intellectual fashion, at which Adam Smith, Ricardo, John Stuart Mill, Bagehot and Alfred Marshall would certainly have knit their brows." [Henderson (1949, pp. 9–10)]

It is also relevant to note that the newly developed theories of balance of payments lacking an explicit consideration of the monetary aspects were already criticized concomitantly with the appearance of the *General Theory* [Keynes (1936)]. An illustration of these sentiments was expressed by Kindleberger:

> "If in this world, too, monetary economists tacitly agree that a national money income which either remains stable or increases at a steady pace should be the objective of monetary policy, then it is necessary for the international trade economist to orient his thinking in terms of monetary, as well as real, factors." [Kindleberger (1937, p. 239)]

In view of the current revival of the monetary approach to the balance of payments, an intriguing question that remains to be answered is what in effect were the socio-economic conditions and intellectual environment that induced the prolonged popularity of theories deviating so much from the monetary approach.

References

Bagehot, W., 1880, Economic studies (R. H. Hutton, ed., London).

Bastable, S. F., 1889, On some applications of the theory of international trade, Quarterly Journal of Economics IV, pp. 1–17.

Bresciani-Turroni, C., 1932, Inductive verification of the theory of international payments (Noury and Son, Cairo).

[14]This and other examples of the Keynesian impact are discussed in Henderson (1949). My tentative conclusions, based on a preliminary study of that problem, tend to agree with Sir Hubert Henderson's. Some evidence were presented in an earlier version of this paper that was presented at the Third Paris–Dauphine Conference on Money and International Monetary Problems, Paris, March 28–30, 1974.

Cantillon, R., 1755, Essai sur la nature du commerce en general, reprinted in: A. E. Monroe, ed., 1927, Early economic thought (Harvard University Press, Cambridge, Mass.).
Dornbusch, R., 1973, Devaluation, money and nontraded goods, American Economic Review LXIII, no. 5, pp. 871–880.
Dornbusch, R., 1976a, Flexible exchange rates, capital mobility and macroeconomic equilibrium, chapter 9.1 in this volume.
Dornbusch, R., 1976b, Capital mobility and portfolio balance, in: R. Z. Aliber, ed., The political economy of monetary reform (Macmillan, London).
Frenkel, J. A., 1971, A theory of money trade and the balance of payments in a model of accumulation, Journal of International Economics I, no. 2, pp. 159–187.
Frenkel, J. A. and C. A. Rodriguez, 1975, Portfolio equilibrium and the balance of payments: A monetary approach, American Economic Review LXV, no. 4, pp. 674–688.
Fullerton, J., 1845, On the regulation of currencies, 2nd ed.
Gervaise, I., 1720, The system or theory of the trade of the world, reprinted in: Economic tracts (Johns Hopkins Press, Baltimore, Md.).
Haberler, G., 1936, The theory of international trade (Hodge, London).
Harrod, R. F., 1933, International economics, 1st ed. (2nd ed.: 1939, 4th ed.: 1957).
Hawtrey, R. G., 1926, The gold standard and the balance of payments, Economic Journal XXXVI, pp. 50–68.
Hawtrey, R. G., 1927, Currency and credit, 3rd ed. (Longmans, Green and Co., London).
Hawtrey, R. G., 1932, The art of central banking (Longmans, Green and Co., London).
Henderson, H., 1949, The function of exchange rates, Oxford Economic Papers I, no. 1, pp. 1–17.
Hicks, J., 1969, Automatists, Hawtreyans and Keynesians, Journal of Money, Credit and Banking I, no. 3, pp. 307–317.
Hume, D., 1752, Political discourses, reprinted in: E. Rotwein, 1955, David Hume, Writings on economics (Nelson, London).
Iversen, C., 1935, Aspects of the theory of international capital movements (Oxford University Press, London).
Johnson, H. G., 1958, International trade and economic growth (Allen & Unwin, London) pp. 153–168.
Johnson, H. G., 1972, The monetary approach to balance of payments theory, Journal of Financial and Quantitative Analysis VII, pp. 1555–1572.
Johnson, H. G., 1976, The monetary theory of balance of payments policies, in: J. A. Frenkel and H. G. Johnson, eds., The monetary approach to the balance of payments (Allen & Unwin, London, and University of Toronto Press, Toronto).
Keynes, M., 1929, The German transfer problem, Economic Journal XXXIX, pp. 1–7.
Keynes, J. M., 1930, A treatise on money, vol. II (Harcourt, Brace and Co., New York).
Keynes, J. M., 1936, The general theory of employment interest and income (Macmillan, London).
Keynes, J. M., 1973, The collected writings of John Maynard Keynes, vol. XIII (Macmillan, London).
Kindleberger, C. P., 1937, International short-term capital movements (Columbia University Press, New York).
Laughlin, J. L., 1903, The principles of money (Charles Scribner's Sons, New York).
Machlup, F., 1943, International trade and the national income multiplier (Blakiston Co., Philadelphia, Penn.).
Machlup, F., 1964, International payments, debts and gold (Charles Scribner's Sons, New York).
McCloskey, D. and R. Zecher, 1976, How did the gold standard work, 1880–1913, in: J. A. Frenkel and H. G. Johnson, eds., The monetary approach to the balance of payments (Allen & Unwin, London, and University of Toronto Press, Toronto).
Mill, J. S., 1874, Essay on some unsettled questions of political economy, 2nd ed. (London).
Mill, J. S., 1893, Principles of political economy, 5th ed. (Appleton and Co., New York).
Mundell, R. A., 1968, International economics (Macmillan, New York).
Mundell, R. A., 1971, Monetary theory (Goodyear, Pacific Palisades).

Mussa, M., 1971, Twice the transfer problem plus David Hume, unpublished manuscript (University of Chicago, Chicago, Ill.).

Mussa, M., 1976, Tariffs and the balance of payments: A monetary approach, in: J. A. Frenkel and H. G. Johnson, eds., The monetary approach to the balance of payments (Allen & Unwin, London, and University of Toronto Press, Toronto).

Nicholson, J. S., 1897, Principles of political economy, vol. II (London).

Ohlin, B., 1929, The reparation problem: A discussion, Economic Journal XXXIX, pp. 172–178.

Ohlin, B., 1933, Interregional and international trade (Harvard University Press, Cambridge, Mass.).

Ricardo, D., 1821, Principles of political economy and taxation, 3rd ed.

Ricardo, D., 1846, The high price of bullion, McCulloch ed.

Robertson, D. H., 1931, The transfer problem, in: A. C. Pigou and D. H. Robertson, eds., Economic essays and addresses (P. S. King and Son, London).

Robinson, J., 1935, Banking policy and the exchange, Review of Economic Studies III, pp. 226–229.

Rueff, J., 1929, Mr. Keynes' views on the transfer problem: I. A criticism, Economic Journal XXXIX, no. 155, pp. 388–399.

Samuelson, P. A., 1971, An exact Hume–Ricardo–Marshall model of international trade, Journal of International Economics I, no. 1, pp. 1–18.

Sekine, T. T., 1973, The discovery of international monetary equilibrium by Vanderlint, Cantillon, Gervaise and Hume, Economia Internazionale XXVI, no. 2, pp. 262–282.

Triffin, R., 1964, The evolution of the international monetary system, Princeton Studies in International Finance, no. 12 (Princeton, N.J.).

Viner, J., 1937, Studies in the theory of international trade (Harper, New York).

Whale, B. P., 1937, The working of the pre-war gold standard, Economica IV, pp. 18–32.

Whewell, W., 1856, Mathematical exposition of some doctrines of political economy, Second Memoir, Transactions of the Cambridge Philosophical Society IX, part I.

Wicksell, K., 1918, International freights and prices, Quarterly Journal of Economics XXXII, pp. 404–410.

Chapter 2.2

SUMMARY OF THE DISCUSSION ON FRENKEL

Fritz MACHLUP, *Chairman*

Jacob Frenkel first challenged the idea which had been expressed by *Jacques Melitz* according to which the monetary approach of the balance of payments had to deal with convertible money but not with inconvertible money, in which case the authorities could control the quantity of paper money. In fact, inconvertibility is exactly the story which explains why the theory is so powerful. We find exchange controls because the central authorities cannot control what they want to control in the absence of exchange controls.

Milton Friedman came back to earlier discussions, the one between Wolfgang Stützel and Alexander Swoboda (see the discussion of the paper by Swoboda, p. 27) and the one between Jacob Frenkel and Jacques Melitz, just above. In his opinion Jacques Melitz used the word "inconvertibility" by referring to the nineteenth century situation in which inconvertibility meant that you could not convert paper into gold at a fixed rate, whereas Jacob Frenkel used it by referring to the twentieth century system under which inconvertibility means that you need permission of an authority to go from one currency to another one, and this difference is precisely the one Wolfgang Stützel made between a world with a unified currency and a world with a collection of national currencies linked together by fixed rates. In a truly unified currency world, there is no problem of running out of reserves.

In Milton Friedman's opinion the monetary theory of the balance of payments has an extraordinary power and value, but it is much limited by having restricted itself to the case of a unified currency and having treated the case of national currencies linked by fixed rates as if it could be approximated by a unified currency world, which cannot be done. Now, the interesting point is that it seems very straightforward to go from a unified currency world to a collection of national currencies linked by variable rates. In fact, when the bullionists and other economists in the nineteenth century were talking about inconvertibility they were talking about the fact that the exchange rate could change and that there was a free floating exchange rate. All of the analysis of the monetary theory of the balance of payments carries over perfectly to that case.

But it is much more difficult to introduce central banks into the scenario, when there is a collection of different national currencies linked by fixed rates. In Jacob Frenkel's or Alexander Swoboda's presentations the central banks are irrelevant institutions, somehow playing around a game in which they are distributing the unified currency around the world. But in the real world they do matter. Keynes, for instance, had in mind a national currency linked by a fixed rate to other countries' currencies with the possibility that this fixed rate may be manipulated by the central bank or be enforced by a series of restrictions and controls. Once you introduce them it is crystal-clear that the notion of a single price in the world is no longer valid. The whole purpose of national controls is to preserve rigid exchange rates but not unified money, to break the law of a single price around the world. This is not criticism of the monetary approach, but just a suggestion for further work.

David Laidler made a clear distinction for the nineteenth century. The bullionist/anti-bullionist controversy was about the determination of the quantity of money: the bullionists said that the quantity of money came back to its initial level, the anti-bullionists said that the banking system simply makes available the money which is necessary to support the price level.

The currency school/banking school debate was quite different: for the banking school convertibility was sufficient to guarantee that you get the price level that the rest of the world has, whereas the currency school held that this situation could be obtained only in a system of a hundred percent reserve requirements against the domestic money supply.

Sven Arndt expressed doubts about the relevance for policy-making either of the short-term Keynesian analysis or of the excessively long-term recent analysis, where there is no growth, or a natural rate of growth on which one does not want to exercise any control, where there is no problem about clearing the labour market, etc. Over the cycle, capacity changes so that we have not only to care about terms of trade between traded and non-traded goods, between export and import goods, but also between capital formation and consumption. The way in which the adjustment mechanism proceeds over the cycle is in some sense determined not only in the manner in which prices change but also in the manner in which income and output change. By manipulating controls and other devices, the authorities believe that they can manipulate the rate of change of output over the cycle and that affects the adjustment mechanism.

Alexander Swoboda, going back to a terms-of-trade argument raised by *Jacques Melitz*, said that terms of trade often play a very important role in the classical adjustment mechanism, not because money influences the terms of trade, but because very often the source of the disturbance that is considered may have been an exogenous change in the terms of trade to which the monetary system had to adapt. In that respect most textbooks are confusing when explaining the classical gold standard, because they do not specify what the initial disturbance was. If the initial disturbance is a drop in demand or a change in taste, the problem is to know how a potential change in the terms of trade, i.e., in real terms, is translated into money prices and by which adjustment mechanism. It is not money which causes the change in the terms of trade, it is the change in the terms of trade which causes money flows, which will bring back an equilibrium distribution of money corresponding to the new terms of trade and their implicit redistribution of incomes in the world.

Rudiger Dornbusch underlined that the relative prices of traded goods could not be systematically affected by a monetary disturbance, so that the fiction that there are two different goods, an import good and an export good, is obviously incorrect. There is no systematic effect on the average price of exports relative to the average price of imports. But there is a systematic effect on the relative price of goods which are not traded. It rises and falls over the cycle relatively to the prices of traded goods, and it is essential to the transmission mechanism so that it has to be included into macro-models.

William Branson recalled that in Jacob Frenkel's presentation, the demand for money is a stable function of the interest rate, the level of income and the price level. As he assumes that all three variables are constant, a change in the supply of money affects directly the balance of payments. But the monetary approach does not require those assumptions. It also holds in a world where there are variations, at least in the short run, in the price level, the interest rate and the level of income.

Chapter 3.1

DEVALUATION, TRADED GOODS, AND INTERNATIONAL ASSETS

Michael CONNOLLY and Dean TAYLOR

Our aim in this paper is to focus attention on the paths of adjustment of prices, reserves, and capital following a devaluation in a small, open economy. The analysis stresses the transitional nature of liquidity effects resulting from price rises. These effects act so as to create an excess demand for nominal cash balances, which translates itself into both a curtailment of expenditure on goods and a sale of assets abroad. Consequently, the trade balance and the capital account improve as a result of devaluation. The model develops the transitional paths of adjustment toward the new equilibrium. In particular, section 1 begins with the simple case of a small economy with all goods traded, then section 2 incorporates holdings of international assets.

In addition to the expenditure dampening effects of devaluation that are now a familiar part of the monetary approach to the balance of payments, a major feature of the model is the suggestion that a temporary improvement in the capital account following devaluation will shift part of the burden away from short-run improvement in the trade account, thereby serving as a cushion in the adjustment process.

Before beginning the formal analysis, it is perhaps appropriate to stress that we assume throughout that devaluation itself is totally unanticipated, so that the adjustment in the capital account which we derive is not a result of profit-taking repatriation following speculative capital outflows.

1. Dynamics of Devaluation

We begin with a very rudimentary type of economy: there exists only money and goods, all goods are traded, and the foreign price of every good is fixed in terms of foreign currency. The economy may be thought of as a small, open one with no capital market. With all goods traded[1] any excess domestic supply

[1]For an analysis of the transitional dynamics of devaluation with non-traded goods, see Connolly and Taylor (1976).

of output can be sold on the world market. The real demand for money is assumed to be proportional to permanent income, or $L/p = k'y$. Permanent income, y, is assumed not to vary over the time period in question. Under these assumptions, the demand for money assumes the following form where $(k = k'y)$

$$L = kp, \qquad \text{[Money Demand]} \tag{1}$$

L being the nominal demand for money, k desired real money balances, and p the level of domestic prices.

The second relationship we postulate is the dynamic flow one that the value of the *excess* demand for goods (demand for imports less supply of exports) depends upon the discrepancy between actual and desired money balances. In other words an excess supply of money leads individuals to increase their expenditure on goods to rid themselves of money, and conversely, in order to accumulate cash balances, expenditures on goods falls. Consequently, an excess supply of money will translate itself directly into a deficit, while an excess demand will imply a surplus. To sum up, individuals in an open economy reduce or increase their cash balances by running a deficit or surplus, respectively. This adjustment mechanism is summarized as follows:

$$B = \mathrm{d}R/\mathrm{d}t = \lambda(L - M), \qquad \text{[Balance of Payments]} \tag{2}$$

where λ is the speed at which individuals adjust to the discrepancy between actual and desired cash balances. If money demands exceeds money supply, expenditures fall short of receipts and the home country will accumulate reserves at the rate $\mathrm{d}R/\mathrm{d}t$. The balance of payments is measured here in terms of home currency.

With a surplus, receipts of foreign exchange exceed payments in foreign exchange. Domestic residents are assumed not to hold balances of foreign currency, implying that the excess supply of foreign exchange must be purchased by the governmental authorities with domestic money in order to maintain a fixed parity. Domestic money is thus issued for foreign money, and in the absence of a banking system, the rate of issue of domestic money must just equal the rate of increase of reserves held by the government. We have, therefore,

$$\mathrm{d}M/\mathrm{d}t = \mathrm{d}R/\mathrm{d}t. \qquad \text{[Money Increase]} \tag{3}$$

Essentially, the monetary authorities change the money supply through their foreign exchange operations.

We can now take up the monetary dynamics of devaluation. Let r_0 be the initial exchange rate, and $\bar{r}$ the deviation from its initial level. The rate of devaluation is thus $\bar{r}/r_0$.[2] Initially, we assume equilibrium in all markets, and since every good is traded its price equals the exchange rate times the price in foreign currency. Since world prices are assumed constant, we can set the foreign currency price of each good equal to unity at no loss in generality. Prior to the devaluation, therefore, $p = r$, or the domestic price of each good equals the exchange rate. This is the arbitrage relationship. Following the devaluation, however, we would not expect domestic prices to rise instantaneously. Importers may sell off their stocks at a price somewhat below the new international one, then raise prices only after they replenish their stocks. Similarly, producers may temporarily sell to exporters at a price below the international one. However, arbitrage and competition will eventually bid the price of traded goods up to the world price.

We will assume that the change in domestic prices, p, is proportional to the discrepancy between the world price and the domestic one, or r and p. Furthermore, the constant of proportionality is assumed the same for all goods. Therefore,

$$\mathrm{d}p/\mathrm{d}t = \alpha(r - p). \qquad \text{[Degree of Arbitrage]} \tag{4}$$

The variables in equation (4) can be written as deviations from their initial positions, or $p = p_0 + \bar{p}$ and $r = r_0 + \bar{r}$. Noting that $\mathrm{d}p/\mathrm{d}t = \mathrm{d}\bar{p}/\mathrm{d}t$, and $r_0 = p_0$, we have

$$\alpha\bar{p} + \mathrm{d}\bar{p}/\mathrm{d}t = \alpha\bar{r}. \tag{5}$$

Multiplying by $\mathrm{e}^{\alpha t}$ and integrating,

$$\int_0^t \frac{\mathrm{d}}{\mathrm{d}\tau}(\mathrm{e}^{\alpha\tau}\bar{p})\,\mathrm{d}\tau = \int_0^t \alpha\bar{r}\,\mathrm{e}^{\alpha\tau}\,\mathrm{d}\tau. \tag{6}$$

At $t = 0$, $\bar{p} = 0$, and for discrete changes in the exchange rate, $\bar{r}$ may be removed from the integrand[3] giving

$$\bar{p} = (1 - \mathrm{e}^{-\alpha t})\bar{r}, \qquad \text{[Response of Prices to Devaluation]} \tag{7}$$

depicted graphically in figure 1.

From (1), the demand for money is proportional to the domestic price of

[2]Throughout, the analysis ignores the accounting revaluation of official holdings of foreign reserves as a result of devaluation. Section 2, however, analyzes the effect of the revaluation of *private* holdings of international assets.

[3]Strictly speaking, $\int_0^t \bar{r}\alpha\,\mathrm{e}^{\alpha\tau}\,\mathrm{d}\tau = \lim_{\varepsilon\to 0^+}\int_\varepsilon^t \bar{r}\alpha\,\mathrm{e}^{\alpha\tau}\,\mathrm{d}\tau = \lim_{\varepsilon\to 0^+}[\bar{r}(\mathrm{e}^{\alpha\tau} - \mathrm{e}^{\alpha\varepsilon})] = \bar{r}(\mathrm{e}^{\alpha\tau} - 1)$ giving (7) following simplification. This results from $\bar{r} = 0$ at $t = 0$ but $\bar{r}$ is a positive constant for $t > 0$.

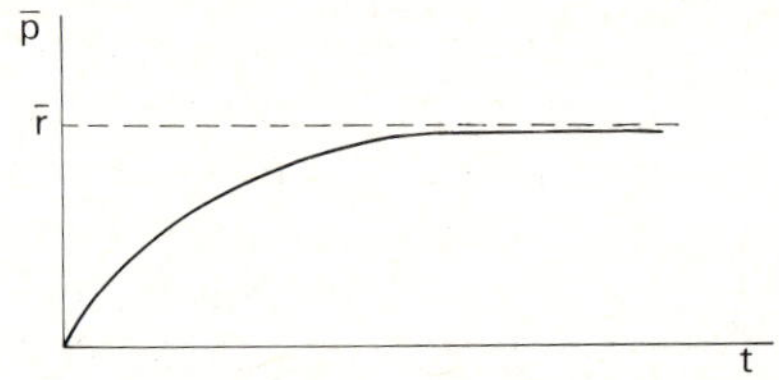

FIGURE 1. Effect of devaluation on domestic prices.

goods, or $L = kp$. Substituting (7) into (1) gives the time path of changes in money demand,

$$\bar{L} = k(1 - e^{-\alpha t})\bar{r}. \tag{8}$$

Substituting (8) into the adjustment equation (2) and (3), $\mathrm{d}M/\mathrm{d}t = \lambda(L - M)$, noting that initially $M_0 = kp_0$ and $p_0 = r_0$, and expressing in terms of deviations gives

$$\lambda\bar{M} + \mathrm{d}\bar{M}/\mathrm{d}t = \lambda k(1 - e^{-\alpha t})\bar{r}. \tag{9}$$

Multiplying by $e^{\lambda t}$ and integrating, we can solve for the response of the money supply and foreign reserves to devaluation,

$$\int_0^t \frac{\mathrm{d}}{\mathrm{d}\tau}(\bar{M}e^{\lambda\tau})\,\mathrm{d}\tau = \int_0^t \lambda k[e^{\lambda\tau} - e^{(\lambda-\alpha)\tau}]\bar{r}\,\mathrm{d}\tau. \tag{10}$$

Once again, $\bar{r}$ is constant from 0 to t and may be removed from the integrand. Also, at $t = 0$, $\bar{M} = 0$. Multiplying by $e^{-\lambda t}$, and simplifying,

$$\bar{M} = k\left[1 + \frac{\lambda}{\alpha - \lambda}e^{-\alpha t} - \frac{\alpha}{\alpha - \lambda}e^{-\lambda t}\right]\bar{r}. \qquad \text{[Response of Reserves and Money Supply]} \tag{11}$$

The effect of devaluation on the balance of payments is found by differentiating (11), or[4]

$$B = \frac{\mathrm{d}\bar{M}}{\mathrm{d}t} = k\frac{\alpha\lambda}{\alpha - \lambda}(e^{-\lambda t} - e^{-\alpha t})\bar{r}. \qquad \text{[Effect on Balance of Payments]} \tag{12}$$

Graphically, these relationships are depicted in figure 2.

Evaluating (12) it is clear that the change in reserves is everywhere positive. However, the curve for reserve change is initially convex, then concave, as can be verified by differentiating (12).[5]

[4]Recall that, by definition, $B = \mathrm{d}M/\mathrm{d}t$ and $M = M_0 + \bar{M}$. Therefore, $\mathrm{d}M/\mathrm{d}t = \mathrm{d}\bar{M}/\mathrm{d}t = B$.

[5]That is, $\mathrm{d}^2M/\mathrm{d}t^2 = k\alpha\lambda\bar{r} > 0$ as $t \to 0$, and the point of inflection in reserves or maximum rate of improvement in the balance of payments, is at $t = (1/(\lambda - \alpha))\ln(\lambda/\alpha)$ found by setting $\mathrm{d}^2M/\mathrm{d}t^2 = 0$. The balance of payments simply reflects changes in the slope of the reserve change curve.

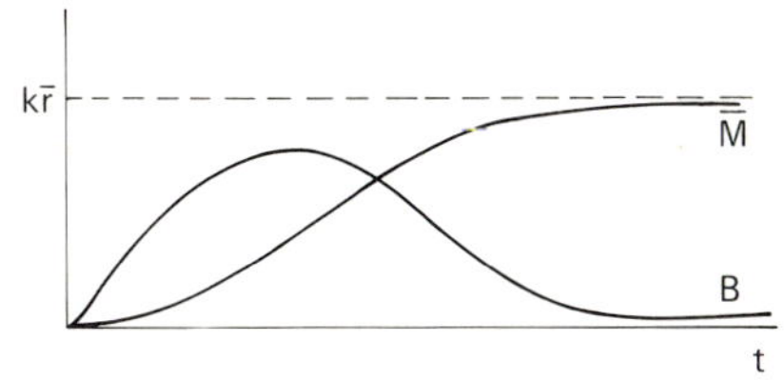

FIGURE 2. Effect of devaluation on the balance of payments, money and reserves.

A case of special interest arises when arbitrage is perfect and domestic prices of traded goods rise instantaneously by the amount of the devaluation. This means that $\alpha = \infty$, and the behavior of reserves and the balance of payments assume the following special forms:

$$\bar{M} = k(1 - e^{-\lambda t})\bar{r}, \tag{13}$$

$$B = d\bar{M}/dt = k\lambda\, e^{-\lambda t}\bar{r}, \tag{14}$$

depicted graphically in figure 3.

In section 2, an international asset is introduced and the assumption is made that following devaluation, the price of goods does in fact rise instantaneously. This particular assumption does not greatly reduce the generality of the analysis, and permits us to highlight the cushioning effect of an international asset.

We may summarize the results of this section in the following way. Devaluation causes domestic prices to rise, leading to an increase in the nominal demand for money balances. The excess demand for money translates itself into a rise in receipts relative to payments or a surplus which eventually replenishes real cash balances. The path of adjustment depends upon the rate of adjustment in domestic prices, α, the rate of adjustment in the money market, λ, the rate of devaluation, $\bar{r}$, and desired real cash balances, k. Ultimately, domestic prices rise by the same amount as the devaluation, $\bar{p} = \bar{r}$,

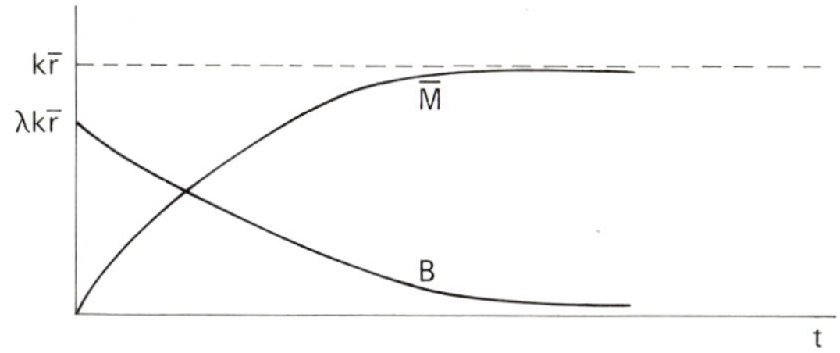

FIGURE 3. Reserves and balance of payments with immediate adjustment in home prices.

and the level of reserves (and money supply) rise by $k\bar{r}$, or just that amount sufficient to restore the initial real cash balance position.

2. Devaluation and International Assets

A major deficiency of the literature on devaluation is its neglect of the impact of devaluation on the capital account of the balance of payments. This section suggests a possible approach to incorporating capital movements into the adjustment process. Our basic reasoning is that the attempt to replenish real cash balances following a devaluation need not entail solely a trade surplus, but also the sale of assets abroad. Indeed, the sale of international assets may serve as a cushion to the trade balance during the adjustment process. In what follows, we stress the short-run improvement in the capital account which eases the eventual long-run adjustment through the trade account. Once again, the analysis focuses upon a situation in which devaluation is unanticipated so that speculative capital outflows followed by repatriation after the devaluation are not assumed to take place. Rather, we stress the impact of the improvement in the capital account as a result of the attempt to increase domestic liquidity.[6]

For our purposes, the main characteristic of the international asset is that its nominal value in foreign currency remains constant following the home currency's devaluation, and therefore its home currency price appreciates by the amount of the devaluation. The international asset may represent, for instance, holdings of foreign currency or securities whose price in foreign currency and rate of interest is unaffected by the devaluation. The constancy of price and rate of return reflects our assumption that the home country plays a negligible role in the world capital market.

With a devaluation, the international asset will initially be sold off in order to replenish money balances thereby improving the capital account along with the general reduction in expenditure on goods which improves the balance of trade. In the long run, the stock of international assets will be restored by maintaining a trade surplus until the previous level of holdings of foreign assets is reached. In short, the international asset plays a role only during the adjustment process, serving as a buffer to adjustment in the trade balance, while its real value is restored in the steady state. This suggests that the capital account should improve following a devaluation, entirely apart from considerations of profit-taking and speculation.

[6]For a recent dynamic analysis that is similar in several respects to what follows, see Frenkel and Rodriguez (1975, pp. 674–688).

To simplify matters, assume that the prices of goods are rigidly linked to the exchange rate via arbitrage. In terms of the analysis in section 1, $\alpha = \infty$. By an appropriate choice of units, the foreign currency price of all goods can be set equal to unity so that their domestic price equals r, the exchange rate. Following devaluation, the international asset appreciates in terms of home currency. If immediately before the devaluation, the stock of international assets valued in home currency is A_0, then immediately after the devaluation the stock of this asset will be valued in home currency at $A_0(1+\bar{r}/r_0)$. (Recall that domestic prices, p, and the exchange rate, r, are equal by the assumption of perfect arbitrage.)

We can assume, with an unchanged rate of return, that domestic residents desire to keep a constant fraction of real wealth in the form of international assets. Therefore, the desired level of holdings of international assets measured in home currency, K, is proportional to the exchange rate,

$$K = k_2 r. \qquad \text{[Demand for International Asset]} \qquad (15)$$

Once again, noting that interest rates are internationally determined and do not vary, the demand for money is proportional to the price level, or exchange rate, with all goods traded,

$$L = k_1 r. \qquad \text{[Demand for Money]} \qquad (16)$$

The excess demand for traded goods (the demand for imports less export supply) rz is assumed to be proportional to any discrepancy between actual money balances M and desired money balances L, and *also* any discrepancy between actual asset holdings A and desired asset holdings K, or

$$rz = \lambda(M-L)+\delta(A-K). \qquad \text{[Excess Demand for Goods]} \qquad (17)$$

Capital outflows, $\mathrm{d}C/\mathrm{d}t$ (which increase asset holdings) are positively related to the excess stock of money and negatively related to the excess of international assets,[7]

$$\mathrm{d}C/\mathrm{d}t = \mu(M-L)-\beta(A-K). \qquad \text{[Capital Outflow]} \qquad (18)$$

The change in the money supply and the balance of payments are identical, and must both equal the excess supply of international goods *less* capital outflows,[8]

$$B = \mathrm{d}M/\mathrm{d}t = -(rz+\mathrm{d}C/\mathrm{d}t). \qquad \text{[Balance of Payments]} \qquad (19)$$

[7]Due to the capital appreciation of international assets, capital flows are not precisely equal to $\mathrm{d}A/\mathrm{d}t$. On this, see equation (22).

[8]We ignore possible effects on the balance of payments of any interest rebates from capital flows. In the case of foreign currency, there would, of course, be no interest payments.

Substituting (15), (16), and (19) into (17) and (18) gives

$$\mathrm{d}M/\mathrm{d}t + \mathrm{d}C/\mathrm{d}t = -\lambda(M - k_1 r) - \delta(A - k_2 r), \tag{20}$$

and

$$\mathrm{d}C/\mathrm{d}t = \mu(M - k_1 r) - \beta(A - k_2 r). \tag{21}$$

To analyze the effect of devaluation, assume that the system is in equilibrium at the time of devaluation. Note that the domestic price of the international asset increases in proportion to the devaluation, so that the market for the foreign asset is not initially disturbed. Following the devaluation, actual asset holdings in home currency will therefore equal the initial asset holdings, A_0, appreciated by the percentage of the devaluation *plus* assets accumulated after the devaluation, $\bar{C}$. That is,

$$A = A_0(1 + \bar{r}/r_0) + \bar{C}. \tag{22}$$

However, the domestic money supply does not change, so that the rise in prices contingent upon devaluation causes an initial excess demand for money. Equations (20) and (21) can therefore be re-written as

$$\mathrm{d}\bar{M}/\mathrm{d}t + \mathrm{d}\bar{C}/\mathrm{d}t = -\lambda(\bar{M} - k_1\bar{r}) - \delta\bar{C}, \tag{23}$$

and

$$\mathrm{d}\bar{C}/\mathrm{d}t = \mu(\bar{M} - k_1\bar{r}) - \beta\bar{C}, \tag{24}$$

where $\bar{M}$, $\bar{r}$, and $\bar{C}$ measure deviations from their original positions.

Solving the system (see appendix) we find that the time path of the total change in the money supply (and in foreign reserves) is summarized by

$$\bar{M} = k_1\left[1 + \frac{\rho_2 - (\lambda + \mu)}{\rho_1 - \rho_2}\mathrm{e}^{-\rho_1 t} - \frac{\rho_1 - (\lambda + \mu)}{\rho_1 - \rho_2}\mathrm{e}^{-\rho_2 t}\right]\bar{r},$$

[Total Change in Money Supply] (25)

where $-\rho_1$ and $-\rho_2$ are the roots of the characteristic equation derived in the appendix satisfying $\rho_1\rho_2 = \lambda\beta + \mu\delta$ and $\rho_1 + \rho_2 = \lambda + \beta + \mu$. Similarly, the change in international assets held by the public is

$$\bar{C} = k_1\left[\frac{\mu}{\rho_1 - \rho_2}\mathrm{e}^{-\rho_1 t} - \frac{\mu}{\rho_1 - \rho_2}\mathrm{e}^{-\rho_2 t}\right]\bar{r}.$$

[Change in International Assets] (26)

As before, the time response of the balance of payments can be derived by differentiating $\bar{M}$, and the time path of the capital flow by differentiating $\bar{C}$, both with respect to time. By deducting the capital inflow from the total improvement in the balance of payments, the export surplus can also be derived as a function of time.

If we first examine the impact of devaluation on capital flows, we have

$$\begin{aligned} d\bar{C}/dt &= \frac{k_1\mu}{\rho_1-\rho_2}[\rho_2 e^{-\rho_2 t} - \rho_1 e^{-\rho_1 t}]\,\bar{r} \\ &= -k_1\mu\bar{r} < 0 \qquad \text{as} \qquad t \to 0. \end{aligned} \tag{27}$$

That is, immediately following the devaluation sales of international assets take place. Differentiating again, we note that $d^2\bar{C}/dt^2 = k_1\mu(\rho_1+\rho_2)\bar{r} > 0$ as $t \to 0$. Consequently, the initial segment of the asset sales curve is convex. Eventually, holdings of international assets are restored, or $\bar{C}$ approaches zero as $t \to \infty$ in equation (26). The path taken toward the ultimate return to the initial international asset position may, however, be direct or oscillatory depending upon the relative values of the parameters.[9] We may therefore summarize the two basic paths of adjustment of international assets in figure 4.

Next we examine the impact effect of devaluation on the money supply and the balance of payments. By differentiating (25) we find that

$$B = d\bar{M}/dt = k_1(\lambda+\mu)\bar{r} > 0 \qquad \text{as} \qquad t \to 0, \tag{28}$$

which means that the balance of payments immediately improves. Also, from equation (19) we can see that as $t \to 0$ the balance of trade is $k_1\lambda\bar{r}$.

The impact effect on the balance of payments is thus composed of two effects: *the liquidity effect on the balance of trade*, $k_1\lambda\bar{r}$, and the *liquidity effect on holdings of international assets*, $k_1\mu\bar{r}$. Both work so as to improve the overall balance of payments: expenditure is reduced and foreign assets are sold off for the same motives namely, to restore the real value of cash balances. [This is perhaps more easily understood by noting the two effects show up

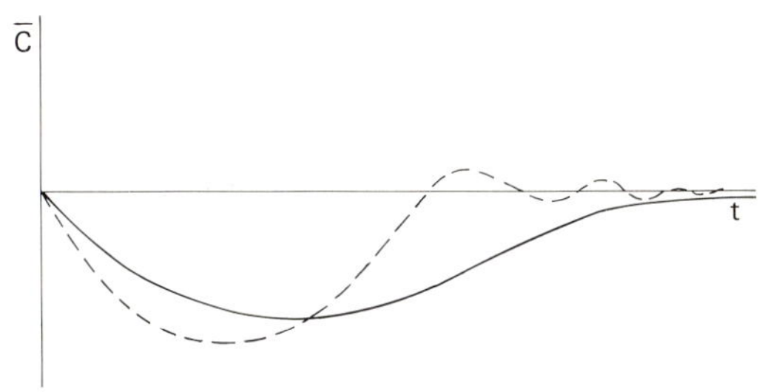

FIGURE 4. Change in holdings of international assets.

[9]Specifically, oscillation arises if $(\lambda+\beta+\mu)^2 < 4(\lambda\beta+\mu\delta)$. Simplifying this condition, it can be seen that relatively large values of δ lead to oscillation.

directly in equations (17) and (18) where a devaluation disturbs the money market through a price rise.]

Taking the second derivative of (25) we find that

$$dB/dt = d^2M/dt^2 = k_1[\mu(\delta - \beta) - (\lambda + \mu)^2]\bar{r} \qquad \text{as} \qquad t \to 0. \tag{29}$$

Therefore the path of the money supply will be either concave or convex depending on the relative size of δ. The possible paths of adjustment of reserves and money are illustrated below for the case where the roots are real.

If the roots are complex, the path of the money supply can be either initially concave or complex but will eventually approach the new equilibrium in dampened cycles.

Finally, we should note that the balance of payments ultimately reverts to equilibrium, or $d\bar{M}/dt$ approaches zero as $t \to \infty$. This reflects the fact that whenever the system is out of equilibrium, for whatever the cause, forces tend to come into play which restore the equilibrium. This happens to hold for devaluations also.

3. *Conclusion*

A devaluation in a small, open economy causes domestic prices to rise, leading to an increase in the nominal demand for money balances. The consequent expenditure reduction leads to a surplus in the balance of trade, which, in turn, eventually restores real cash balances. The path of adjustment depends upon a number of things, including (1) the rate of adjustment in domestic prices, (2) the speed of adjustment in the money market, (3) the rate of devaluation, and (4) the level of desired real cash balances.

With all goods traded and holdings of international assets, the path of

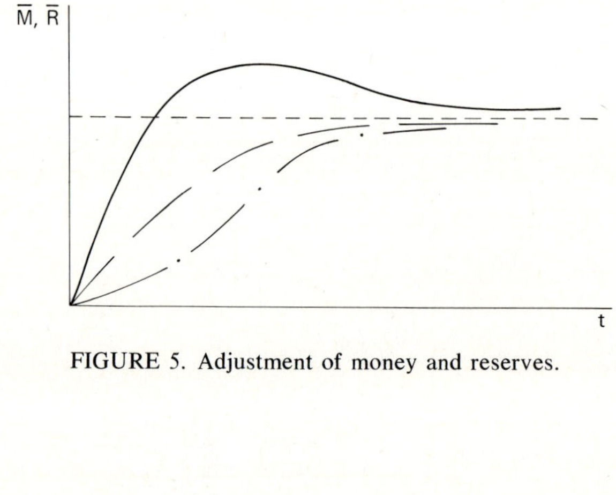

FIGURE 5. Adjustment of money and reserves.

adjustment depends in addition upon the rate of adjustment in the asset market. Of particular interest is the finding that a temporary improvement in the capital account may serve as a buffer to the ultimate long-run adjustment via the current account. This conclusion holds even when devaluation is unanticipated.

Appendix

Expressed in matrix notation, the equations (23) and (24) become

$$\begin{bmatrix} \lambda+D & \delta+D \\ -\mu & \beta+D \end{bmatrix} \begin{bmatrix} \bar{M} \\ \bar{C} \end{bmatrix} = \begin{bmatrix} \lambda k_1 \bar{r} \\ -\mu k_1 \bar{r} \end{bmatrix}, \tag{A.1}$$

where D is the differential operator $\mathrm{d}/\mathrm{d}t$.

This system has the characteristic equation

$$\lambda\beta + \mu\delta + (\lambda + \beta + \mu)D + D^2 = 0.$$

Using Cramer's rule, the differential equation for $\bar{M}$ is

$$[\lambda\beta + \mu\delta + (\lambda + \beta + \mu)D + D^2]\bar{M} = [(\lambda\beta + \mu\delta)k_1 + (\lambda + \mu)k_1 D]\bar{r}, \tag{A.2}$$

and for $\bar{C}$ it is

$$[\lambda\beta + \mu\delta + (\lambda + \beta + \mu)D + D^2]\bar{C} = -\mu k_1 D\bar{r}. \tag{A.3}$$

If we let $-\rho_1$ and $-\rho_2$ be the roots of the characteristic equation, then equation (A.2) becomes

$$(\rho_1 + D)(\rho_2 + D)\bar{M} = [\rho_1\rho_2 k_1 + (\lambda + \mu)k_1 D]\bar{r}. \tag{A.4}$$

A convenient method for solving equations such as (A.4) with step changes such as a devaluation is that of Laplace transforms, as outlined in Allen (1967, pp. 357–362). As discussed there, we need only specify the initial conditions just *before* the step change in the exchange rate, then apply the technique of Laplace transforms. Prior to the devaluation, the initial conditions are $\bar{M} = D\bar{M} = D^2\bar{M} = 0$.

If the initial conditions are as specified, then the solution of $\bar{M}$ with a change in the exchange rate of $\bar{r}$ has Laplace transform $m(s) = \int_0^\infty \mathrm{e}^{-st}\bar{M}(t)\,\mathrm{d}t$ given by[10]

$$m(s) = \frac{\rho_1\rho_2 k_1 + (\lambda + \mu)k_1 s}{(\rho_1 + s)(\rho_2 + s)s}\,\bar{r}. \tag{A.5}$$

[10]See Allen (1967, p. 358).

Equation (A.5) can be written in partial fractions[11] as

$$m(s) = k_1 \left[\frac{1}{s} + \left(\frac{\rho_2 - (\lambda + \mu)}{\rho_1 - \rho_2}\right)\left(\frac{1}{\rho_1 + s}\right) - \left(\frac{\rho_1 - (\lambda + \mu)}{\rho_1 - \rho_2}\right)\left(\frac{1}{\rho_2 + s}\right)\right] \bar{r}. \tag{A.6}$$

The Laplace transform of 1 is $1/s$ and the Laplace transform of $e^{-\rho_1 t}$ is $1/(\rho_1 + s)$ – see Allen (1959, p. 160). Therefore the inverse Laplace transform for (A.6) is

$$\bar{M} = k_1 \left[1 + \frac{\rho_2 - (\lambda + \mu)}{\rho_1 - \rho_2} e^{-\rho_1 t} - \frac{\rho_1 - (\lambda + \mu)}{\rho_1 - \rho_2} e^{-\rho_2 t}\right] \bar{r}, \tag{A.7}$$

giving equation (25) for the change in the money supply following devaluation. Equation (26) giving the change in the international asset can be solved for similarly.

References

Allen, R. G. D., 1959, Mathematical economics (Macmillan, London).

Allen, R. G. D., 1967, Macro-economic theory (Macmillan, London).

Connolly, M. and D. Taylor, 1976, Adjustment to devaluation with money and non-traded goods.

Dornbusch, R., 1973, Currency depreciation, hoarding and relative prices, Journal of Political Economy, July/Aug.

Dornbusch, R., 1973, Devaluation, money and non-traded goods, American Economic Review, Dec.

Frenkel, J. A. and C. Rodriguez, 1975, Portfolio equilibrium and the balance of payments; A monetary approach, American Economic Review, Sept.

Johnson, H. G., 1973, The monetary approach to balance of payments theory, in: M. Connolly and A. Swoboda, eds., International trade and money (Allen & Unwin, London, and University of Toronto Press, Toronto).

Kemp, M., 1969, The pure theory of international trade (Prentice Hall, Englewood Cliffs, N.J.) ch. 14.

Mundell, R., 1968, International economics (Macmillan Company, New York).

Mundell, R., 1971, Monetary theory (Goodyear, Pacific Palisades).

Negishi, T., 1968, Approaches to the analysis of devaluation, International Economic Review, June.

Prais, S., 1961, Some mathematical notes on the quantity theory of money in an open economy, IMF Staff Papers, May.

[11] See Allen (1959, pp. 155–166).

Chapter 3.2

COMMENT ON CONNOLLY AND TAYLOR

Robert MUNDELL

I welcome this paper very much because it represents in one sense a breakthrough into a development that is very badly needed and quickly needed in view of the current changes in exchange rates that are going on today and the interpretation of these. Why I find it useful is that we are getting into the solution path following devaluation and all of us are looking at the figures and wanting to know what evidence we can draw from actual changes in the ups and downs of the exchange rates in recent world that will lend or fortify one or the other theories of the balance of payments. In that sense I consider the paper as an extremely useful one; in particular because I know there is a very extensive empirical work which is backing it.

I would first say something about the construction of models. There are many models of devaluation, as could be expected, because when one tries to integrate the theory and the real world, many real variables and financial variables are involved. For model-building it is hard to cope with all the variables at the same time and it is necessary to deal with very extreme, very simple cases in order to illustrate a point. Therefore, economists really have to show how each model is a special case of international general equilibrium analysis, and they should write down the dynamic view of general equilibrium they have and then show which variables were kept constant for the sake of the particular analysis.

In the development of this model, one thing that emerges very clearly is the immediate effect of the devaluation on the price of imports, the price of international goods, and the slow reaction on the price of domestic goods. That may or may not be the case in the real world and there are a lot of reasons why it is quite possible that domestic good prices rise very quickly even in relation to international goods. The almost instantaneous adjustment of the import price levels to the exchange rates is true in a world without inventories, but if there are large inventories, then it would not really be expected to be the case. When a country devalues, the first impact is on the stock market, and it surely has an effect on the rate of growth of land prices. Land is a good example of a purely domestic good, but the pure and immediate speculative impact of these effects can be considerable. If, for instance, one assumes a very large devaluation – let me say 75% in a small country – people will first shift from money to land, and prices of domestic goods will go up instantaneously. The path of adjustment will be quite different from the one described in the Connolly–Taylor model.

The inventory effect is terribly significant in actual balance-of-payments results. But let us go back to the simple model where all goods are traded. Devalue and suppose all prices go up instantly. It creates a negative effect on real money balances, the liquidity effect. Meanwhile, there is a secondary effect because people are off their portfolio balance line, the ratio of money to capital having been disturbed. But before this wealth effect comes into play, people suffer from a tax on cash from the devaluation. A part of people's wealth is confiscated by the loss in the real value of their cash. They will sell inventories to rebuild their cash balances. The country which devalues is selling off its inventories to foreigners in order to rebuild its liquidity position. This effect, which is a portfolio effect, could be called a wealth tax and it may completely dominate the trade balance over the time period considered. It is only in the longer run that the real wealth effect will come into play and then the economy will move back to equilibrium because people, who have been robbed of a fraction of their wealth, will rebuild it by saving, which means an improvement in the trade balance.

These two effects are going to be completely confounded in trade figures and it is quite important to separate them.

When we move back to equilibrium, in fact the economy will not go exactly to the same position as before since people are taxed by their own central bank, which has got the reserves and it is likely that the private sector will not get any extra utility from the fact that the central bank has more reserves. If part of the people's wealth is thus destroyed, the whole future is different since the lifetime consumption has been hurt.

Contrarily to the opinion of some economists, for instance John Stuart Mill and Ricardo, there is no long-run neutrality of money, since a barter economy and a money economy are just completely different.

Chapter 3.3

SUMMARY OF THE DISCUSSION ON CONNOLLY AND TAYLOR

Fritz MACHLUP, *Chairman*

Michael Connolly emphasized that Dean Taylor and himself had developed a model with capital adjustment, along the lines suggested by Robert Mundell. Following the devaluation, stocks of foreign assets were sold immediately, and the full burden of adjustment in the longer run was taken over by the trade balance, while the capital balance returned to its initial position.

Serge-Christophe Kolm underlined that there was a reason, in addition to the one raised by Robert Mundell, for the final equilibrium to be different from the initial one after a devaluation: general equilibrium theory has shown that there is a high probability to have a large number of equilibrium points in a limited space. As a devaluation is a large price change, there are a lot of chances that the economy is going to another equilibrium point.

Dean Taylor asked why one can say a priori that there would be multiple equilibrium points.

Michael Parkin criticized the fact that the rate of price change in the non-traded good market depends only on the excess demand of that good. Standard new microeconomic theory of price dynamics would in fact require that a further variable is introduced as an argument in the function, namely the expected rate of change of the price of the non-tradable good, with a coefficient of unity in order to avoid long-run money illusion. Then, one must add the specification of how the expected rate of change of the non-traded good price will behave. Typically, we would be content to suppose that the price would change or would be expected to change by some kind of adaptive expectation hypothesis or error-learning process. However, at a point in time when the exchange rate is changed, it would be foolish to live with that particular assumption. It would be necessary to allow the expected rate of change of price change at least for a limited period. It would normally be higher since the exchange rate has brought about a rather large change in the nominal price of tradable goods and therefore a rather large change in relative prices, which presumably nobody believes can be sustained for ever. In terms of the model under discussion it is clear that the rather slow response of the non-traded good price to the devaluation would be speeded up and that might change the time paths and their properties. It would presumably get us a little closer to the sorts of experience that we have had in countries which have devalued by substantial amounts.

The equilibrium results would certainly not be modified. However, in cases where there is a country with a continuous higher inflation than other countries and with a steady rate of devaluation, there would be persistent excess demand for the non-traded good and a real effect, relative prices changing throughout the process, so that money could not be said to be neutral.

Dean Taylor accepted this suggestion of incorporating price expectations and making them a function of exchange rate changes. Naturally, the paper under discussion assumes rather naive behaviors and the model would not apply to economies where devaluations have occurred several times.

Sven Arndt suggested to look at the substitution effect not only from the demand side but also from the supply side. If a change in the composition of output was allowed for, the conditions under which the substitution effect is smaller than the liquidity effect, involving an excess supply of non-traded goods, would be affected. There would also be an impact on the rate at which the price of the non-traded good approaches the price of the traded good and, thirdly, there would be a wealth effect, depending on whether the non-traded good or the traded good was a capital good.

Ronald Jones asked whether, in the empirical work made by Michael Connolly and Dean Taylor, the authors had found significant relative price changes, namely an absolute fall in the price of the non-traded good and a rise in the price of the non-traded good relative to the traded good during some period. The authors answered that they had not the price variations for the non-traded goods, but they registered, for instance, a decline in the price of exports in the third quarter following a devaluation or negative rates of change in import prices. Thus, there is a quick upward adjustment in the prices of traded goods, a continued further upward adjustment and then, in many instances, a decline from that level. As demand and supply conditions changed, the evidence is not quite conclusive, but, however, oscillatory behaviors have been observed.

Alexander Swoboda asked whether the fact that the price of the non-traded good fall at some point of time was consistent with a gross-substitute assumption. *Michael Connolly* answered that in this particular case, goods would be complements and the wealth effect would dominate the substitution effect.

PART II

The Optimizing Approach to the Demand for International Reserves

Chapter 4.1

THE OPTIMIZING APPROACH TO THE DEMAND FOR INTERNATIONAL RESERVES: A SURVEY

Emil-Maria CLAASSEN*

1. The Demand for International Reserves: An Oversurvey

The theory of the demand for international reserves is a rather recent branch in international economics. Only since the mid-60's some "aesthetic models" have been developed replacing the journalistic style of international monetary economics by technical rigour and awarding the recent literature on this subject more credibility among professional economists. Given the relatively small amount of scientific output in this field, it is surprising that the literature on the demand for reserves has already been surveyed five times – by Clower and Lipsey (1968), by Niehans (1970), Grubel (1971), Williamson (1973) and by Cohen (1974) – even though all of them treat not only the demand for reserves but also the interrelated questions of the definition, of the composition and of the supply of reserves on the one hand and the normative aspect of international liquidity on the other hand (i.e., the reform proposals concerning the management of international liquidity).

A survey of the existing surveys with respect to the literature on the *demand* for international reserves could be organized around the different sets of variables which are considered as the main determinants of the demand for reserves. They can be classified in three categories.

1.1. The Oldest and Youngest Approach

The oldest approach to the demand for reserves is that which is relevant for a gold-standard world in which there is a direct functional relationship between

*I should like to thank the participants of the Conference, in particular Milton Friedman, Peter Kenen, Michael Kuszynski and Fritz Machlup for their very helpful comments. A similar version has been published in *Weltwirtschaftliches Archiv* 110, no. 3 (1974).

desired reserves and the *domestic money supply.* The base money is gold held by central banks and similar to today's reserves of commercial banks the money supply can only be increased if "high powered" money – reserves in form of gold – increases. Behind this "technical" relationship for the management of the domestic money supply stands not only the idea that token money was redeemable in commodity money but that this conversion would be undertaken in the case of an increase in the demand for foreign goods which could happen not only as a consequence of a shift in the demand from domestic goods to foreign goods but also – according to the "youngest" approach to the demand for reserves, the monetary approach – as a consequence of an excess supply in the money market.

Supposing that the actual cash holdings (money supply) are higher than desired cash holdings (money demand) either because of a ceteris paribus increase in the money supply or a ceteris paribus decrease in the money demand. This divergence has its counterpart in an excess of aggregate expenditures over aggregate output with the consequence of an increased demand for foreign goods and thus of a balance-of-payments deficit. The expansionary pressure in the internal economy pushes output and/or prices upwards involving an increase in the demand for money and the external deficit is associated with a loss in reserves and consequently with a reduction in the money supply; there is again an overall internal and external equilibrium if the money demand equates the money supply.

From this "monetary approach to balance-of-payments theory" one gets the normative conclusion for central banks' reserve management that the demand for reserves *should* be related to the domestic money supply in order to avoid crisis because a higher amount of outstanding money supply increases the potential conversions by individuals from national currency into international goods. This monetary approach has been advanced by Johnson (1958) and Scitovsky (1958, ch. 9), tested without negative results by Machlup (1966) and Courchene–Youssef (1967) and it has been revived recently by its inventor, Johnson (1972, ch. 3; 1973), and his disciples.

1.2. The Standard Approach

The most traditional attempts and the standard approach until 1960 were the belief expressed uncritically by Harrod (1953) and the I.M.F. (1958) that there is a direct functional relationship between reserves and the *level of imports*, or in a more general form (in analogy to the Cambridge equation of the demand-for-money function) that there is a direct link between the demand for reserves and the total volume of international transactions. This proposition has met many criticisms, in particular by Machlup (1966) who argued that the demand for reserves should be related to the *variability of international payments* rather than to their total volume because reserves are only needed for "bridging the gap" between payments and receipts.

Brown (1964) had already attempted an empirical study of reserve behaviour with respect to the overall external imbalance. But his type of study and subsequent empirical analysis encountered one awkward problem – the simultaneity problem. If one uses ex-post measures instead of ex-ante measures for external imbalances, the first ones also reflect adjustment policies (of the concerned country and of the other countries) which were adopted previously in order to correct certain imbalances for the case that reserves were deficient or too large. Later studies like those of Kenen and Yudin (1965, 1967) – using regression techniques and a stochastic approach to potential reserve outcomes – and of Archibald and Richmond (1971) took these problems into account without solving them completely.

On a purely theoretical level, Olivera (1969) argues that the demand for reserves should be a function of the variance of annual changes in the level of imports and that it is equal to the square root of the level of international transactions. If such a square root law dominated the demand for international reserves, projections often associated with the standard approach and based on an assumed need for a constant reserve/import ratio would be extremely overestimated.

1.3. The Optimizing Approach

The probability distribution of potential external imbalance figures as an input to the third approach, which assumes that a country acts rationally by choosing its appropriate level of reserves on the basis of an optimal decision in analogy to standard demand analysis under conditions of risk and uncertainty. The government is treated as no different from any other economic unit whose demand for an asset is determined by weighing the marginal cost of asset holding against its marginal return. The *costs of holding reserves* are opportunity costs and as proxies for this variable may be chosen the long-term rate of interest [Kenen–Yudin (1965) and Courchene–Youssef (1967)], domestic per-capita income [as used by Clark (1970) and Flanders (1971), but which is an inappropriate variable because it is a measure of the level of development], the growth rate [Flanders (1971)], or some other more meaningful variable which indicates correctly the amount of real reserves a (non-reserve) country gives up by accumulating reserves. The *return of holding reserves* is identical to the cost of not holding reserves. The alternative of financing an external imbalance by reserve variations consists of correcting this imbalance by adjustment policies so that the return of holding reserves is represented by the cost of alternative adjustment policies.

The first authors who propose such a cost–benefit analysis of the demand for reserves (including some testing of the hypothesis) are Heller (1966), Clark (1970) and Kelly (1970). One possible optimizing procedure consists of minimizing the total cost of reserve holding and adjustment policies as it has been suggested by Heller. Another one adopted by Clark–Kelly is conducted in terms of welfare maximization which has to be applied in all those cases where the cost dimension of reserve holding and the cost dimension of adjustment policies are not numerically comparable.

The optimizing approach of reserve holdings includes or can include elements of the first two approaches. As already mentioned the statistical description of the behaviour of reserves over time in terms of the probability of reserve depletion and/or of adopting adjustment policies constitutes one important "input" of the analysis. On the other hand, much recent work has been done on evaluating the costs of various adjustment policies (i.e., the return of reserve holdings), and these costs depend not only on the specific type or bundle of adjustment policies but they also depend on the theoretical view of how any adjustment policy affects the internal and external (i.e. balance-of-payments) variables of the economy among which one possible view is that of the monetary approach.

The optimizing approach to the demand for international reserves assumes that central bankers have some trace of economic rationality. This is a view which has been strongly opposed by Machlup (1966) who argues that the demand for reserves is not a function of any identifiable variable but that it is governed by the insatiable desire of countries to have their reserves grow – a behaviour which could be explained in terms of "Mrs. Machlup's Wardrobe Theory of Monetary Reserves", as Clower and Lipsey (1968, p. 587) termed it. The "need" for reserves can certainly be rather infinite, but the "demand" for reserves which is the need expressed within the limits of the budget constraint of a country will not be infinite and its level will depend on the comparison between the return and cost of reserve holdings giving the "optimum" level of reserves.

The notion of the "optimum" of reserves will be interpreted in this paper as equivalent to the notion of the "equilibrium" amount of the demand for reserves as an outcome of the "optimizing" approach to the demand for reserves. The other notion often used which is that of the "adequacy" of reserves should be reserved to the case where the demand for reserves is equal to the supply of reserves (in the context of world demand and world supply). Finally, the "optimum" of reserve holdings can also be interpreted as the "*optimum optimorum*" in analogy to the optimum quantity of money. These last two notions will be discussed at the end of our analysis while the "equilibrium demand" for international reserves is the main theme of this study.

In this paper some effort will be made to apply existing monetary theory to international monetary phenomena. There is nothing new about such an endeavour in international monetary economics even though some authors are not quite conscious about the analogies one can draw between these two fields of research. It will be shown that there are many similarities between the demand function for precautionary balances by individuals and the demand function for international reserves by central banks. The purpose of such analytical comparison is – so we believe – to permit a better understanding of the recent models for the demand function of international reserves and to provide a possible framework for the analysis which still remains to be done on this subject.

The argument will be developed in the following order. Section 2 answers a preliminary question concerning the demand for *international money* which is the demand for *foreign currencies* by the private sector and the demand for *international reserves* by central banks. It will be shown that the three traditional motives of holding money, the transactions–speculation–precaution motives, are fully applicable to the demand for foreign currencies by *individuals* – a domain which has received very little attention in international monetary economics despite its extreme importance for the actual behaviour of the balance of payments. As far as the demand for international reserves by *central banks* is concerned, only the precautionary motive is applicable. Section 3 develops the "equilibrium demand" for reserves as an outcome of an "objective" trade-off between reserves and adjustment policies and of a "subjective" trade-off between the disutility attached to the opportunity cost of reserve holdings and the disutility associated with the variability of internal variables induced by the adjustment policies. This basic idea can be found in the first fundamental contributions to the optimizing approach of reserve holdings which are those by Clark (1970) and Kelly (1970). Their basic assumptions, however, are a caricature of actual central banker's behaviour. On the one hand, the speed at which adjustment policies will be put into action is neither continuous nor symmetrical with respect to the departure of actual from desired reserves. There is nothing irrational in central banks' behaviour if they give priority to the internal stability target in case of temporarily persistent balance-of-payments surpluses whereas both stability targets, the internal and external one, are seriously taken into account in case of persistent deficits. On the other hand, the monetary authorities are not restricted in their policy choice to expenditure-changing policies as the only alternative to reserve holdings. The "optimum combination" of adjustment policies is the object of section 4. Diminishing returns or increasing disutilities from larger doses of any adjustment policy call for a mixture of available adjustment policies. Furthermore, recognition of uncertainty breaks down the simple pairing of *n* instruments with *n* targets and the application of the portfolio diversification principle makes it more efficient to assign several adjustment policies to the balance-of-payments target. Finally, one special issue will be discussed which concerns the optimal degree of flexibility of the exchange rate as part of the optimum mix of adjustment policies. Section 5 provides some conclusions of the theoretical results for the policy questions of the "adequacy" and the "optimality" of international reserves.

2. Motives for Holding International Money

Each economist seems to have his own Keynes. This may be equally valid for the interpretation of the Keynesian motives for holding cash even though in present literature a certain accordance can be noted with respect to the delimitation of the three motives of the demand for money, notwithstanding what the master really meant by them. The models of the demand for money which were developed in the 50's for the transactions purpose (Baumol–Tobin) and the speculative purpose (Markowitz–Tobin) have contributed to a clarification of the transactions and speculation motives. The first one arises from the imperfect synchronization of payments and receipts under the (implicit) assumption of complete foresight with respect to their timing. The second one is based on uncertainty with respect to future prices of assets.

Both attempts, however, have to be considered as insufficient with regard to their dominant role for the explication of the demand for money. As far as the portfolio theoretical approach is concerned one could presume that not money but rather other equivalent stores of value being moreover interest-bearing assets constitute the speculative "cash balances". On the other hand, the inventory theoretical approach of transactions balances is only useful for those situations in which the fiction of perfect foresight can be maintained as is the case for certain payments and receipts which are periodically "institutionalized". Consequently, the main explanation for the demand for money is given by the precautionary motive which stands for all those cases where the timing and the total volume of certain payments and receipts are not completely known in advance.

In analyzing the motives for holding international money one could ask whether *all three motives* of the demand for money could be used to explain the demand for international money. As we shall see the answer is unambiguous as far as the demand for international money by the private sector of the economy is concerned, while the demand by the central banks which is called the demand for international *reserves* will be sensible only for one or two of the three motives.

2.1. The Transactions Motive

This motive for holding international money exists only for individuals who undertake purchases and sales abroad. If the central bank was engaged in foreign trade, it would also have to hold transactions balances. The characteristic feature of the private sector's transactions demand for international money is that it comprises not only *the* international money – concretely the dollar because gold and special drawing rights are only used between central banks – but also all other currencies, and the choice which other currencies the individual holds, depends on with which country or countries he operates foreign transactions.

In principle, the Baumol–Tobin model can be applied to the (private) transactions demand for foreign currencies. The existence of transaction costs – the costs of conversion from one currency into another one – provides the rational explanation for the holding of foreign currencies. However, the savings of transaction costs has to be weighed with the additional costs arising as Swoboda (1968, pp. 39–41) has shown from a higher level of desired transactions cash balances than it would be necessary in the hypothetical case where only one single currency exists. On the basis of this simple comparison of costs two important facts can be explained. On the one hand there is a specialization of a group of economic units – banks and exchange-brokers – on the holding of foreign currencies. On the other hand there is a specialization on a few foreign currencies, in particular on the U.S. dollar, among the total stock of currencies held by individuals as has been shown by Heller (1968) and Grassman (1973). This last phenomenon is only an application of the "monetary component" of the economic principle according to which the transaction cost (including the numéraire-cost) are the lowest, provided that the world economy disposes of a single currency available for national and international payments.

2.2. The Speculative Motive

However, if one considers the problem of the optimum number of currencies under the aspect of the speculative motive, a higher number of currencies increases the expected return of a portfolio according to the principle of risk reduction via diversification. Under the aspect of its external value money does not constitute any more a perfect store of value because its exchange rate does not remain unchanged even in a system of "fixed" exchange rates. The individual's speculative demand for all (convertible) foreign currencies is nothing else than an extension of the traditional portfolio analysis because the menu of disposable assets is increased by foreign assets of a special kind characterized by perfect marketability. The derivation of the speculative demand for foreign currencies is the domain of the portfolio theory of international capital movements such as it has been developed, for instance, by Branson (e.g., 1970).

A speculative demand for foreign currencies by central banks – and here only a speculative demand for international money – can be conceived for the optimum composition of the total stock of international reserves. First attempts at such a portfolio analysis have been proposed by Kenen (1960, 1963), but only for a gold-dollar-standard. In recent time authors like Aliber (1967), Hirsch (1971), Makin (1972) and Fratianni (1974) have equally taken into account the special drawing rights in a portfolio model besides gold and dollars. It is evident that such an approach is only useful if a portfolio choice is possible for central banks, that means if there is convertibility between the different types of reserves. An important element of this portfolio analysis is the interpretation of the central bank's preference function with respect to expected returns and risk for which Tobin's classification in "risk averters", "risk neutrals" and "risk lovers" is of relevance to the extent that risk aversion is of importance under the special aspect of the effects of a single central bank's portfolio shift on the international monetary system and its repercussions on the concerned country so that one most probable portfolio behaviour in interdependent economies may be that which could be compared with oligopolistic behaviour as Officer and Willet (1969, 1970) have pointed out.

Our study will not treat the question of the reserve composition and it will be concerned only with the total stock of reserves. Such a procedure must be considered as very restrictive to the extent that the money quality of various reserve media is different. In particular, if the "oligopolistic good behaviour" of central bankers plays a special role for the composition of reserves, restrictions on this composition may influence the total desired level of international reserves.

There is still a second reason why the speculative motive may have an important effect on the *total level* of desired reserves holdings. It is conceivable that reserves constitute a sound investment of the national wealth because they may yield high earnings. Even in the case where reserves are low yielding assets, the risk diversification argument can play an essential role for the total amount of desired reserves as part of the total portfolio of *national wealth.* In both cases, as a nation acquires greater aggregate wealth, its demand for all types of assets including international reserves should increase; see Heller (1970).

2.3. The Precautionary Motive

Neglecting the above qualifications the precautionary motive remains the only relevant motive to explain the holding of reserves by central banks, while all three motives are applicable to the private demand for foreign currencies. That the precautionary motive can equally be applied to the private demand for foreign currencies arises from the fact that this motive is nothing else than the "transactions motive in a world of uncertainty".[1]

The official demand for international reserves as the outcome of the precautionary motive has to be interpreted as follows. To the extent that the

[1]Theoretical studies of the private precautionary demand for foreign currencies do not exist until now as far as we know. Furthermore, there is a missing link in monetary theory with respect to the interdependence between the demand for domestic currency and the demand for foreign currencies.

A special issue with respect to privately held foreign balances concerns the relationship (if there is any) between the private demand for foreign currencies (as an outcome of all motives or of only the precautionary motive) and the official demand for international reserves. One particular case is that of an official holding of reserves of zero under a system of "clean" floating exchange rates. According to Machlup (1964, pp. 267–270) under such a system private foreign balances would be especially large. They are held to avoid the risk of loss from exchange-rate fluctuations, even though individuals can avoid these exchange risks by hedging operations in the forward market (provided that the cost of such hedging is lower than the loss of interest from holding foreign currencies). If most individuals (i.e., mainly private business firms) rely on hedging, it will be nevertheless profitable for others to hold inventories of foreign balances for reasons of "speculation". These other individuals can be firms or banks getting specialized in holding foreign currencies: as in all sorts of insuring risk-pooling reduces the cost – here the cost of holding reserves (by reducing the "necessary" amount of foreign balances to be held in order to maintain the same degree of risk).

Of course, this risk-pooling can be operated by the central bank by intervening in the market for foreign exchange and, by this, holding a certain volume of foreign currencies or reserves. However, the social cost of official holding of international money may be higher than the social cost of international money held by specialized firms provided that they compete with one another which would compel strict rationality in the determination of the appropriate size of foreign currencies.

Note that the principle of risk-pooling is also applicable to member-countries of a currency area who centralize their holdings of reserves so that (under certain conditions) the community "needs" less reserves than the total of its members; cf., Salant (1973).

central bank wants to influence the exchange rate in the market of foreign exchange via quantitative interventions in form of purchase or sale of international money, it is forced to hold a certain stock of reserves. This "reserve policy" of varying degree is necessary for all imaginable exchange-rate regimes except the system of "purely" flexible exchange rates. However, it is only operational for those balances of payments which are in a "fundamental equilibrium" over some specified period during which random shocks occur pushing temporarily the actual exchange rate above or under the "desired" exchange rate – fluctuations which can be avoided by the "reserve policy".

The assumption of a "fundamental equilibrium" in the analysis of the demand for reserves is equivalent to the assumption that the cumulative expenditures equal cumulative receipts in the analysis of the demand for precautionary balances because otherwise cash balances of reserves would be always insufficient or abundant. Grubel (1971, p. 1152) rejects any analogy between the demand for cash by individuals and the demand for reserves by governments "because cash holders initiate transactions on their own while reserve holders tend to react passively to the consequences of private transactions". Grubel seems to refer his objection to the transactions demand for which there is, indeed, no valid comparison. However, as far as the precautionary demand is concerned, both types of decision units, individuals and governments, find themselves confronted with a pattern of payments and receipts which are distributed randomly. The essential difference between the two kinds of decision-makers lies in the alternative of cash holdings, respectively. In the literature on the precautionary demand for money a lower holding of cash balances implies a higher number of probable portfolio shifts from bonds into money, while in the case of the demand for reserves a lower holding of reserves involves a higher size of probable adjustment policies of the balance of payments. Any disturbance in the balance of payments can be either *financed* by changes in the existing stock of reserves or *eliminated* by adjustment policies influencing international payments by acting on strategical economic variables like income, interest rates, exchange rates, direct controls etc. *or* met by a *mixture* of both; the last case is the most relevant one provided that the government wants to avoid reserve depletion and saturation. Thus, the "return" component of precautionary balances is the saving of transactions costs associated with portfolio conversions and the "return" component of reserve holdings is the saving of adjustment costs as the outcome of balance-of-payments policies.[2]

[2]Note, however, that modern monetary economics begin to take into account the possibility that individuals may influence the payments pattern "imposed" on them when the opportunity cost of

We must still mention one strong argument for the application of the tools of individual cash holding theory to the analysis of reserve holdings and at the same time some qualification to such application, both pointed out by Niehans (1970, pp. 58–60) even though as Grubel, he fails to take into account the proper part of individual cash holdings as a valid base of comparison which is the precautionary demand for money and not the transactions demand. On the one hand international reserves of a single country correspond to the cash balance approach of an *individual* and not to that of the aggregate of individuals so that the analytical framework of the individual's (and not of aggregate) demand for precautionary cash balances could be used. On the other hand there may be a noticeable difference in the probability distribution of temporary imbalances in the payments-receipts pattern of an individual and in that of a country. For the latter the total of international payments and receipts is constituted not only by commodity imports and exports, but also by the flow of capital, whose fluctuations are relatively more violent and less predictable. The demand for reserves can be largely due to the actual and potential variations in capital flows.

Until now we have discussed only one specific type of precautionary motive for holding reserves which constituted the only reason for the demand of reserves such as it is developed in the literature on the optimizing approach to reserve holdings. This specific type of the precautionary motive concerns the "fundamental" assumption of a "fundamental balance-of-payments equilibrium" over a given period, say several months or several years during which considerable deficits and surpluses may turn up temporarily due to random disturbances arising from seasonal imbalances or from cyclical developments in the domestic and international economy. As Cooper (1970, p. 127) points out, besides temporary imbalances there may be permanent ones which give rise to an additional reason to hold reserves. The argument is not that reserves should finance continuously a fundamental disequilibrium but that it may be preferable from the point of view of intertemporal utility maximization to adjourn the current adjustment to future periods which implies, in particular for permanent deficits, the existence of a "sufficient" level of reserves at least for the current period. It seems, according to Williamson (1973, p. 693), that this problem has not been analyzed in the framework of an intertemporal model until now even though there are attempts, by Britto and Heller (1973), of an intertemporal

cash holdings changes considerably (in case of inflation or of interest payments on money), instead of taking the "lack of synchronization" between receipts and payments as an inevitable fate; see, for instance, Claassen (1975a).

optimizing approach to the timing of adjustment policies, but only for a country which is subject to reversible external imbalances.[3]

3. The Equilibrium Demand for Reserves

The two fundamental contributions to the theory of the demand for reserves as an outcome of a rational optimizing decision are those by Clark (1970) and Kelly (1970), which both utilize the same principal factors relevant to the derivation of the demand function of reserves and which have been emphasized already in an earlier study by Heller (1966): the probability of running out of reserves, the return of reserves in terms of the cost of alternative policy measures which would be required if reserves are insufficient, and the opportunity cost of holding reserves. We shall give a brief summary of their approach as the starting point of an extended model suggested at the end of this section.

The actual balance-of-payments surplus or deficit (B) is composed of a random component (ε) and of a desired change in the level of reserves (B^*) induced by policy actions,

$$B = \varepsilon + B^*,$$

where B is the actual change in the level of reserves (R): $B = \Delta R$. *Starting from an initial position of equilibrium* where actual reserves are equal to desired reserves ($R = R^*$), any deviation of actual reserves from desired reserves (ε) may be counteracted, partially or totally, by policy actions,

$$B^* = -\gamma\varepsilon, \qquad 0 \leq \gamma \leq 1,$$

where γ stands for the (marginal) policy response coefficient equal to $\mathrm{d}B^*/\mathrm{d}\varepsilon$ (and where the marginal coefficient is supposed to be equal to the average policy response coefficient B^*/ε). Thus, the actual change in reserves will be

$$B \equiv \Delta R = \varepsilon(1 - \gamma).$$

Note that we abstract from any time-lag arising from today's balance-of-payments policy reaction to yesterday's random disturbance (this time-lag is

[3]There can be listed still two other reasons for holding international reserves on the grounds of the precautionary motive of a very special type; cf., Cooper (1970, p. 126). The first one concerns the holding of reserves serving as a war chest in times when normal internal or external economic relationships are disturbed. The other reason arises from the traditional notion that a currency of a country should be "backed" partially by international reserves in order to maintain the confidence in the financial strength of that currency. This last argument links, to a certain extent, the monetary approach to the demand for reserves.

taken into account by Clark) as well as from tomorrow's balance-of-payments policy impact of today's balance-of-payments policy.

The probability distribution of reserve changes (ΔR) is supposed to have a zero mean which corresponds to the hypothesis that the country is in a fundamental balance-of-payments equilibrium over a given period. The variance of reserves, $V(R)$, expressing the variability of the temporary gap between payments and receipts, is

$$V(R) = E(\Delta R^2) = V(\varepsilon)(1-\gamma)^2,$$

where E denotes the expectation. It is assumed that the random disturbances in the balance of payments are independently distributed such that any autocorrelation of ε during the period, due to cyclical fluctuations in the level of reserves or to speculation where one disturbance generates another one, is ruled out.

A conservative estimate for the probability of running temporarily out of reserves (P) can be derived from Tchebycheff's inequality. According to this theorem, the probability that a variable is away from its mean by more than k times its standard deviation S is equal to or less than $1/k^2$, and in the case of a symmetrical distribution the probability is equal to or less than $1/2k^2$, that is $P \leqslant 1/2k^2$. Because the expected value of reserves changes ($\bar{R}$) is assumed to be zero, reserves can be insufficient by $R - \bar{R} = R = kS$ so that $k = R/S$. Consequently, we have $P \leqslant 1/2(R/S)^2$. The most conservative estimate of the probability that reserves will be exceeded is assumed to be the relevant measure for reserves management behaviour so that the inequality becomes for the maximum probability of running out of reserves,

$$P = \frac{S^2}{2R^2} = \frac{V(R)}{2R^2} = \frac{V(\varepsilon)(1-\gamma)^2}{2R^2}. \tag{1}$$

The determination of the demand for reserves can be analyzed in three successive steps:

(1) Suppose that a minimum of balance-of-payments adjustment policies is envisaged by the central bank so that balance-of-payments deficits have to be financed nearly entirely by the existing stock of reserves. In this case, the choice for the appropriate level of reserves will be determined by the comparison between the cost of reserves in terms of their opportunity cost and the return of reserves in terms of the degree of solvency. The amount of reserve holdings which result from this decision-making will be called the "maximum" demand for reserves.

(2) By taking into account the possibility of balance-of-payments adjustment

policies the ultimate level of desired reserves, their "equilibrium" amount, will be lower than the maximum one arising from choice (1). The outcome of this second-choice decision depends on the comparison between the cost of reserves, here again in terms of their opportunity cost, and the return of reserves which is now constituted by a lower degree of variability of some important internal economic variables.

(3) The *dichotomized* policy choices, (1) and (2), are an "oversimplification" of the Clark–Kelly model. Its "justification" follows from two sources – the relatively easier exposition in geometrical terms and the feasibility to compare the Clark–Kelly model with an extended one in which their assumption of continuous and symmetrical adjustment policies will be abandoned in favour of the more "realistic" central banks' behaviour who adopt adjustment policies discontinuously and less frequently in situations of excessive reserves than for the cases of insufficient reserves.

3.1. The Maximum Level of Reserve Holdings

The country wishes to minimize the probability of running out of reserves, since if it does run out, it is faced at the national and international opprobrium of insolvency and of borrowing abroad abstracting, for the moment, from the possibility of adopting any important internal policy measures beyond the "minimum" ones in order to reduce the deficit.[4] Thus, because of the latter assumption ($\gamma = \gamma_{\min}$) the probability to run out of reserves will be generally higher than prescribed by relation (1) because

$$P = \frac{V(\varepsilon)(1-\gamma_{\min})^2}{2R^2},$$

or

$$R = \frac{S(\varepsilon)}{(2P)^{1/2}}(1-\gamma_{\min}).$$

[4]Even under the assumption of independently distributed disturbances (although the presence of seasonal and cyclical fluctuations in the balance of payments and speculative attacks against currencies would tend to make reserve changes autocorrelated, and therefore increase their variability), if no attempt at all is undertaken to maintain a certain stock of reserves (i.e., if $\gamma = 0$), the variance of reserves, $V(R)$, becomes undefined, i.e., infinite, because the level of reserves is then an infinite sum of random disturbances. For this (mathematical) reason we have to operate with the assumption of $\gamma = \gamma_{\min}$ where $\gamma_{\min}$ is near to zero.

Note that in a recent study (which I have read after revising this paper) by Hipple (1974, pp. 17 et seq.) a similar dichotomy has been proposed: first, the determination of P for an exogenously given γ; second, the determination of the desired levels of γ and R for a given (pre-determined) P.

This relation is traced in the south-west panel of figure 1 as one side of an equilateral hyperbola being asymptotic to the coordinates. As R increases the probability of becoming insolvent (P) decreases at a decreasing rate. P, or more precisely $(0.5-P)$ is the return component of reserves where 0.5 is the maximum value for P (when $R=0$ in the case of a symmetrical probability distribution).

The cost element of reserves consists of net opportunity cost (C) being equal to the difference between the return the reserves could earn on alternative, domestic or foreign, investments and the positive yield paid on reserves. The cost function is plotted in the north-west panel of figure 1 for a given net opportunity cost per unit of reserves (i).

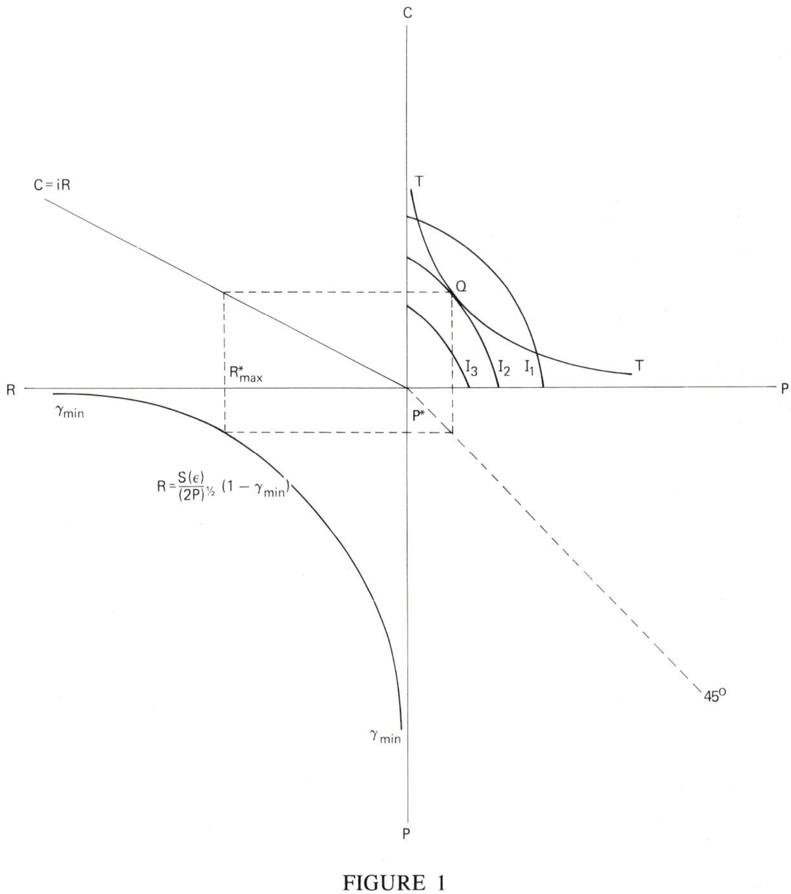

FIGURE 1

More reserves entail higher net opportunity cost and a higher degree of solvability, and vice versa. This trade-off the monetary authorities are faced by for their decision of reserves holding is depicted by the transformation curve *TT* in the north-east panel of figure 1 which is derived from the two curves in the left-hand panels.

Which point of the transformation curve the central banker will choose and by this, which level of reserves he wishes to hold for the hypothetical case of the absence of any balance-of-payments adjustment policy, will depend on the country's preferences for a higher degree of external solvability against a reduced level of opportunity cost. These preferences are summarized in the set of indifference curves for the two "bads", *C* and *P*, in the north-east panel of figure 1 where increasing utility is attained by moving from I_1 to I_2, I_3. The country's utility is maximized at the point of tangency *Q* of the curves I_2 and *TT* indicating the ultimate choice for the desired degree of solvency $(0.5 - P^*)$ for which R^* has to be held, which for a "minimum" of adjustment policies $(\gamma = \gamma_{min})$, is at the same time the highest equilibrium level for *R* (R^*_{max}).

The relevance of the above result is not so much the determination of the maximum level of reserve holdings but that of the desired degree of external solvability P^* (or more precisely, $0.5 - P^*$). This interpretation of P^* may be twofold. If the country faces a degree of insolvency which could only be met by an amount of *R* depassing R^*_{max} (or by a combination of reserve holdings and adjustment policies guaranteeing a higher degree of safety than the target one, $0.5 - P^*$), it may cease the membership of the international monetary system and adopt an international barter trade. Another alternative would be that the country opts for a floating exchange rate or for a higher degree of flexibility in its exchange rate. But this interpretation is only a tentative one and we think that future research has to analyze this question in detail.[5]

3.2. The Equilibrium Level of Reserve Holdings (for Continuous and Symmetrical Adjustment Policies)

The monetary authorities will not necessarily choose R^*_{max} as the desired level of reserve holdings. Any disturbance in the balance of payments can be either financed by changes in the existing stock of reserves *or* eliminated by

[5]Note that the theory of precautionary balances has not answered the (analogical) question for an individual's holding of *liquid assets* which guarantees a certain degree of solvency. The literature on precautionary balances treats only the optimum composition of liquid assets into bonds and cash balances without analyzing the decision of the optimum composition of the portfolio in liquid and non-liquid assets – from the point of view of the precautionary motive.

adjustments within the economy *or* met by a mixture of both. Hence, less reserves will be needed, the higher the rate of internal adjustment policies (γ) will be, *given the target to maintain the degree of external solvability P^**. By re-arranging equation (1) we obtain the trade-off between reserves and internal adjustment policies,

$$R = \frac{S(\varepsilon)}{(2P^*)^{1/2}}(1-\gamma).$$

This relation is traced in the south-west panel of figure 2. In the case where a "minimum" balance-of-payments adjustment policy is undertaken ($\gamma = \gamma_{min}$), the equilibrium level of reserves would be R^*_{max} guaranteeing the desired degree of solvency P^*, which can be achieved as well by any other combinations of

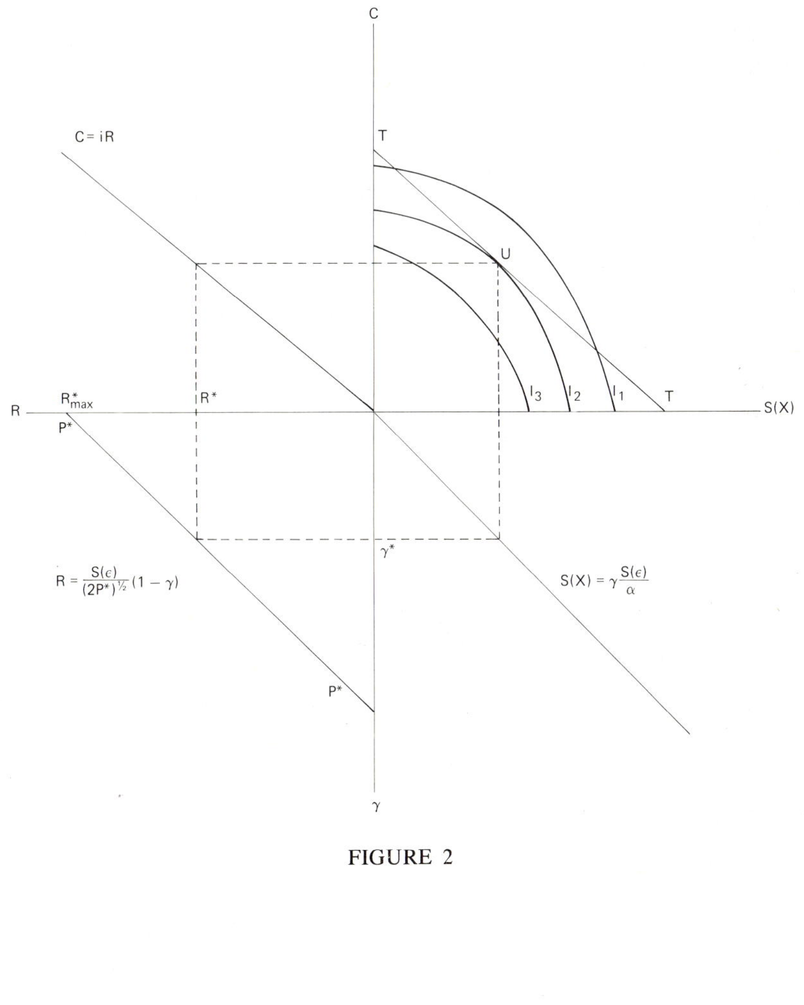

FIGURE 2

R, γ described by the straight line P^*P^*. (In figure 2, R^*_{max} is plotted at $\gamma = 0$ even though it should be traced at γ_{min}, where γ_{min} is near to zero.)

What the final equilibrium level for reserves will be, depends again on the cost–return comparison of reserve holdings. While the cost of reserves is the same net opportunity cost as we know it from the (R, P) decision, traced in the north-west panel of figure 2, the return derived from holding reserves is the avoidance of the costs of adjustment. Since a fundamental equilibrium in the balance of payments is assumed, the action on any internal variable (X) in order to influence the balance of payments via B^* will only be temporary. Consequently the mean value of

$$\Delta X = \beta\varepsilon$$

will be zero where $\beta = \mathrm{d}X/\mathrm{d}\varepsilon$ is the marginal internal policy response coefficient which reflects the impact of the random disturbance on the policy variable X. The variance of X,

$$V(X) = E(\Delta X^2) = \beta^2 V(\varepsilon) = \gamma^2 \frac{V(\varepsilon)}{\alpha^2},$$

expresses the variability of the policy variable, or in terms of the standard deviation,

$$S(X) = \gamma \frac{S(\varepsilon)}{\alpha}, \tag{2}$$

where

$$\gamma = \alpha\beta, \tag{3}$$

that is

$$\frac{\mathrm{d}B^*}{\mathrm{d}\varepsilon} = \frac{\mathrm{d}B^*}{\mathrm{d}X}\frac{\mathrm{d}X}{\mathrm{d}\varepsilon},$$

α being the marginal external (balance-of-payments) response coefficient to a change in the internal variable X. $S(X)$ is the return component of holding reserves since higher reserves decrease the necessity of adopting internal adjustment policies (lower β, and hence, for a given value of α, lower γ) which decreases the variability of X. The relationship (2) is traced in the south-east panel of figure 2.

Which (R, γ) policy mix the monetary authorities can choose in terms of the cost–return alternatives is depicted by the transformation line TT in the north-east panel of figure 2. Higher reserves holdings signify higher opportunity costs on the one hand and a lower variability of some internal economic variables on the other hand, and vice versa. Which cost–return combination the central banker will adopt depends finally on the country's preference function vis-à-vis the opportunity cost and the variability of X represented as a family of concave indifference curves in the north-east panel of figure 2. The shape of the curves assures the attainability of a unique equilibrium at the tangency point U generating the equilibrium value for the reserves holdings, R^*, and for the rate of balance-of-payments adjustment policies, γ^*.

The above dichotomized policy choices, (1) the (R, P) decision and (2) the (R, γ) decision, were based on the implicit assumption that the utility function is separable with respect to its arguments $C, P, S(X)$. A non-separable utility function would have necessitated a simultaneous determination of P, R and γ which would be represented geometrically by the point of tangency between a transformation surface and an indifference surface in a three-dimensional space. This "oversimplification" of the Clark–Kelly model, and in particular of Clark's contribution, consists precisely of this dichotomy, but which "acceptable" probability P^* will be chosen remains unspecified in their model. Furthermore, Clark introduces the element of time into the analysis by proposing a lagged relationship between yesterday's actual reserves movements and today's adjustment policy which he specifies in detail in his article (1972). Thus, it is conceivable that the government adopts an adjustment policy to improve the balance of payments even though it is in surplus at the moment of the policy action while there was a deficit in the past period.

The demand function for reserves on the basis of our simplified model can be written as

$$R^{\mathrm{d}} = p \cdot R^*[i, S(X), S(\varepsilon)], \qquad \frac{\partial R^*}{\partial i} < 0, \quad \frac{\partial R^*}{\partial S(X)} > 0, \quad \frac{\partial R^*}{\partial S(\varepsilon)} > 0.$$

The direction of change of desired reserves holdings is in the first two cases in accord with a priori expectations. With respect to the interpretation of the third derivative, there is an indirect and a direct effect of a change of $S(\varepsilon)$ on R^*. The indirect effect is taken into account by the second derivative because a ceteris paribus increment of $S(\varepsilon)$ increases $S(X)$ according to equation (2): a higher variability in international payments and receipts increases the adjustment cost. The direct effect arises from the (R, P) decisions. An increase in $S(\varepsilon)$ involves a higher P^* and a higher $R^*_{\max}$ the latter inducing a higher R^*; one extreme case would be that P^* remains unchanged so that $R^*_{\max}$ rises proportionately to $S(\varepsilon)$.

Under simple stochastic assumptions there is a proportionate relationship between $S(\varepsilon)$ and $pt\sqrt{N}$, where ptN is the money volume of international transactions: p is the international price level, t the average real value of foreign expenditures and receipts and N the number of foreign expenditures and receipts. A direct proportionality between R^* and $S(\varepsilon)$ – for instance as an outcome of the combined effects $\partial R^*/\partial S(\varepsilon)$ and $\partial R^*/\partial S(X)$ – involves a linear relationship between the demand for nominal reserves and the international price level (and the average real value of international transactions, respectively). The economies of scale for reserve holdings are only applicable with regard to the increased number of international transactions.

A linear relationship between R^* and $S(\varepsilon)$ implies that the real value of the demand for reserves remains unchanged in case of an increase in the international price level. Because short-term disturbances in the balance of payments are generated by "real causes" (such as crop failures, labour disputes, seasonal and political events, etc.), rising international prices transform the "real" disturbances into higher "nominal" random changes such that when deflated by the international price level the variability of the balance of payments remains constant in real terms. Consequently, it will appear sensible to keep the real value of desired reserves intact. However, in the case of a sustained upward trend in the level of international prices and to the extent that the interest rate paid on reserves does not take into account the world inflation rate, the cost of reserve holding will increase in real terms such that the demand of real reserves will diminish similar to the behaviour of the demand for real cash balances.[6]

3.3. *The Equilibrium Level of Reserve Holdings (for Discontinuous and Asymmetrical Adjustment Policies)*

Until now we carried on with a very restrictive assumption in regard to actual central banker's behaviour according to which countries adopt various policy measures *continuously* from the moment onwards where there is any disturbance ε in the balance of payments and *symmetrically* with respect to balance-of-payments surpluses or deficits. In fact, we know from experience that this assumption is ivory-towerish. Actual central banker's behaviour acts rather abruptively. First, only at some significant cumulative deficit or surplus a government begins to use its instruments of adjustment policies. On the other

[6]Shinkai (1973) treats an interesting question with respect to the demand function for reserves by a country which isolates itself from world inflation by steady revaluations while our problem was concerned with a country which has the same inflation path as the rest of the world. However, it seems that he does not clearly distinguish between the cost of *holding* reserves and the cost of *acquiring* reserves, the latter (in particular relevant for inflationary situations) will be treated in the last section.

hand, the policy response is observed to be faster to a deficit than to a surplus. Is there any way to rationalize this discontinuous and asymmetrical behaviour even though its repercussions on the macro-level, that is on the over-all international monetary system, may be disequilibrating?

The last standpoint can be defended on the following grounds. A "discrete-time" adjustment is the sense of less frequent adjustments but at larger lots, could be justified by pointing out that any "continuous-time" adjustment would be in many cases redundant (and more costly in terms of a higher variability of some internal variables). Only if the disturbance has, for a certain time interval, a definite one-way tendency, it will be necessary to adopt internal policy measures.

Figure 3 illustrates one possible speed of adjustment policies in the alternative cases of continuous and discontinuous adjustment. The dotted line indicates one possible time series of the cumulative random disturbance in the balance of payments, $\Sigma\varepsilon(t)$. Thus, in period t_1t_2 there is a continuous deficit (the exchange rate is at the floor) forcing the monetary authorities to intervene by selling foreign exchanges. In period t_2t_3, there is neither a deficit nor a surplus, and from t_3 until t_4 the exchange rate is at the ceiling causing again an intervention by the central bank in the foreign exchange market being now forced to buy foreign exchanges, and so on. (1) If there is a *continuous adjustment* as the Clark–Kelly model suggests "for analytical sake of simplicity" – and it can be conceived as a mechanically regulated system (for instance, only a fixed proportion of reserves outflows and inflows are neutralized with respect to the domestic quantity of money), then we have the line $R_1(t)$ as reflecting the actual behaviour of the level of reserves. The vertical difference between $R_1(t)$ and $\Sigma\varepsilon(t)$ measures the continuous correction of a deficit or surplus by internal policy measures ($\gamma = 0.5$) where one assumes that the latter affect immediately the balance of payments. (2) A *discontinuous adjustment* as depicted by the line $R_2(t)$ has to space the adjustment action points at certain lower and upper limits of actual reserves movements, in figure 3 at zero and R_{max}, respectively, such that by a once-and-for-all internal adjustment measure the balance of payments will "improve" or "deteriorate" bringing back the level of reserves to some desired level, say to R_a. The assumption that the adjustment policies have an immediate impact on the balance of payments justifies setting the lower signal point for policy action at zero. A more realistic analysis would set this lower limit at some positive amount (say at 0 by shifting the origin of the coordinates to 0′); such an analysis has to utilize lagged relationships involving familiar problems of overshooting and undershooting.

Furthermore, by choosing the "reserves-management rule $(0, R_a, R_{max})$" as

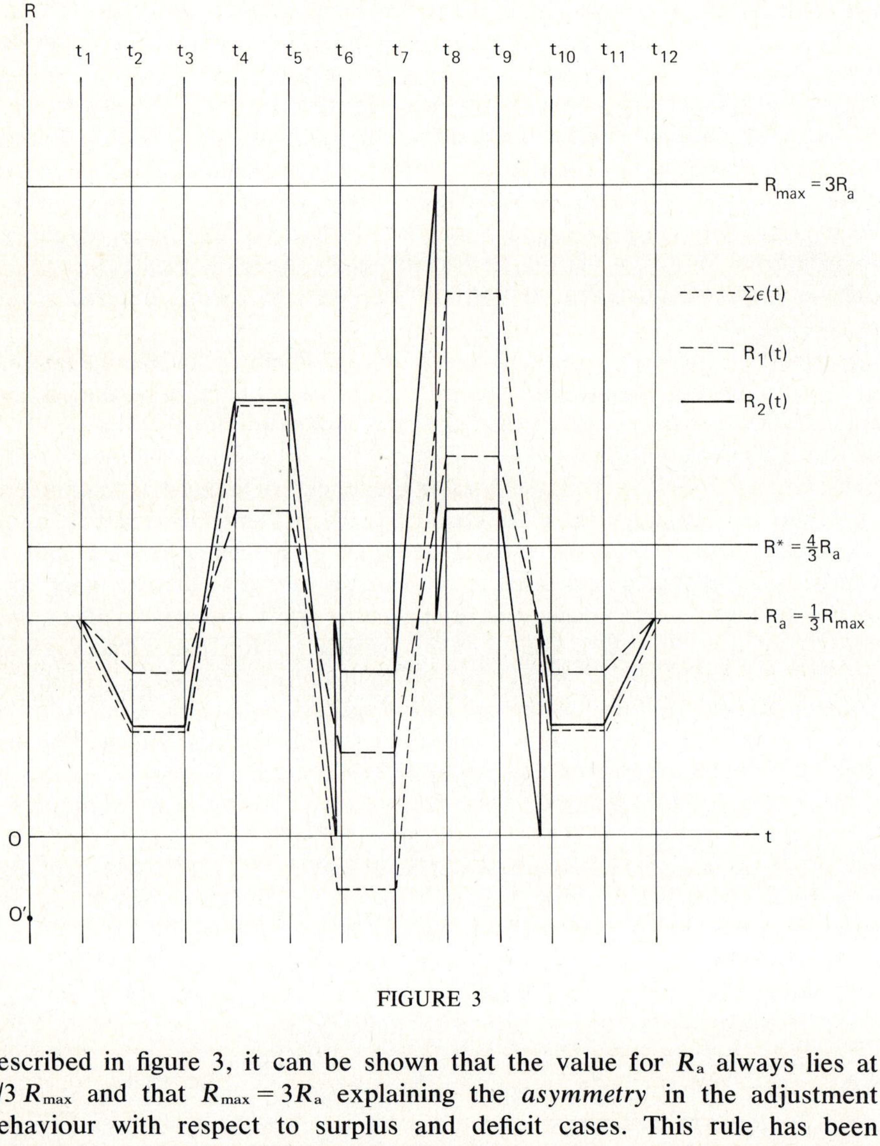

FIGURE 3

described in figure 3, it can be shown that the value for R_a always lies at $1/3\ R_{max}$ and that $R_{max} = 3R_a$ explaining the *asymmetry* in the adjustment behaviour with respect to surplus and deficit cases. This rule has been developed by Claassen (1975) and it can be derived from an analysis developed by Miller–Orr (1966, pp. 420–423) and Orr (1971, pp. 58–60) for the demand for precautionary cash balance by firms whose payments *and* receipts are irregularly timed (as it is the case with central banks) and who manage their cash balances under some "policy of simple form" (as it has been suggested for discrete reserves management by central bankers). Miller and Orr assume that the probability distribution of the net cash flows has a zero mean as we have supposed with respect to the probability distribution for reserves changes since we are dealing with a country being in a fundamental balance-of-payments equilibrium. For the hypothesis of a discontinuous cash-management policy, that is for the case of discontinuous portfolio transfers from bonds to cash or from cash to bonds, they derive two important formulas from probability theory. The first one concerns the probability of a portfolio transfer, $P(A)$ – or in our context the probability how often a balance-of-payments adjustment will be undertaken, that is how often the actual pattern of reserves (cash) will hit either the upper limit R_{max} or the lower zero limit inducing an adjustment policy (a portfolio transfer) to bring back reserves (cash) to the target level R_a,

$$P(A) = \frac{V(\varepsilon)}{R_a(R_{max} - R_a)}. \tag{4}$$

The second formula represents the average level of reserves (cash),[7]

$$R = \frac{R_a + R_{max}}{3}. \tag{5}$$

There are now two problems to be solved. (a) The first one is to know the *relative* level of R_a and R_{max}, that is the optimal ratio R_{max}/R_a. (b) The second one concerns the *absolute* level of R_a and R_{max}, that is the optimum amount of average reserves holdings, R^*.

(a) The solution of the first problem is rather easy to find because it is independent on any return–cost comparison. By definition, R_{max} must exceed R_a, the question is by how much. Suppose that the average desired level is known (which will be analyzed later on). Say, it is of the amount R^*. According to (5) there are many possible combinations of R_a, R_{max} which satisfy the equilibrium amount of R^*, and in this respect the ratio R_{max}/R_a is independent on any return–cost comparison given the amount of R^*. Looking at (4), such a combination will be chosen for which the expression $R_a(R_{max} - R_a)$ is at its maximum value – hence $P(A)$ at its lowest level, subject to the constraint $R^* = (R_a + R_{max})/3$. Because, according to (5), $R_a(R_{max} - R_a)$ is equal to

[7]The derivation of the above formulas (and possible extensions of them) necessitates a rather lengthy and cumbersome analysis in terms of probability theory. The reader interested in the step-by-step derivation should consult Miller and Orr (1966, pp. 420–423) and Orr (1971, pp. 58–60).

$3R^*R_a - 2R_a^2$, we have to maximize this expression with respect to R_a which yields

$$R^* = \frac{4}{3} R_a, \tag{6}$$

and setting the value of R^* given by (5) into (6), we obtain

$$R_{max} = 3R_a. \tag{7}$$

Equations (6) and (7) reveal some interesting properties of the discontinuous adjustment rule for central bankers' reserves-management policy. Despite the assumed symmetrical probability distribution of reserve changes the optimal adjustment behaviour should be asymmetrical implying that situations of temporarily insufficient reserves lead to adjustments with greater average frequency and in a smaller size than adjustments in situations of temporary excessive reserves. The greater size of downwards adjustments in reserves holdings cancels out the greater frequency of upwards adjustments so that the desired average level of reserves will be maintained. It should be noted that this surprising result arises from the fact that any combination of $(R_{max} > R_a)$ maintaining R^* constant does not affect the opportunity cost of average reserves holding but only their return in terms of $P(A)$, that is in terms of lower or higher adjustment costs.

(b) However, as far as the determination of the average volume of desired reserves and, hence, of the absolute level of R_a and R_{max} is concerned, it can only be solved on the basis of a return–cost comparison, similar to the type of analysis exposed in section 3.2. Let us first look at the "technical" trade-off between average reserves holdings, R, and the probable number of adjustments in the reserves $P(A)$. Formula (4) can be re-arranged in the following way by taking into account our previous results for the relations between R^*, R_a and R_{max} expressed by (6) and (7),

$$P(A) = \frac{V(\varepsilon)}{R_a(R_{max} - R_a)} = \frac{V(\varepsilon)}{2R_a^2} = \frac{16}{9}\frac{V(\varepsilon)}{2R^2},$$

or

$$R = \frac{4}{3}\frac{S(\varepsilon)}{[2P(A)]^{1/2}}.$$

This relationship is traced as the asymptotic trade-off curve in the south-west panel of figure 4. As R increases, it becomes less probable that internal adjustment policies have to be undertaken to restore reserves to the level R_a.

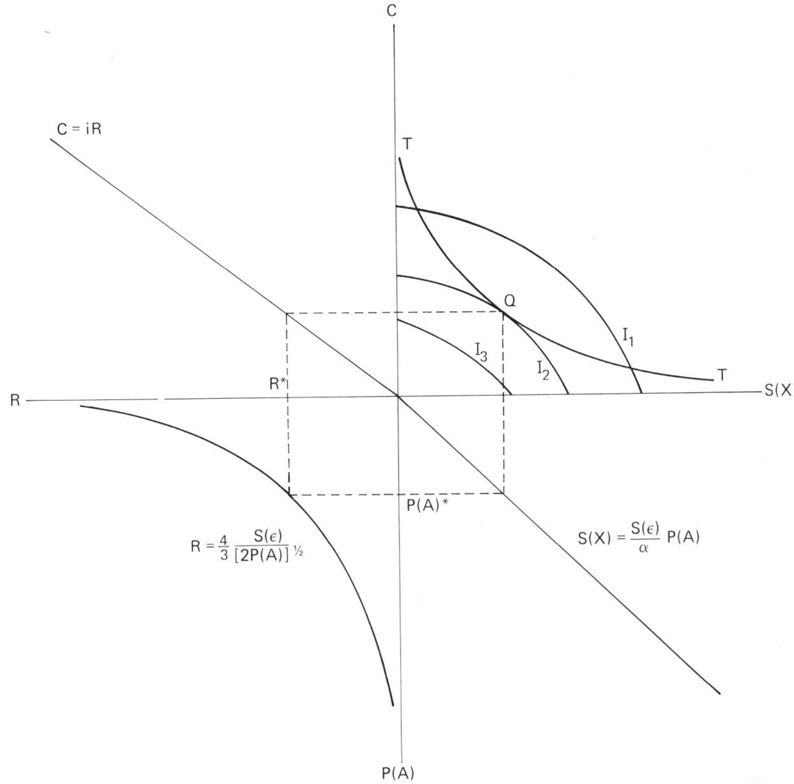

FIGURE 4

[Note that the decision (R, P) as it has been developed in section 3.1 remains valuable so that we still have the same equilibrium values for R^*_{max} and P^*.]

Which point on the trade-off curve will be the optimal one depends on the return–cost comparison of reserves holdings. The *return* consists of the avoidance of the costs of adjustment, the latter represented by the variability of some internal variables X,

$$S(X) = P(A)\frac{S(\varepsilon)}{\alpha}. \tag{8}$$

Expression (8) corresponds to that of (2) provided that γ is replaced by $P(A)$. However, $P(A)$ continues to be equal to $\alpha\beta$ by analogy to formula (3). Relation (8) is represented as a straight line in the south-east panel of figure 4. Higher reserves lead to less frequent adjustments and by this to the benefit of a lower variability of some internal variables. The *cost* of reserves holdings are our familiar opportunity cost traced in the north-west panel of figure 4.

Now, the technical trade-off between R and $P(A)$ can be translated into a trade-off between C and $S(X)$ expressed by the transformation curve TT in the north-east panel of figure 4. Which cost–return combination the central banker will choose depends again on the country's preference function traced as a set of indifference curves in the north-east panel of figure 4. The tangency point Q indicates the equilibrium value for the average reserves holdings, R^*, and for the rate of balance-of-payments adjustment policies, $P(A)^*$.

The above derivation of the "optimum speed" of adjustment policies gives rise to a target level of reserves (R_a) which will be restored discontinuously in time depending on when actual reserve movements hit some maximum level (R_{max}) or fall to some minimum level (zero). The maximum level is always three times higher than the target level which is the rationale of the asymmetrical adjustment behaviour with respect to excessive and deficient reserves. The absolute amount of the target level, and therefore the absolute amount of the maximum level of reserves and of the average level of reserves (R^*), depends in the same way on the interest rate (i), the variability of international payments [$S(\varepsilon)$] and on the internal adjustment cost [$S(X)$] as it was described at the end of section 3.2 for the (average) demand for reserves (for a given "taste" how the "collectivity" judges the two "bads": the domestic income loss due to higher reserves versus the internal adjustment cost due to lower reserves).

Comparing the average level of the equilibrium demand for reserves as the outcome of discontinuous and asymmetrical adjustment policies with that arising from the other extreme of adjustment policies – continuous and symmetrical adjustment, nothing precisely can be stated. At first sight one could argue that average desired reserve holdings are higher in the first case because of less frequent adjustments when the actual balance of payments is in surplus. However, it is conceivable that the target level of reserves (R_a) is relatively low so that the average desired level ($R^* = \frac{4}{3}R_a$) could be equal to that one arising from the hypothetical case of continuous and asymmetrical adjustment.

4. The Optimum Combination of Balance-of-Payments Adjustment Policies

Whatever appropriate trade-off central bankers choose between financing or eliminating a deficit or surplus, both policy choices – "reserve policy" and adjustment policy – are an integrated and simultaneous part of the government's optimum decision-making with respect to the macroeconomic management of the economy and to the behaviour of the balance of payments. The literature on the optimizing approach to the demand for reserves takes into account this interdependence, but its principal attention is directed to the equilibrium amount of desired reserves while the choice of an adjustment policy is made rather on an ad hoc basis guided by analytical convenience. On the other hand, the literature on balance-of-payments adjustment policies is hardly concerned with their alternative which is the reserve policy. It is evident that future research has to be consecrated to a better integration of the above policy choices.

The various aspects of the "optimum combination of balance-of-payments adjustment policies" may be summarized as follows.

(1) A preliminary question is to classify all possible types of adjustment policies in terms of a cost–benefit criterion and to select the *optimal type(s)* of adjustment policy. As already mentioned the present literature on the demand for reserves does only discuss the *optimal size* of an adjustment policy (or in terms of our last section, the equilibrium size of γ^* where γ represents that part of external imbalances which is corrected by an adjustment policy) while – except for one or two authors – the choice of the specific type of adjustment policy is not analyzed. Besides the optimal size and the optimal type of adjustment policy there is also the crucial question of the *optimal speed* of an adjustment policy. We have already treated two kinds of speed: the continuous and symmetrical adjustment γ^* and the discontinuous and asymmetrical adjustment $P(A)^*$. We had also mentioned the fact of lagged adjustment. One possible time-lag for the implementation of an adjustment policy arises from inertia, imperfect information and short-sightedness. Another possibility for a time-lag can be the outcome of a rational intertemporal decision associated with a specific type of adjustment policy.

(2) Diminishing returns or increasing disutilities from larger doses of any adjustment policy or recognition of uncertainty may call for a mixture of available adjustment policies. This question of the "optimal policy mix" is not identical to the Mundellian policy mix whose target is the simultaneous realization of internal and external equilibrium. Because payments imbalances are corrected by adjustment policies *and* financed by reserve variations, a (temporary) balance-of-payments disequilibrium is desired to the extent that an exclusive correction towards an external equilibrium is too costly for the economy.

(3) Another possible aspect of the "optimum combination of adjustment policies" concerns the inclusion of the degree of flexibility of exchange rates into the tool box of adjustment policies. In this respect the demand for reserves becomes a problem of the "optimum policy mix" of financing external imbalances by reserves and correcting external imbalances by adjustment policies including a certain ("optimum") flexibility of exchange rates.

4.1. The Costs of Various Types of Adjustment Policies

A convenient criterion to classify all possible adjustment policies is to ask whether the policy instruments act on aggregate expenditures or on relative prices. The first category is directed to influence the trade balance by using the so-called expenditure-changing policies which include changes in government taxes and expenditures affecting the level rather than the direction of aggregate expenditures and its adjustment costs consist of the variability in domestic income. The second category, the so-called expenditure-switching policies in terms of changes in parities, tariffs, quotas, exchange controls, and so on, is directed to obtain a different allocation of foreign and domestic demand among domestic and foreign output consistent with the desired current account and its adjustment costs are essentially those of distortions in the allocation of resources. There is still a third category of adjustment policies which acts on relative prices *and* aggregate expenditures – i.e., policies to correct external imbalances by changes in the capital account via interest-rate policy, control of capital flows, etc. involving adjustment costs in terms of income variability *and* of distortions in the allocation of resources (even though the first category may have a side-effect on relative prices and the second one on domestic income).

The existing models of the demand for reserves discussed in section 3 are only concerned with expenditure-changing policies so that the internal adjustment cost consists exclusively of the variability in the level of income. In terms of our symbols previously used, the internal economic variable X represents nominal income, so that the internal adjustment cost expressed in equations (2) or (8) must be interpreted in terms of the standard deviation of income; α represents the marginal propensity to import indicating that the internal adjustment cost varies negatively with the openness of the economy. Because the demand for reserves is an increasing function of the adjustment costs, desired reserve holding would be negatively associated with the marginal propensity to import. However, the empirical part of the models by Clark (1970, 1970a) and Kelly (1970) shows a positive relation between reserve holdings and the (average) propensity to import. This factual contradiction does not necessarily refute the theoretical model. On the one hand, the random shocks in external payments may be a positive function of the openness of the economy, in particular for those situations where the disturbances arise from internal sources because in highly open economies internal perturbations are reflected more to the outside world via the balance-of-payments than to the internal economy according to standard macroeconomic models for open economies. On the other hand, a more efficient method of adjustment (i.e., lower adjustment costs) may be the switching technique. Cohen (1971, ch. 7) estimated for the United Kingdom that the cost of restricting trade or capital flows was extremely lower than the cost of expenditure-reducing policies. Frenkel (1974) showed that expenditure switching via a change in the terms of trade leads (in most circumstances) to a demand for reserves which varies positively with the average propensity to import.

Another policy alternative could be an interest rate policy attracting or discouraging capital inflows. Any objection to its effectiveness on the grounds that a change in the interest rate leads only to a once-and-for-all portfolio stock adjustment can be dismissed because of the basic assumption of a fundamental balance-of-payments equilibrium according to which "permanent" deficits or surpluses are excluded. The internal adjustment cost of this policy consists essentially of the variability of interest payments on borrowed funds from abroad affecting the disposable income of the home country's residents. Thus, for instance, a temporary deficit being corrected by a temporary rise in the interest rate leads to net capital inflows – its impact depending on the openness of the economy (α) measured now in terms of the sensitivity of capital flows to changes in the interest rate – and to a higher transfer of interest payments to foreigners reducing disposable income. The amount of these additional interest payments will depend on a variety of factors – the extent of the rise in the interest rate and in net liabilities to foreigners and the extent of refinancing existing debts to foreigners at the higher interest rate as Willet (1968) and Willet–Forte (1969) have shown. While income changes caused by the expenditure-changing policies are some multiple of the desired change in the balance of payments, changes in disposable income may be only a fraction of the desired change in the balance of payments. However, there may be still another item in the adjustment cost of the interest policy and which concerns the possibility of the variability in future income provided that changes in interest rates (upwards and downwards) affect domestic investment and creates a variability in the capital stock and thus in future income. An interesting aspect of the interest-rate policy (which can probably be extended to reserves borrowed or lent by the monetary authorities) has been pointed out by Britto and Heller (1973) who show in a framework of multi-period analysis that borrowing or lending enables a country to convert an initial real adjustment in its current account into a series of smaller real adjustments in future periods which may be less costly for the economy.

There is no doubt that at the present time the theory of adjustment costs and the empirical attempt to measure them remain to be developed, not only for a single economy but in the more coherent general framework of interdependent economies. Such an effort is essential for the proper relation between the demand for reserves and the balance-of-payments adjustment policies because the calculation of desired reserves depends crucially on the policy alternatives.

4.2. The Mix of Adjustment Policies

It is conceivable that the monetary authorities choose a policy instrument in a deficit situation being different from the instrument used in a surplus situation. Thus, reluctant to create any unemployment, an expenditure-increasing policy could be chosen during surpluses and a tight interest-rate policy (for instance, according to the prescriptions of Mundell's policy mix) or restrictions and controls during deficits.

On the other hand, even several instruments may be used simultaneously during either situations. Diminishing returns of policy instruments, that is absolutely and relatively increasing internal adjustment cost of any policy instrument will lead to a combination of policy actions. In figure 5 the efficiency of two policy instruments, γ_1, γ_2 [or $P(A)_1$ and $P(A)_2$], is illustrated in terms of "marginal cost schedules", *AA* for γ_1 and *BB* for γ_2, the latter being measured from right to left. For a given desired dose of adjustment policies (γ^*) determined in section 3, the combination (γ_1^*, γ_2^*) will be chosen at which the total internal adjustment cost is minimized: the shaded area represents still lower cost than the unique utilization of γ_2 having an "absolute advantage" (the integral of curve *BB*) over γ_1.

Even if there cannot be detected any "law of diminishing returns" – of course, only an extended and detailed analysis of the internal adjustment cost of each conceivable balance-of-payments adjustment policy will give an answer to this hypothesis, another explanation for the optimum combination (γ_1^*, γ_2^*) can be suggested by interpreting *AA* and *BB* as "marginal disutility schedules" (assuming that the preference function of γ_1 and γ_2 is separable). Particularly under the aspect that each instrument (or pair of instruments) may disadvantage a different group of individuals within the community, a government may be keen to disperse the "burden of adjustment" on several groups instead of on a single one.

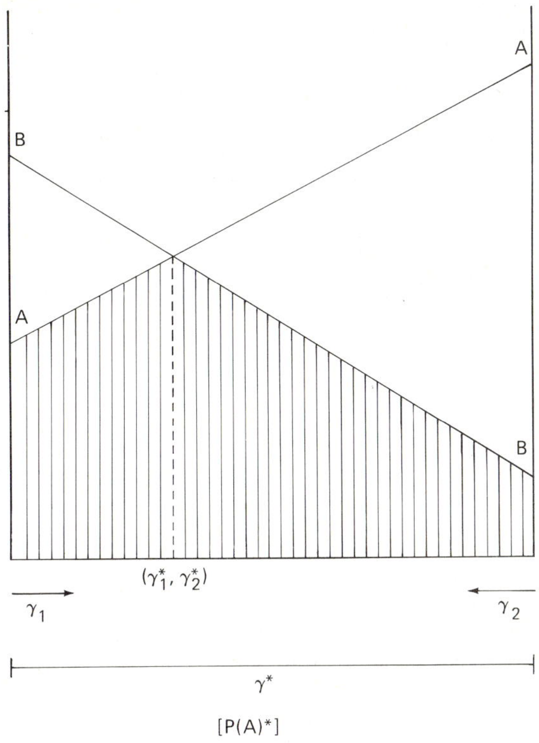

FIGURE 5

An alternative and even stronger argument for the optimum combination of adjustment policies can be made when one leaves the implicitly assumed world of certainty with respect to the "known" response of the balance of payments to any adjustment policy. It has been shown by Brainard (1967) in a theory of policy under uncertainty that with one target and two (n) instruments it will generally be optimal to use some combination of both (n) instruments. This basic idea can be illustrated by figure 6. Suppose that a random disturbance in the balance of payments calls for a balance-of-payments adjustment by the amount of $\bar{B}^*$. The attainment of $\bar{B}^*$ is now an expected value because there is uncertainty by how much any instrument used affects the internal variable (X) *and* by how much this latter influences the balance of payments; the degree of uncertainty to undershoot or overshoot the target value is represented by the standard deviation, that is by $S(B^*)$. Indifference curves, showing various combinations of B^* and $S(B^*)$, are drawn as concentric circles around $\bar{B}^*$; the

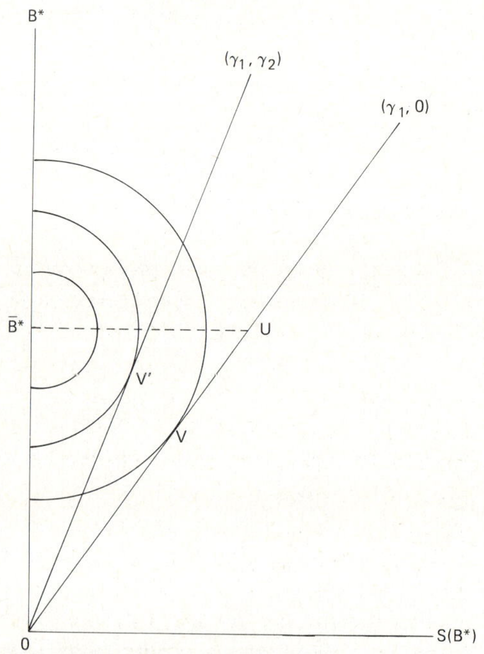

FIGURE 6

highest expected utility is realized where an indifference "curve" coincides with point $\bar{B}^*$. The utilization of *one* policy instrument, say γ_1, could attain the target $\bar{B}^*$ but with the risk indicated by point U on the ray $0(\gamma_1, 0)$. Given the preference function, the authorities will choose point V. In the presence of two policy instruments, however, the risk will be reduced as illustrated by the ray $0(\gamma_1, \gamma_2)$. The reason for a relative lower risk stems from the principle of risk diversification, that is in our context from the "diversification of policy instruments". Even if the second policy instrument had the same degree of risk (if it would have the same opportunity locus as γ_1), there will be economies from diversification which are mainly (not uniquely) due to the assumption that there is not a perfect correlation between the impacts of the two instruments. In the case of figure 6, the mix of adjustment policies would be fixed at the tangency point V' realizing a nearer point to the balance-of-payments target, accompanied by lower risk to attain the target.

Although it cannot be shown which specific combination of γ_1 and γ_2 will be chosen within the limited space of this present article (and which is only an application of the general argument developed by Brainard), two interesting results can be derived from this analytical exercise: firstly that it never pays to attain exactly $\bar{B}^*$, and secondly that the optimum "portfolio" of balance-of-payments adjustment policies will generally include the utilization of all n available instruments.

4.3. The Choice of Exchange Rate Flexibility

Why should economists bother about the demand for reserves when the "first best" solution to external imbalances would consist of (purely) flexible exchange rates? The answer to it may be of two sorts. Either economists consider fixed (or adjustable or dirtily floating) exchange rates as a constraint imposed by (badly informed) politicians and they derive the demand-for-reserves function within the given "institutional" framework, or they take into account the flexibility of exchange rates as an alternative to reserve holding (and to traditional adjustment policies).

Freely floating exchange rates transmit payments imbalances (which are self-reversing or offset by disturbances with opposite effect, originating domestically or abroad) upon certain variables of the domestic economy. Even if one retains all assumptions underlying the case for full flexible exchange rate [à la Friedman (1953) and Sohmen (1969), by assuming away irresponsible governments, destabilizing speculation, excessive costs of forward cover to eliminate traders' exchange risks, speculators' and traders' imperfect competition, . . .], freely floating rates will produce negative externalities. According to Grubel (1973), these social costs consist of three kinds. There will be an instability of the domestic price level caused by the fluctuation in the domestic prices of tradable goods and involving the negative welfare effect of reducing the usefulness of domestic money – that is of reducing its moneyness in terms of a unit of account, medium of exchange and store of value [or in more "modern" terms, more real resources will be devoted to the "transactions activity", see Claassen (1975a)]. Furthermore, there will be fluctuations of real resources between industries producing tradable and non-tradable goods with the consequence of higher frictional costs (cost of moving, job search, temporary unemployment, retraining of labour) and, thus, of lower real income. Finally, there will be a variability of earnings from assets which decreases welfare provided that welfare is not only a function of the level but also of the stability of earnings. The question whether these three types of social costs are significant or not is another matter. One direct evidence on them can be gained from the literature on the criteria of optimum currency areas as they have been developed by Mundell (1961) and McKinnon (1963). Smaller regions or countries opting for flexible exchange rates are exposed to higher instability in prices and income than larger regions or countries (or currency areas) such that the above cited social costs are an inverse function of the size of the concerned economy.

The above argument "against" flexibility where the weight of the against depends on the size of the country can be formulated still in other terms as it has been rigorously done by Mundell (1973). Reserve holdings (or the use of a common currency within currency area) allow a country – in contrast to flexible exchange rates – to distribute through time the burden of random fluctuations. Internal or external shocks which, for instance, reduce real income, can be cushioned by running down reserves which enables the country to draw on the resources of other countries. Reserve holdings fulfil the "Irving Fisher" function of spreading the cost of adjustment more smoothly over the future.

As already mentioned, the question of exchange-rate flexibility (or in other terms the question of reserve holdings) is closely related to the optimum currency–area issue. According to Mundell (1973), a small economy whose local currency has not the quality of high international moneyness and which relies nonetheless on the exchange market by using a flexible exchange rate, will absorb less efficiently shocks than in the case of cushioning disturbances by reserve variations (even though in case of a high depreciation stabilizing speculation provides some shock absorber – that is extra resources – by attracting a capital inflow). Consequently, the advantage of reserve holdings (the degree of flexibility) stands in inverse (direct) relationship to the size of the country and to the moneyness of the domestic currency, respectively. The "marginal return" of reserves in terms of the cost of alternative policies – the adjustment policies including a flexible exchange rate – will be higher for small countries (or currency areas) than for large ones.

5. Concluding Remarks on the Adequacy and Optimality of International Reserves

The present paper has shown probably more problems than solutions to a quantitative evaluation of a well-defined demand-for-reserves function. There is no doubt that much greater sophistication is needed for constructing a better theory and for making the transition from theory to application instead of renouncing any further attempt of quantification or of pointing out the irrationality of government's behaviour.

The quantification of a stable function of the demand for reserves gives some insight for the solution of the problems of adequacy and optimality of reserves. Analytically, the question of adequacy which was defined as the equality of demand and *supply* of reserves can be subdivided into two distinct problems. (1) Given the desired stock of reserve holding for a single country (which is nothing else than the above discussed "demand for reserves") what is the best time path of acquiring reserves in order to achieve their desired stock. This time path will be determined by the minimization of the costs of acquiring reserves via internal adjustment. (2) The second problem of adequacy concerns equally the process of adjustment, but now from the "macroeconomic" view for the whole international monetary system. Are there any mechanisms which maintain the adequacy of reserves of the system in the sense that the demand for reserves will be satisfied by a corresponding supply. (3) Finally, the question of optimality will be mentioned. Reserves may be adequate but socially suboptimal (the adjustment costs are not minimized) – in analogy to the theory of the optimum quantity of money.

5.1. The Adequacy of Reserves of a Single Country

Until now our analysis was silent on the issue during which time length the country acquires reserves in order to reach its long-run "full-stock equilibrium" of reserves. Our previous analysis – and in general the literature on the demand for reserves – assumed implicitly that this desired long-run stock has been attained, and that random disturbances in the balance of payments calls for a combination of reserve changes and adjustment policies. The problem which is now briefly examined is analogous to the stock–flow problem of capital–investment theory or of wealth–savings theory. (And it gets still more complicated if one takes into account a growing context in which the desired long-run – or "steady state" – stock of reserve holding is some direct function of the international trade volume and of the world price level.)

The problem of the optimal time path of reserve accumulation (or decumulation) towards the desired stock has necessarily a dynamic (i.e., intertemporal) context. It has been treated partly by Williamson (1971), Korkman (1973) and Nyberg–Viotti (1976). To put the essential properties of the problem in its simplest form, consider figure 7 which is constructed in analogy to Archibald and Lipsey's (1958) flow–stock equilibrium of the demand for money in a stationary economy. $\bar{Y}$ represents a given domestic output, and A stands for domestic absorption. The desired (steady state) stock of reserves is R^*, while actual reserve holdings are assumed to be at a lower level, say at R_1 in period 1. One possible stock adjustment would be the extreme case where the lacking desired reserves of R_1R^* are immediately acquired by a fall in absorption of domestic output by the amount of R_1R^*. However, due to the principle of

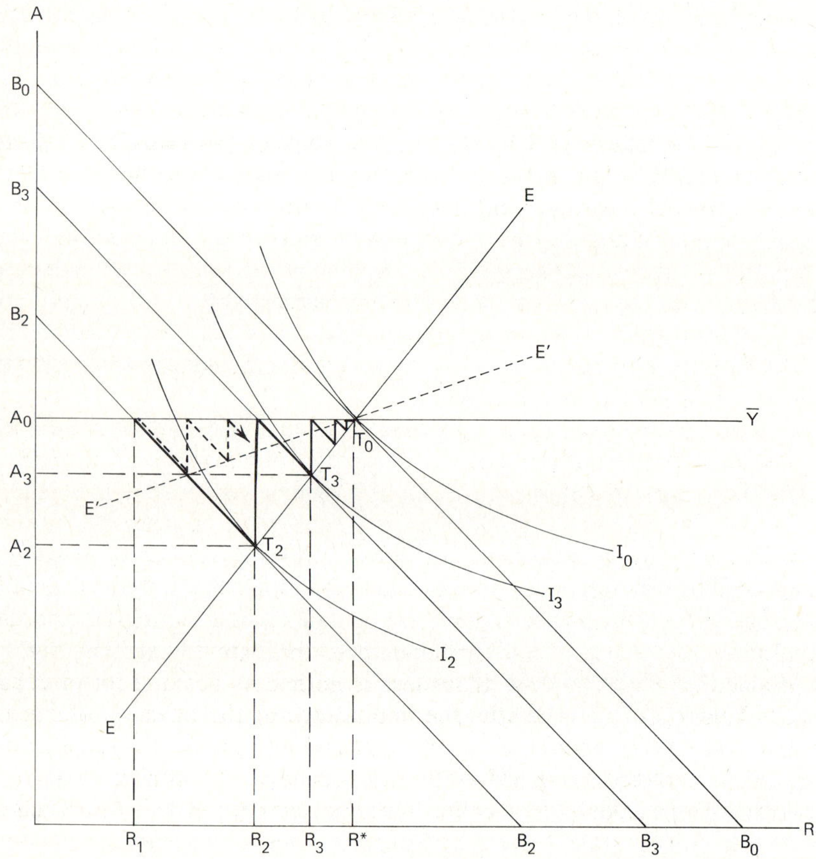

FIGURE 7

diminishing utility (à la Irving Fisher or because of systematic preference for the present) a series of smaller adjustments in several future periods is preferable to one single (and, thus, large) adjustment. Figure 7 traces a possible adjustment path which is primarily determined by the behaviour of the indifference curves I_2, I_3, $I_0, \ldots$, each of them describing, for a given utility level, the terms at which the marginal disutility of an absorption reduction in this period is equal to the marginal utility of a permanent increase of reserves. Consequently, the costs of reserves are not only those of holding reserves (permanent opportunity costs), but also those of acquiring them, represented by a temporary reduction of domestic absorption. The tangency points of the indifferent curves with the budget lines, B_2B_2, B_3B_3, etc. indicate the evolution of reserves (R_2, R_3, etc.) towards their long-run "full-equilibrium" level R^*, where absorption will be equal to domestic output. The budget lines (for instance, $B_2B_2 = \bar{Y} + R_1$) have been drawn under the simplified assumption that reserves are not interest-yielding. If, for example, the government has a higher time preference – it wants to postpone the real adjustment to future periods at a higher rate, the absorption–reserve expansion path will not be EE, but $E'E'$ such that the stock adjustment speed will be slower and distributed over a greater number of periods.[8]

5.2. The Adequacy of Reserves of the International Economy

The concept of inadequate reserves is as much slippery as that of involuntary unemployment. In the absolute sense, everybody "wants" to do whatever he is doing at the moment. Similarly, if reserves are inadequate, the government wants them to be at that level otherwise it would have taken action or would take action to restore them to the "adequate" level. A country behaving in accordance with a severe budget constraint – that is a behaviour described by the ordinary demand and supply curves of economic theory – may be poor and unhappy, but its reserves will be adequate to the extent that it is "on" its demand curve for reserves *and* that there is no excess demand for or excess supply of reserves. Consequently, the importance of the question of reserve "adequacy" concerns the problem of whether there are any "equilibrating" forces in the international economy which assure that countries' demand for reserves will be satisfied, or in other terms that any gap between the desired and existing stock of reserves will be closed by some "invisible hand", i.e., by some quantity or price mechanism.

Despite the huge – and in many cases superfluous – literature on this subject, let us briefly concentrate on one problem which is connected with the demand for reserves and which concerns the question of whether there can be

[8]It should be noted that this aspect of the stock adjustment mechanism interprets the equilibrium concept of the balance of payments in terms of a certain surplus during several periods (or of a certain deficit if $R > R^*$) where the judgement of the country towards assessing its "equilibrium" position will be governed by the stocks of reserves and its rate of reserve growth. Even if the desired reserve stock R^* has been reached, equilibrium of the balance of payments will not become a fixed target because as we have seen in previous sections, any (temporary) disequilibrium will be matched by a mix of financing and correcting the external imbalances. As Williamson (1973, p. 693) suggests, even the case of a fundamental disequilibrium should be incorporated into the intertemporal model of the demand for reserves since a partial financing of fundamental imbalances may be less costly in terms of time preference than a single adjustment in one period.

conceived some sort of "international quantity theory" [Williamson (1973, p. 709)]. According to this theory, provided that there is a stable demand function for reserves, the level of *real* reserves would be determined by the countries' target for desired real reserve holdings whatever may be the *nominal* supply of reserves. (a) Take first the case of deficient reserve holdings. Restrictions and controls on both current and capital accounts could be the answer of the concerned countries revealing that reserves constitute rather a constraint than an objective even though by reducing the volume of international transactions reserve holdings become more "adequate". Internal deflation measures by expenditure-reducing policies could be another reaction, but looking at the past history the most frequent adjustment policies were those of a devaluation of the exchange rate bidding up the real value of reserves. (b) For the case of excess reserve holdings one could enumerate the same catalogue of adjustment reactions with opposite signs due to undesired reserve holdings. The most frequent case in the past was that of internal inflation (instead of revaluations) lowering the real value of outstanding reserves.

The above (factual) cases may cover situations of "fundamental disequilibria", at least for deficit countries whose principal target was the internal one pursuing high employment at the cost of higher inflation than the world average. On the other hand, surplus countries (whose asymmetrical behaviour has been rationalized in section 3) adjusted eventually by diminishing the real value of reserves. Admittedly, the issue of the validity of an international quantity theory is difficult, but it should be a starting point, in particular to the phenomenon of world inflation (in a dollar-standard world) which has to be attributed to an excess of international reserves in terms of the rate of growth rather than the level of existing stocks of reserves; cf., Johnson (1972a). The consequence of an increase in the nominal rate of reserve creation and by this in the rate of world inflation, would be to reduce the *real* level of reserves central banks wish to hold (assuming that the rate of interest on reserves does not fully take into account the inflation rate) according to the prescription of the demand-for-reserves function; cf., Mundell (1971). The consequence would be faster adjustment policies with the possibility of a higher number of "crises" involved by a lower degree of reserve "ease" or reserve "adequacy" – here in the sense that real reserve holdings are more remote from their "optimum" level.

5.3. *The Optimality of Reserves*

Knowledge of individual countries' demand-for-reserves function can play an important role in determining the "optimum" quantity of reserves. In the upper panel of figure 8, the equilibrium demand for reserves of a country is drawn as a decreasing function of their net opportunity cost, *i*. The demand schedule represents the marginal return of reserves. Its negative shape arises from the principle of diminishing marginal returns encountered generally in economies. According to the arguments advanced in sections 3 and 4 it can be explained as follows. A higher equilibrium reserve stock, for instance, from R_1^* to R_0^* because the net opportunity cost has fallen from i_1 to i_0, reduces the size of balance-of-payments adjustment from γ_1^* to γ_1 provided that the country maintains the probability of running out of reserves, P_1^* (which corresponds to an upward movement *on* the trade-off line $P_1^*P_1^*$ in the lower panel of figure 8). However, not only the size of adjustment will be reduced, but also the probability of a reserve run-out will decline, say to P_0^* (see the new trade-off line $P_0^*P_0^*$ in the lower panel) such that the size of adjustment is *less* reduced (γ_0^* instead of γ_1). Or, in other terms, each additional unit of reserves yields a lower return because of the reduced likelihood of reserves to be needed to finance imbalances; cf., Clark (1972, p. 546).

The recent theorizing on the optimum quantity of reserves by Mundell (1971, ch. 17), Clark (1972), Johnson (1972) and Grubel (1973) – along the lines of the optimum quantity of money for the domestic case (including all the caveats this theory has provoked; see Williamson (1973, pp. 726–727) – has come to the conclusion that a *necessary* condition for Pareto optimality is the equality between the (private) marginal return of reserves and the (social) marginal cost of creating them. Suppose that the marginal cost of producing and administering reserves (by the reserve currency country or by the I.M.F.) is equal to c_R in figure 8. In setting the opportunity cost of reserve holdings at i_0, by fixing an interest rate on reserves equal to i_R, the country will be induced to hold the optimum quantity of R_0^*. The country is better off because it enjoys higher solvability (P_0^*) and a lower size of adjustment (γ_0^*) and, thus, lower internal adjustment costs in terms of a reduced variability in internal variables. These two kinds of welfare gains are described by the surface *B* in figure 8 while surface *A* represents the transfer of the previous seigniorage gain (in case of the dollar) from the reserve currency country to the reserve holding country: the total sum of interest payments is equal to $R_0^*i_R$.

There are many special issues with regard to the concrete realization and viability of such a scheme as they have been pointed out by the above authors: there would be positive cost of acquiring reserves in a dollar standard while they are zero in a SDR-standard; there will be no inflationary consequences from larger reserve creation because the interest payments provide the incentive to hold the larger stock; the interest rate to be paid on reserves is a nominal rate which should be linked to a world price index in case of world inflation; due to imperfections in private capital markets the interest rate on

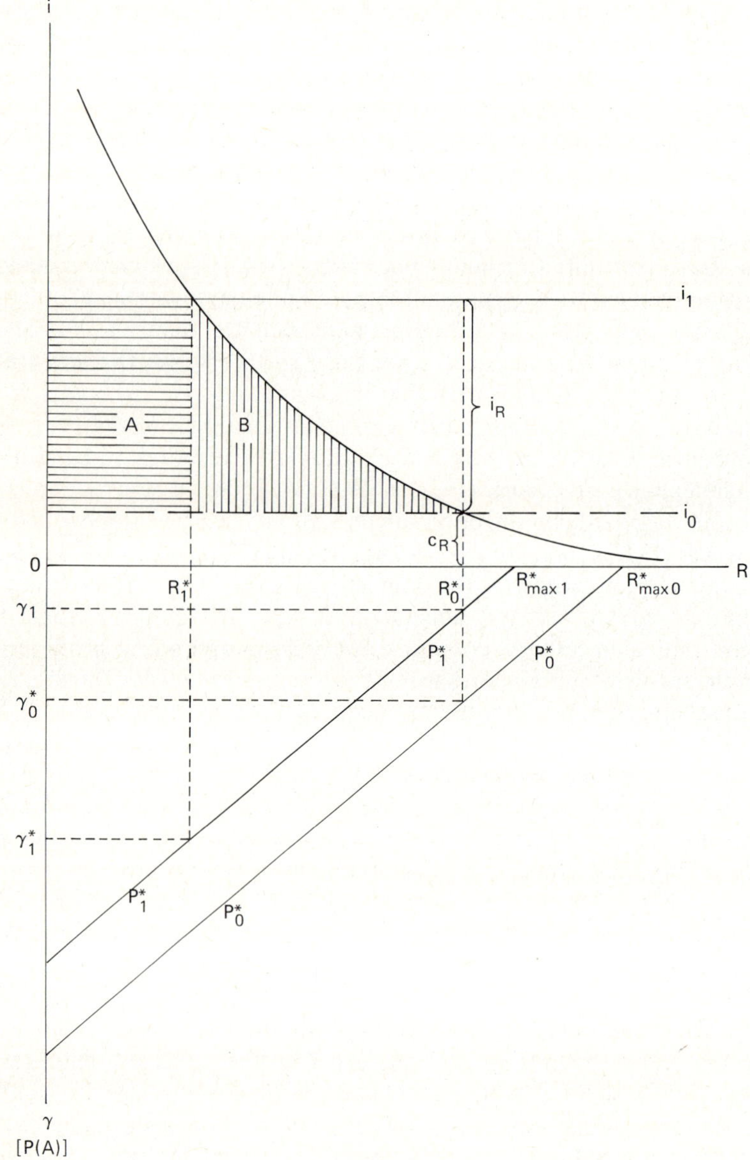

FIGURE 8

reserves should not be higher than the lowest rate of return on capital prevailing in any country, otherwise a higher rate would induce certain countries to exchange permanently real resources against reserves; in the present SDR's system – whatever the interest rate on SDR's may be – there is no net addition to the total stock of SDR's by means of interest payments because countries which utilize SDR's pay the interest charges to those of which the stock has increased beyond the initial amount of allocated SDR's; in the hypothetical case of perfect capital markets and Golden Rule growth (where the growth rate is equal to the rate of return on capital) the stock supply of reserves will grow at the rate of all other variables in the economies (assuming that the marginal cost of creating reserves is zero), and the demand for reserves will only grow at the same rate if payments disturbances occur at a certain increasing rate . . .

References

Aliber, R. Z., 1967, Gresham's law, asset preferences, and the demand for international reserves, Quarterly Journal of Economics, Nov.

Archibald, G. C. and R. G. Lipsey, 1968, Monetary and value theory: A critique of Lange and Patinkin, Review of Economic Studies, no. 1.

Archibald, G. C. and J. Richmond, 1971, On the theory of foreign exchange reserve requirements, Review of Economic Studies, April.

Brainard, W., 1967, Uncertainty and the effectiveness of policy, American Economic Review, Papers and Proceedings, May.

Branson, W. H., 1970, Monetary policy and the new view of international capital movements, Brookings Papers on Economic Activity, no. 2.

Britto, R. and H. R. Heller, 1973, International adjustment and optimal reserves, International Economic Review, March.

Brown, W. M., 1964, The external liquidity of an advanced country, Princeton Studies in International Finance, no. 14 (Princeton University, Princeton, N.J.).

Claassen, E. M., 1975, Demand for international reserves and the optimum mix and speed of adjustment policies, American Economic Review, June.

Claassen, E. M., 1975a, On the indirect productivity of money, Journal of Political Economy, April.

Clark, P. B., 1970, Optimum international reserves and the speed of adjustment, Journal of Political Economy, March.

Clark, P. B., 1970a, The demand for international reserves: A cross-country analysis, Canadian Journal of Economics, Nov.

Clark, P. B., 1972, Interest payments and the rate of return on an international fiat currency, Weltwirtschaftliches Archiv, no. 4.

Clower, R. W. and R. G. Lipsey, 1968, The present state of international liquidity theory, American Economic Review, May.

Cohen, B. J., 1971, The future of sterling as an international currency (Macmillan, London).

Cohen, B. J., 1974, International reserves and liquidity: A survey, Conference on Research in International Trade and Finance (Princeton University, Princeton, N.J.).

Cooper, R. N., 1970, International liquidity and balance of payments adjustment, in: I.M.F., International reverves, needs and availability (I.M.F., Washington, D.C.).

Courchene, T. J. and G. M. Youssef, 1967, The demand for international reserves, Journal of Political Economy, Aug.

Flanders, M. J., 1971, The demand for international reserves, Princeton Studies in International Finance, no. 27 (Princeton University, Princeton, N.J.).

Fratianni, M., 1974, The problem of coexistence of SDRs and a reserve currency: A comment, Journal of Money, Credit and Banking, Feb.

Frenkel, J. A., 1974, Openness and the demand for international reserves, in: R. Z. Aliber, ed., National monetary policies and the international financial system (University of Chicago Press, Chicago, Ill.).

Friedman, M., 1953, The case for flexible exchange rates, in: M. Friedman, Essays in positive economics (University of Chicago Press, Chicago, Ill.).

Grassman, S., 1973, A fundamental symmetry in international payment patterns, Journal of International Economics, Aug.

Grubel, H. G., 1971, The demand for international reserves: A critical review of the literature, Journal of Economic Literature, Dec.

Grubel, H. G., 1973, The case for optimum exchange rate stability, Weltwirtschaftliches Archiv, no. 3.

Harrod, R., 1953, Imbalance of international payments, I.M.F. Staff Papers, April.

Heller, H. R., 1966, Optimal international reserves, Economic Journal, June.

Heller, H. R., 1968, The transactions demand for international means of payment, Journal of Political Economy, Jan.

Heller, H. R., 1970, Wealth and international reserves, Review of Economics and Statistics, May.

Hipple, F. S., 1974, The disturbances approach to the demand for international reserves, Princeton Studies in International Finance, no. 35 (Princeton University, Princeton, N.J.).

Hirsch, F., 1971, SDRs and the working of the gold exchange standard, I.M.F. Staff Papers, July.

I.M.F., 1958, International reserves and liquidity (I.M.F., Washington, D.C.).

Johnson, H. G., 1958, Towards a general theory of the balance of payments, in: H. G. Johnson, International trade and economic growth (Harvard University Press, Cambridge, Mass.).

Johnson, H. G., 1972, Inflation and the monetarist controversy (North-Holland, Amsterdam).

Johnson, H. G., 1972a, A critical appraisal of the Bretton Woods monetary system, unpublished.

Johnson, H. G., 1972b, Efficiency in international money supply, in: H. G. Johnson, Further essays in monetary economics (Allen & Unwin, London).

Johnson, H. G., 1973, The monetary approach to balance of payments theory, in: M. B. Connolly and A. K. Swoboda, eds., International trade and money (Allen & Unwin, London).

Kelly, M. G., 1970, The demand for international reserves, American Economic Review, Sept.

Kenen, P. B., 1960, International liquidity and the balance of payments of a reserve-currency country, Quarterly Journal of Economics, Nov.

Kenen, P. B., 1963, Reserve-asset preferences of central banks and stability of the gold exchange standard, Princeton Studies in International Finance, no. 10 (Princeton University, Princeton, N.J.).

Kenen, P. B. and E. Yudin, 1965, The demand for international reserves, Review of Economics and Statistics, Aug.

Kenen, P. B. and E. Yudin, 1967, The demand for international reserves: A reply, Review of Economics and Statistics, Nov.

Korkman, S., 1973, Foreign exchange reserves and the adjustment mechanism, Seminar Paper no. 31 (Institute for International Economic Studies, University of Stockholm, Stockholm) unpublished.

Machlup, F., 1964, International payments, debts, and gold (Scribner's, New York).

Machlup, F., 1966, The need for monetary reserves, Banca Nazionale del Lavoro Quarterly Review, Sept.

Makin, J. H., 1972, The problem of coexistence of SDRs and a reserve currency, Journal of Money, Credit and Banking, Aug.

McKinnon, R. I., 1963, Optimum currency areas, American Economic Review, Sept.

Miller, M. H. and D. Orr, 1966, A model of the demand for money by firms, Quarterly Journal of Economics, Aug.

Mundell, R. A., 1961, A theory of optimum currency areas, American Economic Review, Nov.

Mundell, R. A., 1971, Monetary theory: Inflation, interest and growth in the world economy (Goodyear, Pacific Palisades, Calif.).

Mundell, R. A., 1973, Uncommon arguments for common currencies, in: H. G. Johnson and A. K. Swoboda, eds., The economics of common currencies (Allen & Unwin, London).

Niehans, J., 1970, The need for reserves of a single country, in: I.M.F., International reserves, needs and availability (I.M.F., Washington, D.C.).

Nyberg, L. and S. Viotti, 1976, Optimal reserves and adjustment policies, in: E. M. Claassen and P. Salin, eds., Recent issues in international monetary economics (North-Holland, Amsterdam).

Officer, L. H. and T. D. Willett, 1969, Reserve-asset preferences and the confidence problem in the crisis zone, Quarterly Journal of Economics, Nov.

Officer, L. H. and T. D. Willett, 1970, The interaction of adjustment and gold-conversion policies in a reserve-currency system, Western Economic Journal, March.

Olivera, J. H. G., 1969, A note on the optimal rate of growth of international reserves, Journal of Political Economy, March.

Orr, D., 1971, Cash management and the demand for money (Praeger, New York).

Salant, W. S., 1973, Implications for international reserves, in: L. B. Krause and W. S. Salant, eds., European monetary unification and its meaning for the United States (The Brookings Institution, Washington, D.C.).

Scitovsky, T., 1958, Economic theory and Western European integration (Allen & Unwin, London).

Shinkai, Y., 1973, The accumulation of international reserves under an inflationary pressure, Zeitschrift für Nationalökonomie, no. 1–2.

Sohmen, E., 1969, Flexible exchange rates, theory and controversy (University of Chicago Press, Chicago, Ill.).

Swoboda, A. K., 1968, The Euro-dollar market: An interpretation, Princeton Essays in International Finance, no. 64 (Princeton University, Princeton, N.J.).

Willet, T. D., 1968, Official versus market financing of international deficits, Kyklos, no. 3.

Willet, T. D. and F. Forte, 1969, Interest rate policy and external balance, Quarterly Journal of Economics, May.

Williamson, J., 1971, On the normative theory of balance of payments adjustment, in: G. Clayton, J. C. Gilbert and R. Sedgwick, eds., Monetary theory and monetary policy in the 1970s (Oxford University Press, Oxford).

Williamson, J., 1973, Surveys in applied economics: International liquidity, Economic Journal, Sept.

Chapter 4.2

COMMENT ON CLAASSEN

Michael KUCZYNSKI

I propose to concentrate these comments on the central part of Professor Claassen's encyclopedic paper. He is concerned here with explanations of official reserve holdings which run along the lines of stochastic multi-period inventory theory. Their common starting-point are countries whose foreign-exchange authorities face balance-of-payments disturbances randomly distributed about a mean of zero ("fundamental equilibrium"); the authorities may either finance each disturbance to the extent of their reserves, or they may "adjust" to reduce or even fully eliminate the requisite movement in their reserves. "Adjustment" carries a cost in terms of temporary departures from equilibrium income growth, while holdings of official reserves earn a smaller return than alternative investments, domestic or foreign. (The fashion, followed by Claassen, is to treat only the former cost as a random variable.) The authorities choose their rules of "adjustment" and their average reserve levels in such a way as to minimize the sum of these costs without letting the risk of insolvency rise above a small figure. There are no recognition lags, and the action of "adjustment" is instantly effective.

Claassen contrasts the "continuous adjustment" rule assigned to the authorities by Clark and by Kelly with a two-bin, or (S, s), rule of his own devising. Under the former the authorities ever offset a constant proportion of each balance-of-payments disturbance, while for Claassen they act only when their reserves rise or fall to certain extremes, and then they "adjust" so as to return in one go to some benchmark level. It is well-known that under two-bin rules of this sort the benchmark S (Claassen's R_a) need not lie half-way between the two extremes of the inventory: in the particular case at hand, the costs of reserve-holding (in terms of lower yields) rise monotonically from zero at one end to a maximum at the other, while "adjustment" costs are likely to be high at both ends and low in the middle of the range; thus the average towards which reserve holdings tend under these total-cost minimizing rules should be closer to the minimum end than to the maximum; and countries following the rules would be seen to be "adjusting" more frequently to smaller reserve losses and less frequently to larger reserve gains. Claassen claims support for his interpretation from the casual observation of such patterns of asymmetrical adjustment in the real world.

Our authors envisage "adjustment" primarily as a change in the management of aggregate demand in response to exogenous, random, and reversible payments disturbances; and their models are grounded in a firm distinction between "reserves" and "adjustment" in situations of "fundamental equilibrium". But the distinction is deceptive in just such situations, especially if there is a modicum of capital mobility and the margins of exchange-rate variation are not zero. Also, to be useful, a fiction must admit generalization: yet it is strenuous to suppose that several countries, all interrelated in "fundamental equilibrium", could long continue to respond to these random disturbances (quite how generated?), in ways of their own choosing, without breaking the stochastic pattern. Indeed, foreign-exchange authorities are more likely to hold reserves against the uncertainties inherent in their use of policy in a world of imperfectly-perceived trends and cycles, than against stationary random walks of disturbances. All told, "fundamental equilibrium" does not seem the best place to look for the explanation of asymmetrical attitudes to reserve gains and losses.

(1) In situations of "fundamental equilibrium", conflict between internal and external balance is ruled out. Payments deficits (or surpluses) are more likely to coincide with excess demand than with spare capacity (or vice versa). Therefore it is conceivable that, when reserve movements are such as to call for our authors' "adjustment" (continuously for Clark and for Kelly, occasionally for Claassen), the requisite change in the management of aggregate demand will amount to a *return* to equilibrium income growth rather than a *departure* from it. Any such instance of the classical gold-standard mechanism would invalidate our authors' procedure, relying as it does on costs of "adjustment" which increase rather than diminish with the size of the reserve movement to be reversed.

(Incidentally, the probability calculus which Claassen has adopted from Miller and Orr's work requires that the cost in question be constant per *instance* rather than per *unit* of "adjustment" – a lump sum rather than something proportional to the reserve movement involved. The sort of adjustment discussed in paragraph (3) below might fit the bill better than changes in the management of aggregate demand.)

(2) To turn the point around, reserve movements – unless "neutralized" – will affect aggregate demand through their association with changes in the distribution of income, in the money supply, and in rates of interest. Such

changes constitute the classical mechanism whereby a net balance-of-payments disturbance may be reversed. To neutralize them is just as likely, in situations of "fundamental equilibrium", to cause a departure from equilibrium income growth as to prevent one. Yet, in order to preserve a meaningful distinction between "reserves" and "adjustment", Claassen requires an unspecified form of neutralization while there is no "adjustment" proper. In contrast, we can interpret Clark's and Kelly's "continuous adjustment" as the classical mechanism at work (with lags, to be sure), their "coefficient of policy response" (Claassen's phrase), γ, being *known* rather than *chosen*.[1]

(3) In any case, "adjustment" is seldom confined to the management of aggregate demand. If official reserves are taken to consist only of owned assets of a certain liquidity, then "adjustment" may run the gamut of actions on capital account, from major changes in controls to small inducements to foreign borrowing or lending, before it gets to any direct action on expenditure. No doubt national income is affected, but in ways which it is hard for the authorities to quantify as the discounted expected costs of departures from equilibrium income growth. (What is the cost of a change of heart about the regulation of foreign direct investment?) From this standpoint, the official reserves of countries in "fundamental equilibrium" would appear, not as precautionary balances against random payments disturbances, but as an instance of risk-aversion against the uncertain costs of other forms of "adjustment" – a textbook case of liquidity preference. The greater part of these uncertain costs might well be a lump sum, like a brokerage fee. In any event the point is that, if capital markets were good enough, in the sense of offering perfectly predictable terms to each country's authorities, there might be no need for any official reserves at all in situations of "fundamental equilibrium".[2] (If official reserves are stretched to include some of these items

[1]Kelly purports to derive his "optimum" level of reserves from a utility function in which both reduced income (due to reserve holding) and reduced instability of income (due to reserve use) appear as arguments. In fact, however, either his model is undetermined, or he takes the coefficient of policy response – Claassen's γ, his f – as given. In the latter case "optimum" reserves are quite mechanically determined once the minimum risk of insolvency has been chosen, and the utility function adds nothing. Indeed, the exercise amounts to deducing the utility function which is consistent with such a mechanically-determined average level of reserves being optimal. (I am indebted to Fred-Olav Sørensen of the International Monetary Fund for confirmation of this point.) Automatic adjustment of the gold-standard variety would be consistent with a given γ, but there would be problems of international consistency if this coefficient did not vary appropriately from country to country.

[2]See, for instance, Egon Sohmen, in: International Monetary Fund, *International Reserves: Needs and Availabilities* (1970).

"above the line", so that "adjustment" is confined to the management of aggregate demand, we run into the difficulties already noted.)

(4) It is hard to envisage the simultaneous application of Claassen's rules by all countries in "fundamental equilibrium". Similar strictures apply to the work of Clark and of Kelly. If the definitions of "reserves" and "adjustment" are uniform from country to country, then the international economy would have to be endowed with peculiarly accommodating properties: like a kaleidoscope, it would have to turn out to each country a random walk of *net* balance-of-payments disturbances, and yet arrange for the more frequent offsets to smaller reserve losses of some countries to coincide with the less frequent offsets to the larger gains of the others. This is a far-fetched construction, when trend and cycle (alas, ruled out by these models) more readily account for internationally-consistent disturbances to each country. The alternative is to suppose *either* that at least one country in "fundamental equilibrium" furnishes the requisite degree of freedom by abstaining from Claassen's rules, *or* that the definitions of "reserves" and "adjustment" do vary. We cannot draw any support for the former from the real world, because the obvious candidates, the reserve centres, have never (almost by definition) belonged to the set of countries in "fundamental equilibrium". Thus variations in the definitions must be our refuge.

Chapter 4.3

SUMMARY OF THE DISCUSSION ON CLAASSEN

Milton FRIEDMAN, *Chairman*

Two main issues were discussed: (1) the existence and notion of a demand function for reserves, and (2) the types and costs of adjustment policies.

(1) *Milton Friedman* asked the question whether it is conceivable that there does not exist any demand for international reserves by central banks, because this possibility had been mentioned in Claassen's papers, *Emil Claassen* answered that in such a case one has to assume a certain type of irrational behaviour by central bankers or that the country does not respect its budget constraint. To this *Milton Friedman* pointed out that an irrational person will have a demand function even though this demand function may be irrational. After a vivid discussion between *Assar Lindbeck* and *Milton Friedman* it turned out that a central bank even if it does not directly make a decision on a certain desired amount of reserves to hold, it will optimize indirectly the holdings of reserves.

Marcus Miller referred to Claassen's treatment of the demand for reserves in analogy to the demand for precautionary balances by firms. He raised the question what would be the optimum amount of reserve holdings if one accepts the Hicksian argument according to which the precautionary demand for money is the result of a second best. The first best would be not to hold precautionary balances at all; to the extent that credit markets are perfect, any amount of cash in the event of a liquidity shortage could be obtained by borrowing. To the extent that credit markets are not efficient, it could be difficult to arrange this sort of borrowing so that one has to hold money for precautionary reasons; by this, the welfare analysis of precautionary cash balances – and, by analogy of reserve holdings – is an exercise in the theory of the second best.

Milton Friedman pointed out that the conclusion of the Hicksian argument is that the optimum quantity of money would be zero – a conclusion which shows what is wrong with the Hicksian analysis. On the other hand, a question which should be asked in connection with the demand for reserves and which has not been properly dealt with in the literature is the inter-relationship between private and public holdings of reserves. According to Friedman, a case is conceivable in which a change in central bank's reserves is completely irrelevant to the extent that it is balanced dollar-for-dollar by a corresponding change in private holdings of international money; consequently, it may well be that the appropriate demand function for reserves is the function which sums up public plus private holdings of reserves. *Fritz Machlup* mentioned that an early essay by him dealt with this question; there he showed that the total demand for reserves would be different (i.e., lower) from the sum of the private and official demand if the latter would be pooled.

Another issue which was mentioned by Machlup was related to the variables in the demand function for reserves. In analogy to the normal demand curve for a good, he asked which variable should be chosen on the vertical axis of the demand curve for reserves. Should it be a rate of interest, a quantity of domestic money or anything else? *Peter Kenen* and *Emil Claassen* argued that this question had been dealt with properly in recent literature. On the one hand, the proper price of reserves is the interest rate as the opportunity cost of holding reserves and the reduction of absorption as the opportunity cost of acquiring reserves (Kenen). On the other hand, the actual theoretical problem is not that of the interpretation of the vertical axis but that of knowing how the area under the demand curve should be interpreted; this area representing the total return of reserve holdings could be interpreted in terms of external solvability and of less internal adjustment policies (Claassen).

(2) As far the second subject of the discussion, the types and costs of adjustment policies, is concerned, one of the first questions raised by *Milton Friedman* was related to the extreme case where no adjustment policy is undertaken. Such a case must necessarily imply a complete dollar-for-dollar sterilization of the domestic quantity of money following changes in reserves.

Jacob Frenkel suggested that with respect to the types of adjustment policies one has to distinguish between automatic adjustment policies (for instance, the case of no sterilization by monetary authorities) and discretionary adjustment policies, this distinction would avoid the possible misunderstanding between adjustment policies and adjustment mechanisms.

Sven Arndt argued that the distinction between expenditure-changing policies and expenditure-switching policies is highly questionable when one takes into account the time dimension to the extent that the adjustment process requires time. Thus, for instance, an expenditure-changing policy is equally, from the inter-temporal point of view, an expenditure-switching policy in the sense that certain expenditures are postponed from the present period to the future period, and vice versa.

With respect to the costs of adjustment policies, *Jacob Frenkel* raised the question whether these costs are all that important if the adjustment takes place through a change in relative prices instead of a change in the employment level the costs of which are probably significant. And *Sven Arndt* meant that such a change in relative prices could even eliminate previous distortions in the allocation of resources which were created by certain policies.

Chapter 5.1

OPTIMAL RESERVES AND ADJUSTMENT POLICIES

Lars NYBERG and Staffan VIOTTI*

1. Introduction

Among the first pieces of knowledge we extract from the textbooks on international finance is how to handle a deficit in the balance of payments. We may either finance by drawing on the stock of foreign reserves, or we may force the economy to adjust. Thus it is clear that the problem of adjustment is closely related to the question of the optimal size of foreign reserves. Yet in the literature on the adjustment mechanism, reserves are largely neglected, while in the writings on optimal reserves nothing is said about the problem of adjustment.[1]

A main reason for this unfortunate separation can be found in the treatment of the external target. In the adjustment models the interest is in the *change* of reserves, equal to the surplus or deficit in the balance of payments. The optimal reserve models, on the other hand, deal with the *level* of reserves. They regard reserves mainly as buffers against random fluctuations in international payments, and derive demand functions for international liquidity.

In this paper we aim at *integrating the adjustment models with the theory of international reserves.* We formulate the external target in stock terms and assume that there is a criterion function aiding the policy-makers in the choice between this target and the internal ones. From this we can derive the optimal level of reserves, *as well as the optimal way of adjustment.* Since the analysis is dynamic, we are able to take into account the fact that adjustment and the building up of reserves cannot be done immediately. We obtain unique time paths for the policy variables, showing the optimal policies at any moment of time until the final equilibrium is reached.

The analysis will also have some relevance for the so-called assignment

*We are grateful to William Branson and Lars Svensson for comments on an earlier version of this paper.

[1]On adjustment, see e.g. Niehans (1968), Sohmen (1969), Cooper (1969), Whitman (1970), Swoboda (1972), Mundell (1968). The literature on optimal reserves is reviewed in Clower and Lipsey (1968) and Grubel (1972).

problem. In our model, which bears strong resemblance to the assignment models, we may obtain policy rules of the same general structure. *Assigning certain instruments to certain targets will, however, never be optimal.*

The forces influencing the optimal reserve level and the adjustment process will of course be discussed. For instance, we find that an increase in the international dependence will raise the optimal speed of adjustment and that an exogenous increase in capital mobility will make the optimal level of reserves higher.

The outline of the paper is as follows. We begin in section 2 by presenting the model and stating the optimal conditions. Section 3 contains the flow analysis of the problem and carries the argument over to section 4, which covers the adjustment of the stock of reserves. The most important policy conclusions are drawn in section 5. Some general criticism of the model, aiming at further research, is discussed in the concluding section. Most of the mathematical analysis is handled in an appendix.

2. The Analytical Framework

To describe the economy we use a standard income–expenditure model with a balance-of-payments constraint,

$$Y = E(Y, i) + X - I(Y) + G, \tag{1}$$

$$L(Y, i) = M, \tag{2}$$

$$\dot{R} = X - I(Y) + F(Y, i). \tag{3}$$

R is the level of foreign reserves and $\dot{R}$ denotes its time derivative, i.e., the surplus or deficit of the balance of payments. All other symbols have their usual meaning, and the signs of the relevant partial derivatives are also standard (see appendix). It is well observed in the literature [cf., Jones (1968), Swoboda (1972)] that complications may arise from the association of net capital inflow with domestic income. To the ordinary assumption $F_Y > 0$ [Johnson (1972, part II)] we add in some instances the further restriction $F_Y < I_Y$, which amounts to assuming that an increase in domestic income will have a net negative effect on the balance of payments.[2]

In order to make comparisons possible we have chosen the same model as that often used in the analyses of adjustment. Our treatment of it will be quite

[2]If an increase in income has a net *positive* effect on the balance of payments ($I_Y - F_Y < 0$), then *unique* optimal policies can in general not be found. Cf., Johnson (1972, pp. 151–166).

different, though. The usual procedure is to put $\dot{R} = 0$ in equation (3), add some ad hoc dynamic postulates – e.g., assignment rules, then linearize and study the stability properties of the system. The analyses can be illustrated in an *IS–LM* diagram with a balance-of-payments line added.[3]

Since our interest is in the development of reserves over time, we shall not require that $\dot{R} = 0$. We use equation (3) as a definition of the balance of payments rather than as an equilibrium condition. Neither do we need any ad hoc assumptions of dynamic behaviour. Instead we make use of a government utility function,

$$U = U(Y, i, R). \tag{4}$$

The government derives satisfaction from high levels of income (employment) and reserves, but also from a low level of the rate of interest. Having the rate of interest as a target variable may seem a bit unusual, but is very realistic in many countries (such as Sweden) where high priority is given to keeping down housing costs. Note also that R, not $\dot{R}$, is used as the external target in the function.[4]

The policy-makers presumably act to maximize their utility over time. They are constrained, however, by the conflict between the targets that is expressed in equation (3). Raising Y or diminishing i will worsen the balance of payments and hence affect the reserve target negatively. The problem can be stated formally as

$$\text{Max. } \Omega = \int_0^\infty e^{-rt} U(Y, i, R)\, dt,$$

subject to

$$\dot{R} = X - I(Y) + F(Y, i), \tag{5}$$

r is the rate of time preference, expressing the way in which the policy-makers weigh the future versus the present.

A few things should be noted before we proceed to the solution of the problem. First, U denotes the instantaneous utility, while Ω stands for total utility over the entire time period. To distinguish the two, we shall rename U and call it *felicity*. Second, the fact that we consider a period from the present

[3]Dynamic approaches related to ours can be found in Williamson (1971) and Korkman (1973).

[4]The question of *how* utility is derived from reserves is treated in the literature on optimal reserves referred to above. The present model rests on that literature when it comes to explicit specification of the utility function. In this paper further specification will not be necessary, however.

(0) to infinity (∞) does *not* necessarily mean that the analysis is long-run. The mathematical concept of infinity and the economic concept of long-run should be kept apart. In fact, the problems dealt with in this paper are typically short-run in nature. Third, it may seem that the *IS–LM* system (1)–(2) has disappeared in the formulation (5). It has not. It determines how G and M affect i and Y. Fourth, it should be noted that all variables are functions of time, though this is not explicitly written out. Of course, the solutions to the problem will also be time paths of the different variables. Fifth, to simplify the analysis, the utility function (4) is assumed to be separable.

Optimum Conditions

The problem as stated in (5) may be solved by the Maximum Principle (see appendix). To facilitate the interpretation of the necessary first-order conditions we group them according to their dynamic status.

(A) *Optimal flow conditions*

$$U_G + \lambda \dot{R}_G = 0, \tag{6}$$

and

$$U_M + \lambda \dot{R}_M = 0. \tag{7}$$

A new variable, λ, is introduced here. Define $\mu = e^{-rt}\lambda$. Then μ is the dynamic equivalent of a Lagrange multiplier and can be shown to have similar economic interpretations. Conditions (6) and (7) are the static conditions of the system, defining flow equilibrium. How the system moves over time is determined by:

(B) *Optimal stock adjustment conditions*

$$\dot{\lambda} = r\lambda - U_R, \tag{8}$$

and

$$\dot{R} = X - I(Y) + F(Y, i). \tag{9}$$

Apart from the conditions under (A) and (B) we shall need some information on our system at the starting point and some knowledge of what will happen when $t \to \infty$. The initial stock of reserves will be known, of course, satisfying the first need. Regarding the second issue, it is sufficient to assume that the parameters of the utility function are such as to prevent infinitely large values of Y, i and R from being optimal. This can be shown to imply (11) below.

(C) *Optimal "end" conditions*

$$R(0) = R_0, \quad \text{[initial condition]} \tag{10}$$

and

$$\lim_{t\to\infty} \mu = 0. \qquad \text{[transversality condition]} \tag{11}$$

Since μ is the shadow price of reserves, as shown below, condition (11) states that this implicit price must approach zero as $t \to \infty$.

The stock adjustment condition (8) was implied by the canonical equation $\dot{\mu} = -e^{-rt} U_R$. Integrating this formula we find that

$$\mu(t) = \int_t^\infty e^{-r\tau} U_R(\tau)\,d\tau, \tag{12}$$

which looks a little awkward but has a clear economic interpretation. At any point of time, μ is the sum of the discounted values of all future contributions to utility that is derived from a change in reserves. But this is equal to the marginal effect on the optimal values of the utility functional Ω from a unitary change in reserves, i.e.,

$$\mu = \delta\Omega^+/\delta R, \tag{13}$$

where + indicates optimality. In other words, μ can be looked upon as the *shadow price of reserves.*

The optimal conditions derived above are quite closely related to those of ordinary static Lagrange techniques.[5] Conditions (6) and (7) can be shown to imply (see appendix)

$$\mu = -(U_Y/\dot{R}_Y)\,e^{-rt} = -(\delta\Omega^+/\delta Y)/(\delta\dot{R}/\delta Y). \tag{14}$$

Using (13) and (14) we can derive a relation of familiar nature,

$$(\delta\Omega^+/\delta Y)/(\delta\Omega^+/\delta R) = -\,\delta\dot{R}/\delta Y, \tag{15}$$

according to which the marginal rate of substitution between the level of income in this period and the level of reserves over the relevant time horizon should equal the trade-off existing between income and balance of payments. Another way to state this is to say that the marginal disutility of an income

[5]See Nyberg–Viotti (1973b, pp. 16–19) for a further development of these relations.

reduction in this period should equal the marginal benefit of a permanent increase of reserves. Similar results can be derived for the other flow target, *i*.

3. The Optimal Policies

The necessary conditions derived can be used to study the optimal mix of fiscal and monetary policy in the process of adjustment. From the flow conditions (6) and (7) we immediately obtain

$$U_M / U_G = \dot{R}_M / \dot{R}_G. \tag{16}$$

We may regard our problem as one of allocation between instantaneous utility (i.e., felicity) and future utility, derived by increasing reserves. Then (16) states that the two instruments, M and G, should be used in such a mix that the ratio of their marginal effects (their marginal rate of substitution) is the same on instantaneous and on future utility. In other words, *apply the instruments up to the point where no comparative advantages remain.*[6] This policy rule can be illustrated in a diagram, recognizing that the left-hand side of (16) can be interpreted as the slope of a family of constant felicity curves in the G–M space, while the right-hand side traces a family of curves where the change in reserves is constant. In figure 1 we illustrate the case where the curve families are "well-behaved".

From the assumption on the derivatives made earlier it follows that higher indifference curves give higher utility in the usual way, while higher reserve changes are represented by lower $\dot{R}$ curves. For a given level of felicity, the best $\dot{R}$ curve possible is the one tangent to the felicity curve. By changing the level of felicity, we can then trace out combinations of felicity and reserve changes that all satisfy the optimal condition (14). The locus of such combinations is the P–P curve in figure 1.

To illustrate the policy rule, consider for instance a point such as A. If we reduce M slightly, moving horizontally to the left in the diagram, we can compensate the loss in felicity by somewhat increasing G. Staying on the same $\dot{R}$ curve as before will require a further increase in G. Thus G has a comparative advantage in affecting felicity (and M has a similar advantage in influencing reserve changes). Then it is obvious that, keeping $\dot{R}$ constant, we gain higher felicity by decreasing M and increasing G, and that this policy should continue until all comparative advantages have disappeared.

[6]This policy rule is the same as the one derived by Niehans (1968). Niehans used a static model, however, having $\dot{R}$ instead of R as a target variable.

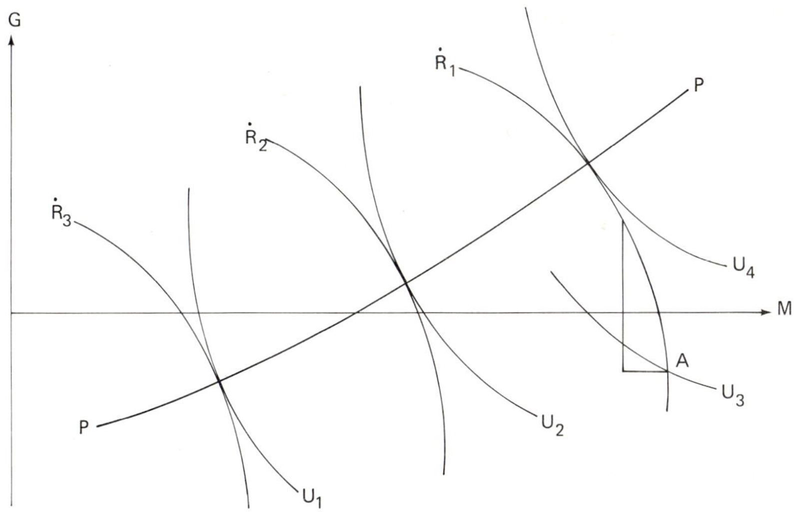

FIGURE 1

It is easy to verify that the policy rule is valid regardless of the number of instruments available.[7] We do not require, as in static linear analysis, that the number of instruments should equal the number of targets. *All* instruments must be used until their comparative advantages disappear. Also, the assignment of certain targets to certain instruments will not in general be optimal.

If we transpose the P–P curve into the U–$\dot{R}$ space we arrive at an equivalent of the ordinary production-possibility frontier, giving combinations of U and $\dot{R}$ – which can be interpreted as instantaneous and future utility – that efficiently utilize the two instruments, G and M. This efficiency locus is shown as the P–P curve in figure 2. Whatever the level of reserves we must be somewhere on this locus if we use our two instruments in the best possible way.

The P–P locus was derived by eliminating λ in the flow conditions (6) and (7). It is therefore independent of λ. It is also independent of R, the total stock of reserves, since reserves are not influenced directly by M and G and thus never enter the flow conditions. But R and λ are the variables determining the time development of the system, as can be seen from the adjustment equations (8) and (9). *Thus the P–P curve stays where it is, independent of time.* This is very reasonable from an economic standpoint, since it means that the *efficient*

[7]See Nyberg–Viotti (1973b).

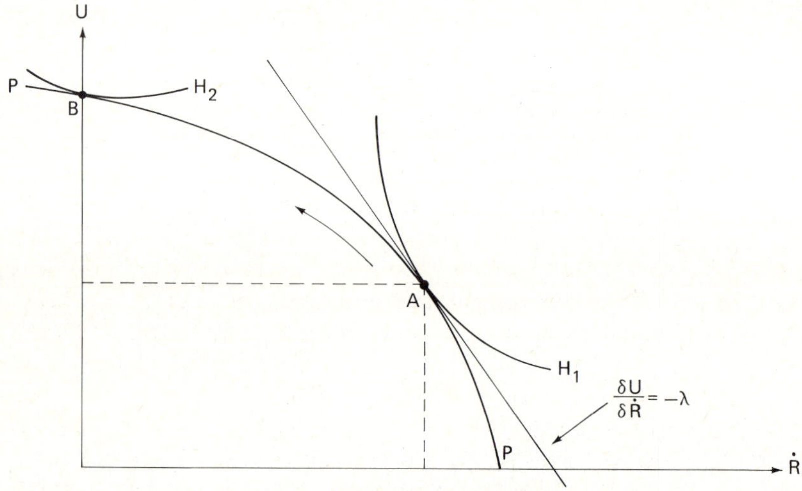

FIGURE 2

ways of combining fiscal and monetary policy are *not* dependent on the level of reserves or of its implicit value.

As usual, an efficient choice is a necessary prerequisite for optimality, but it is not enough. What is now needed to complete the analysis is of course a "utility function", showing us how to choose between present and future, i.e., between felicity and reserve changes. This part is played by the Hamiltonian, the expression corresponding to the Lagrangean function of static optimization theory, and from which the necessary conditions (6)–(9) were derived (see appendix),

$$H = e^{-rt} \cdot U(Y, i, R) + \mu \cdot \dot{R}. \tag{17}$$

The two arguments can be interpreted simply as present and future utility.

In any given time period we should, in analogy to similar diagrams in welfare theory, expect an optimum where the slope of the Hamiltonian is equal to the slope of the P–P curve. The slope of the P–P curve we know to be equal to the trade-off between reserve changes and felicity, $\delta U/\delta \dot{R}$. The slope of the Hamiltonian for any given level of reserves is derived from implicit differentiation of (17),

$$\delta U/\delta \dot{R}|_{H=\bar{H}} = -\mu \cdot e^{rt} = -\lambda. \tag{18}$$

In optimum $\delta U/\delta \dot{R} = -\lambda$, which is what should be expected considering the conditions (6) and (7). Here the P–P curve and the Hamiltonian are tangent to each other as shown in point A in figure 2.

This completes the illustration of the *flow* mechanism of the model. Before proceeding to the explicit analysis of the *adjustment* mechanism we show how it will affect the argument illustrated in figure 2.

The above analysis is valid for every instant of time, since, keeping R constant, we can consider the Hamiltonian as a utility function in U and $\dot{R}$. The decision taken on the values of U and $\dot{R}$ at a certain time point will, however, change R and thereby the position of the Hamiltonian. Thus this curve – in contrast to the P–P curve – moves with time. As will be found in the following analysis, starting for example at a point such as A in figure 2, $\dot{R}$ will diminish over time till it reaches zero. The "utility" curve will then have changed position so that the new optimum (steady-state) position is where the P–P curve cuts the vertical axis in figure 2 – i.e., when changes in reserves no longer occur. Of course, we may also have too large reserves at the starting point, i.e., too large compared to the optimal reserve level. We then start in the second quadrant of figure 2, diminishing reserves over time, but still ending up at the same position (B).

4. Adjustment of the Reserve Level

We now proceed to an explicit study of the optimal growth of foreign reserves. For convenience, we restate the stock adjustment conditions (8) and (9),

$$\dot{\lambda} = r\lambda - U_R,$$

and

$$\dot{R} = X - I(Y) + F(Y, i).$$

This system of differential equations in reserves and its instantaneous shadow price will serve to determine the development of all variables in the model. Knowing λ, we can solve for G, M, i and Y via the flow conditions (6) and (7) and the Keynesian system (1) and (2).

Explicit solutions to the equation system (8)–(9) cannot be obtained, since nothing has been assumed about the form of the functions involved – in particular no linearity assumptions have been introduced. The system can, however, be qualitatively analyzed in a phase diagram (figure 3). Starting with the combinations of R and λ, which imply that either of them is unchanged over time, we get

$$\mathrm{d}\lambda/\mathrm{d}R|_{\dot{\lambda}=0} = U_{RR}/r < 0, \qquad \mathrm{d}\lambda/\mathrm{d}R|_{\dot{R}=0} = 0, \tag{19}$$

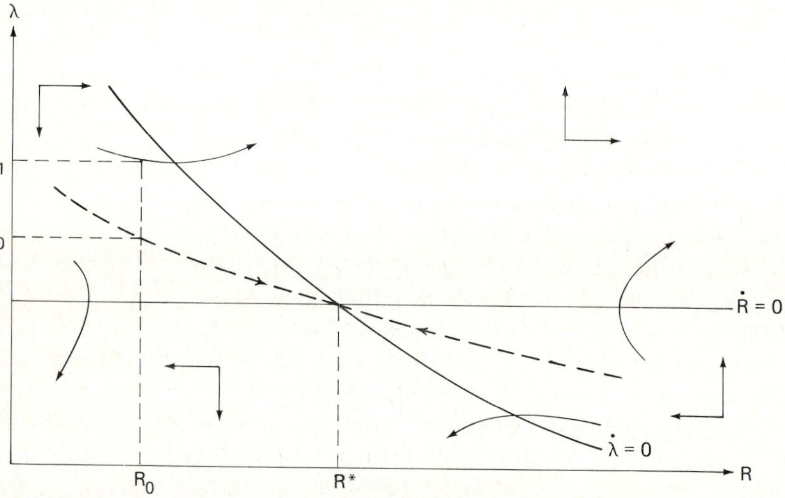

FIGURE 3

as shown in figure 3. For the properties of solutions at an arbitrary point in the (R, λ) space we consider

$$\delta\dot{\lambda}/\delta R = -U_{RR} > 0, \tag{20}$$

implying the small vertical arrows in the diagram, and

$$\delta\dot{R}/\delta\lambda = -(I_Y - F_Y)Y_\lambda + F_i i_\lambda > 0, \tag{21}$$

which is indicated by the small horizontal arrows. We use here the assumption that $I_Y > F_Y$ and also that $Y_\lambda = Y_M M_\lambda + Y_G G_\lambda < 0$ and $i_\lambda = i_M M_\lambda + i_G G_\lambda > 0$, which are sufficient (but *not* necessary) conditions for (21) to hold.[8]

These assumptions are easily interpreted in economic terms. When λ, the implicit valuation of reserves, increases, M and G are adjusted so as to make Y smaller, thus decreasing imports and holding back capital inflow – the net effect being an improvement in the balance of payments. The interest rate effect is seen to work in the same direction. Thus what is assumed in (21) is in fact that the negative effect on the balance of payments from the income sensitivity of capital flows will be outweighed by the positive effects stemming from the real

[8]The signs of Y_λ and i_λ can be derived from the flow system (6) and (7) and some further assumptions on the second-order characteristics of the Keynesian system. A linear balance-of-payments constraint together with the separability of the utility function would do, for example (see appendix).

side and from the interest sensitivity of capital. The higher this sensitivity (F_i), the more likely it is that (21) is true.

The intersection of the $\dot{\lambda} = 0$ and $\dot{R} = 0$ curves represents the stationary equilibrium or steady state. Under the assumptions given, this stationary point is a saddle. But this implies that, whatever the initial size of reserves, there is a *unique* optimal path leading to the final optimal reserve level. This is shown by the heavy dashed arrows in the diagram. Starting, for instance, with the reserve level R_0, we must choose M and G (and hence Y and i) so as to render λ equal to λ_0. If, instead, we make $\lambda = \lambda_1$, we do of course satisfy the optimal conditions (6)–(9) – those which so far have been discussed. We do not fulfill the transversality condition (11), however, since both λ and R will grow infinitely large if we follow a path starting at (R_0, λ_1).

In conclusion, for any given initial stock of reserves, there will be *a unique equilibrium level and a unique optimal path along which to approach it. The monetary and fiscal policy used to keep the economy on this path will also give the optimal levels of employment and the rate of interest.*

The adjustment path has one characteristic of particular interest. No matter where the starting point is, it will be true that *the adjustment towards the steady state is quickest in the beginning.*[9] Thus, once we have calculated the equilibrium value of reserves, the optimal way to approach it will not be direct, nor by equal amounts every period – i.e., linearly – but by comparatively greater efforts in the beginning. Indeed, if we specify the government utility function as quadratic and the constraint as linear [see, e.g., Theil (1964)], we find that a certain fraction of the discrepancy between actual and equilibrium reserves should be closed in every period, i.e., $\dot{R} = k(R - R^*)$, $k < 0$. As will be shown below we can also draw specific conclusions about the assignment of instruments.

Optimal Policy versus "Assignment"

To get some further information of how to adjust our policy parameters, we can assume a quadratic utility function and make the basic system (1)–(3) linear. Alternatively, we can linearize our original system of differential equations (8)–(9) around the stationary equilibrium, confining our interest to the vicinity of that point. The results derived below will hold for both interpretations.

The optimal time path of reserve accumulation can be shown to be

[9]This follows directly from (21).

$$R(t) = R^* + (R_0 - R^*)\, e^{\phi t}, \tag{22}$$

where ϕ is the negative characteristic root of the system (8)–(9). This can be written in a closed loop form

$$\dot{R} = \phi(R - R^*), \tag{23}$$

which is the one we discussed in the previous section. The similarities between (23) and stock adjustment equations in the theory of capital and investment should be obvious.

From the solutions given above we can derive time paths for the policy variables,

$$\dot{M} = h_1(R - R^*), \qquad \dot{G} = h_2(R - R^*), \tag{24}$$

where h_1 and h_2 are constants.[10] Thus the optimal changes in the policy variables are also fractions of the discrepancy between actual and steady-state reserves. It is interesting to compare these policy rules with the "assignment" policies often discussed in connection with models such as (1)–(3).[11] Typically, fiscal policy would be assigned to internal balance, while monetary policy would be assigned to external balance,

$$\dot{M} = c_1(\dot{R} - 0), \qquad \dot{G} = c_2(Y - Y^*), \tag{25}$$

where Y^* is the desired income target (full employment), and c_1 and c_2 are constants.

Though the structure of (24) and (25) is similar, the differences are apparent. (24) are *results* of an optimization process. They are optimal, not only with respect to reserves, but also with respect to the flow targets, income and the rate of interest. No assignment of certain instruments to certain targets is implied. In (25), on the other hand, the rules are ad hoc dynamic *assumptions* about the policy-makers' behaviour. Together with the static equilibrium conditions implied by (1)–(3) (where $\dot{R} = 0$) they constitute a dynamic system. Given this, it is possible to study whether the assignment is stable or not, and to compare it with various alternative assignments. This is about all, however.[12,13]

[10]This is a standard result in optimal control theory where the criterion function is quadratic and the constraint is linear. h_1 and h_2 are then solutions to the matrix Ricatti equation. See, e.g., Athans and Falb (1966).

[11]See Mundell (1968) and Swoboda (1972).

[12]The difference between the two approaches corresponds to that in control theory betwee- synthesis by analytical and by optimal methods.

[13]In the assignment models, an additional assumption of incomplete information or of decen ized decision-making is required to give reasonable economic interpretations [Swoboda (19

5. Planning and Replanning

We return now to the general non-linear problem as posed in (5). To solve this problem, i.e., to find the optimal paths of the policy variables, the government must be assumed to know (or have estimates of) all parameters and exogenous variables, present and future. Clearly, this is not realistic. We therefore assume that the government plans on the basis of expectations (certainty equivalents), and then replans when expectations are revised. Alternatively, different plans may be made for different possible developments of the exogenous variables, e.g., export behaviour. This is probably the way much planning is done today, since the introduction of stochastic elements complicates the process considerably.[14]

To analyze optimal replanning, we study the comparative dynamics of the model,[15] i.e., we investigate the effects on the optimal paths of various changes in parameters. For the purpose of illustration we assume that the initial stock of reserves is below R_1^*. Consider first the situation where expectations of a currency revaluation arise. This will shift the capital flow function $F(Y, i)$ upwards, i.e., increase capital mobility. The same effect may arise from an increase of investment by foreigners caused in turn, say, by the discovery of rich new raw material deposits (Norwegian oil).

In the phase diagram, this will shift the $\dot{R} = 0$ curve downwards from $\dot{R}_1$ to $\dot{R}_2$ while the $\dot{\lambda} = 0$ curve is left unchanged, as shown in figure 4. The stationary equilibrium level of reserves will rise from R_1^* to R_2^*. Furthermore, we can show that *the new optimal path will always lie below the old one*. This means that the implicit valuation of reserves for a given reserve level will always be smaller on the new path, reflecting the fact that the increase of F has made the conflict between present and future targets less severe. Since the cost of increasing reserves is smaller, the optimal policy will shift in favour of the flow targets, Y and i. This is achieved by more active fiscal and/or monetary policy.

The effect on the optimal adjustment path is shown by the dotted line in figure 4. The optimal policies conduct the economy along the "old" path leading to R_1^*. Then new information is received by the authorities and the optimal policies are recalculated. When this is done, we change over to the "new" path leading to R_2^*.

An exogenous increase in exports will have about the same effect as an upward shift in the capital flow function. The steady state level of reserves rises,

[14]A more detailed discussion of the planning problems of a similar model can be found in Nyberg–Viotti (1973a).

[15]The technique used is briefly explained in the appendix. For further reference, see Treadway (1969) and Gould (1970).

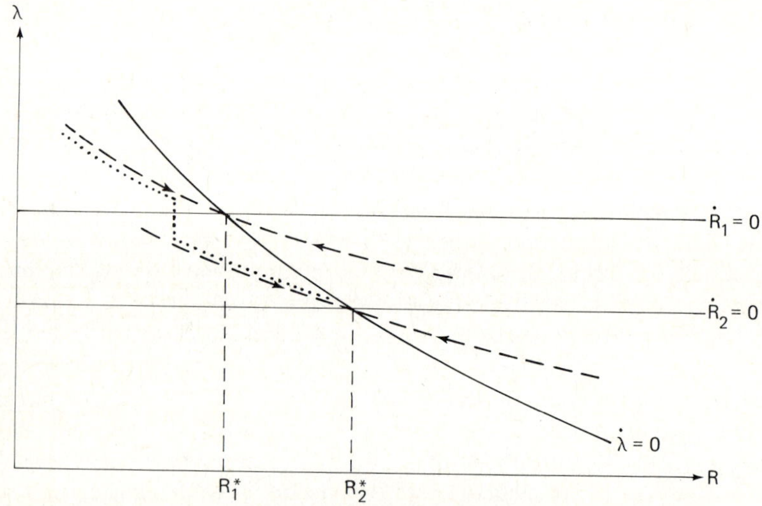

FIGURE 4

and over the whole path we can favour our flow targets, the activity level and the rate of interest, again by means of more expansive monetary and fiscal policies.

To sum up, so far, an increase in capital mobility or exports will increase the optimal level of foreign exchange reserves. But it will also be optimal to conduct an economic policy so as to increase current satisfaction as reflected in the values of Y and i.

In the case of an increase in imports – an upward shift in the import function – we get, as expected, the opposite response to that of an increase in exports. The $\dot{R} = 0$ curve shifts upwards, thus decreasing the optimal level of reserves by making reserve accumulation more costly in terms of the income and interest rate targets.

If there is a change in government preferences in favour of the external balance target, the U_R curve will rise. This will shift the $\lambda = 0$ curve upwards but leave the $\dot{R} = 0$ curve unchanged as shown in figure 5. The stationary equilibrium of reserves will increase, and the new optimal path will always be above the old one. *It is clear in this case that the "immediate" effect will be a rise in λ and hence a lower domestic activity and/or a higher interest rate. In the final equilibrium R_2^*, the optimal policies will be just the same as in R_1^*, however.* This can be verified in the figure by noting that the steady state value

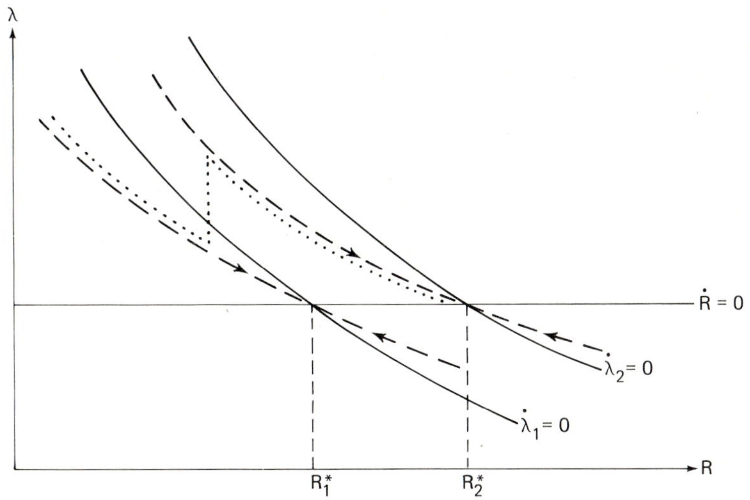

FIGURE 5

of λ is unchanged. Since comparing the two stationary equilibria is exactly what is done in ordinary comparative statics, we see that the dynamic analysis has important information to add here.

Finally, we note that a rise in the rate of time preference, *r*, has an effect opposite to that which was obtained from an upward shift in the U_R curve. This is plausible, because it indicates that the policy-makers will concentrate more heavily on the purely short-run targets, *Y* and *i*, when the time horizon gets more narrow (because, for instance, of a near election).

For reference, we collect the results concerning the target variables in a table. The symbol ~ is used to notify the "immediate" effects.

	$F\uparrow$	$I\uparrow$	$X\uparrow$	$U_R\uparrow$	$r\uparrow$
R^*	+	−?	+	+	−
Y^*	+	−?	+	0	0
$\tilde{Y}$	+	−?	+	−	+
i^*	+	−?	+	0	0
$\tilde{i}$	+	−?	+	−	+

The Speed of Adjustment

If we return again to the linear framework some further results may be obtained. It is seen from (23) that the speed of adjustment is completely determined by ϕ where

$$\phi = \tfrac{1}{2}\{r - \sqrt{(r^2 - 4U_{RR}Q)}\}. \tag{26}$$

If we assume a linear balance-of-payments constraint and a separable utility function, then

$$Q = \frac{\delta \dot{R}}{\delta \lambda} = -\left[\frac{(I_Y - F_Y)^2}{U_{YY}} + \frac{F_i^2}{U_{ii}}\right].^{16} \tag{27}$$

The effects on the speed of adjustment from an increase in any of the parameters are summarized below:[17]

	I_Y	F_Y	F_i	U_{YY}	U_{ii}	U_{RR}	r
$-\phi$	+	−	+	+	+	−	−

A rise in the import propensity or in the interest sensitivity of capital movements will always increase the optimal speed of adjustment. *In other words, when international dependence increases, the desired adjustment process will become faster.* The explanation to this is of course that an increase in I_Y and F_i always mitigates the conflict between Y, R and i, so that in every period of time it will be less costly in terms of changes in Y and i to accumulate reserves. It can also be shown that if capital shows high interest mobility ($F_i \to \infty$), then changes in F_Y and I_Y will have negligible effects on the adjustment speed.

All three targets in the utility function are by assumption subject to diminishing marginal utility. Considering the reserve target, we see that the closer the utility function is to linearity (U_{RR} increases), the slower will be the speed of adjustment. For the flow targets the opposite holds, as would be expected.

Finally, an increase in the rate of time preference – which can be thought of as a shortening of the planning horizon – will diminish the speed of adjustment. Thus the more shortsighted the politicians, the more will they care for the flow targets which yield utility today, and the slower will they adjust reserves.

[16]See appendix and compare with (21).
[17]ϕ is negative so $-\phi$ is the speed of adjustment.

6. Summary and Conclusion

Received literature in international finance has treated the problem of adjustment as separate from that of finding an optimal reserve level. *The main contribution in this paper has been to show how optimal reserves and optimal adjustment can be handled simultaneously.* Given the criterion function of the government we have been able to find the stationary equilibrium level of foreign reserves and of the internal targets. This optimal reserve level is *independent of the initial stock of reserves.* We also establish the optimal way to proceed to the final equilibrium, i.e., *the best possible time development of both the external and the internal targets.* On the optimal path, adjustment of reserves will be *quickest in the beginning* of the planning period. Furthermore, we have shown that a *unique choice of fiscal and monetary policy* will lead to the stationary value, and that *the instruments should be used so as to fully explore their comparative advantages. All available instruments should be used* regardless of the number of targets, and *assignment of instruments to targets will not be optimal.* The response of the model to changes in parameters is summarized in section 5. In general, *the "immediate" dynamic effects of parameter changes may differ in sign and size from the stationary equilibrium (comparative statics) effects.*

In order to make comparisons possible, we tied the model fairly closely to those used in the traditional adjustment literature. It should be clear, however, that the analysis disregards some mechanisms of economic importance. First, there is one assumption implicit in our treatment of the money supply as an instrument variable, viz. that the change in foreign reserves can always be sterilized by the government. Second, the relation between the rate of interest and the *flow* of capital is discomforting. If the capital flow function were derived from a proper portfolio analysis, we should expect the *change* in the domestic relative to the *change* in the foreign interest rate as the explanatory variable. Our traditional way of handling the interest rate could perhaps be defended by arguing that capital is imperfectly mobile in the short run, due to credit commitments etc. Third, in the Keynesian framework we use, there is no room for prices. Thus we are unable to study the remaining important internal target, price stability.

Consequently, further research should focus on a model where reserve changes affect the money supply, where an explicit portfolio analysis is introduced, and where prices are permitted to play an important part. The authors are presently working with such a model.

Appendix

(A) The symbols used are

Y = national income,
R = level of foreign reserves,
X = exports,
I = imports,
F = net capital inflow,
i = rate of interest,
E = total private expenditure,
L = demand for money,
M = stock of money,
G = net government spending,
r = rate of time preference,
μ = the shadow price of reserves (discounted),
λ = the shadow price of reserves (not discounted),
Ω = total utility (the entire planning period),
U = instantaneous utility or *felicity*.

A dot over a variable denotes time derivative. Partial derivatives are denoted by subscripts, e.g., E_Y, when not written out completely. An asterisk (*) indicates steady state values of the variables while a plus (+) means that the solution so marked is optimal.

(B) In the sytem (1)–(3) we assume

$$1 > E_Y > 0; \quad E_i < 0; \quad 1 > L_Y > 0; \quad L_i < 0;$$
$$I_Y > 0; \quad F_i > 0; \quad I_Y > F_Y > 0,$$

then

$$\begin{aligned} Y_G &= L_i/\Delta > 0, \qquad i_G = -L_Y/\Delta > 0, \\ Y_M &= E_i/\Delta > 0, \qquad i_M = (1 - E_Y + I_Y)/\Delta < 0, \end{aligned} \tag{B.1}$$

where $\Delta = L_i(1 - E_Y + I_Y) + E_i L_Y < 0$.

The assumptions on the felicity function U are

$$U_Y > 0, \qquad U_R > 0, \qquad U_i < 0,$$
$$U_{YY} < 0, \qquad U_{RR} < 0, \qquad U_{ii} < 0.$$

(C) The problem (5) is a dynamic optimization problem with one state variable (R), two control variables (M and G) and two output variables (Y and i). All functions involved are assumed continuous and twice-differentiable. The problem is solved by the Maximum Principle [cf., Athans–Falb (1966)]. The Hamiltonian is

$$H = e^{-rt}[U(Y, i, R) + \lambda(X - I(Y) + F(Y, i))]. \tag{C.1}$$

Differentiating with respect to the control variables gives

$$\delta H/\delta G = Y_G[U_Y - \lambda(I_Y - F_Y)] + i_G(U_i + \lambda F_i) = 0, \tag{C.2}$$

and

$$\delta H/\delta M = Y_M[U_Y - \lambda(I_Y - F_Y)] + i_G(U_i + \lambda F_i) = 0. \tag{C.3}$$

These are equal to (6) and (7). Considering the signs of the multipliers in (B.1) they imply

$$U_Y = \lambda(I_Y - F_Y), \tag{C.4}$$

and

$$U_i = -\lambda F_i. \tag{C.5}$$

These are the conditions that would be obtained if Y and i (not M and G) were used as control variables.

Differentiating the Hamiltonian with respect to R gives

$$H_R = U_R\, e^{-rt}. \tag{C.6}$$

Since

$$\dot{\mu} = e^{-rt}(\dot{\lambda} - r\lambda), \tag{C.7}$$

the first canonical equation $-H_R = \dot{\mu}$ reduces to (8), while the second produces the constraint (9).

λ is a continuous function of Y and i (C.4)–(C.5). The condition that optimal values of Y and i are finite will assure that λ is bounded. This implies the transversality condition (11),

$$\lim_{t\to\infty} \lambda\, e^{-rt} = 0. \tag{C.8}$$

Condition (C.4) implies that

$$\lambda = -U_Y/\dot{R}_Y \quad \text{equal to} \quad \mu = -(U_Y/\dot{R}_Y)\, e^{-rt}. \tag{C.9}$$

Since $U_Y\, e^{-rt} = \delta\Omega^+/\delta Y$ we obtain (14).

(D) Differentiating totally (C.4) and (C.5) we obtain

$$[U_{YY} - \lambda(I_{YY} - F_{YY})]Y_\lambda + [U_{Yi} - \lambda(I_{Yi} - F_{Yi})]i_\lambda = I_Y - F_Y, \tag{D.1}$$

and

$$[U_{iY} + \lambda F_{iY}]Y_\lambda + [U_{ii} + \lambda F_{ii}]i_\lambda = -F_i. \tag{D.2}$$

If the felicity function U is separable, and if the balance-of-payments constraint is linear, then (D.1) and (D.2) reduces to

$$Y_\lambda = (I_Y - F_Y)/U_{YY} < 0, \qquad i_\lambda = -F_i/U_{ii} > 0. \tag{D.3}$$

Linearizing (8) and (9) we arrive at

$$\dot{\lambda} = r(\lambda - \lambda^*) - U_{RR}(R - R^*), \tag{D.4}$$

and

$$\dot{R} = Q(\lambda - \lambda^*), \tag{D.5}$$

where $Q = \delta\dot{R}/\delta\lambda$ as defined in (21).

Solving for R (and considering the transversality condition) we obtain (22). Using the fact that $R_0 = (R - R^*)\,e^{-\phi t} + R^*$, we find the closed loop form (23).

(E) *Comparative dynamics.* Consider as an example the effect of an upward shift in the capital flow function, i.e., $F_1(Y, i) < F_2(Y, i)$. From (8) and (9) it is clear that the $\dot{R} = 0$ curve associated with F_2 will be below the one associated with F_1 in the (R, λ) phase space and that there is no change in the $\dot{\lambda} = 0$ curve, so that $R_1^* < R_2^*$.

We then show that it is impossible for the two optimal paths to intersect. Since the slopes of the optimal paths are negative, there could be no intersection for $R_1^* < R < R_2^*$. If the optimal paths even intersect to the left of R_1^*, the first such intersection must have

$$\mathrm{d}\lambda/\mathrm{d}R|_{F_1} > \mathrm{d}\lambda/\mathrm{d}R|_{F_2}. \tag{E.1}$$

We have from (8) and (9) that

$$\mathrm{d}\lambda/\mathrm{d}R|_{F_j} = \dot{\lambda}/\dot{R}|_{F_j} = (r\lambda - U_R)/[X - I(Y) + F_j(Y, i)]. \tag{E.2}$$

At a point of intersection in this region of the phase space the inequality (E.1) holds only if $F_1 > F_2$ ($\dot{\lambda}$ is negative in this region), which is a contradiction. A similar contradiction can be established for intersections to the right of R_2^*. Thus we have shown that, when the capital flow function is shifted upward in the (λ, R) phase space, the optimal policy path is shifted downward and the stationary level of R will be decreased (see figure 4).

References

Athans, M. and P. L. Falb, 1966, Optimal control: An introduction to the theory and its applications (McGraw-Hill, New York).

Clower, R. and R. Lipsey, 1968, The present state of international liquidity theory, AER, pp. 586–595.

Cooper, R. N., 1969, Macro-economic policy adjustment in interdependent economies, QJE, pp. 1–24.

Gould, I. P., 1970, Diffusion processes and optimal advertising policy, in: Phelps et al., Microeconomic foundations of employment and inflation theory (New York).

Grubel, H. G., 1971, The demand for international reserves; A critical review of the literature, JEL, Dec.

Johnson, H. G., 1972, Further essays in monetary economics (London).

Jones, R. W., 1968, Monetary and fiscal policy for an open economy with fixed exchange rates, JPE, July/Aug.

Korkman, S., 1973, Foreign exchange reserves and the adjustment mechanism, Seminar Paper no. 31 (Institute for International Economic Studies, Stockholm).

Mundell, R. A., 1968, International economics (New York).

Niehans, J., 1968, Monetary and fiscal policies in open economies under fixed exchange rates: An optimizing approach, JPE, pp. 893–920.

Nyberg, L. and S. Viotti, 1973a, Quasi-dynamic and dynamic methods in an economic planning problem, Seminar Paper no. 29 (Institute for International Economic Studies, Stockholm).

Nyberg, L. and S. Viotti, 1973b, The policy conflict between internal and external balance under fixed exchange rates: An optimizing approach, Seminar Paper no. 30 (Institute for International Economic Studies, Stockholm).

Sohmen, E., 1969, Flexible exchange rates (Chicago).

Swoboda, A.K., 1972, On limited information and the assignment problem, in: Claassen and Salin, eds., Stabilization policies in interdependent economies (Amsterdam).

Theil, H., 1964, Optimal decision rules for government and industry (Amsterdam).

Treadway, A. B., 1969, On rational entrepreneurial behaviour and the demand for investment, RES, April.

Whitman, M., 1970, Policies for internal and external balance, Special Papers in International Finance, no. 9 (Princeton).

Williamson, J., 1971, On the normative theory of balance of payments adjustment, in: Clayton, Gilbert, and Sedgwich, eds., Monetary theory and policy in the 1970s (London) pp. 233–257.

Chapter 5.2

COMMENT ON NYBERG AND VIOTTI

Jacques L'HUILLIER

As Professors Nyberg and Viotti point out in their remarkable essay, two theories have greatly improved in recent years, but the one ignoring the other: the theory of adjustment and that of optimal reserves.

The two authors of the paper try to synthesize these two theoretical developments.

In theories of adjustment, the problem is to find the combination of economic policies – monetary and fiscal policy – which allows simultaneous attainment of an internal target, almost without exception full employment, and an external target, equilibrium in the balance of payments. The originality of the paper lies in the substitution of the stock of reserves for this external target.

The authors demonstrate first all combinations of the levels of employment and balance-of-payments surpluses which imply optimal utilization of available policies, in the sense that any alternative assignment can only yield a similar level of employment at the cost of a smaller balance-of-payments surplus, or inversely. The choice between these efficient combinations is made via a community utility function whereby the marginal disutility of a reduction in the level of employment is balanced against the marginal utility of an addition in the stock of reserves. The authors' proof in the analysis is a skilful accomplishment because the external target cannot be reached in one move: the whole process is dynamic. It is superfluous to add anything further here for it is only through reading the paper that we can appreciate the rigour and elegance of thought of its authors.

My modest contribution to the discussion will deal neither with the combination of instruments nor with the paths to be followed in order to reach the targets but will concentrate upon the targets themselves.

In theories of adjustment, the target of external equilibrium does not appear, upon reflection, to be on the same plane as that of internal equilibrium. Even if we question what level of activity signifies full employment, nobody ponders too long over the desirability of full employment. Implicitly, we recognize that a chronic deficit cannot be sustained, and thus, it is necessary to be in external equilibrium. But, it can be equally argued that to make permanent external equilibrium an imperative is to impose a constraint that can prove very awkward. And it is the merit of the theory of optimal reserves to focus attention upon this aspect of the problem.

It is one thing to argue that it is useful to have some reserves in order that the slightest deficit of the balance does not upset national economic policy. It is another to define an optimum level for these reserves. The ingenious idea of the authors of the paper is that this level cannot be defined absolutely but varies significantly with the sacrifices that the building-up of reserves imply in terms of employment. With respect to this, we might at the same time ask if recognition of this possible conflict between the internal target of employment and the external target of growth in reserves arises because the paper adopts a national viewpoint. For, if we view the problem globally, we see that growth in reserves is not necessarily linked with the existence of surpluses in the balance of payments. It is enough to create, for example, some SDR without toil.

But it can be questioned if the real problem lies there. A target located within the domain of international payments cannot be an ultimate goal simply because the system of international payments is only an instrument for international trade, more precisely for the gain from international trade.

It is clear that under a regime of fixed exchange rates a certain level of international liquidity is essential in order that deficit countries avoid taking hasty corrective measures. Nevertheless, if we are convinced that disequilibrium in the balance of payments diminishes the gain from international trade, this will affect the level of reserves that we deem to be globally desirable.

In order to show the damage inflicted by external disequilibrium on the gain from international trade, we shall take a very simple case where trade takes place only in goods and services. So, disequilibrium pertains to the current balance.

We can distinguish between two sources of disequilibrium: (1) Disequilibrium due to a change in real variables, a modification of relative condition productions or of the structure of demand. This is the type of disequilibrium that the classical school had in mind. It is inevitable. The important thing is not to allow the disequilibrium to continue forever. (2) The other cause of disequilibrium lies in divergences between policies of demand regulation followed by different countries.

Since 1960, it is not excessive to assert that the disequilibria have been primarily of the second type. They have been provoked by differences in the degree of inflation tolerated by national economic policies. Under a regime of fixed exchange rates, the country which follows the most inflationary policy can live for a certain period above its means at the cost of other economies; it finishes by living below its means during the adjustment phase of its external balance. With this second type of disequilibrium, it is not only its persistence but also the disequilibrium itself which is harmful.

In the diagram attached we show "à la Meade" the position of the production block of a country A in a state of external equilibrium. Assuming free trade, its marginal rates of transformation of production and substitution of consumption (tangent common to the point of tangency *Ta* of the production transformation curve of goods *X* and *Y* and of the community indifference curve) – in quadrant I – are equal to the international terms of trade *t* – in quadrant II. This is a Pareto optimum.

Now suppose the authorities undertake an expansionary policy, starting from a situation of full employment – even if there is some frictional unemployment – and inflate money income, a policy which allows country A to live above its means. Its production block shifts north-west. We assume that the income–consumption line, given the international terms of trade, is a straight line from the origin and passing through *Ta.* Let us add a further assumption that by extending this line in quadrant III, we determine the point *Tb* where the production block of country B – rest of the world – is tangent to a community indifference curve, the common tangent being parallel to the line *t*

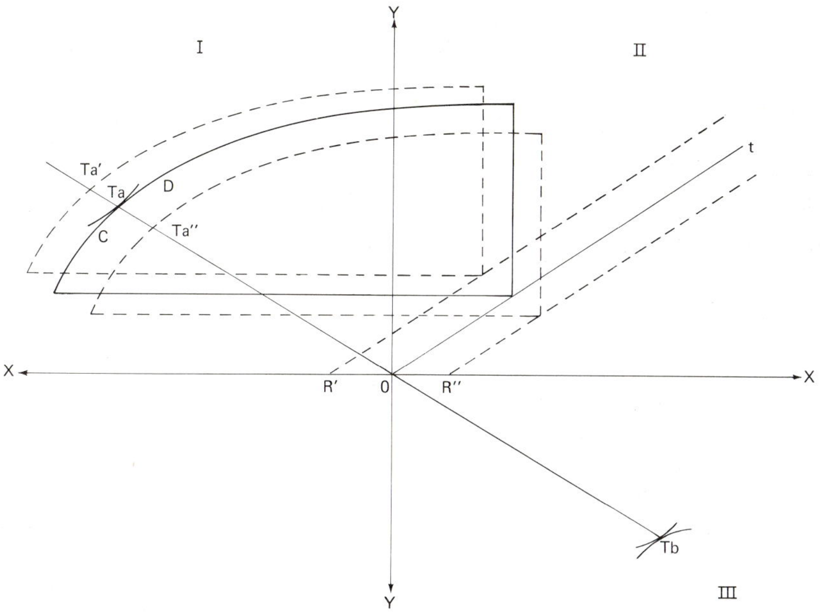

FIGURE 1

of the international terms of trade. This line joining 0 to *Tb* is the income–consumption line of country B.

Under these assumptions there is no reason for the international terms of trade to alter, because the relative contraction of money income in B frees *X* and *Y* in the same proportion that consumption of the two goods increases in A. During the deficit phase of the current balance in A, its production block is in the position indicated by the dotted curve, with *Ta'* north-west of *Ta*. Expressed in terms of *X*, the deficit equals $0R'$. The new point of tangency between the production block of A and an indifference curve, higher than the old one, is *Ta'*.

Then, during the adjustment phase, the production block shifts south-east, with a surplus $0R''$, always expressed in terms of *X*.

We see that country A has consumed exactly the same amount of *X* and *Y* in the course of the two successive periods: deficit (point of consumption *Ta'* with respect to the axes of quadrant I); then surplus (point of consumption *Ta"*) as if it had lived for the whole span of time within the limits set by its means (point of consumption *Ta*). It is only the distribution of this consumption over time which differs; in that sense that it has in fact been irregular.

Whether we adhere to the concept of marginal utility of income or that of consumption regulated according to permanent income, we are correct in thinking that the population of A would have preferred – its tastes unchanged throughout the process – to remain permanently for the whole span of time at *Ta*, rather than move successively from *Ta* to *Ta'* and then to *Ta"*. The disequilibrium, therefore, reduces its welfare. The same argument can be applied to country B.

A further injury is added if we relax the assumption that the income–consumption lines of the two countries are such that one is the extension of the other, from the origin. For under these new conditions, the successive disequilibria – deficit, then surplus of the balance of A – will necessarily be accompanied by changes in the international terms of trade. And, as we are always in free trade, this implies that the internal terms of trade also alter for the two countries. Consequently, they will move along their production transformation curves. Now, these transformations of *X* into *Y*, then *Y* into *X*, or inversely, in the two countries, are done at increasing cost.

It is no longer then solely a question of a different distribution over time, for A and B, of consumption of the same world production as in the absence of disequilibrium. World production itself has changed.

This suggests that even if we had redistributed over time the consumption of this world production to make it even, A and B could not have attained the same level of welfare as *Ta* and *Tb*, respectively. For example, for A, we see that the process of detrimental change in the structure of production, during the two phases of disequilibrium, would have brought about a movement along the production transformation curve, successively from *Ta* to a point like *C*, then from *C* to a point like *D*, or inversely. Now, whether we are at *C* or at *D*, it is impossible to reach the indifference curve passing through *Ta*.

We have not been concerned here with the sharing of these losses between A and B. It would depend in particular upon the change in the value of international liquidity, between the time it is given up by A (deficit) and when it is recovered by A (surplus), with respect to goods *X* and *Y*. If it depreciates rapidly in real terms, the burden of the losses will fall mainly upon B.

Chapter 5.3

SUMMARY OF THE DISCUSSION ON NYBERG AND VIOTTI

Milton FRIEDMAN, *Chairman*

Because of the detailed presentation of the papers by the authors and the lengthy comment by Jacques L'Huillier, only the three following points could be briefly discussed.

For which reason should the rate of interest be included in the utility function? *Milton Friedman* and *Allan Meltzer* suggested that the (nominal) interest rate could be treated as a proxy for the inflation rate such that the utility function embodies not only the internal target of employment but also the internal target of inflation; however, for such an interpretation of the interest rate, one could no longer linearize the utility function because a very low (negative) interest rate corresponding to a certain deflation could be undesirable just as a very high interest rate associated with a certain inflation. *Sven Arndt* proposed another reason for including the interest rate in the utility function. To the extent that government expenditures are financed by a bond issue, this latter could depend on the interest rate and involved a different government indebtedness and, by this, changes in the outstanding stock of assets. To the objection of the limited value of introducing the interest rate into the utility function (*Alexander Swoboda*), *William Branson* on the one hand and *Lars Nyberg* and *Staffan Viotti* on the other hand objected that it does not make any difference for the final result of the model if there is an interest rate in the utility function or not.

The second main point during the discussion was concerned with the level of reserves as an argument of the utility function. *Allan Meltzer* thought that this would bring us back to the pre-Adam Smithian mercantilist time. *Helmut Frisch* argued that the concept of the utility function is fundamentally an empty box and that for operational reasons the level of reserves should be considered as a constraint rather than as a target such that reserves produce an indirect utility as it had already pointed out by Jacques L'Huillier. *Lars Nyberg* and *Staffan Viotti* answered that nothing important would be changed in their model if the level of reserves was regarded as an ultimate or as an intermediate goal of government behaviour; and with respect to L'Huillier's comment they emphasized the analytical framework of their model which is concerned only with an open economy and not with a two-country world.

A third criticism was directed towards the possible inappropriate kind of model the authors had used. As *Rudiger Dornbusch* put it, the essential feature of the model is the intertemporal optimization problem involving the adjustment of the stocks of assets towards their final full equilibrium for which a Keynesian model cannot be used with the exception of the analysis of the impact effects. Furthermore, the authors assume a world of perfect information for which Mundell's assignment principle is of complete irrelevance as *Jacob Frenkel* and *Alexander Swoboda* pointed out. *Robert Mundell* argued that his assignment principle could be formulated not only in terms of a decentralized pairing of instruments to targets (relevant for the case of incomplete information), but also in terms of a "multi-general equilibrium pairing" as the comment by Jacques L'Huillier suggested. Thus, for instance, if there is a shift in the terms of trade affecting the trade balance, the question to be asked is to which extent the capital market must bear the burden (in terms of allocation effects) of this disequilibrium. In defending the author's model *William Branson* argued that one cannot ask for a model which explains everything at once. It is better to carve out a small piece of the world and to observe what happens if we apply a certain line of analysis in comparison to an exercise which models the whole world before anybody will buy any part of it.

Chapter 6.1

A COMPARISON OF EXCHANGE-RATE REGIMES: STABILITY, PROFITABILITY, AND SPECULATION*

Peter KENEN

1. Introduction

This paper reports on part of a more ambitious study. The larger project seeks to appraise and compare alternative methods for changing exchange rates. It examines the behavior of trade volume and value, spot exchange rates, and central-bank reserves when exchange rates are determined by the market, are pegged permanently by official intervention, are allowed to float temporarily, or are governed by rules that mandate regular changes in parities. The comparisons take place within a single, simple model of a foreign-exchange market programmed to generate a month-by-month history of trade, exchange rates, and reserves, so that the several exchange-rate regimes can be studied in the same controlled environment.

The model and program used in the study invite a large number of experiments. One can ask how the several exchange-rate regimes behave in the face of various disturbances – once-over, progressive, and stochastic changes in domestic prices or import volume. One can ask how they behave when the adjustment of trade volume to prices occurs rapidly or with long lags and how these lags interact with price elasticities. One can vary the size of the band surrounding parity, the frequency and sizes of the parity changes, and the parameters defining the conditions under which each regime triggers a change. Finally, one can ask how the performance of the model and regimes is affected by the way in which foreign-exchange speculators form their expectations and in which they adjust their holdings of home and foreign currency.

I shall report in other papers on work with the disturbances, lags, and

*Work on this project has been financed by the National Science Foundation (Grant GS 41498) and by the International Finance Section, Princeton University. The present versions of the model and program reflect suggestions made in seminars at The Johns Hopkins University, the University of Pennsylvania, Princeton University, the U.S. Treasury, and the International Monetary Fund. I am grateful to Dennis Warner and Nancy Happe for research assistance.

elasticities, with the size and frequency of parity changes, and with variations in the parameters used to mandate the parity changes.[1] Here, I deal only with the role of speculation in the foreign-exchange market and its effects on the efficiency of the various exchange-rate regimes. I look at the effects of speculation on the speed with which the foreign-exchange market adjusts to a particular exogenous disturbance (a permanent five percent increase in home prices spread evenly across the first twelve months of every single hypothetical history), at its impact on the size of fluctuations in the volume of trade, spot exchange rate, and reserves set up by the disturbance and subsequent adjustment, and at the relationship of these phenomena to the profitability of speculation.

2. The Model

Detailed descriptions of the basic model and of the computer program used to study it are available elsewhere.[2] Here, then, I furnish only a sketch – enough for you to know how the model functions and to evaluate the results of the experiments reported below.

The model simulates behavior in a single spot market for foreign exchange. The participants in that market are traders who buy home and foreign currency to pay for goods ordered in earlier months, speculators who buy or sell home currency to profit from expected changes in the spot exchange rate, and a central bank that intervenes to peg the exchange rate whenever it reaches an upper or lower limit defined in relation to a predetermined parity.

Orders for home and foreign goods depend on the terms of trade prevailing in the months when the orders are placed. Formally,

$$XO(I) = AX \cdot TT(I)^{-EX}, \tag{1}$$

$$MO(I) = AM \cdot TT(I)^{EM}, \tag{2}$$

and

$$TT(I) = PH(I)/[PF(I) \cdot RM(I)], \tag{3}$$

where $XO(I)$ is the volume of export orders placed in the Ith month, $MO(I)$ is the volume of import orders, $TT(I)$ is the terms of trade, $PH(I)$ is the level of home prices, $PF(I)$ is the level of foreign prices, and $RM(I)$ is the spot

[1]See, in particular, Kenen (1975).

[2]See Kenen (1974). The notation used in this description of the model is a simplification of the vocabulary used in the FORTRAN IV version of the computer program (MXRT-III) written to study it.

exchange rate in units of home currency per unit of foreign currency. The scalars AX and AM are chosen so that the annual volume of trade will be 100 when the terms of trade are unity, and each simulation starts with $PH(I) = PF(I) = RM(I) = 1$, so that the terms of trade also start at unity. The price elasticities, EX and EM, can be varied from one simulation to the next, but are set at unity in the ones reported here.[3]

The current demand for home currency to pay for exports depends on past values of export orders, and the current demand for foreign currency to pay for imports depends on past values of import orders:

$$XP(I) = \sum_J W_J \cdot XO(I-J) \cdot PH(I-J), \tag{4}$$

and

$$MP(I) = \sum_J W_J \cdot MO(I-J) \cdot PF(I-J). \tag{5}$$

In the simulations under study here, goods are delivered rapidly; the W_J are tightly bunched ($W_1 = W_6 = 0.10$, $W_2 = W_5 = 0.15$, and $W_3 = W_4 = 0.25$).

One other trade series, current export volume, is used to measure certain effects of changes in exchange rates:

$$XV(I) = \sum_J W_J \cdot XO(I-J). \tag{6}$$

This series is compared with a hypothetical measure of export volume, $XQ(I)$, obtained in two steps. First, write

$$XQ(I) = AX \cdot TQ(I)^{-EX}, \tag{7}$$

$$MQ(I) = AM \cdot TQ(I)^{EM}, \tag{8}$$

and

$$TQ(I) = PH(I)/[PF(I) \cdot EQ(I)], \tag{9}$$

where $EQ(I)$ is the spot exchange rate which would clear the market in the absence of all lags, speculation, and official intervention (the comparative-static equilibrium rate). Second, write

$$XQ(I) \cdot PH(I) - MQ(I) \cdot PF(I) \cdot EQ(I) = 0, \tag{10}$$

solve for $EQ(I)$, and calculate $XQ(I)$ using this solution.

The treatment of trade described here has two major implications. First, it

[3]To generate the permanent exogenous disturbance studied in this paper, I augment $PH(I)$ by (0.05/12) in each of the first 12 months of each simulation, then fix it at 1.05 permanently. [The foreign price index, $PF(I)$, is set at unity.]

asserts that traders are naive. They place orders on the basis of prices prevailing when the orders are logged, making no allowance for possible changes in prices and the spot exchange rate during the months that must elapse before goods are delivered and payment is made. Furthermore, they make no attempt to cover their currency needs by dealing in spot or forward exchange at the time they place their orders. The second implication of equations (1) through (5) is even more important. As trade volume is not sensitive to the current spot exchange rate, there must be speculation – movements of private funds responsive to expectations – to bridge temporarily inevitable gaps between the traders' demands and supplies.

There are, of course, many ways in which one might model the behavior of speculators. Are they "gnomes" who bet against the current parity or against the rules for altering the parity? Do they, in fact, know the rules used by the central bank? And how much money will they stake on their own judgments concerning future movements in the exchange rate?

The answers given by this model are not apt to satisfy anyone who watches foreign-exchange markets. They are far too simple to be realistic. This same simplicity, however, has its advantages, permitting me to look at several modes of speculation without making major changes in the model or the program as I move from mode to mode.

I assume that speculators have perfect faith in the rules governing the maintenance of the parity, but know those rules only to a first approximation. They do not stage massive "raids" on the foreign-exchange market when there are large movements of official reserves, but neither do they know exactly when or why the central bank will change the parity. Each month, moreover, the speculators come to market with a point estimate of the future spot rate – an expectation formed from experience by methods set out below – and do not alter that point estimate during the course of the month, no matter what happens in the open market.[4]

The first and second methods for forming expectations are *regressive* modes, based upon the notion that there is a "normal" rate and that the market rate will always tend toward it,

$$AR(I) = RM(I-1) + C[NR(I) - RM(I-1)], \qquad 0 \leqslant C \leqslant 1, \tag{11}$$

where $AR(I)$ is the point expectation, $RM(I-1)$ is the spot rate one month ago, and $NR(I)$ is the "normal" rate to which $RM(I)$ must tend. In the first model of speculation, however, the "normal" rate is based upon parity, $PA(I)$, adjusted for the rate of change suggested by experience,

[4]This supposition is not as drastic as it sounds, since the parity can only change from month to month, not within a single month.

$$NR(I) = PA(I) + [PA(I) - PA(I-12)]/12. \tag{12}$$

In the second mode, the "normal" rate is a moving average of the equilibrium rates defined by equation (10) above,

$$NR(I) = [EQ(I-3+L) + EQ(I-2+L) + EQ(I-1+L)]/3, \tag{13}$$

where L is a lag operator.

Under the *par-value* mode given by equation (12), speculators gamble on the supposition that the market rate will tend to a value in the vicinity of parity. The coefficient C tells us how fast they expect it to do so.[5] Under the *equilibrium* mode given by equation (13), speculators gamble on the supposition that the market rate will tend to a value in the vicinity of the comparative-static equilibrium rate defined by the basic trade equations and the price or trade disturbance.[6] In this instance, however, we can give them more or less foresight by altering the operator L. When, for example, $L = 0$, as in the first experiments reported below, speculators cannot even see into the present; when, by contrast, $L = 3$, as in other trials, they are made to see three months ahead. Note, finally, that when $C = 0$, the first two modes of speculation collapse into one; speculators are deemed to believe that the spot rate will not change.

The third mode of speculation is *adaptive*. Speculators are made to correct their prior expectation by some fraction of the error they made last month,

$$AR(I) = AR(I-1) + D[RM(I-1) - AR(I-1)], \qquad 0 \leq D \leq 1. \tag{14}$$

When, of course, $D = 0$, expectations cannot change; when $D = 1$, speculators are made to believe that the spot rate will not change.

The fourth mode of speculation is *extrapolative*. Once again, speculators change their prior expectations on the basis of recent experience, but use the recent change in the market rate, not their own past error,

$$AR(I) = AR(I-1) + E[RM(I-1) - RM(I-2)], \qquad 0 \leq E \leq 1. \tag{15}$$

We have now to answer the final question posed above: How much money will the speculators stake on their own judgments concerning the future? My model and program give two answers. The first is a stock-adjustment response. The second is a simple flow response.

[5]Under a flexible-rate system, there is no change in parity, so that $AR(I)$ is fixed forever (at unity) when $C = 1.0$. The more serious anomaly, however, occurs in respect of temporary floats; there is a discontinuous change in expectations, but only when the parity is altered, not when the float begins.

[6]This mode has kinship to models in which speculators form "rational" expectations; see, e.g., Black (1972).

In the *stock-adjustment* case, the size of the prospective profit from speculation – the difference between expected and actual spot rates – regulates the speculators' desired short position in foreign currency,

$$SFA(I) = S[RM(I) - AR(I)]/AR(I). \tag{16}$$

The right-hand side of this equation measures the prospective profitability of two transactions taken together: A speculator selling a unit of foreign currency obtains at once $RM(I)$ units of home currency. He hopes to sell these at the expected rate, $1/AR(I)$, thereby to earn a profit of $[RM(I)/AR(I) - 1]$ per unit of foreign currency sold. The coefficient S, linking the profit rate to the desired short position, is scaled in multiples of initial exports (at 10 and 20 times initial monthly exports in the experiments reported below). The long position in home currency corresponding to $SFA(I)$ is

$$SHA(I) = RM(I) \cdot SFA(I), \tag{17}$$

and speculators are assumed to reach this position by the familiar Koyck-type process. Their current sales of foreign currency are defined by

$$SS(I) = Q[SHA(I) - SH(I-1)]/RM(I), \tag{18}$$

where $SS(I)$ is the number of units of foreign currency sold in the Ith month, $SH(I-1)$ is the actual long position in home currency at the close of the previous month, and Q is the stock-adjustment coefficient (which cannot exceed unity). At the beginning of each simulation, $SH(I)$ is set at zero; thereafter, it is defined by

$$SH(I) = SH(I-1) + SS(I) \cdot RM(I). \tag{19}$$

In the *flow* case, speculators show no interest in positions per se. The profit calculation given by equation (16) is deemed to regulate directly the speculators' current sales of foreign currency,

$$SS(I) = (S/3) \cdot [RM(I) - AR(I)]/AR(I). \tag{20}$$

The coefficient S is re-scaled arbitrarily at one-third of its "stock" value, reflecting the plausible supposition that a prospective profit of given size will not have as much impact on a month-by-month flow (which could continue indefinitely) as on the determination of a desired stock.

In stock and flow cases alike, the speculators' short position in foreign currency is given by

$$SF(I) = \sum_J SS(J), \qquad J = 0, 1, \ldots, I. \tag{21}$$

How should one measure the profits realized by the speculators? This is quite easy when, at the end of any simulation, speculators' holdings of home currency have gone to zero: The terminal value of the speculators' holdings of foreign currency measures the accumulated profit or loss across the simulation. (If they are long, they have made profits; if they are short, they have suffered losses.) But when $SH(I)$ is not zero at the end, one has to ask how much foreign currency speculators could obtain in exchange for their holdings of home currency and, therefore, to decide which exchange rate to employ in profit calculations.[7] The current version of the program calculates three distinct measures of profit, including unrealized profit. It computes

$$PPM(I) = SH(I)/RM(I) - SF(I), \tag{22}$$

$$PPA(I) = SH(I)/AR(I) - SF(I), \tag{23}$$

$$PPE(I) = SH(I)/EQ(I) - SF(I). \tag{24}$$

The first calculation makes the supposition that speculators could dispose of their home-currency holdings at the market rate prevailing in the Ith month. The second supposes that they could sell their holdings at the rate which they themselves forecast for the future. The third supposes that they could sell their holdings at the comparative-static equilibrium rate.

The determination of the current market rate, $RM(I)$ calls first for the solution of a market-clearing equation,

$$XP(I)/RMT(I) - MP(I) + SS(I) = 0, \tag{25}$$

where $RMT(I)$ is a tentative market rate.[8] When, of course, exchange rates are fully flexible (or floating temporarily), $RM(I) = RMT(I)$. The calculation is complete. When, however, rates are pegged, there is more to be done. One must compute the upper and lower limits for exchange-rate fluctuations,

$$PU(I) = PA(I)[1 + BD/100], \tag{26}$$

and

$$PL(I) = PA(I)[1 - BD/100], \tag{27}$$

where $PA(I)$ is the current parity, discussed below, and BD is the allowable margin for fluctuations expressed as a percentage of the current parity. In all simulations reported here, BD is set at 2.5 percent. Next, one must compare $RMT(I)$ with these limits and set $RM(I)$ accordingly: If $PL(I) \leqslant RMT(I) \leqslant PU(I)$, then $RM(I) = RMT(I)$, as with flexible (or tem-

[7]The difficulty here resembles one identified by Telser (1959) in his critique of Baumol (1957); see also Sohmen (1961, ch. 3).

[8]Equation (25) is quadratic in $RMT(I)$, so that $RMT(I)$ may have more than one value (or may have no real value). For analytic and computational implications, see Kenen (1974).

porarily floating) rates. If $PL(I) > RMT(I)$, then $RM(I) = PL(I)$, but the central bank must intervene (buy foreign currency) to keep $RM(I)$ from falling to $RMT(I)$. If, finally, $RMT(I) > PU(I)$, then $RM(I) = PU(I)$, but the central bank must intervene (sell foreign currency) to keep $RM(I)$ from rising to $RMT(I)$.

To measure the amount of intervention required to peg the rate at one of its limits, compute

$$DF(I) = XP(I)/RM(I) - MP(I) + SS(I). \tag{28}$$

The end-of-month level of central-bank reserves is then given by

$$RE(I) = RE(I-1) + DF(I). \tag{29}$$

In all simulations reported here, $RE(I)$ starts at 20.0 (at 20 percent of the initial annual value of exports).

3. *The Exchange-Rate Regimes*

The current version of the model studies seven distinct ways of altering exchange rates:

In the first (Regime 1.0), the rate is fully flexible. The central bank abstains from intervention, and $RM(I) = RMT(I)$ in each and every month.

In the second (Regime 2.0), there is a fixed parity, $PA(I) = 1.0$, and the market rate is constrained forever between fixed values of $PL(I)$ and $PU(I)$. There are, however, two permutations of this regime. In one (Regime 2.1), the market rate is set free to float temporarily when (a) reserves have fallen to 75 percent of their initial level and $RM(I) > RMT(I)$, or (b) reserves have risen to 125 percent of their initial level and $RM(I) < PL(I)$. The float is allowed to continue until the market rate has settled down, at which time a new parity is announced.[9] In the other (Regime 2.2), the rules for floating are the same, but the float is made to last exactly one year.

The third and fourth regimes embody *rate-based* rules for altering parity. In the third, I flatter central banks and governments. I assume that they can recognize $EQ(I)$, the comparative-static equilibrium rate, and will change the parity whenever it differs sufficiently from a moving average,

$$MA(I) = [EQ(I-3+K) + EQ(I-2+K) + EQ(I-1+K)]/3, \tag{30}$$

[9]The new parity is given by $PA(I) = [RM(I-1) + RM(I-2)]/2$. New trigger points are also set to govern future floats [at 75 and 125 percent of $RE(I)$ in the month when the float began].

where K is a lag operator much like L in equation (13), but is set at zero in the work reported here. In the fourth, I use a rule suggested by Murphy (1965) among others,[10] taking a moving average of recent market rates,

$$MA(I) = \sum_J RM(I-J), \qquad J = 1, 2, \ldots, 6. \tag{31}$$

In the *discontinuous* versions of these systems (Regimes 3.1 and 4.1), the size of the parity change is fixed at GD percent per annum (or $GD/120$ 'cents' per month), and $GD = 5.0$ in work reported here. Furthermore, there can be no change in parity unless $MA(I)$ differs from $PA(I-1)$ by at least PLM 'cents' (set at 2.0 for this paper). Hence, when $[MA(I) - PA(I-1)] \geqslant PLM$, $PA(I) = PA(I-1) + (GD/120)$; when $[PA(I-1) - MA(I)] \geqslant PLM$, $PA(I) = PA(I-1) - (GD/120)$; and when these conditions do not obtain, $PA(I) = PA(I-1)$.

In the *continuous* versions of these systems (Regimes 3.0 and 4.0), the size of the parity change is not fixed; it depends on the size of the gap between $MA(I)$ and $PA(I-1)$. And there is no threshold for parity changes. But GD and PLM are used to standardize the parity changes,

$$PA(I) = PA(I-1) + \left(\frac{GD/120}{4 \cdot PLM}\right)[MA(I) - PA(I-1)]. \tag{32}$$

The decision to multiply PLM by four came from inspection of early results in which the continuous rule caused large cumulative changes in parity.

There is one more permutation of the third system (Regime 3.2) in which the central bank displays to the limit the courage of its convictions. It keeps the parity in line with the moving average of equilibrium rates, so that $PA(I) = MA(I)$ at all times. There is an additional discontinuous permutation of the fourth system (Regime 4.2), in which the moving average of market rates spans a full year, not the six months specified in equation (31).

The fifth system studied here is an automatic counterpart of the "presumptive indicator" proposed by the United States in recent international negotiations [see, e.g., U.S. Treasury (1973)].[11] It uses as the trigger for parity changes the difference between the current *level* of reserves, $RE(I)$, and the initial level, 20.0, treated here as the target or desired level. There is, again, a discontinuous case (Regime 5.1) in which the size of the parity change is fixed and there can be no change at all unless reserves differ from their initial level by

[10]For other antecedents, see Underwood (1973) who traces the origins of several rules studied in this paper; also Sacchetti (1972) and Halm (1970).

[11]Modigliani and Kenen (1966) and Triffin [in Hinshaw (1971)] made similar proposals. Underwood (1973) shows that the same notion was central to the Keynes plan for the postwar system.

at least *RLM* percent of that initial level: When $RE(I-1) \leqslant (1 - RLM/100) \cdot 20$ *and* $RE(I-1) \leqslant RE(I-2)$, then $PA(I) = PA(I-1) + (GD/120)$; when $RE(I-1) \geqslant (1 + RLM/100) \cdot 20$ *and* $RE(I-1) \geqslant RE(I-2)$, then $PA(I) = PA(I-1) - (GD/120)$; otherwise, $PA(I) = PA(I-1)$.[12] The continuous form (Regime 5.0) uses a formula much like equation (32), replacing $(4 \cdot PLM)$ with $(4 \cdot RLM \cdot 20/100)$ and $[MA(I) - PA(I-1)]$ with $[RE(I-1) - 20.0]$. Finally, a third permutation (Regime 5.2), modifies the discontinuous formulation. It cancels any signal to devalue if the "basic" balance of payments is in surplus and any signal to revalue if the "basic" balance is in deficit. Here, of course, there are no long-term capital flows, so that the "basic" balance is the trade balance,

$$BB(I) = XP(I)/RM(I) = MP(I). \tag{33}$$

In all experiments reported here, *RLM* is set at 15 percent.

The sixth and seventh systems studied here use *flow-based* rules for regulating parity. The sixth resembles a suggestion by Cooper (1970), using recent changes in reserves. The seventh resembles a suggestion by Bergsten (1972), using recent levels of the "basic" balance. To state the sixth system formally define a flow indicator, $FL(I)$,

$$FL(I) = DF(I-1), \tag{34a}$$

and

$$FL(I-1) = DF(I-2). \tag{34b}$$

To state the seventh formally redefine the indicator,

$$FL(I) = [BB(I-1) + BB(I-2) + BB(I-3)]/3, \tag{35a}$$

and

$$FL(I-1) = [BB(I-4) + BB(I-5) + BB(I-6)]/3. \tag{35b}$$

In the discontinuous cases (Regimes 6.1 and 7.1), the parity is made to change whenever $FL(I)$ and $FL(I-1)$ exceed a fixed limit, *DLM*, set at 0.250 reserve units per month in experiments reported here. (The sign of the parity change is, of course, opposite to the sign of the imbalance.) In the continuous cases (Regimes 6.0 and 7.0), the formula resembles equation (32), with $(4 \cdot DLM)$ replacing $(4 \cdot PLM)$ and $FL(I)$ itself replacing $[MA(I) - PA(I-1)]$. In additional permutations of the discontinuous rules (Regimes 6.2 and 7.2), there is a

[12]The additional condition in $RE(I-1)$ and $RE(I-2)$ is meant to preclude corrective action after the reserve position has started to improve. Analogous conditions are employed in the next two regimes.

supplementary change in parity when, after one full year without any change, there is a continuing imbalance [$FL(I) \neq 0$], no matter how small, thereby to eliminate small deficits or surpluses which, in the sixth regime, could cause endless movements of reserves.

4. The Effects of Speculation

Several simulations were performed to explore the implications for exchange rates and foreign trade of the ways in which speculators might behave. I shall review first three large-scale computations which used, ad seriatum, all four modes of speculation (par-value regressive, equilibrium regressive, adaptive, and extrapolative) and contrasted stock adjustment with flow cases.[13] Thereafter, I shall summarize simulations designed to identify the principal effects of altering the scale of speculation [the coefficient S in equations (16) and (20)], the speed with which actual stocks are adjusted [the coefficient Q in equation (18)], and the span of speculators' foresight [the operator L in equation (13)].

The first three large-scale simulations are distinguished by the values chosen for parameters featured in equations (11), (14) and (15). The coefficient C used in the regressive modes was set first at 1.00, causing speculators to believe that the market rate will move directly to its "normal" level, then at 0.75 and at 0.50, causing them to give less weight to the "normal" rate. The coefficient D used in the adaptive mode was set first at 0.05, then increased to 0.10 and to 0.20, causing speculators to take fuller account of their own past errors. The coefficient E used in the extrapolative mode was set first at 0.10, then at 0.25 and at 0.50, causing speculators to weigh more heavily the most recent change in the market rate.[14] (In each case, however, the coefficient S, relating desired stocks and flows to prospective profitability, was set at 10 times the initial monthly export level, and the stock-adjustment coefficient was set at unity, its upper limit. The disturbance is a permanent five percent increase in home prices, spread across the first twelve months.

Summary statistics for the flexible-exchange-rate cases are arrayed in table 1.A (for stock-adjustment speculation) and table 1.B (for flow speculation);

[13] The program MXRT-III produces output in four parts (one for each mode of speculation), with two *sets* in each part (one for stock-adjustment speculation, the other for flow speculation). Each set, in turn, contains one or more experiments with each of the seven exchange-rate regimes.

[14] The range of values chosen for this set of experiments is based in part on earlier work with the model. We found, for example, that runs with $C < 0.50$, $D > 0.20$, and $E > 0$ aborted within the first ten years; large movements in $RM(I)$ induced by (and inducing) large movements in $SS(I)$ led quickly to large swings in the volume of trade, and the model could not find a real market-clearing rate.

TABLE 1.A
Adjustment under flexible exchange rates; final effects of a five percent increase in home prices with stock-adjustment speculation ($S = 10.0$, $Q = 1.00$); simulation covering 10 years.

Mode of speculation	Market rate			Final values		RMSQDEV[a]		Final profit at		
	Min.	Max.	Final	$AR(I)$	$SH(I)$	$RM(I)$	$XV(I)$	$RM(I)$	$AR(I)$	$EQ(I)$
Regressive (to par value):										
$C = 1.00$	1.000	1.052	1.050	1.000	4.374[f]	0.0080	0.0631	−0.094	0.114	−0.094
$C = 0.75$	1.000	1.060	1.050	1.013	3.240[f]	0.0072	0.0554	−0.072	0.042	−0.072
$C = 0.50$	0.998	1.105	1.086[e]	1.048[e]	3.301[c]	0.0293	0.2093	−0.267	−0.156	−0.162
Regressive (to equilibrium):										
$C = 1.00$	1.000	1.073	1.050	1.050	0.000[f]	0.0054	0.0416	−0.037	−0.037	−0.037
$C = 0.75$	1.000	1.081	1.050	1.050	0.000[f]	0.0077	0.0582	−0.042	−0.042	−0.042
$C = 0.50$	0.880	1.254	0.887[e]	0.994	−7.969[e]	0.0814	0.5866	−1.710	−0.741	−0.315
Adaptive:										
$D = 0.05$	1.000	1.078	1.050	1.050	−0.001[b]	0.0119	0.0931	−0.146	−0.146	−0.146
$D = 0.10$	1.000	1.102	1.064[d]	1.059[d]	0.413[b]	0.0245	0.1892	−0.448	−0.446	−0.442
$D = 0.20$	No Solution at Month 73 [Quadratic Has No Real Roots]									
Extrapolative:										
$E = 0.10$	1.000	1.054	1.050	1.005	3.920[f]	0.0076	0.0592	−0.085	0.082	−0.085
$E = 0.25$	1.000	1.060	1.050	1.013	3.244[f]	0.0072	0.0554	−0.072	0.042	−0.072
$E = 0.50$	0.998	1.105	1.086[e]	1.048[e]	3.304[e]	0.0293	0.2093	−0.267	−0.156	−0.162

[a]Root mean squared deviations of market from equilibrium exchange rate and export volume from equilibrium export volume.
[b]Converging to zero.
[c]Converging to a positive level.
[d]Converging to equilibrium level.
[e]Moving without apparent convergence.
[f]Stable.

TABLE 1.B
Adjustment under flexible exchange rates; final effects of a five percent increase in home prices with flow speculation ($S = 10.0$); simulation covering 10 years.

Mode of speculation	Market rate			Final values		RMSQDEV[a]		Final profit at		
	Min.	Max.	Final	$AR(I)$	$SH(I)$	$RM(I)$	$XV(I)$	$RM(I)$	$AR(I)$	$EQ(I)$
Regressive (to par value):										
$C = 1.00$	1.000	1.012	1.011[f]	1.000	36.184[e]	0.0365	0.2854	−0.007	0.402	−1.321
$C = 0.75$	1.000	1.015	1.014[f]	1.004	33.757[e]	0.0340	0.2653	−0.008	0.345	−1.144
$C = 0.50$	1.000	1.021	1.019[f]	1.009	29.785[e]	0.0298	0.2324	−0.007	0.262	−0.332
Regressive (to equilibrium):										
$C = 1.00$	1.000	1.053	1.050	1.050	1.768[f]	0.0013	0.0085	−0.028	−0.028	−0.028
$C = 0.75$	1.000	1.055	1.050	1.050	1.741[f]	0.0015	0.0089	−0.026	−0.026	−0.026
$C = 0.50$	1.000	1.056	1.050	1.050	1.698[c]	0.0023	0.0124	−0.022	−0.022	−0.022
Adaptive:										
$D = 0.05$	1.000	1.040	1.040[d]	1.037[d]	21.005[c]	0.0211	0.1666	−0.288	−0.227	−0.472
$D = 0.10$	1.000	1.048	1.048[d]	1.047[d]	13.292[c]	0.0147	0.1164	−0.227	−0.219	−0.250
$D = 0.20$	1.000	1.050	1.050	1.050	6.990[f]	0.0095	0.0748	−0.125	−0.125	−0.125
Extrapolative:										
$E = 0.10$	1.000	1.013	1.012[f]	1.001[f]	35.354[e]	0.0357	0.2785	−0.007	0.382	−1.258
$E = 0.25$	1.000	1.015	1.014[f]	1.004[f]	33.774[e]	0.0340	0.2654	−0.008	0.345	−1.145
$E = 0.50$	1.000	1.021	1.019[f]	1.009[f]	29.802[e]	0.0298	0.2326	−0.007	0.263	−0.883

[a]Root mean squared deviations of market from equilibrium exchange rate and export volume from equilibrium export volume.
[b]Converging to zero.
[c]Converging to a positive level.
[d]Converging to equilibrium level.
[e]Moving without apparent convergence.
[f]Stable.

TABLE 2.A
Adjustment under fixed exchange rates; final effects of a five percent increase in home prices with stock-adjustment speculation ($S = 10.0$, $Q = 1.00$); simulation covering 10 years.

Mode of speculation	Final values						Final profit at		
	$RM(I)$	$AR(I)$	$DR(I)$	$RE(I)$	$SH(I)$	$SS(I)$	$RM(I)$	$AR(I)$	$EQ(I)$
Regressive (to par value):									
$C = 1.00$	1.025	1.000	−0.203	−1.941[c]	2.135[e]	0.000	−0.023	0.029	−0.072
$C = 0.75$	1.025	1.006	−0.203	−2.300[c]	1.592[e]	0.000	−0.018	0.011	−0.055
$C = 0.50$	1.025	1.013	−0.203	−2.673[c]	1.055[e]	0.000	−0.014	−0.002	−0.039
Regressive (to equilibrium):									
$C = 1.00$	1.025	1.050	−0.203	−4.902[c]	−2.034[e]	0.000	−0.005	0.043	0.043
$C = 0.75$	1.025	1.044	−0.203	−4.449[c]	−1.534[e]	0.000	−0.005	0.022	0.031
$C = 0.50$	1.025	1.038	−0.203	−4.017[c]	−1.029[e]	0.000	−0.005	0.007	0.019
Adaptive:									
$D = 0.05$	1.025	1.025	−0.203	−3.930[c]	0.008[b]	0.000	−0.020	−0.020	−0.020
$D = 0.10$	1.025	1.025	−0.203	−3.871[c]	0.001[b]	0.000	−0.018	−0.018	−0.018
$D = 0.20$	1.025	1.025	−0.203	−3.775[c]	0.000[e]	0.000	−0.016	−0.016	−0.016
Extrapolative:									
$E = 0.10$	1.025	1.003	−0.203	−2.085[c]	1.918[e]	0.000	−0.021	0.021	−0.065
$E = 0.25$	1.025	1.006	−0.203	−2.300[c]	1.592[e]	0.000	−0.018	0.011	−0.055
$E = 0.50$	1.025	1.013	−0.203	−2.673[c]	1.055[e]	0.000	−0.014	−0.002	−0.039

[a]Identical to corresponding flexible exchange-rate case.
[b]Converging to zero.
[c]Falling (algebraically).
[d]Rising (algebraically).
[e]Stable.

TABLE 2.B
Adjustment under fixed exchange rates; final effects of a five percent increase in home prices with flow speculation ($S = 10.0$); simulation covering 10 years.

Mode of speculation	Final values						Final profit at		
	$RM(I)$	$AR(I)$	$DR(I)$	$RE(I)$	$SH(I)$	$SS(I)$	$RM(I)$	$AR(I)$	$EQ(I)$
Regressive (to par value):									
$C = 1.00$[a]	1.011[e]	1.000	0.000	20.000	36.184[d]	0.318	−0.007	0.402	−1.321
$C = 0.75$[a]	1.014[e]	1.004	0.000	20.000	33.757[d]	0.294	−0.008	0.345	−1.144
$C = 0.50$[a]	1.019[e]	1.009	0.000	20.000	29.785[d]	0.256	−0.007	0.262	−0.882
Regressive (to equilibrium):									
$C = 1.00$	1.025	1.050	−0.865	−74.616[c]	−73.544[c]	−0.661	−0.004	1.705	1.705
$C = 0.75$	1.025	1.044	−0.702	−56.863[c]	−55.337[c]	−0.499	−0.004	0.966	1.232
$C = 0.50$	1.025	1.038	−0.538	−38.946[c]	−36.933[c]	−0.335	−0.005	0.430	0.853
Adaptive:									
$D = 0.05$	1.025	1.025	−0.199	8.257[c]	13.943[d]	0.004	−0.067	−0.065	−0.391
$D = 0.10$	1.025	1.025	−0.203	2.465[c]	7.014[e]	0.000	−0.035	−0.035	−0.198
$D = 0.20$	1.025	1.025	−0.203	−0.477[c]	3.509[e]	0.000	−0.021	−0.021	−0.102
Extrapolative:									
$E = 0.10$[a]	1.012[e]	1.001	0.000	20.000	35.354[d]	0.310	−0.007	0.382	−1.258
$E = 0.25$[a]	1.014[e]	1.004	0.000	20.000	33.774[d]	0.295	−0.008	0.345	−1.145
$E = 0.50$[a]	1.019[e]	1.009	0.000	20.000	29.802[d]	0.256	−0.007	0.263	−0.883

[a]Identical to corresponding flexible exchange-rate case.
[b]Converging to zero.
[c]Falling (algebraically).
[d]Rising (algebraically).
[e]Stable.

summary statistics for the fixed exchange-rate cases are arrayed in table 2.A (for stock-adjustment speculation) and table 2.B (for flow speculation). These limiting cases dramatize differences among the modes of speculation but also identify important regularities.

Consider first the columns of tables 1.A and 1.B relating to the market rate, $RM(I)$. In seven of twelve cases shown by table 1.A, $RM(I)$ has come to rest by month 120 and finishes at 1.050 in every such instance. This is, of course, the equilibrium rate, $EQ(I)$, corresponding to the five percent price disturbance introduced at the start of the first month. In four of the remaining cases, $RM(I)$ is still moving, but one of these (adaptive speculation with $D = 0.10$) displays convergence on 1.050. [In the remaining case, $RM(I)$ cannot come to rest; equation (25) defining $RMT(I)$ has no real roots at month 73.] In no case shown by table 1.A does $RM(I)$ settle down at a level different from the equilibrium rate. In ten of twelve cases shown by table 1.B, the market rate comes to rest, and it is converging on 1.050 in the other two. In six separate cases, however, the final market rate differs substantially from $EQ(I)$. This first major difference between the two tables is due directly to the fundamental difference between stock-adjustment and flow speculation. With the former, a constant difference between $RM(I)$ and $AR(I)$, the market and expected rates, leads speculators to take up a *fixed position*, $SH(I)$, in home currency. They cease to deal in foreign currency, ceasing to "support" or "raid" the market. Consequently, trade flows are forced gradually into line by movements in the spot exchange rate, and these flows cannot come completely into line until $RM(I)$ is equal to $EQ(I)$.[15] With flow speculation, by contrast, a constant difference between $RM(I)$ and $AR(I)$ leads speculators to *increase* their home-currency positions at a constant rate. They go on dealing in foreign currency and may support $RM(I)$ forever. This is precisely what happens in the first regressive mode and, again, in the extrapolative mode. Speculators build up huge long positions in home currency, and $RM(I)$ does not rise to 1.050.[16]

Similar phenomena emerge in tables 2.A and 2.B. With stock-adjustment speculation, $RM(I)$ ends always at 1.0250, the upper limit of the band through which it can move. The central bank is forced to intervene, and reserves,

[15]In the first regressive mode of speculation, the position in home currency does not go to zero; speculators continue mistakenly to gamble on a movement of $RM(I)$ to (or toward) parity. The same thing is true in the fourth mode of speculation (which is very like the first in all important properties, despite the conceptual differences between them). In the other regressive mode and in the adaptive mode, $AR(I)$ and $RM(I)$ are not different when the model comes to rest, and $SH(I)$ goes to zero.

[16]Although speculators sell some home currency in the other regressive mode and in the adaptive mode – they do so as soon as $AR(I)$ comes to exceed $RM(I)$ – their (early) purchases of home currency exceed their (later) sales, and $SH(I)$ is positive in month 120.

$RE(I)$, turn negative in every case. Speculators have net positions in home currency in three of the four modes, for $RM(I)$ does not equal $AR(I)$ at month 120, but those net positions are not changing.[17] Notice, however, the signs of those positions. $SH(I)$ is positive in the first and fourth modes; speculators think that $RM(I)$ will fall to levels lower than 1.0250. $SH(I)$ is negative in the second mode; speculators think that $RM(I)$ will rise. When, then, we turn to flow speculation, we find that $RM(I)$ has come to rest inside its upper limit in the first and fourth modes; speculators buy large quantities of home currency, preventing $RM(I)$ from reaching its limit. The authorities do not lose reserves – the speculators do all of their work for them – and the outcome is identical to full flexibility. In the second mode, however, speculators sell large quantities of home currency, and the outcome is much like a speculative "raid" in anticipation of devaluation. The balance of payments shows very large deficits (much larger than the "basic" deficit of -0.203 reserve units), and the authorities are deeply in debt.

We turn now to look at the effects of speculation on the variance of export volume – our measure of instability – and its relationship to profitability.[18] First, a few comments on the index itself and, separately, on profitability:

There is a strong positive relationship between the instability of export volume and the time it takes for the model to settle down after introduction of the price disturbance. Whenever $RM(I)$ is still moving at the end of 120 months, the index of instability is very large. It is also very large when the market rate is stable in month 120 but is different from the equilibrium rate. This is because the volume of exports is stabilized when $RM(I)$ is stabilized, but cannot equal equilibrium volume unless $RM(I)$ equals $EQ(I)$.[19]

Profits evaluated at $RM(I)$ are negative in every case shown by tables 1.A and 1.B and tables 2.A and 2.B. This, we shall see, is due to the fact that speculators have no foresight. Even in the second regressive mode, where they can look only at past levels of $EQ(I)$, the lag operator L is zero in these simulations. Profits evaluated at $AR(I)$ are, of course, positive in several instances. But this can give the speculators very little comfort – wishful thinking has no place in the foreign-exchange market – and this measure of profitability

[17]The positions are zero in the adaptive mode, because the speculators come finally to believe that the market rate will stay at 0.0250. They take no notice of the fact that the central bank has run out of reserves.

[18]We could use the other index shown in the tables – the variability of $RM(I)$ itself. The two, however, are highly correlated, and the one we have chosen would seem in any case to measure more directly real costs. Fluctuations in trade volume imply fluctuations in production or, at the very least, in producers' inventories.

[19]It should perhaps be noted that there can be no case in which instability can be zero. The model operates with lags.

will not be used hereafter. I mention it only because it provides an internal logical check. It says that the speculators would have fared well if they had made accurate forecasts.

I come now to tests of Friedman's (1950) conjecture concerning stability and profitability. Putting that conjecture in relative form, I ask if there is a positive correlation between the stability of export volume and the total profits of foreign-exchange speculators.

There are several ways to look for this correlation, and I shall begin with the simplest, comparing similar flexible-exchange-rate cases. One can, of course, make two independent comparisons within each group of three simulations in tables 1.A and 1.B, furnishing a maximum of 16 comparisons. But one of these was lost, as one run ended prematurely. We have, then, 15 independent pairs, and can group them for convenience into three classes: (a) pairs in which the market rate has come to rest (whether or not at equilibrium); (b) pairs in which the market rate has not come to rest; and (c) pairs in which the outcomes differ in this respect.

Tables 1.A and 1.B give us nine pairs belonging to group (a), and five of them display the "right" relationship between stability and profitability.[20] To illustrate, consider the first two lines of table 1.A: The index of instability falls from 0.0631 on the first line to 0.0554 on the second, while profits at $RM(I)$ rise from -0.094 to -0.072. Contrast, however, the first and second lines of table 1.B: Export instability falls from 0.2854 to 0.2653, but profits fall from -0.007 to -0.008. There is, next, one pair belonging to group (b), and it displays the "right" relationship.[21] There are five pairs belonging to group (c), and they display the "right" relationship.[22] To summarize:

Nature of Final Outcome	"Right"	"Wrong"
Pairs in which $RM(I)$ is at rest	5	4
Pairs in which $RM(I)$ is not at rest	1	0
Pairs in which outcomes differ	4	0

[20]There are three in table 1.A; the first par-value regressive pair ($C = 1.00$ and $C = 0.75$); the first equilibrium regressive pair; and the first extrapolative pair. There are six in table 1.B; the two par-value regressive pairs; the two equilibrium regressive pairs; and the two extrapolative pairs.

[21]In table 1.B: the first adaptive pair.

[22]In table 1.A: the second par-value regressive pair; the second equilibrium regressive pair; the one adaptive pair; and the second extrapolative pair. In table 1.B: the second adaptive pair.

Do these results constitute a correlation between stability and profitability? The formal statistical answer is inconclusive. If "right" and "wrong" cases were equi-probable – the usual null hypothesis – the probability of drawing by pure chance 11 or more "right" cases in 15 would be 0.059, a bit below conventional levels of significance.[23]

But one can make similar pairwise comparisons using the 24 fixed-rate cases shown in tables 2.A and 2.B and the other exchange-rate regimes described by the previous section of this paper, and when one does so the outcome is decisive. Pairwise comparisons for each regime are shown in groups by table 3.[24] Summaries for all regimes are listed at the end. The probability of each result happening by chance is less than 0.001 in every instance.[25] There *is* a strong positive correlation between stability and profitability within any one mode of speculation and any one exchange-rate regime.[26]

Table 3 contains additional information worthy of brief note. It shows, for example, that certain regimes are more likely to achieve complete adjustment when the model is disturbed. Subtract from the total number of simulations (24 for each regime) the number in which the outcome was identical to the corresponding fixed- or flexible-rate case, and look at the frequency with which each regime was able to produce stable or convergent outcomes:[27]

[23]This is an exact computation using the binomial distribution. The ones mentioned hereafter are approximations using the normal distribution.

[24]These comparisons derive from data like those arrayed in the appendix.

[25]Using a normal approximation, $t > 5.0$ in the first and second cases, and $t > 4.0$ in the third. For the 225 cases together, $t = 6.71$.

[26]There is little difference among modes and between the stock-adjustment and flow cases in the frequency of "wrong" results:

	Stock		Flow	
	Total	Wrong	Total	Wrong
Par-value regressive	37	6	16	4
Equilibrium regressive	37	2	32	8
Adaptive	36	6	20	1
Extrapolative	35	9	12	1

[27]I omit Regime 2.1 which does not differ much from Regime 2.2. I also omit the continuous formulations; with one minor exception (Regime 4.0), these gave results no better than the discontinuous formulations.

TABLE 3
Summary of three full-scale simulations covering 10 years (each with four modes of stock-adjustment and flow speculation); key characteristics of final positions and paired relationships between stability and profitability (numbers of simulations).

Exchange rate regime	Characteristics of final position					Feasible pairwise comparisons[b]	"Wrong" results with		
	Replicates fixed or flexible	$RM(I)$ stable		$RM(I)$ changing			$MR(I)$ & $RE(I)$ stationary	$RM(I)$ or $RE(I)$ moving	Different final states
		Reserves stable	Reserves changing	Convergent[a]	Non-convergent				
1.0	—	17	0	3	4[c]	15	4	0	0
2.0	6	0	18[d]	0	0	12	0	0	0
2.1	5	10	3[e]	4	2[d]	12	0	0	0
2.2	5	10	3[e]	4	2[d]	12	0	0	2
3.0	3	13	3	1	4[d]	14	0	0	3
3.1	9	9	0	1	4[d]	9	2	0	1
3.2	7	6	3	4	4[d]	10	1	0	1
4.0	6	9	0	5	4[d]	12	0	0	2
4.1	8	10	0	2	4[d]	10	0	0	1
4.2	8	11	0	1	4[d]	10	0	0	0

5.0	6	0	0	2	16[d]	12	0	5	0
5.1	6	0	11[d,f]	2	5	12	0	1	1
5.2	6	0	9[f]	3	6[d]	10	0	1	2
6.0	6	1	14[d]	1	2	12	0	0	0
6.1	7	4	13[d]	0	0	11	0	0	1
6.2	8	9	0	4	3[d]	8	0	0	0
7.0	2	2	18[d]	2	0	14	0	2	0
7.1	1	11	5	4	3[d]	15	1	0	1
7.2	1	7	0	5	11[d]	15	0	1	1
Total, "wrong" relationships						—	8	10	19
Total, "right" relationships						—	45	79	64
Grand total						225	53	89	83

[a]Based on an inspection of calculations extending through month 240.

[b]The number of independent pairs (sixteen) *less* those in which one or both members of the pair resembled the fixed- or flexible-rate case (or did not complete 120 months).

[c]Includes one flexible-exchange-rate simulation terminated in month 73.

[d]Includes the counterparts of the simulation terminated in month 73.

[e]Rate would be set free to float again after month 120.

[f]Rate would start to change again as cumulative movement in reserves led to additional changes in parity.

Exchange-rate regime	Simulations differ from 1.0 & 2.0	Simulations stable or convergent
1.0 Flexible	24	20
2.0 Fixed	18	0
2.2 Fixed with temporary float	19	14
3.1 Equilibrium-rate based	15	10
3.2 Equilibrium-rate exact	17	10
4.1 Market-rate based (6 month average)	16	12
5.1 Reserve level	18	2
5.2 Reserve level with override	18	3
6.1 Reserve change	17	4
6.2 Reserve change with supplementary	16	13
7.1 Basic balance	23	15
7.2 Basic balance with supplementary	23	12

The two reserve-level rules do very badly. This is because they marry a stock target to a flow control. Exchange rates can regulate the rate of change of reserves; they cannot regulate the level of reserves.[28] It would appear, of course, that Regime 6.1, the one that marries the two variables properly, does no better than the reserve-level rules. Its defect, however, is less serious and is remedied completely by Regime 6.2, which introduces "supplementary" parity changes. The defect is the frequency with which Regime 6.1 fails to eliminate imbalances entirely, allowing residual movements in reserves. Regime 6.2, dealing with these movements, is one of the best systems in the list, followed closely by the moving-average rules. Parity changes based on the basic balance or the equilibrium exchange rate are somewhat less successful in achieving stable outcomes.

The findings summarized above furnish information for an answer to another question: Is there any correlation *across* exchange regimes between stability and profitability? To answer this question, I choose a subset of regimes able to generate stable outcomes and to furnish "right" results in table 3, above. I rank

[28]Notice, moreover, that Regime 5.1 gave one of the weakest correlations between stability and profitability (3 "wrong" results in 10). Regime 3.1 does as badly, followed by 1.0. It seems strange that flexibility gives results inferior to those obtained by other ways of altering exchange rates. The difficulty, however, seems to reside entirely in table 1.B, with flow speculation. All four "wrong" results occur in the par-value regressive mode and the (similar) extrapolative mode, and each of these results is due to a very small reduction in profitability when $C = 0.075$ (and $E = 0.25$).

them by stability and profitability and look for concordance between the two rankings. To illustrate, consider the adaptive mode (with $D = 0.10$) and the stock-adjustment case:

Exchange-rate regime	Stability		Profitability	
	Absolute	Rank	Absolute	Rank
1.0 Flexible	0.1892	6	−0.448	6
2.0 Fixed with temporary float	0.1238	5	−0.105	4
3.1 Equilibrium-rate based	0.0628	1	−0.100	3
4.1 Market-rate based	0.0941	4	−0.111	5
6.2 Reserve change with supplementary	0.0688	3	−0.046	1
7.1 Basic balance	0.0672	2	−0.090	2

I find no correlation between these two rankings, nor can I find one for most other modes of speculation.[29]

Consider, next, the impact of changes in the volume of the funds that speculators put into the market – of raising from 10.0 to 20.0 *times* export volume the coefficient S in equation (16). A line-by-line comparison of two full simulations gives this distribution of "right" and "wrong" results:[30]

[29]There is a strong rank correlation in only one instance (par-value regressive with stock-adjustment speculation and $C = 0.75$):

Exchange-rate regime	Stability		Profitability	
	Absolute	Rank	Absolute	Rank
1.0	0.0554	2	−0.072	4
2.2	0.1208	6	−0.179	6
3.1	0.0357	1	−0.041	1
4.1	0.0770	4	−0.071	3
6.2	0.0837	5	−0.123	5
7.1	0.0596	3	−0.059	2

There are, however, certain other regularities, especially in absolute ranking by stability. The equilibrium-based method, for example, seems always to rank first in overall stability; temporary floats seem always to rank fifth or sixth (probably because adjustment is deferred until reserves have fallen to the point at which a float can start). Rankings of this sort may be most germane to the choice among exchange-rate regimes, but this is not the chief aim of the present paper. [For more on rankings by absolute stability, see Kenen (1975).]

[30]When profits changed sign between two observations, the outcome was classified according to their sign when $S = 10.0$.

"*Right*":	Increased instability and larger losses	75
	Decreased instability and smaller losses *or* increased instability and smaller profits *or* decreased instability and larger profits	16
"*Wrong*":	Increased instability and larger profits	11
	Increased instability and smaller losses *or* decreased instability and larger losses *or* decreased instability and smaller profits	12

These statistics seem to say that an increase in the volume of speculation strengthens the positive correlation between stability and profitability; there is little likelihood of obtaining by pure chance 91 "right" results in this many trials. The test itself, however, may be badly biased. If an increase in the volume of speculation served typically to augment the variability of exports but also worked to magnify absolutely the size of the speculators' profits and losses, the increase in volume would appear to strengthen the positive correlation between stability and profitability. This is because the simulations under study here generate losses more often than profits, so that a simple "scale" effect would generate more "right" than "wrong" results. And when I work only with cases in which there are profits, the results are inconclusive. The 27 cases are distributed as follows:

Increased instability and smaller profits *or* decreased instability and larger profits	13
Increased instability and larger profits *or* increased instability and smaller profits	14

The outcome is too close for decisive inference.[31]

Every simulation described heretofore has assumed instantaneous stock adjustment, by setting Q at unity in equation (18). What happens to stability taken by itself and to its relationship to profitability when one slows the rate of stock adjustment by cutting Q in half? I find first an unambiguous decline in the instability of export volume. The variance declines in 69 of 74 cases studied.[32] I also find a strong positive correlation between the changes in stability and the changes in profitability. There are 67 "right" results.

[31]Notice, however, that this test is biased *against* "right" relationships. The effects of pure "scale" would appear as "wrong" results.

[32]The relevant simulations are summarized in the appendix.

What, finally, is the consequence for profitability of letting the speculators look ahead? Replace $L = 0$ with $L = 3$ in equation (13) to see if profits increase in the regressive mode when the speculators' views about "normal" market rates are based on the equilibrium rate, $EQ(I)$, during the forthcoming quarter (including the current month). Profits are enlarged or losses reduced in 35 of 36 instances, and 24 of these show the "right" relationship between stability and profitability.[33]

5. Conclusion

This paper has concentrated on one aspect of my current work with the several ways to regulate exchange rates. It has not tried to rank directly rival rules or regimes. This task calls for many additional simulations to look at their performance. I plan indeed to study a wide range of disturbances, including stochastic fluctuations in trade and prices, the consequence of lengthening delivery lags and raising price elasticities, the impact of narrow and wide bands for exchange-rate variations, and the implications for each exchange regime of altering the size and frequency of the permissible parity changes. Here, I have tried to explore in detail one dimension of the problem – the behavior of the basic model and of the regimes under a wide range of suppositions concerning the ways in which speculators operate. I find a strong positive correlation between the stability of export volume and the profitability of foreign-exchange speculation, showing that the model replicates consistently the relationship forecast by Friedman (1950). I find, further, that profits correlate with foresight, an outcome that is reassuring if not surprising, and that stability correlates inversely with the speed at which speculators bring positions into line with expectations. I cannot show, however, that more speculation strengthens the correlation between stability and profitability. More of a good thing may not be better.

Appendix – Summaries of Simulations

The tables that follow summarize some of the simulations used to generate tables 1 through 3 above. Each of them examines the effects of a five percent increase in home prices. The first *part* of each job deals with par-value

[33]The first result reported in the text is not apt to occur by pure chance. The second could be due to chance. Using the normal approximation to the binomial, the probability of 24 or more "right" results works out at 0.02275.

(regressive) expectations; the second with equilibrium-rate (regressive) expectations; the third with adaptive expectations; and the fourth part deals with extrapolative expectations. The first *set* in each part deals with stock-adjustment speculation and sets $Q = 1.0$; the second deals with flow speculation. In Job 2.00, shown in its entirety, $S = 10$ *times* monthly export value, $Q = 1.00$, and $L = 0$. In Job 2.10, shown in part, Q is cut in half; in Job 2.20, L is raised to 3; in Job 2.30, S is doubled.

The "stability code" in the final column describes the condition of each simulation at the end of 120 months. A zero in the first (left-most) column indicates that the parity was not changing during the final year; a zero in the second column that the market rate was not changing; a zero in the third column that reserves were not changing; and a zero in the fourth column indicates that the home-currency position was not changing. The letters attached to certain entries in this column call attention to special situations:

- a Simulation cut short before month 120 (no real roots).
- c Simulation stable or strongly convergent at the end of month 240.
- d Simulation cut short after month 120 but before month 240 (no real roots).
- f Identical to corresponding fixed-rate case.
- n No supplemental parity changes.

SIMULATION OF EXCHANGE REGIMES, JOB 2.00 COVERING 10 YEARS
THIS IS PART 1 OF 4, SET 1 OF 2. BEGIN EXCHANGE REGIME 1

REG	BAND	SIZE GLDE	FREQ GIDE	RMSQDV FX VOL	RMSQDV BF SUR	NUM CH PARITY	PARITY DATA MAXIM	PARITY DATA MINIM	PARITY DATA FINAL	MKT RATE DATA MAXIM	MKT RATE DATA MINIM	MKT RATE DATA FINAL	RESERVES DATA MAXIM	RESERVES DATA MINIM	RESERVES DATA FINAL	SPC PROF AT FRM	STAB CODE
1.0	2.5	5	0	0.0554	0.0	0	1.000	1.000	1.000	1.060	1.000	1.050	20.0	20.0	20.0	-0.072	0000
2.0	2.5	5	0	0.1876	0.1915	0	1.000	1.000	1.000	1.025	1.000	1.025	20.0	-2.3	-2.3	-0.018	0010
2.1	2.5	5	0	0.1205	0.2044	1	1.058	1.000	1.058	1.084	1.000	1.050	20.0	12.3	12.5	-0.177	0101 C
2.2	2.5	5	0	0.1208	0.2018	1	1.058	1.000	1.058	1.085	1.000	1.050	20.0	12.4	12.5	-0.179	0101 C
3.0	2.5	5	12	0.0461	0.0521	78	1.049	1.000	1.049	1.059	1.000	1.050	20.0	18.1	18.1	-0.052	0001
3.1	2.5	5	12	0.0357	0.0531	8	1.033	1.000	1.033	1.059	1.000	1.050	20.0	18.8	18.8	-0.041	0000
3.2	2.5	5	12	0.0515	0.0186	14	1.050	1.000	1.050	1.076	1.000	1.050	20.0	19.6	19.6	-0.041	0000
4.0	2.5	5	12	0.0719	0.0760	56	1.050	1.000	1.050	1.061	1.000	1.050	20.0	16.2	16.2	-0.065	0001
4.1	2.5	5	12	0.0770	0.0808	12	1.050	1.000	1.050	1.071	1.000	1.050	20.0	16.6	16.6	-0.071	0001
4.2	2.5	5	12	0.0822	0.0907	10	1.042	1.000	1.042	1.061	1.000	1.050	20.0	15.1	15.1	-0.061	0001
5.0	2.5	5	12	0.1902	0.1806	104	1.121	1.000	1.108	1.093	1.000	1.080	25.3	14.5	25.3	-0.050	1111
5.1	2.5	5	12	0.2129	0.1913	54	1.108	0.992	0.992	1.091	1.000	1.016	26.5	14.3	25.7	-0.219	1111
5.2	2.5	5	12	0.1777	0.1686	29	1.100	1.000	1.079	1.103	1.000	1.052	24.5	14.3	24.5	-0.123	1111
6.0	2.5	5	12	0.0742	0.0825	51	1.022	1.000	1.022	1.047	1.000	1.047	20.0	13.6	13.6	-0.051	0010
6.1	2.5	5	12	0.1315	0.1364	2	1.008	1.000	1.008	1.034	1.000	1.034	20.0	4.6	4.6	-0.031	0010
6.2	2.5	5	12	0.0837	0.0951	6	1.025	1.000	1.025	1.051	1.000	1.050	20.0	13.1	13.1	-0.055	0001
7.0	2.5	5	12	0.0606	0.0692	46	1.022	1.000	1.022	1.047	1.000	1.047	20.0	14.9	14.9	-0.048	0010
7.1	2.5	5	12	0.0596	0.0765	8	1.033	1.000	1.033	1.059	1.000	1.050	20.0	17.3	17.3	-0.059	0000
7.2	2.5	5	12	0.0722	0.0770	15	1.033	1.000	1.029	1.059	1.000	1.046	20.0	17.1	17.1	-0.064	1101

SIMULATION OF EXCHANGE REGIMES, JOB 2.00 COVERING 10 YEARS
THIS IS PART 1 OF 4, SET 2 OF 2. BEGIN EXCHANGE REGIME 1

PEG	BAND	SIZE GLDE	FREQ GLDF	RMSQDV EX VOL	RMSQDV BP SUR	NUM CH PARITY	PARITY DATA MAXIM	MINIM	FINAL	MKT RATE DATA MAXIM	MINIM	FINAL	RESERVES DATA MAXIM	MINIM	FINAL	SPC PROF AT FRM	STAB CODE
1.0	2.5	5	0	0.2653	0.0	0	1.000	1.000	1.000	1.015	1.000	1.014	20.0	20.0	20.0	-0.008	0001
2.0	2.5	5	0			IDENTICAL TO FLEXIBLE RATE CASE FOR THIS PART AND SET											
2.1	2.5	5	0			IDENTICAL TO FLEXIBLE RATE CASE FOR THIS PART AND SET											
2.2	2.5	5	0			IDENTICAL TO FLEXIBLE RATE CASE FOR THIS PART AND SET											
3.0	2.5	5	12	0.0685	0.0	78	1.049	1.000	1.049	1.050	1.000	1.049	20.0	20.0	20.0	-0.106	0001
3.1	2.5	5	12	0.0910	0.0	8	1.033	1.000	1.033	1.042	1.000	1.038	20.0	20.0	20.0	-0.022	0001
3.2	2.5	5	12	0.0094	0.0	14	1.050	1.000	1.050	1.058	1.000	1.050	20.0	20.0	20.0	-0.024	0000
4.0	2.5	5	12	0.1460	0.0	114	1.040	1.000	1.040	1.043	1.000	1.043	20.0	20.0	20.0	-0.257	1101c
4.1	2.5	5	12			IDENTICAL TO FLEXIBLE RATE CASE FOR THIS PART AND SET											
4.2	2.5	5	12			IDENTICAL TO FLEXIBLE RATE CASE FOR THIS PART AND SET											
5.0	2.5	5	12			IDENTICAL TO FLEXIBLE RATE CASE FOR THIS PART AND SET											
5.1	2.5	5	12			IDENTICAL TO FLEXIBLE RATE CASE FOR THIS PART AND SET											
5.2	2.5	5	12			IDENTICAL TO FLEXIBLE RATE CASE FOR THIS PART AND SET											
6.0	2.5	5	12			IDENTICAL TO FLEXIBLE RATE CASE FOR THIS PART AND SET											
6.1	2.5	5	12			IDENTICAL TO FLEXIBLE RATE CASE FOR THIS PART AND SET											
6.2	2.5	5	12			IDENTICAL TO FLEXIBLE RATE CASE FOR THIS PART AND SET											
7.0	2.5	5	12	0.0990	0.0	98	1.045	1.000	1.045	1.047	1.000	1.047	20.0	20.0	20.0	-0.156	0001
7.1	2.5	5	12	0.0968	0.0	9	1.037	1.000	1.037	1.047	1.000	1.041	20.0	20.0	20.0	-0.078	0001
7.2	2.5	5	12	0.0803	0.0	15	1.050	1.000	1.046	1.054	1.000	1.046	20.0	20.0	20.0	-0.101	1101

SIMULATION OF EXCHANGE REGIMES, JOB 2.00 COVERING 10 YEARS
THIS IS PART 2 OF 4, SET 1 OF 2. BEGIN EXCHANGE REGIMF 1

REG	BAND	SIZE GLDE	FREQ GLDE	RMSQDV EX VOL	RMSQDV BP SUR	NUM CH PARITY	PARITY DATA MAXIM	PARITY DATA MINIM	PARITY DATA FINAL	MKT RATE DATA MAXIM	MKT RATE DATA MINIM	MKT RATE DATA FINAL	RESERVES DATA MAXIM	RESERVES DATA MINIM	RESERVES DATA FINAL	SPC PROF AT FPM	STAB CODE
1.0	2.5	5	0	0.0582	0.0	0	1.000	1.000	1.000	1.081	1.000	1.050	20.0	20.0	20.0	-0.042	0000
2.0	2.5	5	0	0.1830	0.2078	0	1.000	1.000	1.000	1.025	1.000	1.025	20.0	-4.4	-4.4	-0.005	0010
2.1	2.5	5	0	0.0754	0.1097	1	1.060	1.000	1.060	1.061	1.000	1.050	20.0	14.9	14.9	0.015	0000
2.2	2.5	5	0	0.0754	0.1097	1	1.060	1.000	1.060	1.061	1.000	1.050	20.0	14.9	14.9	0.015	0000
3.0	2.5	5	12	0.0237	0.0699	78	1.049	1.000	1.049	1.054	1.000	1.050	20.0	17.7	17.7	-0.002	0000
3.1	2.5	5	12	0.0165	0.0466	8	1.033	1.000	1.033	1.057	1.000	1.050	20.0	18.7	18.7	-0.021	0000
3.2	2.5	5	12	0.0500	0.0128	14	1.050	1.000	1.050	1.076	1.000	1.050	20.0	19.8	19.8	-0.041	0000
4.0	2.5	5	12	0.0389	0.0829	33	1.049	1.000	1.049	1.053	1.000	1.050	20.0	16.6	16.6	0.006	0000
4.1	2.5	5	12	0.0311	0.0904	9	1.037	1.000	1.037	1.055	1.000	1.050	20.0	17.4	17.4	0.006	0000
4.2	2.5	5	12	0.0544	0.1031	8	1.033	1.000	1.033	1.052	1.000	1.050	20.0	15.5	15.5	0.014	0000
5.0	2.5	5	12	0.1088	0.1337	109	1.103	1.000	1.094	1.075	1.000	1.067	22.8	15.7	22.8	0.004	1111
5.1	2.5	5	12	0.0550	0.0979	19	1.079	1.000	1.079	1.061	1.000	1.052	20.0	16.7	18.4	0.015	0010
5.2	2.5	5	12	0.0800	0.1142	21	1.087	1.000	1.087	1.061	1.000	1.060	22.4	16.7	22.4	0.013	0010
6.0	2.5	5	12	0.0476	0.0859	57	1.021	1.000	1.021	1.047	1.000	1.047	20.0	13.4	13.4	0.003	0010
6.1	2.5	5	12	0.0316	0.1269	3	1.012	1.000	1.012	1.038	1.000	1.038	20.0	7.1	7.1	0.001	0010
6.2	2.5	5	12	0.0480	0.0988	6	1.025	1.000	1.025	1.051	1.000	1.050	20.0	14.9	14.9	0.005	0000
7.0	2.5	5	12	0.0561	0.0948	56	1.022	1.000	1.022	1.047	1.000	1.047	20.0	13.1	13.1	0.006	0010
7.1	2.5	5	12	0.0689	0.1051	9	1.037	1.000	1.037	1.061	1.000	1.050	20.0	15.5	15.5	0.015	0000
7.2	2.5	5	12	0.0641	0.1041	13	1.033	1.000	1.029	1.059	1.000	1.050	20.0	15.6	15.6	0.015	0000

SIMULATION OF EXCHANGE REGIMES, JOB 2.00 COVERING 10 YEARS
THIS IS PART 2 OF 4, SET 2 OF 2. BEGIN EXCHANGE REGIME 1

REG	BAND	SIZE GLDE	FREQ GLDE	RMSQDV EX VOL	RMSQDV BP SUF	NUM CH PARITY	PARITY DATA MAXIM	PARITY DATA MINIM	PARITY DATA FINAL	MKT RATE DATA MAXIM	MKT RATE DATA MINIM	MKT RATE DATA FINAL	RESERVES DATA MAXIM	RESERVES DATA MINIM	RESERVES DATA FINAL	SPC PROF AT FRM	STAB CODE
1.0	2.5	5	0	0.0089	0.0	0	1.000	1.000	1.000	1.055	1.000	1.050	20.0	20.0	20.0	-0.026	0000
2.0	2.5	5	0	0.1828	0.6501	0	1.000	1.000	1.000	1.025	1.000	1.025	20.0	-56.9	-56.9	-0.004	0011
2.1	2.5	5	0	0.0495	0.1532	1	1.046	1.000	1.046	1.073	1.000	1.050	20.0	14.8	14.8	0.108	0000
2.2	2.5	5	0	0.0495	0.1532	1	1.057	1.000	1.057	1.073	1.000	1.050	20.0	14.8	14.8	0.108	0000
3.0	2.5	5	12	0.0219	0.0647	78	1.049	1.000	1.049	1.052	1.000	1.050	20.0	17.6	17.6	-0.014	0000
3.1	2.5	5	12			SIMILAR TO FLEXIBLE RATE CASE FOR THIS PART AND SET											
3.2	2.5	5	12			SIMILAR TO FLEXIBLE RATE CASE FOR THIS PART AND SET											
4.0	2.5	5	12	0.0362	0.1195	84	1.049	1.000	1.049	1.052	1.000	1.050	20.0	14.5	14.5	0.018	0000
4.1	2.5	5	12	0.0251	0.0749	8	1.033	1.000	1.033	1.053	1.000	1.050	20.0	17.1	17.1	-0.006	0000
4.2	2.5	5	12	0.0523	0.1763	8	1.033	1.000	1.033	1.051	1.000	1.050	20.0	11.0	11.0	0.073	0000
5.0	2.5	5	12	0.1450	0.5124	109	1.109	0.985	0.997	1.081	1.000	1.022	29.9	10.9	10.9	0.709	1111
5.1	2.5	5	12	0.0510	0.1677	19	1.079	1.000	1.079	1.057	1.000	1.052	20.0	13.5	18.7	0.070	0011
5.2	2.5	5	12	0.0507	0.1668	19	1.079	1.000	1.079	1.057	1.000	1.052	20.0	13.5	18.1	0.070	0011
6.0	2.5	5	12	0.0354	0.1136	22	1.024	1.000	1.024	1.049	1.000	1.049	20.0	13.3	13.3	0.014	0011
6.1	2.5	5	12	0.0294	0.0866	6	1.025	1.000	1.025	1.051	1.000	1.050	20.0	16.8	16.8	0.004	0000
6.2	2.5	5	12	0.0294	0.0866	6	1.025	1.000	1.025	1.051	1.000	1.050	20.0	16.8	16.8	0.004	0000
7.0	2.5	5	12	0.0562	0.1926	56	1.022	1.000	1.022	1.047	1.000	1.047	20.0	2.3	2.3	0.058	0011
7.1	2.5	5	12	0.0654	0.2216	8	1.033	1.000	1.033	1.057	1.000	1.050	20.0	9.3	9.3	0.136	0000
7.2	2.5	5	12	0.0607	0.2047	10	1.033	1.000	1.033	1.057	1.000	1.050	20.0	10.4	10.4	0.113	0000

SIMULATION OF EXCHANGE REGIMES, JOB 2.00 COVERING 10 YEARS
THIS IS PART 3 OF 4, SET 1 OF 2. BEGIN EXCHANGE REGIME 1

REG	BAND	SIZE GLDE	FREQ GLDE	RMSQDV EX VOL	RMSQDV BE SUF	NUM CH PARITY	PARITY DATA MAXIM	PARITY DATA MINIM	PARITY DATA FINAL	MKT RATE DATA MAXIM	MKT RATE DATA MINIM	MKT RATE DATA FINAL	RESERVES DATA MAXIM	RESERVES DATA MINIM	RESERVES DATA FINAL	SPC PROF AT FRM	STAB CODE
1.0	2.5	5	0	0.1392	0.0	0	1.000	1.000	1.000	1.102	1.000	1.064	20.0	20.0	20.0	-0.448	0101[c]
2.0	2.5	5	0	0.1878	0.2076	0	1.000	1.000	1.000	1.025	1.000	1.025	20.0	-3.9	-3.9	-0.018	0010
2.1	2.5	5	0	0.1238	0.1230	2	1.083	1.000	1.054	1.083	1.000	1.049	20.0	14.9	18.6	-0.105	1111[c]
2.2	2.5	5	0	0.1205	0.1169	1	1.074	1.000	1.074	1.083	1.000	1.049	20.0	14.9	16.1	-0.112	0101[c]
3.0	2.5	5	12	0.0706	0.0685	78	1.049	1.000	1.049	1.063	1.000	1.053	20.0	17.5	17.5	-0.097	0101[c]
3.1	2.5	5	12	0.0628	0.0696	8	1.033	1.000	1.033	1.059	1.000	1.053	20.0	17.8	17.8	-0.100	0101[c]
3.2	2.5	5	12	0.1063	0.0516	14	1.050	1.000	1.050	1.076	1.000	1.057	20.0	18.8	18.8	-0.192	0101[c]
4.0	2.5	5	12	0.0787	0.0901	101	1.052	1.000	1.050	1.062	1.000	1.047	20.0	15.6	15.6	-0.068	1101[c]
4.1	2.5	5	12	0.0941	0.0928	12	1.050	1.000	1.050	1.070	1.000	1.053	20.0	16.8	16.8	-0.111	0101[c]
4.2	2.5	5	12	0.0851	0.1142	10	1.042	1.000	1.042	1.060	1.000	1.046	20.0	14.3	14.3	-0.052	0101[c]
5.0	2.5	5	12	0.1553	0.1498	104	1.110	1.000	1.100	1.083	1.000	1.073	23.5	14.7	23.5	-0.076	1111
5.1	2.5	5	12	0.1677	0.1454	47	1.100	1.000	1.004	1.083	1.000	1.029	23.2	16.4	21.2	-0.162	0011
5.2	2.5	5	12	0.1185	0.1004	18	1.075	1.000	1.075	1.083	1.000	1.050	20.0	16.4	17.3	-0.143	0101[c]
6.0	2.5	5	12	0.0679	0.0923	38	1.024	1.000	1.024	1.050	1.000	1.050	20.0	14.2	14.2	-0.046	0010
6.1	2.5	5	12	0.0720	0.1083	5	1.021	1.000	1.021	1.046	1.000	1.046	20.0	12.4	12.4	-0.043	0010
6.2	2.5	5	12	0.0688	0.1055	7	1.029	1.000	1.029	1.053	1.000	1.050	20.0	14.7	14.7	-0.046	0101[c]
7.0	2.5	5	12	0.0623	0.0884	42	1.022	1.000	1.022	1.047	1.000	1.047	20.0	13.4	13.4	-0.051	0010
7.1	2.5	5	12	0.0672	0.0695	8	1.033	1.000	1.033	1.059	1.000	1.052	20.0	17.2	17.2	-0.090	0101[c]
7.2	2.5	5	12	0.0630	0.0758	15	1.033	1.000	1.029	1.059	1.000	1.049	20.0	16.8	16.8	-0.083	1101[c]

SIMULATION OF EXCHANGE REGIMES, JOB 2.00 COVERING 10 YEARS
THIS IS PART 3 OF 4, SET 2 OF 2. BEGIN EXCHANGE REGIME 1

REG	BAND	SIZE GLDE	FREQ GLDE	RMSQDV EX VOL	RMSQDV BP SUR	NUM CH PARITY	PARITY DATA MAXIM	PARITY DATA MINIM	PARITY DATA FINAL	MKT RATE DATA MAXIM	MKT RATE DATA MINIM	MKT RATE DATA FINAL	RESERVES DATA MAXIM	RESERVES DATA MINIM	RESERVES DATA FINAL	SEC PROF AT FRM	STAB CODE
1.0	2.5	5	0	0.1164	0.C	0	1.000	1.000	1.000	1.048	1.000	1.048	20.0	20.0	20.0	-0.227	0101[c]
2.0	2.5	5	0	0.1925	0.1632	0	1.000	1.000	1.000	1.025	1.000	1.025	20.0	2.5	2.5	-0.035	C010
2.1	2.5	5	0	0.1467	0.0808	1	1.036	1.000	1.036	1.046	1.000	1.046	20.0	15.0	15.0	-0.212	0101[c]
2.2	2.5	5	0	0.1467	0.0808	1	1.037	1.000	1.037	1.046	1.000	1.046	20.0	15.0	15.0	-0.212	0101[c]
3.0	2.5	5	0			SIMILAR TO FLEXIBLE RATE CASE FOR THIS PART AND SET											
3.1	2.5	5	0			SIMILAR TO FLEXIBLE RATE CASE FOR THIS PART AND SET											
3.2	2.5	5	12	0.1107	0.0172	14	1.050	1.000	1.050	1.048	1.000	1.048	20.6	20.0	20.6	-0.222	0101[c]
4.0	2.5	5	12			SIMILAR TO FLEXIBLE RATE CASE FOR THIS PART AND SET											
4.1	2.5	5	12			SIMILAR TO FLEXIBLE RATE CASE FOR THIS PART AND SET											
4.2	2.5	5	12			SIMILAR TO FLEXIBLE RATE CASE FOR THIS PART AND SET											
5.0	2.5	5	12	0.1317	0.0436	88	1.059	1.000	1.059	1.047	1.000	1.047	20.0	17.6	17.6	-0.227	1101[c]
5.1	2.5	5	12	0.1364	0.0648	17	1.071	1.000	1.071	1.048	1.000	1.048	20.0	16.6	17.3	-0.224	0101[c]
5.2	2.5	5	12	0.1364	0.0648	17	1.071	1.000	1.071	1.048	1.000	1.048	20.0	16.6	17.3	-0.224	0101[c]
6.0	2.5	5	12	0.1390	0.0528	94	1.017	1.000	1.017	1.043	1.000	1.043	20.0	14.4	14.4	-0.180	1111[c,d]
6.1	2.5	5	12	0.1792	0.1375	1	1.004	1.000	1.004	1.029	1.000	1.029	20.0	5.3	5.3	-0.064	C011
6.2	2.5	5	12	0.1224	0.0208	6	1.025	1.000	1.025	1.048	1.000	1.048	20.0	18.8	18.8	-0.225	0101[c]
7.0	2.5	5	12			SIMILAR TO FLEXIBLE RATE CASE FOR THIS PART AND SET											
7.1	2.5	5	12	0.1154	0.1890	21	1.087	1.000	1.087	1.060	1.000	1.060	35.8	20.0	35.8	-0.262	C010
7.2	2.5	5	12	0.0997	0.1719	27	1.087	1.000	1.062	1.060	1.000	1.051	29.4	20.0	29.4	-0.131	1001[c]

SIMULATION OF EXCHANGE REGIMES, JOB 2.00 COVERING 10 YEARS
THIS IS PART 4 OF 4, SET 1 OF 2. BEGIN EXCHANGE REGIME 1

REG	BAND	SIZE GLDE	FREQ GLDE	RMSQDV EX VOL	RMSQDV BP SUR	NUM CH PARITY	PARITY DATA MAXIM	PARITY DATA MINIM	PARITY DATA FINAL	MKT RATE DATA MAXIM	MKT RATE DATA MINIM	MKT RATE DATA FINAL	RESERVES DATA MAXIM	RESERVES DATA MINIM	RESERVES DATA FINAL	SPC PROP AT FEM	STAB CODE
1.0	2.5	5	0	0.0554	0.0	0	1.000	1.000	1.000	1.060	1.000	1.050	20.0	20.0	20.0	-0.072	0000
2.0	2.5	5	0	0.1876	0.1915	0	1.000	1.000	1.000	1.025	1.000	1.025	20.0	-2.3	-2.3	-0.018	0010
2.1	2.5	5	0	0.1023	0.0939	1	1.058	1.000	1.058	1.058	1.000	1.050	20.0	15.0	15.0	-0.072	0000
2.2	2.5	5	0	0.1023	0.0939	1	1.058	1.000	1.058	1.058	1.000	1.050	20.0	15.0	15.0	-0.072	0000
3.0	2.5	5	12	0.0533	0.0240	78	1.049	1.000	1.049	1.053	1.000	1.050	20.0	19.5	19.5	-0.073	0000
3.1	2.5	5	12	0.0546	0.0070	8	1.033	1.000	1.033	1.059	1.000	1.050	20.0	19.9	19.9	-0.072	0000
3.2	2.5	5	12				SIMILAR TO FLEXIBLE RATE CASE FOR THIS PART AND SET										
4.0	2.5	5	12	0.0668	0.0501	85	1.049	1.000	1.049	1.052	1.000	1.050	20.0	18.0	18.0	-0.073	0000
4.1	2.5	5	12	0.0647	0.0530	9	1.037	1.000	1.037	1.054	1.000	1.050	20.0	18.6	18.6	-0.073	0000
4.2	2.5	5	12	0.0794	0.0753	8	1.033	1.000	1.033	1.052	1.000	1.050	20.0	16.7	16.7	-0.073	0000
5.0	2.5	5	12	0.1072	0.1030	102	1.100	1.000	1.099	1.072	1.000	1.072	20.6	16.1	20.6	-0.151	1111
5.1	2.5	5	12	0.0901	0.0804	19	1.079	1.000	1.079	1.058	1.000	1.052	20.0	16.6	18.0	-0.079	0010
5.2	2.5	5	12	0.1042	0.0987	21	1.087	1.000	1.087	1.061	1.000	1.060	21.4	16.6	21.4	-0.105	0010
6.0	2.5	5	12	0.0825	0.0723	68	1.021	1.000	1.021	1.047	1.000	1.047	20.0	13.7	13.7	-0.065	0010
6.1	2.5	5	12	0.1317	0.1318	2	1.008	1.000	1.008	1.034	1.000	1.034	20.0	5.1	5.1	-0.033	0010
6.2	2.5	5	12	0.0848	0.0820	6	1.025	1.000	1.025	1.051	1.000	1.050	20.0	14.5	14.5	-0.073	0000
7.0	2.5	5	12	0.0624	0.0448	41	1.022	1.000	1.022	1.047	1.000	1.047	20.0	16.2	16.2	-0.065	0010
7.1	2.5	5	12	0.0593	0.0347	8	1.033	1.000	1.033	1.059	1.000	1.050	20.0	19.6	19.6	-0.072	0000
7.2	2.5	5	12	0.0593	0.0347	12	1.033	1.000	1.033	1.059	1.000	1.050	20.0	19.6	19.6	-0.072	0000

SIMULATION OF EXCHANGE REGIMES, JOB 2.00 COVERING 10 YEARS
THIS IS PART 4 OF 4, SET 2 OF 2. BEGIN EXCHANGE REGIME 1

REG	BAND	SIZE GLDE	FREQ GLDE	RMSQDV EX VOL	RMSQDV BP SUR	NUM CH PARITY	PARITY DATA MAXIM	PARITY DATA MINIM	PARITY DATA FINAL	MKT RATE DATA MAXIM	MKT RATE DATA MINIM	MKT RATE DATA FINAL	RESERVES DATA MAXIM	RESERVES DATA MINIM	RESERVES DATA FINAL	SPC PROF AT FRM	STAB CODE
1.0	2.5	5	0	0.2654	0.0	0	1.000	1.000	1.000	1.015	1.000	1.014	20.0	20.0	20.0	-0.008	0001
2.0	2.5	5	0			IDENTICAL TO FLEXIBLE RATE CASE FOR THIS PART AND SET											
2.1	2.5	5	0			IDENTICAL TO FLEXIBLE RATE CASE FOR THIS PART AND SET											
2.2	2.5	5	0			IDENTICAL TO FLEXIBLE RATE CASE FOR THIS PART AND SET											
3.0	2.5	5	12	0.2293	0.1739	78	1.049	1.000	1.049	1.023	1.000	1.023	36.7	20.0	36.7	-0.128	0011
3.1	2.5	5	12			SIMILAR TO FLEXIBLE RATE CASE FOR THIS PART AND SET											
3.2	2.5	5	12	0.1984	0.2536	14	1.050	1.000	1.050	1.024	1.000	1.024	49.5	20.0	49.5	-0.024	0011
4.0	2.5	5	12			SIMILAR TO FLEXIBLE RATE CASE FOR THIS PART AND SET											
4.1	2.5	5	12			IDENTICAL TO FLEXIBLE RATE CASE FOR THIS PART AND SET											
4.2	2.5	5	12			IDENTICAL TO FLEXIBLE RATE CASE FOR THIS PART AND SET											
5.0	2.5	5	12			IDENTICAL TO FLEXIBLE RATE CASE FOR THIS PART AND SET											
5.1	2.5	5	12			IDENTICAL TO FLEXIBLE RATE CASE FOR THIS PART AND SET											
5.2	2.5	5	12			IDENTICAL TO FLEXIBLE RATE CASE FOR THIS PART AND SET											
6.0	2.5	5	12			IDENTICAL TO FLEXIBLE RATE CASE FOR THIS PART AND SET											
6.1	2.5	5	12			IDENTICAL TO FLEXIBLE RATE CASE FOR THIS PART AND SET											
6.2	2.5	5	12			IDENTICAL TO FLEXIBLE RATE CASE FOR THIS PART AND SET											
7.0	2.5	5	12	0.1594	0.6546	88	1.074	1.000	1.074	1.047	1.000	1.047	83.3	20.0	83.3	-0.563	0011
7.1	2.5	5	12	0.1289	1.0978	21	1.087	1.000	1.087	1.060	1.000	1.060	138.1	20.0	138.1	-0.372	0011
7.2	2.5	5	12	0.1152	0.9334	27	1.087	1.000	1.079	1.060	1.000	1.052	120.3	20.0	120.3	-0.190	1111

SIMULATION OF EXCHANGE REGIMES, JOB 2.10 COVERING 10 YEARS
THIS IS PART 2 OF 4, SET 1 OF 2. BEGIN EXCHANGE REGIME 1

REG	BAND	SIZE GLDE	FREQ GLDE	RMSQDV EX VOL	RMSQDV BP SUR	NUM CH PARITY	PARITY DATA MAXIM	PARITY DATA MINIM	PARITY DATA FINAL	MKT RATE DATA MAXIM	MKT RATE DATA MINIM	MKT RATE DATA FINAL	RESERVES DATA MAXIM	RESERVES DATA MINIM	RESERVES DATA FINAL	SPC PROF AT FRM	STAB CODE
1.0	2.5	5	0	0.0455	0.0	0	1.000	1.000	1.000	1.076	1.000	1.050	20.0	20.0	20.0	-0.031	0000
2.0	2.5	5	0	0.1828	0.2053	0	1.000	1.000	1.000	1.025	1.000	1.025	20.0	-4.4	-4.4	-0.0[illegible]4	0010
2.1	2.5	5	0	0.0713	0.1050	1	1.057	1.000	1.057	1.057	1.000	1.050	20.0	14.9	14.9	0.023	0000
2.2	2.5	5	0	0.0713	0.1050	1	1.053	1.000	1.053	1.057	1.000	1.050	20.0	14.9	14.9	0.023	0000
3.0	2.5	5	12	0.0220	0.0632	78	1.049	1.000	1.049	1.052	1.000	1.050	20.0	17.7	17.7	-0.002	0000
3.1	2.5	5	12	0.0160	0.0356	8	1.033	1.000	1.033	1.059	1.000	1.050	20.0	18.8	18.8	-0.019	0000
3.2	2.5	5	12	0.0441	0.0026	14	1.050	1.000	1.050	1.075	1.000	1.050	20.0	20.0	20.0	-0.031	0000
4.0	2.5	5	12	0.0366	0.0765	84	1.049	1.000	1.049	1.051	1.000	1.050	20.0	16.7	16.7	0.005	0000
4.1	2.5	5	12	0.0254	0.0694	8	1.033	1.000	1.033	1.052	1.000	1.050	20.0	17.5	17.5	0.0[illegible]3	0000
4.2	2.5	5	12	0.0526	0.0930	8	1.033	1.000	1.033	1.051	1.000	1.050	20.0	15.7	15.7	0.016	0000
5.0	2.5	5	12	0.1149	0.1362	109	1.104	1.000	1.092	1.076	1.000	1.064	23.3	15.6	23.3	0.010	1111
5.1	2.5	5	12	0.0654	0.1008	20	1.083	1.000	1.083	1.056	1.000	1.056	20.5	16.3	20.5	0.020	0010
5.2	2.5	5	12	0.0541	0.0928	19	1.079	1.000	1.079	1.055	1.000	1.052	20.0	16.3	17.6	0.021	0010
6.0	2.5	5	12	0.0491	0.0830	56	1.021	1.000	1.021	1.046	1.000	1.046	20.0	13.2	13.2	0.003	0010
6.1	2.5	5	12	0.0913	0.1162	3	1.012	1.000	1.012	1.038	1.000	1.038	20.0	7.1	7.1	-0.001	0010
6.2	2.5	5	12	0.0468	0.0837	6	1.025	1.000	1.025	1.051	1.000	1.050	20.0	15.0	15.0	0.005	0000
7.0	2.5	5	12	0.0562	0.0906	56	1.022	1.000	1.022	1.047	1.000	1.047	20.0	13.2	13.2	0.007	0010
7.1	2.5	5	12	0.0657	0.1007	8	1.033	1.000	1.033	1.055	1.000	1.050	20.0	15.3	15.3	0.021	0000
7.2	2.5	5	12	0.0610	0.0983	10	1.033	1.000	1.025	1.055	1.000	1.050	20.0	15.6	15.6	0.020	0000

SIMULATION OF EXCHANGE REGIMES, JCE 2.20 COVERING 10 YEARS
THIS IS PART 2 OF 4, SET 1 OF 2. BEGIN EXCHANGE REGIME 1

REG	BAND	SIZE GLDE	FREQ GLDE	RMSQDV EX VOL	RMSQDV BP SUR	NUM CH PARITY	PARITY DATA MAXIM	MINIM	FINAL	MKT RATE DATA MAXIM	MINIM	FINAL	RESERVES DATA MAXIM	MINIM	FINAL	SPC PROF AT FRM	STAB CODE
1.0	2.5	5	0	0.0371	0.0	0	1.000	1.000	1.000	1.065	1.000	1.050	20.0	20.0	20.0	-0.023	0000
2.0	2.5	5	0	0.1828	0.1988	0	1.000	1.000	1.000	1.025	1.000	1.025	20.0	-3.9	-3.9	-0.003	0010
2.1	2.5	5	0	0.0810	0.0967	1	1.060	1.000	1.060	1.061	1.000	1.050	20.0	14.8	14.8	0.016	0000
2.2	2.5	5	0	0.0810	0.0967	1	1.060	1.000	1.060	1.061	1.000	1.050	20.0	14.8	14.8	0.016	0000
3.0	2.5	5	12	0.0234	0.0539	78	1.049	1.000	1.049	1.054	1.000	1.050	20.0	18.3	18.3	0.007	0000
3.1	2.5	5	12	0.0129	0.0471	8	1.033	1.000	1.033	1.055	1.000	1.050	20.0	19.1	19.1	0.001	0000
3.2	2.5	5	12	0.0365	0.0019	14	1.050	1.000	1.050	1.064	1.000	1.050	20.0	20.0	20.0	-0.023	0000
4.0	2.5	5	12	0.0298	0.0578	83	1.049	1.000	1.049	1.053	1.000	1.050	20.0	17.8	17.8	0.007	0000
4.1	2.5	5	12	0.0226	0.0637	9	1.037	1.000	1.037	1.055	1.000	1.050	20.0	18.3	18.3	0.009	0000
4.2	2.5	5	12	0.0474	0.0800	8	1.033	1.000	1.033	1.052	1.000	1.050	20.0	16.5	16.5	0.015	0000
5.0	2.5	5	12	0.0956	0.1113	111	1.100	1.000	1.096	1.072	1.000	1.069	21.9	16.1	21.9	0.004	1111
5.1	2.5	5	12	0.0624	0.0830	19	1.079	1.000	1.079	1.061	1.000	1.052	20.0	16.6	18.3	0.016	0010
5.2	2.5	5	12	0.0844	0.1010	21	1.087	1.000	1.087	1.061	1.000	1.060	22.1	16.6	22.1	0.014	0010
6.0	2.5	5	12	0.0540	0.0758	67	1.021	1.000	1.021	1.047	1.000	1.047	20.0	13.4	13.4	0.008	0010
6.1	2.5	5	12	0.1203	0.1375	2	1.008	1.000	1.008	1.034	1.000	1.034	20.0	4.1	4.1	0.001	0010
6.2	2.5	5	12	0.0569	0.0847	6	1.025	1.000	1.025	1.051	1.000	1.050	20.0	14.5	14.5	0.009	0000
7.0	2.5	5	12	0.0630	0.0839	57	1.022	1.000	1.022	1.047	1.000	1.047	20.0	13.2	13.2	0.012	0010
7.1	2.5	5	12	0.0685	0.0859	9	1.037	1.000	1.037	1.061	1.000	1.050	20.0	16.0	16.0	0.016	0000
7.2	2.5	5	12	0.0637	0.0847	13	1.033	1.000	1.029	1.059	1.000	1.050	20.0	16.2	16.2	0.016	0000

SIMULATION OF EXCHANGE REGIMES, JCE 2.30 COVERING 10 YEARS
THIS IS PART 2 OF 4, SET 1 OF 2. BEGIN EXCHANGE REGIME 1

REG	BAND	SIZE GLDE	FREQ GLDE	RMSQDV EX VOL	RMSQDV BP SUR	NUM CH PARITY	PARITY DATA MAXIM	MINIM	FINAL	MKT RATE DATA MAXIM	MINIM	FINAL	RESERVES DATA MAXIM	MINIM	FINAL	SPC PROF AT FRE	STAB CODE
1.0	2.5	5	0	0.0375	0.0	0	1.000	1.000	1.000	1.067	1.000	1.050	20.0	20.0	20.0	-0.041	0000
2.0	2.5	5	0	0.1831	0.2392	0	1.000	1.000	1.000	1.025	1.000	1.025	20.0	-6.0	-6.0	-0.005	0010
2.1	2.5	5	0	0.0616	0.1531	1	1.045	1.000	1.045	1.050	1.000	1.050	20.0	14.9	14.9	0.031	0000
2.2	2.5	5	0	0.0616	0.1531	1	1.044	1.000	1.044	1.050	1.000	1.050	20.0	14.9	14.9	0.031	0000
3.0	2.5	5	12	0.0253	0.0985	78	1.049	1.000	1.049	1.050	1.000	1.050	20.0	17.2	17.2	0.001	0000
3.1	2.5	5	12	0.0190	0.0587	8	1.033	1.000	1.033	1.057	1.000	1.050	20.0	18.9	18.9	-0.034	0000
3.2	2.5	5	12	SIMILAR TO FLEXIBLE RATE CASE FOR THIS PART AND SET													
4.0	2.5	5	12	0.0408	0.1204	86	1.049	1.000	1.049	1.050	1.000	1.050	20.0	16.2	16.2	0.017	0000
4.1	2.5	5	12	0.0343	0.1348	8	1.033	1.000	1.033	1.050	1.000	1.050	20.0	16.7	16.7	0.017	0000
4.2	2.5	5	12	0.0595	0.1531	8	1.033	1.000	1.033	1.050	1.000	1.050	20.0	14.7	14.7	0.031	0000
5.0	2.5	5	12	0.0888	0.1577	108	1.096	1.000	1.086	1.069	1.000	1.059	22.1	15.8	22.1	0.021	1111
5.1	2.5	5	12	0.0795	0.1673	30	1.087	1.000	1.050	1.061	1.000	1.054	23.1	16.1	23.1	0.030	1111
5.2	2.5	5	12	0.0795	0.1673	30	1.087	1.000	1.050	1.061	1.000	1.054	23.1	16.1	23.1	0.030	1111
6.0	2.5	5	12	0.0417	0.1387	35	1.022	1.000	1.022	1.047	1.000	1.047	20.0	13.8	13.8	0.009	0010
6.1	2.5	5	12	0.0933	0.1671	3	1.012	1.000	1.012	1.038	1.000	1.038	20.0	6.1	6.1	0.010	0010
6.2	2.5	5	12	0.0529	0.1464	6	1.025	1.000	1.025	1.050	1.000	1.050	20.0	14.3	14.3	0.019	0000
7.0	2.5	5	12	0.0552	0.1298	55	1.022	1.000	1.022	1.047	1.000	1.047	20.0	13.0	13.0	0.016	0010
7.1	2.5	5	12	0.0732	0.1584	9	1.037	1.000	1.037	1.050	1.000	1.050	20.0	13.9	13.9	0.031	0000
7.2	2.5	5	12	0.0676	0.1563	8	1.033	1.000	1.033	1.050	1.000	1.050	20.0	14.3	14.3	0.031	0000

References

Baumol, W. J., 1957, Speculation, profitability, and stability, Review of Economics and Statistics, Aug.

Bergsten, C. F., 1972, Reforming the dollar (Council on Foreign Relations, Washington, D.C.).

Black, S. W., 1972, The use of rational expectations in models of speculation, Review of Economics and Statistics, May.

Cooper, R. N., 1970, Sliding parities: A proposal for presumptive rules, in: G. N. Halm, ed., Approaches to greater flexibility of exchange rates (Princeton University Press, Princeton, N.J.).

Friedman, M., 1950, Essays in positive economics (University of Chicago Press, Chicago, Ill.) pp. 157–203.

Halm, G. N., 1970, Toward limited flexibility of exchange rates, in: G. N. Halm, ed., Approaches to greater flexibility of exchange rates (Princeton University Press, Princeton, N.J.).

Hinshaw, R., ed., 1971, The economics of international adjustment (The Johns Hopkins Press, Baltimore, Md.).

Kenen, P. B., 1974, Alternative rules for changing exchange rates: The model, program, and selected solutions, International Finance Section Working Papers in International Economics, G-74-01 (Princeton University, Princeton, N.J.).

Kenen, P. B., 1975, Floats, glides and indicators: A comparison of methods for changing exchange rates, Journal of International Economics, May.

Modigliani, F. and P. B. Kenen, 1966, A suggestion for solving the international liquidity problem, Banca Nazionale del Lavoro Quarterly Review, March.

Murphy, J. C., 1965, Moderated exchange rate variability, National Banking Review, Dec.

Sacchetti, U., 1972, Mechanico-discretionary tools for parity changes, Banca Nationale del Lavoro Quarterly Review, Dec.

Sohmen, E., 1961, Flexible exchange rates (University of Chicago Press, Chicago, Ill.).

Telser, L. G., 1959, A theory of speculation relating profitability and stability, Review of Economics and Statistics, Aug.

Underwood, T. G., 1973, Analysis of proposals for using objective indicators as a guide to exchange rate changes, International Monetary Fund Staff Papers, March.

United States Treasury, 1973, The U.S. proposals for using reserves as an indicator of the need for balance-of-payments adjustment, reprinted in: Economic Report of the President (Washington, D.C.).

Chapter 6.2

COMMENT ON KENEN

Francis WOEHRLING

Professor Kenen has started in a large-scale project aimed at simulating the exchange markets and at using these simulations to evaluate various alternative exchange-rate regimes that have been proposed as part of the Reformed International Monetary System. This is an ambitious, pioneering and most welcome study. We are privileged to attend and, I hope, to assist the first steps of his youngest brain-child!

I must however add that we have here only a very small excerpt of the complete study and that it is therefore difficult to appreciate exactly all the facets of the paper submitted to our attention. I shall limit my comments to examining whether Professor Kenen's *model* is satisfactory on theoretical grounds or whether, as I believe, it requires the addition of an essential element.

Before investigating the theoretical structure of the model, I would however like to point out that the work is still entirely aprioristic and that its validity is, therefore, limited: Professor Kenen makes assumptions concerning some possible patterns of speculative behaviour. Many more patterns could be imagined and an even greater number of variants of the model could be simulated. As there are no empirical inputs, the many computer runs can offer interesting results but cannot carry the conviction that one exchange regime will, *in practice*, be superior to another. At this stage of the work, the experiment can only test the logical consistency of the human mind reflecting on the exchange-rate regime – a test which is indeed important and useful – but it does not "*test*" the realism of the model. Because of this, the correlation coefficients derived in the paper under review are of a special nature: they are indicators of consistency between various features of intellectual constructions.

The Main Features of the Model

The model simulates the exchange market for a currency without specifying, even by proxy, its economic environment: the domestic economy and the "rest of the world" are not represented. The model consists therefore of only a single foreign sector comprising:

(a) *A trade sector* with exporters and importers whose reaction to an exogenous price disturbance is lagged. The lag produces a typical, "*J*"-curve type deficit or surplus but, in the long run, the current account is, *in principle*, always in equilibrium since exports and imports are assumed, in the computer runs used in the study under review, to be of unitary elasticity.

(b) *A speculators' sector.* The speculators' behaviour is also lagged but less than that of the traders; the speculators' function in the model is to supply the traders with extra foreign exchange and thus to bridge the "*J*"-curve type gap in payments for imports and exports. (Technically, the speculators obtain this foreign exchange by engaging in borrowing and lending.)

Traders are always lagged more than speculators.

One feature appears to be crucial for the model: because traders' responses are lagged, everything hinges on speculation. If "correct", speculation will supply the amount of foreign exchange that will produce an equilibrium rate; if inadequate it will *impose* a rate that will lead the system to cumulative imbalances (even though the basic data of the trade sector – the elasticities – are potent factors of equilibrium). This feature can be considered at two levels: first, for the functioning of the model, the speculators' reaction is the crucial element. Secondly, however, and more important for the economic *theory* that appears to underpin the model, the speculators' behaviour is a money supply mechanism: the speculators' function is to provide the traders with foreign exchange to bridge the "gap" between receipts and expenditures (Kenen, section 2).

I shall examine the implications of this "theoretical structure" after having taken a look at the model's treatment of the financial and monetary sectors.

The Financial and Monetary Sector

The absence of any financial sector should come as a shock to those conversant with the conventional interpretation of contemporary speculative crises. In this interpretation the development of the international money and capital markets is considered to be a major cause of these crises for two reasons:

(a) Liquid capital plays a *permissive* role: the larger the stock of financial assets, the larger the possible speculation. It is indeed believed that speculation depends to a great extent on (i) the availability of money and finance denominated in the currency under attack (assets which can easily be *mobilized for* speculation), (ii) the availability of financial assets denominated in the appreciating currency (assets *in which* the speculators can temporarily invest their funds).

(b) Liquid capital plays a *causative* role: shifts may occur in the demand for the money(s) of one or more countries independently of changes in the trade account.[1] These shifts – which can be prompted by *economic* factors as well as by psycho-political ones – can create a disequilibrium in the balance of payments no less than an exogenous change in prices.

Many people believe, indeed, that the Bretton Woods system broke down, largely because it could not cope with the increasing masses of financial assets that had developed within this system.

The neglect of this aspect of the real world could be considered to be no more than a paradox (and it is paradoxical indeed to present, to a gathering of monetarists, a paper on speculation that does not emphasize the financial sectors). However, this paradox may well *not* be the result of a simplification, that does away with useless refinements, but of an unresolved difficulty of the model: to wit the absence of a clearly specified money supply and demand function *even though* "money", i.e., foreign exchange, is at the same time a key explanatory variable in the model.

The Theory Behind the Role of "Speculation"

The function of the speculators is to provide temporary foreign exchange to the traders and thus enable them to bridge an imbalance between payments and receipts (in foreign exchange) until equilibrium is restored. Then the speculators can again leave the scene.

If this speculation provides an adequate amount of foreign exchange, the system will return to equilibrium; if the amount is inadequate, the speculators will set a disequilibrium rate.

The "theoretical structure" of Professor Kenen's model thus appears to be a straightforward classical monetary model: money (in this model: foreign exchange) is a short-term phenomenon used to bridge a discrepancy. In the long run, money disappears again. Yet, as in early explanations of the business

[1]Autonomous shifts in the demand for other financial assets independent of changes in the current account, are not mentioned here because Professor Kenen's model could be expanded to include long-term capital flows in his "trade" sector.

cycle, the equilibrium or disequilibrium depends entirely on the money (or foreign exchange) supply.

Although, the model appears to be a "real" disequilibrium model (exogenous disturbances in the trading sector), it is in fact one of purely monetary disequilibrium.

Professor Kenen endeavours to examine speculative patterns – and succeeds in doing so – but from the vantage point of theory, these speculative patterns fulfil also the role of a money supply.

Two questions arise: first, at the level of model building, is it possible to consider speculative behaviour in abstraction from monetary conditions? In other words, can we assume that *money supply to speculators* is unlimited? Can we further assume that the speculators' demand for speculative balances (which in turn is the speculators' supply of foreign exchange to the traders) is entirely or primarily a function of speculative psychology. In other words, can we assume that, up to a point (stock variant of the model) or indefinitely (flow variant), the *speculators' demand for money* (i.e., for long or short positions), also is unlimited!

Second, and more fundamentally, what is the kind of monetary theory used by the model? What is the role and nature of "foreign exchange". What is the link between monetary and real variables?

"Money" Supply and Demand Functions in the Model

Let us now examine the model on my assumption that speculation is the model's money supply "policy". Are the mechanisms through which the speculators supply foreign exchange to the traders properly specified, that is (i) what is the demand function for speculative balances and (ii) how does the system supply money to speculators?

To answer the second question first: foreign exchange is a free good in this system; available at zero cost to whatever extent it is demanded by speculators.

Speculators' demand for money (which is the money supply function for the trade sector) is constructed in two ways:

(a) *In the flow case*, this demand is a function exclusively of the behaviour of speculators: when a discrepancy appears between traders' demand and supply of foreign currencies, the speculators rush in to balance the foreign exchange market (at some level consistent with their expectations). This is not really a demand function; to transform the actual mechanism into a genuine economic function, account should be taken of other investment possibilities for "foreign exchange"; it would then be possible to construct a less rigid demand for speculative funds. For example, funds available for speculation would *increase* as speculation becomes *more* profitable and decrease as other investment opportunities become *more* attractive. Similarly, as funds rush into speculation its profitability would decline and other investment opportunities would become more appealing.

(b) *In the stock case*, the demand is a function of speculators' opinions [as in above (a)] but also of the scalar S that *limits* this demand to a multiple of foreign trade. This scalar is a very rudimentary demand or function indeed. Why should foreign exchange, i.e., *private reserves*, be a multiple of trade? Is this not the old quantitativist theory ($m = v \cdot y$) coming back in disguise?

In answer to these observations, Professor Kenen could reply that he endeavoured exclusively to examine speculative behaviour, mainly that which would underly various proposed exchange-rate systems, and that he did not seek to examine the effects of monetary policy. Yet the question must be raised whether monetary conditions are not a crucial determinant of such behaviour and it must be noted that while all important aspects of the *real* sectors, domestic and foreign, can be incorporated in the model (at least under the form of a proxy such as the elasticities of imports and exports, so that the trade sector of the model is complete), this does not seem to be the case for the monetary sector. It therefore appears necessary for the monetary conditions to be explicitly included, so that the monetary side can also be formally complete. Incidentally, it may be for this reason that the model performs better when there is even a rudimentary proxy of money supply, as is the case in the stock variants.

Conclusion

It is disturbing that we are confronted with a model whose "theoretical structure" predicates, as it seems to me, its results on the adequacy of the supply of foreign exchange, yet does not explicitly include a supply function for money. This is the more remarkable for the model being basically realistic: at a useful level of abstraction it is probably correct to view traders as lagging behind speculators. Speculators are, therefore, foreign exchange suppliers. But the very excellence of this abstraction raises in my opinion two questions and not one. Viz the questions of (a) speculative behaviour, and (b) monetary conditions.

Professor Kenen has asked a correct question: if there is a disturbance in the real sector (1) how will it be bridged by foreign exchange (i.e., financed through private reserves) and (2) how will adjustment occur? However his answer is incomplete: in the model adjustment and finance are "*regulated*" exclusively by speculation. Actually, adjustment and finance are regulated by a more complex interplay of speculation and monetary policy,[2] or, at least, of speculation and prevailing monetary conditions.

It may be legitimate to raise, *in fine*, a more general question: is it possible that this oblivion of monetary policy and of the financial environment stems from an implicit and unconscious bias in the analysis: the view that adjustment is mainly a matter of exchange markets, of altering the exchange rates, while changes in the *domestic* (monetary) conditions is a less important adjustment instrument. This is perhaps correct in a very large economy where the foreign sector is small and where the supply of speculative funds is indeed practically infinite. But this is, at best, a special case.

[2]The mechanistic pegging of the exchange rate divorced from the liquidity impact of this pegging cannot be considered an acceptable proxy for monetary policy.

Chapter 6.3

SUMMARY OF THE DISCUSSION ON KENEN

Milton FRIEDMAN, *Chairman*

In replying to Francis Woehrling, *Peter Kenen* emphasized that the equilibrium rate of exchange of his model is entirely determined by the trade account. The fact that the Marshall–Lerner condition is equal to unity in the long run does not mean that speculation determines the equilibrium rate. If for instance speculators overvalue the exchange rate, this fact is due to the dynamic movement of the system within a ten-years interval and to the possibility of an explosive evolution. On the other hand, Kenen pointed out that his model concerns only an exchange-market model in which there is no specified demand function for money. Furthermore, he recognized a defect of his model mentioned by *Wolfgang Stützel* and *Jacques Rueff* that speculators commit their funds to speculation on the foreign-exchange market without any regard to the opportunity cost in terms of the interest rate; or, in other terms, he assumes that the cost of borrowing the home or foreign currency is the same and that the (identical) interest rate in both countries is invariant with respect to speculation.

Manfred Willms raised the question of stability with respect to the gliding-parity system. If changes in the exchange rate are related to the trade account or to a certain level of reserves, speculation could always be profitable, but also lend to an unstable system unless the data on the trade account or on reserves are not published. *Peter Kenen* replied that he assumes that the speculators do not gamble against the system itself and that they do not know the rules very well. He agreed that one of the major faults of the gliding-parity proposals consists of giving to the speculator a perfectly certain gamble unless one introduces a stochastic element into the process or that one has to make the changes in the exchange rate so small that it is not worthwhile to speculate.

William Branson suggested a substantial improvement of Kenen's result (to which the author subscribed completely) if he applied the concept of "integral and differential stabilizers" as it had been developed with respect to internal stabilization policy by E. M. Phillips in a series of articles in the Economic Journal during the 50's. For Kenen's case of a reserve indicator the exchange rate moves when reserves being away from their target level are around the indicator level. To the extent that reserves oscillate around the target level, they will not turn back to it and it is conceivable that reserves overshoot their target level with the consequence of a stability problem associated with the "integral stabilizer rule". If one uses instead the "differential stabilizer" consisting of the balance of payments as an indicator, the change in the exchange rate will not be any longer a function of reserves but a function of a certain state of the balance of payments. If reserves are away from their target level and the exchange rate changes according to the balance-of-payments indicator, the latter will be zero and the reserves will not get back to their target level and remain where they were at the moment of the change in the exchange rate; using an adequate combination of the two stabilization rules in terms of a reserve-plus-balance-of-payments indicator could guarantee an efficient realization of the target level.

PART III

Balance-of-Payments Adjustment and Portfolio Theory

Chapter 7.1

BALANCE-OF-PAYMENTS ADJUSTMENT AND PORTFOLIO THEORY: A SURVEY*

Johan MYHRMAN

1. Introduction

This paper covers a broad field with many threads going far back in history. It is surprising how much understanding there was of the international payments system and its functions by authors such as Hume, Ricardo, Thornton and John Stuart Mill. It is even more amazing, though, how so many of these earlier insights could be forgotten for such a long time. It was not until what I have called the Mundell–Johnson epoch in the 1960's that an understanding of the international *monetary* system was once again reached.[1] What remained to be done then and what is being done now is to build models that account for many assets in an increasingly, but perhaps not yet completely, integrated international credit and goods market. The important and difficult future task of designing short-run adjustment models is left to the next generation.

My aim has been to follow the broad lines in the development up to the late 1960's and to report on the results shown by them. Following this there is a more detailed study of most of the contributions in recent years. In these later studies I have tried to give a glimpse of the typical features of the model construction and the main conclusions. It has been my ambition to simplify and to bring forth the important aspects of these models. For this reason I have

*The author has received numerous valuable comments on an earlier draft from Harry G. Johnson and Alexander K. Swoboda and has benefited from discussions with Peter B. Kenen and Michael Parkin. This version is, however, the sole responsibility of the author.

[1]This is to some extent an overstatement. In The Netherlands there existed a "modified" quantity theory approach to macroeconomic equilibrium even during the heyday of Keynesian economics. In this approach the monetary aspects of balance-of-payments problems were often recognized, or at least were implicit in many writings. Due to their publication in Dutch, most of these writings never reached out to the Anglo-Saxon scientific world. Now there are two summaries of the Dutch literature available in English [de Jong (1973) and Holtrop (1972)]. However, the Dutch tradition seems to have influenced work in this field outside The Netherlands through another channel, namely the early work carried out by The International Monetary Fund under J. J. Polak [see Polak (1957/8) and Prais (1960/1)].

written a special section to compare many of the models and to show their similarities and differences. It has not been possible to consider the problems of growth and devaluation and their effects on the balance of payments.

2. Theoretical Background

In the 19th century classical and neoclassical theory dominated most parts of economic theory, and perhaps the strongest influence was in the theory of the balance of payments. For more than a hundred years it was thought that the monetary system operated in such a way that a country's balance of payments always automatically tended to adjust to an equilibrium situation. One way in which an adjustment can take place is through a change in the exchange rate. During this period most countries had adopted the gold standard with fixed exchange rates. The process of adjustment under this system is described in the following way by John Stuart Mill (ch. XXI, pp. 415–416):

> "When, therefore, the state of prices is such that the equation of international demand cannot establish itself, the country requiring more imports than can be paid for by her exports, it is a sign that the country has more of the precious metals or their substitutes, in circulation, than can permanently circulate, and must necessarily part with some of them before the balance can be restored. Her currency is accordingly contracted: prices fall, and among the rest, the prices of exportable articles; for which, accordingly, there arises, in foreign countries, a greater demand: while imported commodities have possibly risen in price, from the influx of money into foreign countries, and at all events have not participated in the general fall. But until the increased cheapness of English goods induces foreign countries to take a greater pecuniary value, or until the increased dearness (positive or comparative) of foreign goods makes England take less pecuniary value, the exports of England will be no nearer to paying for her imports than before, and the stream of the precious metals which had begun to flow out of England, will still flow on. This efflux will continue, until the fall of prices in England brings within reach of the foreign market some commodity which England did not previously send thither; or until the reduced price of the things which she did send has forced a demand abroad for a sufficient quantity to pay for the imports, aided, perhaps, by a reduction of the English demand for foreign goods, from their enhanced price, either positive or comparative.
>
> Now this is the very process which took place on our original suppposi-

tion of barter. Not only, therefore, does the trade between nations tend to the same equilibrium between exports and imports, whether money is employed or not, but the means by which this equilibrium is established are essentially the same."

We note here the following characteristics: the identification of price level and terms of trade change, emphasis on the fact that money does not change a barter economy, the essentially monetary character of the disturbance, and of the adjustment process and the automatic adjustment to equilibrium. "The trade is in a state like that which is called in mechanics a condition of stable equilibrium."[2] We also note that there is no mention of what happens to output and employment. This can be interpreted as an implicit assumption about very flexible prices and wages, which is probably the most common interpretation. However, it is also possible to think of the description as a statement of more long-run comparative static equilibrium conditions. In this case, the interpretation is that even if the prices are not very flexible in the immediate short run, money supply and prices must change if a stable equilibrium is going to be reached in the longer run.

The automaticity was reached in two ways: the first being the reserve or gold outflow and the second the tying of the domestic money supply to the gold reserves.

Many empirical studies in the interwar period revealed the fact that there were surprisingly few gold movements under the gold standard regime. This led many economists to doubt the classical theory and even a specialist like F. W. Taussig was very disturbed by findings of this kind, according to Metzler (1948). It is rather surprising that they seem to have missed one part of the functioning of the gold standard – the exchange rates, which were not completely fixed, but could move between the gold points. This meant that if the imbalance was expected to be rather temporary or if it was of a seasonal character, short-term credits and stabilizing speculation held back the increase in the foreign exchange rate and prevented gold movements. This is recognized by Mill (ch. XX, p. 414):

> "Disturbances, therefore, of the equilibrium of imports and exports, and consequent disturbances of the exchange, may be considered as of two classes: the one causal or accidental, which if not on too large a scale, correct themselves through the premium on bills, without any transmission of the precious metals . . ."

[2]Mill (ch. XXI, p. 415).

This reason for the lack of gold movements may be of small importance compared to another explanation, the income–employment mechanism. Just as the Keynesian revolution completely changed the monetary and macro theories of the closed economy and disregarded price adjustment to a large extent, it also introduced a fundamentally different view of the balance-of-payments adjustment problem. This view was not developed by Keynes himself but by Roy Harrod (1939) and Joan Robinson (1949). This new theory was essentially the export multiplier case of modern textbooks. An increase in the exports from country A leads to a multiplier increase in national income in A and thereby to increased total demand and employment and to an induced increase in imports. The latter balances the export increase and tends to even out the export surplus.

The main adjustment mechanisms in the classical system, the monetary changes and the price level changes, have been discarded and the balance-of-payments adjustment problem is reduced to the achievement of equilibrium in the balance of trade in an economy with fixed wages and prices. This model has held a great popularity for a very long time with the policy-makers and planners as evidenced by e.g., the "full employment b.o.p. deficit"-concept. Parallel to this and even overshadowing it is the popular use of different elasticities in discussing the effects of devaluation. This approach was most popular in the 1940's, but it continued to be used for a long time before it became clear to most economists that too much of it was in partial equilibrium terms. Even more serious is that the elasticity model is a real model, which fails to account for the existence of money and credit and the capital balance, and consequently fails to face the problem of balance-of-payments adjustment as distinguished from balance-of-trade adjustments.

Meade (1951a) was the first to really try to work out some kind of integration of general equilibrium theory and the neo-Keynesian approach.[3] A very complicated exposition reduced the number of readers and, as it appeared at a time when monetary theory was just going to take a step forward, reduced the direct impact of Meade's theories.[4] Perhaps an important influence of this work is through its direct effect via Robert Mundell. It must also be remembered that Meade was the first one to construct a formal macromodel for an open economy, a very important step in the development in this field of economics [Meade (1951b)].

Another contribution in the early 1950's linked the concept of absorption to the formulation of macroeconomic problems in open economies. Sidney

[3]See also Harberger (1950), Laursen and Metzler (1950).

[4]Meade's assumption of pegging the interest rate as a "neutral monetary policy" made his work less attractive.

Alexander (1952) analyzed the problem of the effects of devaluation on the trade balance by concentrating on the effects on real expenditures and real income. He defined an aggregate market for commodities as

$$Y = C + I + X, \tag{1}$$

$$C + I = A, \tag{2}$$

$$X = Y - A, \tag{3}$$

where Y = real income, X = trade balance or net exports, C = consumption, I = investment, and A = absorption.

By formulating the problem in this way he clearly saw that a devaluation has a positive effect only if it increases income more than absorption.

However, Alexander's article is also the first formulation of the commodity market equation in aggregate form in the way that it has been used in many models since then. Alexander was aware of the oversimplification of his model, and in verbal comments he discussed some extensions.

It may be correct to say that Alexander saw the aggregate macro-aspects of the problem, but it was still the simplest type of income–expenditure model, with concentration on the trade balance. It was left to someone well-versed in monetary theory to take the next step: it was time for a Harry G. Johnson. In an important article from 1958, Johnson (1969) sets out to "synthesize and generalize". However, the article is much more than this. Its highest value probably lies in the clear recognition that the balance-of-payments problem is fundamentally a monetary problem, which had been neglected by most economists for more than twenty years. This insight anticipates the work of the next decade by himself and Robert Mundell. Johnson (1969) states:

> "... the formulation of the balance of payments as the difference between aggregate receipts and payments, rather than receipts and payments on international account only, has two major advantages. It brings out the essentially monetary nature of a deficit, which must be accompanied by dishoarding of domestic money or credit creation; and it relates the deficit to the operation of the economy as a whole."

3. The Mundell–Johnson Epoch

During the classical period, writings by Ricardo, Thornton and Mill revealed a remarkable insight into the workings of the international payments system and the problem of internal and external balance in a world economy. The main defect with the classical and the neo-classical analysis was a tendency to concentrate on the equilibrium solutions and to neglect what happened during the adjustment process. This could be one of the reasons that led some central banks to adopt a very crude form of policy. In the second half of the 19th century the Swedish central bank, for instance, had no reserves to mention and no discount rate mechanism. Therefore, when there was a gold outflow the central bank cut down on all its outstanding loans, causing a very abrupt and disastrous deflation.

The interwar period was characterized by a great bewilderment in international monetary relations with floating exchange rates, fixed exchange rates, competing devaluations and exchange controls. At the same time the Keynesian revolution took place and, as often is the case, led to an overreaction among the converted in relegating classical economics into doctrinal history. Unfortunately, Keynes presented his new ideas for a closed economy at this time. Perhaps even more disastrous for the field of international macroeconomics was the strong impact that Keynesian ideas in the Hicks–Hansen formulation had in the U.S. For several reasons, research in economics came to be completely dominated by the work in the U.S. Because the U.S. economy to a large extent approximates a closed economy it was natural that the work on macroeconomic problem was concentrated on closed economy models.

This development meant that the insights and understanding of the classical economists was more or less forgotten for about three decades and had to be rediscovered. The rediscovery was made by Robert Mundell (1968) and Harry Johnson (1972b), who in a series of articles in the 1960's worked out most of the implications for macro-economics of being open economies. The brilliant presentation and the elegant simplification of Mundell's early articles and Harry Johnson's penetrating and illuminating expositions contributed to a great advance in this field. A close reading of the articles today gives the impression of an extraordinary knowledge of the working of the international payments system, especially seen as a system or a world economy, even if the models that were used could not handle some aspects of the problems.

The model that is used by Mundell and Harry Johnson is usually some variant of the ordinary *IS–LM* model but extended to an open economy. One of the important achievements is just this extension in a consistent way to an open economy. It must be emphasized at once, however, that much important knowledge is spread out in their work in the form of comments on the models or as exceptions and is not embedded in the formal model structure.

This is the first time that an aggregate model for an open economy with more than one asset is constructed[5] and its working carefully studied. Because there are two assets in the model that are substitutes we may also say that it is the first portfolio approach to the problem of macroeconomic equilibrium in open economies. [In a way this is not quite true since much of this is already incorporated in Meade (1951a, b), but for some reasons it seems as if its importance and its implications were not recognized until Mundell saw them.][6]

It took much of the 1960's to work out all the implications of this basic model and of different model specifications. The importance of really trying alternative specifications and investigating their effects on the results is often belittled as "technicalities". However, even small changes in the specification can result in important changes in the conclusions, as the treatment of capital mobility shows.

The basic model consists of the following equations:

$$Y = C(Y) + I(i) + X(Y, r), \tag{4}$$

$$\bar{M} = L(i, Y), \tag{5}$$

$$B = X(Y, r) + K(i, r), \tag{6}$$

where i = interest rate, r = exchange rate, $\bar{M}$ = the supply of money, L = the demand for money, B = the balance of payments, and K = net capital inflow.

This is essentially the *IS–LM* model of the closed economy with unemployment and constant wages and prices extended to the open economy in the simplest way. Equation (4) gives the equilibrium condition for the output market, equation (5) for the money market, and equation (6) is the balance-of-payments equation, which in a system of flexible exchange rates is the equilibrium condition for the market for foreign exchange. The country is assumed to be very small so that it cannot affect prices and incomes in the rest of the world.

The three equations are the core of this model type, and they can be solved for the equilibrium values of Y, i and r or B. By changing the specification of the model it is possible to handle many cases. As it now stands, it represents the extreme Keynesian case with fixed wages and fixed prices. With both prices and wages flexible, it is a classical model and with wages fixed and prices flexible, it is an intermediate case. It is also possible to work with different degrees of capital mobility, with or without sterilization policies, and so on. In a

[5]However, see also early attempts by Fleming (1962) and Vanek (1962, ch. 8).

[6]One problem at the time when Meade wrote was that the gold standard was very unpopular and that many of his significant ideas were in that section. In his main model he treats reserve flows as *flows*, not as stock adjustments, and this is one of the crucial new points in, e.g., Johnson (1969).

very clear and useful article Takayama (1969) has assembled all these cases [see also Takayama (1972)].

For the case of flexible exchange rates and the Keynesian assumption, both fiscal policy and monetary policy have positive effects on the level of real income and on employment. If we assume perfect capital mobility, the effect of fiscal policy becomes zero. This is due to the fact that when the interest rate is fixed and the money supply is constant, there is only one income level that can make the demand for money equal to the supply. An increase in government expenditure, therefore, cannot change this "equilibrium" income, but only lead to increased imports and an equal capital outflow.

In the classical case, both fiscal and monetary policy have positive effects on the price level. With perfect capital mobility fiscal policy has no effect and an increase in the money supply leads to a proportional increase in the price level.

Under fixed exchange rates, the balance of payments will not necessarily be balanced. In the Keynesian version of the model, both fiscal and monetary policy have positive effects on the level of income. If there is perfect capital mobility, then monetary policy has no effect on real income, because any change in the interest rate leads immediately to a capital inflow or outflow, adjusting the money supply in the hands of the public to its original level. If, on the other hand, there is complete sterilization by the central bank then the degree of capital mobility does not matter. The analogous conclusions will hold in the classical case. It should be noted that the stability conditions are important for some of these conclusions.

The general conclusion for this type of model is that the more mobile financial capital is, the less effective is fiscal policy under flexible exchange rates. In the limiting case of perfect capital mobility, fiscal policy has no effect under flexible exchange rates and monetary policy has no effect under fixed exchange rates in the absence of sterilization policy. This is also the conclusion reached by Mundell in his original article of 1963, where he also points out that in that case sterilization is not possible [Mundell (1968)].

The articles by Fleming (1962) and Mundell (1968) brought out the importance of the degree of capital mobility and it also led Mundell to formulate his "Principle of Effective Market Classification" and the Assignment Problem that are built on the idea of the differential impact of the two instruments.[7]

The results that have been described here have by now been re-confirmed by many authors. [See e.g. Krueger (1965), von Neuman-Whitman (1967), Helliwell (1969), Fratianni (1972), and Sohmen–Schneeweiss (1969b).] These

[7]This problem will not be discussed any more in this paper, since it is a little outside the main line of interest. See Swoboda (1972a) and Nyberg–Viotti (1974).

results can be said to be standard for this type of short-run aggregate macromodel. However, one more generalization has been made. In the second edition of Sohmen's book (1969b) and in two articles by Swoboda (1972b, 1973) it has been shown that monetary policy has no effect under fixed exchange rates on real income or the interest rate independent of the degree of capital mobility.

This striking result is reached by imposing the equilibrium condition that the rate of change of foreign exchange reserves has to be zero. In that case, this type of model is forced to an equilibrium with unchanged interest rate and real income. (See also below.)

Until now the analysis has been undertaken for a single "small" country, and the assumption has been that its activities cannot influence prices, interest rates and real income in the rest of the world. Mundell (1968) was the first to consider a model with two countries, or one country and the rest of the world. The result of this extension under the assumption of perfect capital mobility was that most of the earlier conclusions were still valid. The main differences were that an increase in government expenditures in one country raised its real income but could either raise or lower the real income of the other country under fixed exchange rates, whereas monetary policy raised income in both countries. Under flexible exchange rates fiscal policy has positive effects in both countries, whereas monetary expansion increases income at home and lowers it abroad.[8] These results seem contrary to the widespread conception that flexible exchange rates make economic policy in two countries independent of each other. As Mundell points out, this result holds only when there is no capital mobility. When such mobility is present we revert to interdependence.

This type of model but with full employment was earlier treated by Metzler (1968), but he never analyzed economic policy. Metzler's model has later been formalized in two articles by Holmes (1972a, b).

This work was continued under any degree of capital mobility by Swoboda and Dornbusch (1973) who find, like Mundell, that the effectiveness of monetary policy varies inversely with the size of the country:

> "Furthermore, if one country, say, the United States, is very large relative to any single foreign country, and if foreign countries do not act in concert, its economic policy will largely determine income and interest-rate trends in the rest of the world (this is of course one feature of the so-called dollar standard). Again, this conclusion holds irrespective of the degree of capital mobility although the latter plays a role in determining the speed with

[8]See also Roper (1971).

> which developments in the dominant country are transmitted to the rest of the world. Second, the model emphasises the importance of monetary factors in determining the impact of transfers and expenditure-switching policies on the level of world income and its distribution among countries. Finally, the concept of a 'natural distribution of specie' retains its importance even in a world of underemployment. This distribution does depend in general, it is true, on autonomous expenditure levels; however, the smaller the interest sensitivity of the demand for money the less the influence of exogenous changes in spending.
>
> The main point is simply that 'Hume's Law' with its monetary mechanism of payments adjustment holds in the face of unemployment and wage rigidities."

This quotation brings out some of the characteristics of the development described in this section. It was mentioned above that the monetary aspects of the balance-of-payments adjustment, after having been totally neglected, were brought into focus again by Harry Johnson in his 1958 article [Johnson (1969)]. During the following period the implications of introducing money in a small aggregate model for open economies was worked out by many scholars, but in particular by Mundell. The multiplier and elasticity models were found to be unsatisfactory. The basic structure of the models used was essentially the *IS–LM* model extended to an open economy.

Parallel to this model-technical development and partly also as a result of it, there was a growing interest in and understanding of the world economy as a system. Mundell and Johnson at an early stage came to the conclusion that most of the balance-of-payments disturbances were monetary disturbances, that the mechanism of adjustment is a monetary mechanism and that a successful working of the system as a whole required an understanding of the necessary "rules of the game" by the central banks (and the economists!). This has later been formulated in a "Monetary Theory of the Balance of Payments" [Johnson (1972b)].

4. Portfolio Balance Proper and Balance-of-Payments Adjustment

In the previous section it was described how money and securities were introduced into aggregate models for open economies in the beginning of the 1960's. Thereby portfolio decisions were also introduced in the form of a choice between money and bonds. Several years of work with this "Keynesian" model led to a growing dissatisfaction with many of its characteristics. Some of the defects could be removed by a respecification. One example is the change from using the interest rate as the monetary policy instrument to using the money supply and finally to using only the domestic component of the monetary base as the proper instrument of monetary control.

There is, however, a much more fundamental deficiency in this model. For the closed economy the *IS–LM* model can be regarded as including a short-run portfolio equilibrium. For the given stocks of money and government bonds the public can be regarded as adjusting until the interest rate and the real income have reached a level where the given stocks of money and bonds are willingly held. [As Mundell (1968) has pointed out, there is a logical fallacy involved here since real capital is growing with the rate of investment and therefore there cannot be any full portfolio equilibrium.] Extended to the open economy, this is the way in which the model was first interpreted. However, it was later recognized that the conditions for portfolio equilibrium were not fulfilled, because in the open economy the money stock is not constant, except under flexible exchange rates, and the stock of bonds is not constant unless there is no capital mobility whatsoever.

A full equilibrium – or portfolio equilibrium or stock–flow equilibrium, or whatever we choose to call it – requires (a) that all stocks are willingly held at the prevailing prices and incomes, and (b) that at these prices and incomes all stocks are constant. The first person to recognize and discuss some aspects of this problem seems to have been Harry Johnson (1969), but there was not any attempt to incorporate these ideas explicitly in the formal model structure until McKinnon and Oates (1966) did so. Let us illustrate the differences in the simplest possible way and start with a model of the type that is behind Mundell's article from 1963 [Mundell (1968)], where he assumes perfect capital mobility. We will apply this to a small country. We then have

$$E(Y, i_0) + X(Y, r_0) - Y = 0, \tag{7}$$

and

$$\bar{D} + R - L(i_0, Y) = 0, \tag{8}$$

where the supply of money has been divided into two components – $\bar{D}$, the exogenous part, which is under the control of the central bank, and R, foreign exchange reserves that are endogenous. To this a definition of the balance of payments can be added, but this is of little importance as long as there is no restriction on the values it can take. There are two equations describing equilibrium in three markets: the output market, the money market and the bond market. However, the two markets in (7) and (8) do not form a simultaneous system of equations. Instead, equation (7) forms a subsystem in which income, Y, is determined. Then, given Y and i_0, the demand for money is determined, and this in turn determines the amount of reserves for given $\bar{D}$.[9]

Assume now that there is less than perfect capital mobility. Then equations (7) and (8) simultaneously determine i and Y and there is equilibrium in this model. We call this a flow equilibrium. If the balance of payments is not zero, however, there will be an inflow of reserves and the money supply will change. There will be no stock equilibrium. This problem was recognized by many authors and it led them to assume it away, or to presume that the monetary authorities pursued a sterilization policy [see, e.g., von Neuman-Whitman (1967, pp. 14–15)].

A more satisfactory solution has been presented by Swoboda, who introduced the extra equilibrium condition that the balance of payments has to be zero for a full equilibrium. This extra condition is a stock equilibrium condition. This gives

$$E(Y, i) + X(Y, r_0) - Y = 0, \tag{9}$$

$$\bar{D} + R - L(i, Y) = 0, \tag{10}$$

$$B = X(Y, r_0) + K(i, r_0) = 0. \tag{11}$$

The system of equations is said to give full equilibrium; monetary policy has no effect on real income and interest rates even without perfect capital mobility. What Swoboda has done is to change the balance-of-payments definition to an equilibrium condition (for the market for foreign exchange). Since an open market purchase tends to lower the interest rate and to increase income, and since both of these work in the same direction on the balance of payments by leading to reserve losses, it follows that monetary policy has no effect except to change the amount of reserves.

Swoboda's formulation takes care of stock equilibrium in the money market. From equation (11) it is seen that a capital movement, $K(i)$, different from zero means that bonds are going in or out of the economy, which implies that there is not stock equilibrium in the bond market.

As mentioned earlier, McKinnon and Oates (1966) explicitly tried to formulate a model with portfolio equilibrium. They considered the case of a model with perfect capital mobility. The model then is

$$E(Y, W, i_0) + X(Y, i_0) - Y = 0, \tag{12}$$

$$X(Y, i_0) = 0, \tag{13}$$

[9]This illustrates Mundell's conclusion that monetary policy has no effect on income in this case. A change in $\bar{D}$, with Y and i_0 given, only changes R.

$$L(Y, W, i_0) - W = 0, \tag{14}$$

where W is the sum of money and bonds in the economy. One equation is dependent on the others and can be eliminated, thereby leaving two equations to determine Y and W. Equation (13) gives the essential difference from Mundell's model. It is now an equilibrium condition that the balance of trade is zero. In this way a portfolio equilibrium is assured in the sense that the net stocks of money and bonds in the private sector of the economy are not changing.

Mundell's conclusions still hold, but this is not so surprising because of the assumption of perfect capital mobility. McKinnon (1969) has extended the model to incorporate less than perfect capital mobility as well as to have real capital as a separate asset. The conclusions of these two studies can be summarized by the following quotation:

> "Therefore, one can conclude that the effectiveness of inside monetary policy in controlling exchange reserves (which may vary in response to exogenous shocks) is lessened by an increase in external capital immobility. However, the effectiveness of outside monetary policy in influencing exchange reserves is, surprisingly, independent of the degree of external capital mobility."[10]

These conclusions must, however, be regarded with some scepticism, since they are drawn from a very particular model specification. The output market is eliminated by Walras' Law; the market for real capital is recursive[11] to the rest of the model and therefore also eliminated.[12] The three remaining equations are used to solve for Y, i, and M. But exports are constant and imports are only a constant proportion of real income. Real income can therefore, by definition, never be changed by any policy measure under fixed exchange rates. Finally, McKinnon distinguishes between an inside monetary policy and an outside monetary policy, but when he draws his conclusions about the effects of these two policies he refers to a model without government. It is not possible,

[10]Inside monetary policy is defined as an open market operation, and outside monetary policy as a change in the stock of money without any change in the stock of bonds.

[11]It is recursive in the sense that real capital has no separate price in this model. Therefore, once Y and i are determined in the simultaneous part of the system, they can be put into the capital equation and the quantity of capital is determined. McKinnon therefore works with a subset of three equations out of the five he started with.

[12]This, however, is not correct either since real capital depends on the interest rate and output demand depends on real capital.

however, to change the money supply unless government expenditures are increased at the same time, when open market operations are ruled out.

Although Meade, Johnson, and Mundell were all aware of the stock–flow problems and commented upon them, Ott and Ott (1965, 1968), McKinnon and Oates (1966), McKinnon (1969) and Oates (1966) were the first to try to introduce portfolio equilibrium explicitly into their models. They chose to use a stock equilibrium constraint to describe and analyze the full, stationary equilibrium rather than to consider any dynamic aspects.

Later another approach to the problem of portfolio equilibrium in an open economy was developed by Branson (1968), Willet (1967) and Willet and Forte (1969). It was built on Tobin's theory of portfolio choice and it analyzed capital movements as either a stock adjustment, which was a once-and-for-all change, or as a result of different growth rates of the whole portfolio, in which case it could be continuous. This approach to capital movements has since been used extensively to study short-term capital movements but it has always been a partial equilibrium analysis since the rest of the economy is not dealt with.

In a series of articles John Floyd (1962a, b; 1972a, b) tackled the problem of incorporating these new ideas about capital movements and portfolio equilibrium into an aggregate macromodel. His model seemed to be different from Mundell's, and our task is therefore to try to explain what this difference is.

Floyd uses Canada as an example of a small country faced with perfect capital mobility. Instead of bonds he uses claims to real capital as the internationally traded asset. The value of these claims is a function of current output,

$$P_K \cdot \bar{K} = f(Y)/i, \tag{15}$$

where P_K is the price of capital assets. Only a fraction, Q, is held by Canadians. They hold no foreign securities. The demand for money is then written as

$$M^{\mathrm{D}} = f(i_0, QPK), \tag{16}$$

or

$$M^{\mathrm{D}} = g(i_0, Q, Y). \tag{17}$$

The whole model is then in our notations

$$E(Y, i_0) + X(Y, r) - Y = 0, \tag{18}$$

$$\bar{M} - L(i_0, Q, Y) = 0, \tag{19}$$

$$B = X(Y, r) + (1 - Q)I - P_K K\dot{Q}, \tag{20}$$

I being real investment. The differences from Mundell are obvious. First, the money supply is treated as a policy parameter. Secondly, the capital account in the balance of payments consists of an inflow due to foreign purchase of new Canadian real capital and an outflow because of an increased demand for capital assets in Canada. Both I and $\dot{Q}$ are changes in stocks and in a stationary equilibrium they have to be zero. If we then also take away the sterilization assumption, we have the same model as McKinnon and Oates with the exception of the Q in the demand for money function and equities instead of bonds.

In Floyd's model the results show that monetary policy has no effect on income in the long run under fixed exchange rates but that fiscal policy is effective. Under flexible exchange rates, both monetary and fiscal policy have positive effects on real income, and fiscal policy has larger effects than under fixed exchange rates. This difference depends in a crucial way on the fact that Mundell has a fixed-price bond with given interest rate while Floyd has an asset with a fixed interest rate but a variable price. In Floyd's model an increase in government expenditures will increase real income. In Mundell's model this was not possible because with a given money supply and a constant interest rate, there would not be equilibrium in the money market with a higher income. Now, in Floyd's model, when real income increases, the value of real capital assets goes up and foreigners demand more of these assets. This means that Q, the domestic holdings of real capital assets, goes down, which reduces the demand for money and counterweights the effect of an increase in real income.

Another attempt to introduce both stock and flow considerations in a macro model for a small open economy is made by Neil Wallace (1970) at about the same time as Floyd. Wallace uses the ordinary *IS–LM* model and adds a balance-of-payments equation, but, just as Floyd, he does not allow changes in the balance of payments to affect the rest of the economy. However, one of the virtues of this study is the elegant and simple derivation of the balance-of-payments equation. In this way it supplements and extends Floyd's articles because it also considers the effects of interest rate changes.[13] A model of essentially the same type is also presented by Levin (1972).

5. Portfolio Balance: Short-Run

All attempts to approach the portfolio analysis that have been mentioned in the previous section have still centered around what is basically the well-known

[13]There is also an interesting discussion of the effects of introducing speculation and forward markets in a model of this type.

IS–LM model in one form or another. Swoboda, McKinnon and Oates imposed a stock equilibrium condition and Floyd and Wallace developed better formulations of the capital account in the balance of payments.

By this time, however, there was a widespread dissatisfaction with this model. Some of the most unsatisfactory characteristics of the model follow:

(1) In its usual form, the model is essentially short-run and is not appropriate for analysis of long-run problems (or better: for stock–flow problems). There are two reasons for this: first, positive savings and investment mean asset accumulation which is inconsistent with stock equilibrium. Secondly, the assumption of fixed wages and/or prices over a period where complete asset adjustment takes place does not seem to be in accordance with either theory or postwar experience.

(2) Wealth is disregarded in the model but has been more and more recognized as an important element in the formation of economic models.

(3) The government budget constraint is not explicitly included in the model. This has serious drawbacks for the analysis of economic policy and for the stock–flow adjustment.

(4) Interest earnings on government and foreign securities are neglected. This is the reason for some strange results mentioned in the literature.

In the previous section some early attempts to avoid or to handle these shortcomings were described. In the subsequent work in this field the aim has been to solve or avoid these problems. We are going to divide this work into two categories, short-run portfolio equilibrium and long-run portfolio equilibrium.

The short-run portfolio equilibrium is characterized by the "normal" assumptions of "ordinary" portfolio analysis, namely that all real variables and the size of the portfolio are held constant. An interesting example of this approach has been developed by Kouri and Porter (1973a, b). Their model postulates the demand for money, domestic bonds and foreign bonds as functions of income, wealth, interest rates and risk factors. Further, it contains a money supply consisting of a foreign component and a domestic component, an exogenous current account balance, a capital account and stock equilibrium conditions for money and bonds. Foreign interest rates and income are held constant. Differentiating the model makes it possible to solve for the domestic interest rate and the foreign reserve changes as a function of the exogenous variables. In this way pure monetary policy comes directly into the estimated equation and its effect on the balance of payments can be observed, as well as the extent of offsetting capital flows.

Karl Brunner has also used a model of this type. In a recent study (1973), he extends to the open economy the elaborate and well-known model of the money supply process that he and Allan Metzler have constructed.[14] His main conclusions are that monetary policy is not without effect in the short run, even with perfect capital mobility, and that the policy complaint in small economies about imported inflation is justified, while the assertion that monetary policy is ineffective because of "offsetting capital flows" is simply incorrect.

In a very recent paper Dornbusch (1973a) reaches a similar conclusion. In both cases this is a portfolio model with wealth, income and prices constant and with both an internationally traded asset and a non-traded asset. In Dornbusch's paper the central bank makes open market operations in the non-traded asset, while an open market operation in Brunner's model is performed in bonds, the traded asset. However, this does not seem to affect the qualitative conclusions.

Girton and Henderson (1973) have extended this type of portfolio model to the two-country, world economy case. Their main conclusion is that there is an automatic mechanism to balance-of-payments adjustment either through money adjustment or through securities adjustment or a combination of the two. They also find that if the small country assumption is abandoned, changes in international reserves and in interest rates are jointly determined.

6. The Monetary Approach to the Balance of Payments

The work by Johnson and Mundell has recently developed into the formulation of what is called the "Monetary Approach to the Balance of Payments" [Johnson (1972b)]. Before taking up the second part of the portfolio approach we will briefly describe its content. This theory is in a sense a modernized version of Hume. It has three basic features: first, it affirms the fundamental proposition that the balance of payments is an essentially monetary phenomenon. Without money, there would not even be a balance of payments. Second, the monetary approach concentrates on the demand for money function and the money supply process as the most important relationships. Third, it deals mainly with long-run aspects of policy consequences for the balance of payments.[15]

As the theory is laid out by Harry Johnson (1972a, b; 1973) for a small country, the interest rate and the prices are given on the world markets. Then

[14] An earlier use of this model for an open economy is to be found in Willms (1971).
[15] See also Mussa (1974) for a good presentation of the basic features.

the demand for money is

$$M^{D} = p \cdot L(y, i). \tag{21}$$

The supply of money is

$$M^{S} = R + D, \tag{22}$$

and if supply and demand are equal,

$$R = M^{D} - D. \tag{23}$$

Define $r = R/(R + D)$, and let $(dR/dt)/R = g_R$, and in the same way for the other variables. Then

$$g_R = \frac{1}{r}(g_p + \eta_y g_y + \eta_i g_i) - \frac{1-r}{r} g_D, \tag{24}$$

where η_y and η_i are the income and interest rate elasticities of the demand for money.

The rate of change of prices and interest rates are assumed to be exogenous, determined on the world markets. If their growth rates are zero, and if the rate of growth of real income is also given and is zero, we have instead

$$g_R = -\frac{1-r}{r} g_D. \tag{25}$$

This says that the rate of growth of reserves is determined by the rate of change of domestic credit creation.

Aside from other merits this presentation of the theory has the virtue of very clearly bringing out some important points. First, contrary to some widespread beliefs, a higher growth rate of domestic output improves the balance of payments. Second, it is normally said that for a devaluation to improve the balance of payments in a situation of rather full employment will require the support of a demand-reducing policy. However, it is clear from equation (24) that with a reduced rate of growth of domestic credit creation the devaluation becomes unnecessary.

7. *Portfolio Balance: Long-Run*

The second approach to portfolio equilibrium is the long-run approach. It is inspired by McKinnon's early attempt to solve this problem [McKinnon (1969)], and works with a careful specification of the full, long-run stock–flow equilibrium and sometimes with the path to this equilibrium as well.[16] These models are aggregate general equilibrium models.

Edward Tower (1972) has published an article describing such a model, where he explicitly introduces stock equilibrium conditions. He finds that both fiscal and monetary policy have effects on real output under fixed exchange rates, but that monetary policy effects under flexible exchange rates are very uncertain, while fiscal policy is still effective. Reserve changes are not constrained to zero and monetary policy is defined as interest rate policy. Output is assumed to be perfectly elastic at prevailing wages and prices as in the usual Keynesian model.

This is also true in the model by William Branson (1972), which is basically a Keynesian model but extended in an interesting way to include a flexible capital stock, dynamic adjustment and portfolio equilibrium. Branson begins with formulating what he calls an "instantaneous" equilibrium. This is a situation where the stocks of money, bonds and real capital are held constant. Equilibrium is reached when real income and the yields on bonds and capital have adjusted to the levels where flow equilibrium exists. Stock adjustment functions are then constructed that describe the desire to accumulate wealth in different forms. Finally, the model is solved for a complete stock–flow equilibrium.

It is perhaps worth pointing out the difference in method from the short-run approach. In that case, income, real capital and wealth are held constant and rates of return and the relative amounts of money and bonds adjust to an equilibrium situation. In this case, money, bonds and real capital are each held constant and rates of return and real income adjust to short-run equilibrium.

In both McKinnon's model [McKinnon (1969)] and in Tower's and Branson's, the capital stock is variable. Now, this implies that a reasonable amount of time has to pass. In a recent paper, Myhrman (1973) argues that it seems unnecessarily unrealistic to ignore the effects on the supply of output and on prices of variations in the capital stock. His model is a long-run stationary state model for a small, open economy. It has flexible prices and output supply varies with the capital stock. There are money, bonds and capital on the asset side and a government budget constraint and portfolio equilibrium conditions are included. The most important conclusion is that under fixed exchange rates monetary policy may or may not be effective depending on what is assumed about reality and the way this is reflected in the model specification. For example, if there is a government budget constraint, then

[16] Another important source of inspiration is Jones' (1969) comment on McKinnon's article.

monetary policy becomes more effective the less capital mobility there is. With perfect capital mobility monetary policy has no effect.

McKinnon and Branson modified the basic Keynesian model. Myhrman constructed a different model with flexible prices and wages and a variable supply of goods depending upon the real capital stock. Frenkel and Rodriguez (1975) have extended this type of model in an elegant way and they are also able to analyze the adjustment path to the long-run stationary equilibrium. They also consider some monetary policy experiments. For instance, a once-and-for-all change in the money stock brought about by an unanticipated governmental transfer will have the impact effect of raising the value of assets which induces a rise in consumption and a deterioration in the trade balance. However, in the long run, the initial equilibrium is restored and there are no effects of the increase in the money supply. If the change in the money stock is instead brought about by an open market operation, then the effects will depend upon whether or not the private sector capitalizes the flow of transfers, when the government is assumed to return the yield on its holdings of securities to the private sector in the form of transfer payments. If it is capitalized, then we get the case equivalent to the other experiment and there are no effects in the long-run equilibrium. On the other hand, if it is not capitalized, there will be a positive effect on, e.g., consumption.

8. Two-Country, World Models

The models under this subtitle are models in which it is assumed that there are two countries, the home country and a foreign country representing the rest of the world. This was also the case earlier in this survey, but in that situation, the rest of the world was assumed to be exogenous to the home country, while it is now assumed that the two economies interact.

The two countries together constitute the whole world and are therefore a closed economy. When this world was on a gold standard (and disregarding changes in the foreign exchange rates between the gold points) it was like a closed economy in our textbooks, or like a common currency union with one central bank. There were different governments, but they can be compared to the local government of the U.S. today. They had their own budgets, their own budget expenditures, the right to tax and the right to borrow by issuing securities. *But they did not have the right to create money.*

In this sense, then, in all important respects, the world is like a closed economy in the analysis of macroproblems, and the concept of "the natural distribution of the species" is relevant. There are circumstances under which it is fruitful to split this world into two parts and to investigate the interaction between these two parts. We may distinguish three cases. First, there is the problem of the world being divided into separate countries, each with its own balance of payments to be concerned about. It may therefore be of some interest to study how equilibrium in the balance of payments is restored after some exogenous disturbance, although no one has yet been interested in how, for instance, California's balance of payments with the rest of the U.S. has returned to equilibrium after a change in the demand for money in California.

The second reason is that the countries in the world of today have given up the strict form of the gold standard; therefore, each separate country can print its own money and choose, if so desired, to finance a budget deficit in the central bank.

Third, the separate countries may also have a system of flexible exchange rates.

An example of the first case is Lloyd Metzler's model from 1960 [Metzler (1968)]. He started from a model that was of the neoclassical type with full employment and with both investment and savings being functions of the rate of interest. He then added a liquidity preference function and introduced trade in commodities and securities. Metzler was mainly interested in the effect of introducing liquidity preference and interest elastic capital flows on the balance-of-payments adjustment process. Would most of the adjustment to a disturbance take place through adjustments in prices and money (gold) flows, or would it be effected via interest rate changes and capital (securities) flows? His conclusion was that this depends upon the internal conditions of saving and investment and not upon the external conditions of the demand for imports. He further concluded that the real variables are unaffected by changes in the demand for money.

In a recent article, James M. Holmes (1973) has formalized Metzler's model, corrected a mistake in the specification of the model, and extended it. His correction consists of a recognition that the capital flows in Metzler's model are functions of the interest rate differentials, which is not a correct specification, and he changes this so that the capital flows and the interest rates in both countries are determined simultaneously. This is the same criticism of portfolio behavior that has earlier been raised by Branson (1968), Willet–Forte (1969), and many others. However, Holmes did not go all the way to the explicit specification of stock equilibrium conditions. Instead, he extended Metzler's model by introducing the terms of trade as an argument in the savings and investment functions. He then found that, contrary to Metzler's results, the adjustment after a disturbance in the foreign investment sector may primarily be through price change instead of monetary flows.

Shortly after the appearance of Metzler's model, Mundell (1968) constructed a similar model but included unemployment and fixed prices. Additional work was later done on this model by Swoboda and Dornbusch (1973) and Roper (1971). At the same time Holmes, in two other articles (1972a, b), solved the Metzler model for the case of unemployment and for the case of full employment but including flexible exchange rates.

All these models are really only variants of the Keynesian, or Hicksian, *IS–LM* model. We can also see that the conclusions are similar, but a few details should be noted. First, the Metzler–Holmes formulation assumes a gold standard, which implies that the separate countries cannot increase their money supply by discretionary measures. Mundell and the others assume a paper standard or a gold exchange standard. Second, all these models are open to criticism from the same basic point of departure; namely, the capital–flow behavior and the lack of a proper stock–flow specification that was extensively discussed in the "small country" case.

As was discussed above, several authors have dealt with the problem of formulating models with a proper specification of the portfolio equilibrium conditions for a small open economy. For the two-country case, however, there have only been a few attempts to do so. The first article dealing with this problem was written by Polly Allen (1973). She used a Keynesian model with fixed prices and wages and introduced explicit conditions for portfolio equilibrium in both countries. From this model she derived the result that a change in the demand for money in one of the countries does not have any effect on real income in any country or on the interest rate. The same is true for an increase in the supply of money. These results are difficult to understand. If prices are fixed and real income and interest rates unchanged, how is an excess supply of money going to be diffused into the portfolios?

In a very recent paper Rudiger Dornbusch (1974) has constructed a model for a two-country, world economy with flexible exchange rates. It is a model with full employment and flexible prices and wages; it deals with both short-run and long-run equilibrium, and it has dynamic adjustment functions. One of the most appealing features of this model is its explicit treatment of the wealth-saving relationship. This is very important, since once we leave the short-run equilibrium the problem of the determinants of asset accumulation has to be faced.

The model has two assets; money and claims on real capital, with one output being produced in both countries. There is trade in output and equities between the two countries. Saving is a function of target wealth and the government budget constraint is explicitly recognized.

This model yields some very interesting results. First, the determination of the exchange rate is seen not so much as equilibrating trade flows but rather as adjusting so that the given money balances in both countries are willingly held.

Second, the exchange rate does not isolate one country from an inflation in the other country. An ongoing inflation in country A due to a persistent budget deficit financed by money creation will increase the demand for equities in country A, which lowers the rate of interest. A lower interest rate increases the demand for real money balances in country B, which reduces the inflation rate in B.

The transmission is brought about through the capital mobility. It is interesting to compare this result with the following conclusion by Mundell (1968, p. 267) ten years earlier: "According to traditional theory, an investment boom in one country is not transmitted abroad under flexible exchange rates. My results show that there is a transmission mechanism at work when capital is mobile."

9. Models With More Than One Sector

In the survey by Anne O. Krueger (1965) she pointed out the potential value of models with traded and non-traded goods. In spite of this, very few such models have appeared in the literature.

Mathieson (1973) has constructed a model with non-traded goods. In this model for a small country three goods are produced: an export good, an import-competing capital good and a non-traded good. Prices of the traded goods and the interest rate on bonds are given on the world market. There are also portfolio balance equations and a government budget constraint. The main conclusions are that Mundell's results are not drastically changed by the presence of non-traded goods, except that fiscal policy under flexible exchange rates now becomes effective. This result and many of the other results as well depend very much on the relative price effect between traded and non-traded goods.

Prachowny (1973) reaches broadly the same conclusions in a similar model. Both Mathieson and Prachowny use "Keynesian-type" models extended in different ways.

A more "classical" model is used by Dornbusch (1973b). He has a two-sector model with flexible wages and prices, full employment and continuous market clearing. The supply of output is a function of real capital and its relative price. There are portfolio equilibrium equations and stock adjustment. It is a model for a small open economy.

In this model an increase in the money supply brought about by an open market operation has no effect on the economy except on the balance sheet of the central bank. This is not surprising because of the perfect capital (bond) mobility. One of the most important conclusions is that if the central bank made the open market operation in equities (that are not traded) instead of in bonds, then there would be an expansionary effect on the economy.[17]

10. Comparison of Different Models

Many authors try to differentiate their products by choosing different notations and by stressing small differences from others instead of pointing out similarities. In this section I am therefore trying to compare the different models to find out where the crucial assumptions are made.

Let us start with Mundell's famous article of 1963 [Mundell (1968)]. If we formalize the model it can be written as

$$E(Y, i) + X(Y) - Y = 0, \tag{26}$$

$$R + D - L(Y, i) = 0, \tag{27}$$

$$B = X(Y) + K(i). \tag{28}$$

Equations (26) and (27) form a system of two equations that simultaneously determine Y and i (the equation for the bond market is eliminated by Walras' law). The third equation is the balance-of-payments equation. Under a fixed exchange-rate system any non-zero value of B affects the supply of money and disturbs the equilibrium in the economy. This has of course been recognized by everyone, but many have chosen to assume that this influence is eliminated by sterilization operations from the central bank. However, a sale of government securities to sterilize an inflow of foreign exchange will raise the interest rate. Then, if there is any capital mobility, more foreign exchange will flow into the country and the central bank has to step in and sterilize again. As Mundell pointed out himself, sterilization is not viable (unless the country is large enough to influence the world interest rate or sterilizes long enough, which would mean an infinite increase in foreign reserves and in future interest payments!).

Mundell came to this conclusion and chose instead to divide the money supply into one domestic component under the control of the central bank, D, and one foreign component, foreign exchange reserves, R, which is not under

[17]However, both with non-traded assets and with non-traded commodities it is important to try to determine why they are not traded and what would make them traded.

the control of the central bank.[18] Earlier, the sterilization assumption made it possible to isolate the first two equations mentioned above to a subset of the model, where Y and i were determined and then B was recursively determined in the third equation without affecting the rest of the system.

This is also the approach of Floyd in the above-mentioned articles. However, this means that the careful work he puts into the specification of the capital flows affects his balance-of-payments equation, *but does not have any effect on the rest of his model.* Therefore it is not possible to compare his results with Mundell's, as Floyd does, without changing this specification.

The same problem exists if monetary policy is defined as a setting of the interest rate, as Mundell stated in his earlier works. When Tower uses this specification, he eliminates the possibility of comparison with Mundell's work and that of most other authors.

Regarding D as the monetary policy variable gives three equations to determine Y, i and R, but Mundell chose to assume perfect capital mobility and could then use the two first equations to determine Y and R. Given i, Y is determined by the first equation and R is then determined by the second equation. The third equation is not used. Dividing the supply of money into the two components R and D and regarding D as the monetary policy variable, attention is immediately focused on an important problem, namely whether it is the level of reserves or the change in reserves that is determined in the model. In the early literature it was not unusual to treat the whole money supply, $R + D$, as the monetary policy parameter and then the three equations determined Y, i and B. As soon as the money supply is divided it is evident that the level of reserves, R, is the relevant variable to be determined in the model together with real income and the interest rate, and that the third equation should be set equal to zero as an equilibrium condition. [This problem is also discussed from a slightly different angle in an article by Aghelvi and Borts (1973), where they reach the conclusion that the level of reserves, R, is the proper policy target by analyzing the dynamic behavior of the model.]

This is done by Swoboda when he drops the assumption of perfect capital mobility and adds the condition that the balance of payments has to be zero. There are now three equations to determine Y, i and R, but once more there is a subsystem – in this case the first and the third equations – for determining Y and i. Here, the second equation recursively determines R. A change in D cannot affect anything in the first and third equations and therefore it only leads to an opposite change in R.

[18]It has to be remembered that there is no banking system in this type of model so the money supply is identical to the supply of base money. With a banking system in the model the central bank determines the composition but not the total of assets backing the money supply.

McKinnon and Oates introduce real non-human wealth in the first equation. They change the third equation so that the trade balance is equal to zero and they assume perfect capital mobility. This time there is a subset of one equation, the third, to determine real income. Then W, real non-human wealth, is determined by the first equation.

Let us continue by considering the "Monetary Approach to the Balance of Payments". Now, the above model is converted to growth rates and prices are flexible, but both prices and interest rates are determined on the world market, and the rate of growth of real income is determined exogenously. Therefore, for given values of interest rates (perfect capital mobility), prices and real income, the first and the third equations are redundant and the demand for money is also exogenously determined. For a given domestic credit creation, D, the rate of change of international reserves is determined in the second equation above, the money equation.

Turning now to the Kouri and Porter model we could say, still comparing with our basic model above, that what they do is essentially to solve equations two and three simultaneously while holding income and wealth constant. They solve for the change in international reserves and in the domestic interest rate. Therefore, when applying the model to empirical issues, they test for the assumption of perfect capital mobility or what they call offsetting capital movements. It must be remembered, though, that this is not a test of the "Monetary Approach to the Balance of Payments", as that theory is a long-run theory while the Kouri–Porter model is typically short-run.

In a separate paper by Kouri–Porter (1973b), they take up the problem of whether monetary policy can be effective under fixed exchange rates and to what extent the answer depends on the degree of capital mobility. This problem runs through so many of the studies under survey that it is worth some extra attention. The implication of the discussion by Kouri and Porter is that they consider a low offset coefficient as an indication of efficient monetary policy. This is also the point at which Mundell once started. Contrary to this conclusion, both Swoboda and the "Monetary Approach to the Balance of Payments" come to the conclusion, though for different reasons, that monetary policy has no effect in the long run, except on the foreign exchange reserves. Both McKinnon and Branson find that monetary policy has no effect on real income. There is also the connected and very important question of whether or not there is an automatic adjustment mechanism at work.

All these questions are closely related to the problem of the government budget constraint. The government budget constraint for a *closed* economy states that any excess of government expenditures over tax receipts must be financed through increases in either the monetary base or government securities,

$$G - T = \Delta D + \Delta S.$$

This has been recognized by many people, among whom we may mention some of the earlier; Ott and Ott, Christ and Silber. One reason for setting up this equation is that it shows that if the government decides on the level of government expenditure and on the tax rates it can further only decide on either ΔB or ΔS. An even more important reason for using this equation is that it spells out the fundamental interrelationships between the private and the public sector in the stock–flow adjustment process. There are rather few economists who have been aware of the real importance of this. One exception is Brunner and Metzler.[19]

In a situation with stock equilibrium, all stocks have to be constant. This implies that the government budget must be balanced; this is then a *stock equilibrium condition*. Now, some authors have added this condition to their model and then differentiated it. As a result they have got

$$\frac{\mathrm{d}Y}{\mathrm{d}G} = \left(\frac{\delta T}{\delta Y}\right)^{-1},$$

and from this they have concluded that fiscal policy has a multiplier effect on real income and that monetary policy has no effect at all in the long run when $\Delta D = \Delta S = 0$.[20] This conclusion is really not warranted, except as a very special case, because government expenditures also depend upon interest payments on the government bond debt, and taxes also depend on the price level.[21] Therefore, using this multiplier expression to deny any effect of monetary policy on real income is too much of defining away the problem.[22]

The government budget constraint for the open economy is even more interesting. It is

$$\Delta R + G - T = \Delta D + \Delta S,$$

or

$$X(\quad) + K(\quad) + G - T = \Delta D + \Delta S,$$

[19]In their latest papers the importance of having this condition in the model is clearly demonstrated. See also Myhrman (1973).

[20]See, e.g., Ott and Ott (1965).

[21]It is here assumed that government expenditures are fixed in nominal terms, otherwise they also depend on the price level.

[22]See also Bent Hansen (1973).

where X is an unspecified trade balance and K the capital account. For stock equilibrium we now have

$$-X(\quad) = G - T.^{23}$$

The stock equilibrium condition for the economy is now that imports minus exports have to equal government expenditure minus taxes or that the deficit on the trade balance has to equal the deficit on the government budget. This situation has been called a quasi-equilibrium by Mundell (1968).

Writing imports and taxes as functions of only real income makes it possible to derive

$$\mathrm{d}Y/\mathrm{d}G = (\delta IM/\delta Y + \delta T/\delta Y)^{-1},$$

where IM = imports and exports are assumed constant.

This has been done by Oates (1966), by McKinnon (1969) and by Branson (1972), and the conclusion is that monetary policy has no effect on real income. This conclusion is even less warranted than for the closed economy because now interest payments to and from foreigners must also be taken into consideration together with the earlier facts.

Swoboda does not mention the government budget constraint, but when he introduces the condition that the balance of payments has to be zero he says that it is to ensure full equilibrium, which is the same as a stock–flow equilibrium. Such a condition in a model with a government budget constraint means that it must be split into two parts, one part being that the balance of payments has to be in equilibrium and the other that the government budget has to balance. However, it is just the property of the government budget constraint as formulated above that it ensures stock–flow equilibrium. All markets are in continuous equilibrium, but there may be a surplus in the balance of payments that is matched by a surplus in the government budget of equal size.

Which assumption is then the better approximation to the world we live in? I will argue that the government budget constraint is the better choice. The assumption of a zero balance of payments is instead the natural assumption under a gold standard. In that case, the supply of money is formally tied to the amount of foreign exchange reserves, i.e., gold, and a deficit in the balance of payments immediately reduces the amount of money available to the public, which reduces expenditures and restores the balance in the balance of payments. Under the Bretton–Woods system this is no longer the case. The

[23]An appropriate balance-of-payments formulation should also include interest payments on outstanding debts and so on. Compare earlier discussion.

direct link between foreign exchange reserves and the domestic money supply is cut off. Consider a situation with a deficit in the balance of payments and an equal deficit in the budget. The balance sheet of the central bank would then be

ΔR	-100	ΔB_1	-100
ΔS_G	$+100$	ΔB_2	$+100$

Here the reserve loss is balanced by an increase in government securities in the central bank. One could also say that the deficit in the balance of payments is financed by the printing of new money by the government. The total effect on the monetary base is zero and all markets in the economy are in equilibrium.

This leads to the important and much debated question of balance-of-payments adjustment. Mundell (1968) calls the Bretton–Woods system a *disequilibrium system*, but for a different reason. His reason seems to be "that there are no equations specifying equilibrium in the balance of payments". However, having added such an equilibrium condition, he goes on to show the automatic adjustment to equilibrium in this system and what he calls Hume's Law. In their paper Girton and Henderson also stress the automatic adjustment.[24] I would also prefer to call this system a disequilibrium system, but for the reason of the possibility of quasi-equilibrium. *In such a situation there are no forces moving the system to balance-of-payments adjustment.* Now the effectiveness of monetary policy is to a large extent dependent on the degree of capital mobility. However, I must here hasten to add that I completely agree with Swoboda that the degree of capital mobility is mainly important for the speed of adjustment.

Of course, a country with a deficit in the balance of payments cannot go on with this forever, because its reserves are limited. However, the important thing is that it may be able to continue with it for some time, say for a couple of years, without the existence of any forces which necessarily would bring the balance of payments back to equilibrium, while under a gold standard the money supply would automatically decrease at the same rate as the balance of payments deficit. Now, if many countries use this degree of freedom and let reserves increase or decrease over an intermediate period, the system will move into a crisis zone. The reason for this is that governments lack foresight. If they had perfect foresight they would change policy at the right moment, but living in a world with incomplete information as we do, they tend to wait too

[24]They do not have the government budget constraint in their model, and it is a gold standard world.

long and are forced to change their exchange rate. Once this has been done reserve accumulation or decumulation will be taken as a sign of an expected exchange-rate change and speculation is started, thereby increasing the tendencies to disequilibrium.

This does not mean that the system always tends to such a situation. It is just an observation of the possibility of quasi-equilibrium. However, this is also a likely situation after, e.g., a base-financed budget deficit, which is not an unusual event.

It can also be noted that although the existence of this government budget constraint may inhibit or delay the balance-of-payments adjustment, it stabilizes the economy from external shocks. Assume that the business cycle upturn for a small country starts with an increase in exports. As a result, money, income and prices will rise, but then taxes will also rise, the government budget becomes overbalanced[25] and money is withdrawn from the economy, which dampens the upturn. The opposite will take place in the recession.

Turning now to the most recent development in general equilibrium, aggregate macromodels as represented by Branson (1972), Myhrman (1973), Dornbusch (1973b, 1976), and Frenkel and Rodriguez (1975), it is a common characteristic that they are all careful in specifying explicit stock equilibrium conditions. They also treat real capital as a separate asset with its own asset price. Therefore, all of these models incorporate a rather satisfactory treatment of the long-run stock–flow equilibrium.[26] Myhrman does not consider short-run equilibrium, but in all the other models there is an explicit treatment of short-run equilibrium and of the dynamics of asset accumulation to the new equilibrium.

The method that is used in these studies takes its inspiration from the book by Foley and Sidrauski (1971). First, all stocks are held constant and the economy is assumed to reach a short-run equilibrium with the help of changes in all prices and current income. The values of these are then assumed to influence the desired stock of assets and eventually induce stock changes. In this way the economy keeps moving until a stationary stock equilibrium is reached. But at each moment in time the economy is in short-run equilibrium.

Now, this is an elegant method, but it requires a very high degree of information in the system. It may therefore be allowed to put a decisive questionmark on this approach, since most of the short-run adjustment problems in the Western economies seem to stem from a lack of relevant

[25]Unless politicians raise G.

[26]However, it is debatable whether it is reasonable to have real capital asset accumulation but no effect of this increase in real capital on the supply of output and on the price level, as in Branson's model.

information. It also follows from this that we have to use extreme caution in connection with policy conclusions for the short run.

11. Conclusions

This paper has covered a very long time span in the history of economics, nearly 250 years. It could have gone even further back in time, to the age of the Spanish gold and silver discoveries. And yet most of the material is from very recent years. Why then look back to misty ages at all? I have done this to show the existence of authors with a good grasp of the workings of the international payments system of their time and its adjustment to disturbances. I think this is the right setting to start from when reviewing more recent developments, since the largest part of the work done by or inspired by the two predominant researchers in this field, Robert Mundell and Harry Johnson, has consisted of regaining this insight and learning to apply it to the world of today. By this I mean that it was not until recently that attempts have been made to regard the problem of balance-of-payments adjustment as a world economy problem and a problem for monetary theory.

It is therefore very interesting and promising that there has been such an acceleration in the number of authors in the last three or four years in this field who have used monetary theory and portfolio theory to analyze balance-of-payments adjustment and monetary and fiscal policy. The use of portfolio models in a narrow interpretation with income and wealth constant has led to a better understanding of the determinants of short-run capital flows, but more work has to be done on extending this approach to include expectations and speculation.

An even more promising line of development is the recent attempts to integrate portfolio theory with aggregate general equilibrium models for an open economy [McKinnon (1969), Branson (1972), Tower (1972), Myhrman (1973)] where asset equilibrium and output or flow equilibrium are analyzed simultaneously. Dornbusch (1973b) and Frenkel and Rodriguez (1975) have carried this work further in some recent papers with an elegant formulation of the wealth-saving relationship.

After penetrating all this material, one is left with one dominating impression. In spite of all discussions about "fundamental disequilibrium in the balance of payments" and related views on "the wrong exchange rate" and so on, it is clearly shown from all this research that *we have had an equilibrium system with automatic adjustment if only the politicians and the central banks would stick to the rules of the system.* These are: (1) do not change the exchange rate, and (2) keep the rate of change of the money supply at the appropriate speed. Under the gold standard these rules were built into the system. Under the Bretton–Woods system, each country could jeopardize the system by letting its money supply increase too much or too little in an attempt to get its rate of inflation to diverge from the rest of the world.

There is of course much room for future research in this field. The following problems seem to present a natural continuation of recent work. First, macromodels for open economies should be worked out with a careful specification of permanent income in the economic relationships in the model, as well as a proper treatment of the government budget as an important element in the stock–flow process. Second, two-sector models with non-traded goods seem to provide an interesting field worth more exploration. Third, it must be time now to start investigating the short-run adjustment behavior of the economy. [Parkin (1972) provides an interesting attempt in this direction.] Fourth, there are also reasons for trying to formulate some models of the behavior under "dirty float" or managed exchange rates. In this connection it is interesting to note that Mundell's conclusions – that under perfect capital mobility monetary policy has no effect under fixed exchange rates but that fiscal policy has, and that the reverse is true for flexible exchange rates – seem to break down under the intermediate case of crawling peg or dirty float. Are, then, both monetary and fiscal policy effective or is neither of them effective?

References

Aghelvi, B. B. and G. H. Borts, 1973, The stability and equilibrium of the balance of payments under a fixed exchange rate, Journal of International Economics, Feb.

Alexander, S., 1952, Effects of a devaluation on a trade balance, IMF Staff Papers, no. 2.

Allen, P., 1973, A portfolio approach to international capital flows, Journal of International Economics, May.

Branson, W., 1968, Financial capital flows in the U.S. balance of payments (North-Holland, Amsterdam).

Branson, W., 1972, Macroeconomic equilibrium with portfolio balance in open economies, Seminar Paper no. 22 (Institute for International Economic Studies, Stockholm).

Brunner, K., 1973, Money supply processes and monetary policy in an open economy, in: M. Connolly and A. Swoboda, eds., International trade and money (Allen & Unwin, London).

Dornbusch, R., 1973, Capital mobility, portfolio balance and nontraded assets, mimeo.

Dornbusch, R., 1975, A portfolio balance model of the open economy, Journal of Monetary Economics, Jan.

Dornbusch, R., 1976, Flexible exchange rates, capital mobility and macroeconomic equilibrium, in: E. Claassen and P. Salin, eds., Recent issues in international monetary economics (North-Holland, Amsterdam).

Fleming, M. J., 1962, Domestic financial policies under fixed and under floating rates, IMF Staff Papers, no. 9.

Floyd, J., 1962a, International capital movements.and monetary equilibrium, American Economic Review, Sept.

Floyd, J., 1969b, Monetary and fiscal policy in a world of capital mobility, The Review of Economic Studies, Nov.
Floyd, J., 1972a, Portfolio equilibrium and the theory of capital movements, in: F. Machlup, W. Salant and L. Tarshis, eds., International mobility and movement of capital (New York).
Floyd, J., 1972b, Alternative fiscal policies in a world of capital mobility, in: E. Claassen and P. Salin, eds., Stabilization policies in interdependent economies (North-Holland, Amsterdam).
Foley, D. and M. Sidrauski, 1971, Monetary and fiscal policy in a growing economy (Macmillan, New York).
Fratianni, M., 1972, On the short-run effectiveness of monetary policy in a regime of fixed exchange rates: An IS–LM interpretation, mimeo.
Frenkel, J. and C. Rodriguez, 1975, Portfolio equilibrium and the balance of payments: A monetary approach, American Economic Review, Sept.
Girton, L. and D. Henderson, 1973, A two-country model of financial capital movements as stock adjustments with emphasis on the effects of central bank policy, mimeo.
Hansen, B., 1973, On the effects of fiscal and monetary policy: A taxonomic discussion, American Economic Review, Sept.
Harberger, A. C., 1950, Currency depreciation, income, and the balance of trade, Journal of Political Economy, Feb.
Harrod, R. F., 1973, International economics (Cambridge University Press, Cambridge, Mass.).
Helliwell, J., 1969, Monetary and fiscal policies for an open economy, Oxford Economic Papers, March.
Holmes, J., 1972a, The existence of capital flows, fixed and flexible exchange rates and full employment, Canadian Journal of Economics, May.
Holmes, J., 1972b, Monetary and fiscal policies in a general equilibrium underemployment trade model under fixed exchange rates, International Economic Review, June.
Holmes, J., 1973, The process of international adjustment under conditions of full employment: A Keynesian view revised, Journal of Political Economy, Nov.
Holtrop, M. W., 1972, Money in an open economy (Stenfert Kroese N.V., Leiden).
Jong, F. J. de, 1973, Developments of monetary theory in the Netherlands (Rotterdam University Press, Rotterdam).
Johnson, H., 1969, Towards a general theory of the balance of payments, in: R. N. Cooper, ed., International finance (Penguin, Baltimore, Md.).
Johnson, H., 1972a, Inflation and the monetarist controversy (North-Holland, Amsterdam).
Johnson, H., 1972b, Further essays in monetary economics (Allen & Unwin, London).
Johnson, H., 1973, Secular inflation and the international monetary system, Journal of Money, Credit and Banking, Feb.
Jones, R., 1969, Comment on McKinnon, in: R. Mundell and A. Swoboda, eds., Monetary problems of the international economy (University of Chicago Press, Chicago, Ill.).
Kouri, P. and M. Porter, 1974, International capital flows and portfolio equilibrium, Journal of Political Economy, May.
Kouri, P., 1975, The hypothesis of offsetting capital flows: A case study of Germany, Journal of Monetary Economics, Jan.
Krueger, A. O., 1965, The impact of alternative government policies under varying exchange systems, Quarterly Journal of Economics, May.
Krueger, A. O., 1969, Balance of payments theory, Journal of Economic Literature, March.
Laursen, S. and L. Metzler, 1950, Flexible exchange rates and the theory of employment, Review of Economics and Statistics.
Levin, J., 1972, International capital mobility and the assignment problem, Oxford Economic Papers, March.
Mathieson, D., 1973, Traded goods, nontraded goods, and the balance of payments, International Economic Review, Oct.
McKinnon, R. and W. Oates, 1966, The implications of international economic integration for monetary, fiscal, and exchange-rate policy, Princeton Studies in International Finance, no. 16.

McKinnon, R., 1969, Portfolio balance and international payments adjustment, in: R. Mundell and A. Swoboda, eds., Monetary problems of the international economy (University of Chicago Press, Chicago, Ill.).

Meade, J. E., 1951a, The theory of international economic policy, The balance of payments, vol. 1 (Oxford University Press, London).

Meade, J. E., 1951b, The balance of payments, mathematical supplement (Oxford University Press, London).

Metzler, L., 1948, The theory of international trade, in: H. Ellis, ed., A survey of contemporary economics, vol. 1 (Irwin, Homewood, Ill.).

Metzler, L., 1968, The process of international adjustment under conditions of full employment: A Keynesian view, in: R. Caves and H. G. Johnson, eds., Readings in international economics (Irwin, Homewood, Ill.).

Mill, J. S., The principles of political economy (Routledge, London).

Mundell, R. A., 1968, International economics (Macmillan, New York).

Mundell, R. A., 1971, Inflation, interest, and growth in the world economy (Goodyear, Pacific Palisades, Calif.).

Mussa, M., 1974, Tariffs and the balance of payments: A monetary approach, in: J. A. Frenkel and H. G. Johnson, eds., The monetary approach to the balance of payments (Allen & Unwin, London).

Myhrman, J., 1973, A macroeconomic model with asset equilibrium for an open economy, Seminar Paper no. 28 (Institute for International Economic Studies, Stockholm).

Neumann-Whitman, M. von, 1967, Policies for internal and external balance, Princeton Studies in International Finance, no. 28.

Nyberg, L. and S. Viotti, 1974, The policy conflict between internal and external balance under fixed exchange rates, An optimizing approach, Swedish Journal of Economics, Dec.

Oates, W., 1966, Budget balance and equilibrium income: A comment on the efficacy of fiscal and monetary policy in an open economy, Journal of Finance, Sept.

Ott, D. and A. Ott, 1965, Budget balance and equilibrium income, Journal of Finance, March.

Ott, D. and A. Ott, 1968, Monetary and fiscal policy: Goals and the choice of instruments, Quarterly Journal of Economics, May.

Parkin, M., 1974, Inflation, the balance of payments and domestic credit expansion in a fixed exchange rate open economy, in: R. Z. Aliber, ed., National monetary policies and the international financial system (University of Chicago Press, Chicago, Ill.).

Polak, J. J., 1957/8, Monetary analysis of income formation and payments problems, IMF Staff Papers.

Prachowny, M., 1973, The effectiveness of stabilization policy in a small, open economy, Weltwirtschaftliches Archiv, no. 2.

Prais, S. J., 1960/1, Some mathematical notes on the quantity theory of money in an open economy, IMF Staff Papers.

Robinson, J., 1949, The foreign exchanges, in: H. Ellis and L. Metzler, eds., Readings in the theory of international trade (Irwin, Homewood, Ill.).

Roper, D., 1971, Macroeconomic policies and the distribution of the world money supply, Quarterly Journal of Economics, Feb.

Sohmen, E. and H. Schneeweiss, 1969a, Fiscal and monetary policies under alternative exchange rate systems, Quarterly Journal of Economics, May.

Sohmen, E. and H. Schneeweiss, 1969b, Flexible exchange rates (Chicago University Press, Chicago, Ill.).

Swoboda, A., 1972a, On limited information and the assignment problem, in: E. Claassen and P. Salin, eds., Stabilization policies in interdependent economies (North-Holland, Amsterdam).

Swoboda, A., 1972b, Equilibrium, quasi-equilibrium, and macroeconomic policy under fixed exchange rates, Quarterly Journal of Economics.

Swoboda, A., 1973, Monetary policy under fixed exchange rates: Effectiveness, the speed of adjustment and proper use, Economica, May.

Swoboda, A. and R. Dornbusch, 1973, Adjustment, policy, and monetary equilibrium in a two-country model, in: M. Connolly and A. Swoboda, eds., International trade and money (Allen & Unwin, London).

Takayama, A., 1969, The effects of fiscal and monetary policies under flexible and fixed exchange rates, Canadian Journal of Economics, May.

Takayama, A., 1972, International trade (Holt, Rinehart and Winston, New York).

Tower, E., 1972, Monetary and fiscal policy under fixed and flexible exchange rates in the inter-run, Journal of Money, Credit and Banking, Nov.

Vanek, J., 1962, International trade: Theory and economic policy (Irwin, Homewood, Ill.).

Wallace, N., 1970, The determination of the stock of reserves and the balance of payments in a neo-Keynesian model, Journal of Money, Credit and Banking, Aug.

Willet, T., 1967, A portfolio theory of international short-term capital movements, Ph. D. Thesis (University of Virginia, Charlottesville, Virg.).

Willet, T. and F. Forte, 1969, Interest rate policy and external balance, Quarterly Journal of Economics, May.

Willms, M., 1971, Controlling money in an open economy: The German case, Federal Reserve Bank of St. Louis Review, April.

Chapter 7.2

SUMMARY OF THE DISCUSSION ON MYHRMAN

Assar LINDBECK, *Chairman*

To Johan Myhrman's proposition that many Keynesian or Keynesian-type models having long-run stationary properties are inconsistent because they ignore changes in the stocks of assets, *Peter Kenen* pointed out that many of the models that Myhrman entitled as wealth or portfolio models with "consistent stationary properties" are not necessarily consistent because a permanent interest rate effect is allowed for, which involves a change in the permanent savings rate and a change in the permanent investment rate and therefore of capital accumulation. Such a result could only be avoided if one could show that monetary policy cannot influence permanently the interest rate.

However, the main discussion was concentrated on the notion and the adequate formulation of the government's budget constraint. *Allan Meltzer* clarified that their (Brunner–Meltzer) budget constraint is less a constraint on the government and more a constraint on the economy's use of resources with the implication of a consistent division of resources between the government sector and the private sector.

William Branson challenged Myhrman's statement that the usual *IS–LM* models did not contain the budget constraint of the government. According to him the *IS* part of the model implies, for a closed economy, that government spending minus tax revenues equals savings minus investment. The *LM* curve specifies that all assets have to be held; if wealth consists only of capital and money, then the time rate of change of wealth minus the time rate of change of capital equals the time rate of change of the money stock. Because savings is the time rate of change of wealth and because investment is the time rate of change of capital, government spending minus tax revenues equals the change in the money stock – one possible formulation of the government budget constraint.

To the question raised by *Allan Meltzer* where to find government debt in this budget constraint, *William Branson* answered that one has to include it in the wealth constraint such that the time rate of change of wealth minus the time rate of change of capital equals the time rate of change in the stock of money plus government debt. *Johan Myhrman* replied that this budget constraint is implicit in the *IS–LM* models to the extent that the *LM* part of the models contains an adequate portfolio equilibrium equation.

At the end of the discussion *David Laidler* stressed the analytical advantages of monetary models, in particular, for describing the adjustment process as simply as possible. Thus, for instance, there are two possible ways to explain how firms plan their output and fix their prices. One can derive their behaviour based on their expectations of the probable volume of sales either from their inventories policy or from their plans for the time path of cash balances. Disappointed plans about cash balances play the same signalling role in the adjustment process as undesired inventories. The advantage of this monetary approach, in opposition to the real approach, is that it is much easier to aggregate money across firms and households and that it is tied more easily to the balance of payments with respect to adjustment problems for open economies.

Chapter 8.1

PORTFOLIO EQUILIBRIUM AND MONETARY POLICY WITH FOREIGN AND NON-TRADED ASSETS*

William H. BRANSON

1. Introduction

The ineffectiveness of monetary policy in an open economy with fixed exchange rates has become part of the conventional wisdom in the international economics literature since Mundell's (1963) paper describing a small open economy with its interest rate fixed by the world market. There seem to be two basic assumptions behind this general conventional wisdom: (a) that the economy is a price-taker on the world market (the "small-country" assumption), and (b) that all earning assets are traded internationally. Two sub-assumptions under (b) could be: (i) that there is only one earning asset and one interest rate, or (ii) that there are some non-traded assets in the system but they are perfectly substitutable in portfolios for traded assets.

The small-country assumption has been relaxed in a recent paper by Girton and Henderson (1973), which studies the resulting effects of monetary policy on domestic and foreign rates. In this paper I retain the small-country assumption, and study a case in which the financial system includes traded and non-traded assets. This seems to me a case more realistic than one with all assets traded, and it presents an interesting parallel to the "Scandinavian model" of the real sector, described in Branson–Myhrman (1973), which emphasizes separation between traded and non-traded goods.

The model described in section 2 and analyzed in sections 3–5 below is an extension of Tobin's (1969) model of the financial sector to include a foreign asset with an interest rate determined by the world market, given exogenously to the open economy being studied. The financial sector also includes two non-traded assets that are imperfectly substitutable. One purpose here is to study what difference it makes for the monetary authorities to do open-market

*This paper is an extension of Branson (1972, sect. III), which discussed a model with a foreign asset and one non-traded asset. The four-asset model described here is based on notes circulated at the Institute for International Economic Studies in Stockholm, May 1973. I am indebted to my colleagues there for helpful comments on this work during my stay in Stockholm in 1972–73.

operations in one asset rather than the other. The model is a pure short-run stock-adjustment model of the financial sector, taking the price level, output, and exchange rates as given and fixed, and ignoring capital gains.

Following Tobin, I assume that a policy change in the financial sector is expansionary if it lowers the financial market rate of return on real assets, stimulating investment activity. Thus the focus of the analysis is on determination of rates of return on domestic assets, and the limited purpose of the paper is to study the effects of inclusion of non-traded assets among them.

The main results are two. First, inclusion of non-traded assets does restore the effectiveness of monetary policy as measured by its ability to change rates of return on domestic assets relative to foreign securities.[1] Second, the relative impact of open-market operations on rates on domestic assets does depend on which asset is the instrument of open-market operations.

2. A Portfolio Equilibrium Model

To study the relationships between domestic interest rates, foreign rates and monetary policy, I will use a variant of Tobin's (1969) model of the financial sector. Asset-holders have demand functions for four imperfectly substitutable assets: K (equities), B (bonds), S (foreign securities), and M (money). Each of these symbols represents the nominal (= real) value of the stock of these assets in private-sector portfolios.[2] The demand for each asset is a function of the rates of return r_k, r_b, r_s, and income Y. The latter is included to represent the transactions demand for money, which I assume has a fixed zero rate of interest. The demand functions can be written as

$$K/W = F^k(r_k, r_b, r_s, Y), \tag{1}$$

$$B/W = F^b(r_k, r_b, r_s, Y), \tag{2}$$

$$S/W = F^s(r_k, r_b, r_s, Y), \tag{3}$$

$$M/W = F^m(r_k, r_b, r_s, Y). \tag{4}$$

I assume assets K, B, S, M are all gross substitutes. This implies that for $i = k, b, s, m$ and $j = r_k, r_b, r_s$, $F^i_j < 0$ for $i \neq j$, and $F^i_j > 0$ for $i = j$. I also assume the transactions demand for money, $F^m_y > 0$, and F^k_y, F^b_y, $F^s_y < 0$. The balance sheet constraint from equations (5) and (6) below implies that $\sum F^i = 1$, $i = k, b,$

[1] The same conclusion is reached by Dornbusch (1974) in a paper including one non-traded asset.

[2] I am ignoring capital gains, whose inclusion would complicate the analysis without adding anything to the results. For a similar model with capital gains, see Branson (1972, sect. III).

s, m, so that if all partials are non-zero, own-partials F^i_j for $i = j$ are larger in absolute value than each cross-partial F^i_j for $i \neq j$. Also $F^m_y = -\Sigma F^i_y$, $i = k, b, s$.

To use this model to study the questions at hand, I assume that equities K and bonds B are non-traded assets, and that domestic asset-holders face an elastic supply of foreign securities S at a fixed interest rate r_s. Domestic asset-holders must hold given stocks of K and B but are free to trade between M and S. Any purchases of S implicitly reduce domestic reserves by that amount. These assumptions yield the two-part wealth, or balance-sheet, constraint,

$$W = K + B + H, \tag{5}$$

where

$$H = M + S. \tag{6}$$

One can imagine domestic asset-holders having an initial endowment of K, B, and H, and then allocating H between M and S to equilibrium.

Substitution of (3) and (4) into (6) yields

$$H = W \cdot F^s(r_k, r_b, r_s, Y) + W \cdot F^m(r_k, r_b, r_s, Y). \tag{7}$$

The three portfolio balance equations (1), (2), (7) are constrained by (5), so they contain two independent equations determining r_k and r_b, given K, B, H, r_s and Y. The discussion below focuses on (2) and (7).

3. Solutions for Domestic Interest Rates

The solution of equations (2) and (7) for r_k, r_b is illustrated in figure 1. There the BB curve gives r_k, r_b pairs that maintain the B market in equilibrium, and the HH curve gives the pairs that maintain combined $M + S = H$ market equilibrium, for given values of K, B, H, r_s, Y. The BB curve is positively sloped since an r_b increase will require an r_k increase to hold the demand for B constant. The HH curve is negatively sloped since an r_b increase will require an offsetting r_k reduction to hold the aggregate $M + S$ demand constant. The intersection of the BB and HH curves determines equilibrium values for r^*_k, r^*_b. Through this intersection also passes the implicit equilibrium curve for the K market, KK. It is positively sloped for reasons similar to BB, and its position is fixed by HH and BB, since in equations (1), (2), (7) there are only two independent equations.

In general, any change in the exogenous variables K, B, H, r_s, and Y will shift both the HH and BB curves, giving a seemingly indeterminant result for the

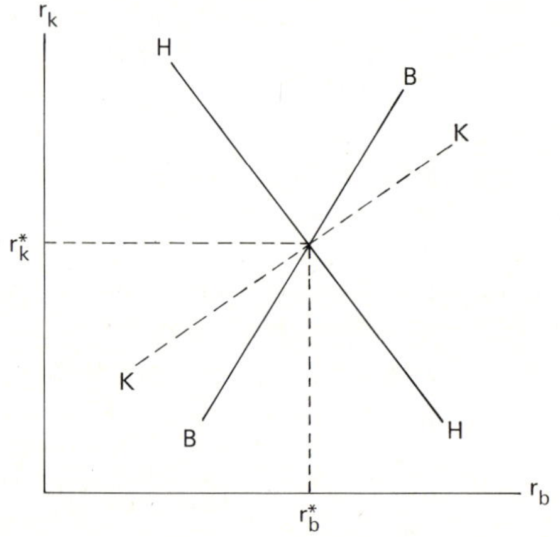

FIGURE 1. Equilibrium r_k, r_b.

direction of movement of one of the rates. Thus analysis of the effects of changes graphically is difficult; it is simpler to go to algebraic solutions using the total differentials of (2) and (7).

Total differentiation of (2) and (7) yields (2′) and (7′), which determine $\mathrm{d}r_k$ and $\mathrm{d}r_b$ as functions of changes in K, B, H, r_s, and Y,

$$WF_k^b\,\mathrm{d}r_k + WF_b^b\,\mathrm{d}r_b = -F^b\,\mathrm{d}K + (1-F^b)\,\mathrm{d}B - F^b\,\mathrm{d}H - WF_s^b\,\mathrm{d}r_s - WF_y^b\,\mathrm{d}Y, \tag{2'}$$

and

$$W(F_k^s + F_k^m)\,\mathrm{d}r_k + W(F_b^s + F_b^m)\,\mathrm{d}r_b = -(F^s + F^m)\,\mathrm{d}K - (F^s + F^m)\,\mathrm{d}B + [1-(F^s + F^m)]\,\mathrm{d}H - W(F_s^s + F_s^m)\,\mathrm{d}r_s - W(F_y^s + F_y^m)\,\mathrm{d}Y. \tag{7'}$$

Here F_k^i is the partial derivative of F^i with respect to r_k, and similarly for F_b^i, F_s^i. F_y^i is the partial derivative with respect to Y. The slope of the BB curve in figure 1, from equation (2′), is

$$(\mathrm{d}r_k/\mathrm{d}r_b)|_{BB} = -F_b^b/F_k^b > 1.$$

The slope of the HH curve from (7′) is

$$\mathrm{d}r_k/\mathrm{d}r_b = -(F_b^s + F_b^m)/(F_k^s + F_k^m) < 0.$$

Equations (2′) and (7′) can be written in matrix form,

$$\overset{A}{\begin{bmatrix} WF_k^b & WF_b^b \\ W(F_k^s+F_k^m) & W(F_b^s+F_b^m) \end{bmatrix}} \begin{pmatrix} \mathrm{d}r_k \\ \mathrm{d}r_b \end{pmatrix}$$

$$= \overset{B}{\begin{bmatrix} -F^b & 1-F^b & -F^b & -WF_s^b & -WF_y^b \\ -(F^s+F^m) & -(F^s+F^m) & 1-(F^s+F^m) & -W(F_s^s+F_s^m) & -W(F_y^s+F_y^m) \end{bmatrix}} \begin{pmatrix} \mathrm{d}K \\ \mathrm{d}B \\ \mathrm{d}H \\ \mathrm{d}r_s \\ \mathrm{d}Y \end{pmatrix}. \tag{8}$$

The coefficient matrices A and B have the following sign patterns for their elements, which will be identified henceforward as a_{ij}, b_{ij},

$$\overset{A}{\begin{bmatrix} - & + \\ - & - \end{bmatrix}} \begin{pmatrix} \mathrm{d}r_k \\ \mathrm{d}r_b \end{pmatrix} = \overset{B}{\begin{bmatrix} - & + & - & + & + \\ - & - & + & - & - \end{bmatrix}} \begin{pmatrix} \mathrm{d}K \\ \mathrm{d}B \\ \mathrm{d}H \\ \mathrm{d}r_s \\ \mathrm{d}Y \end{pmatrix}.$$

The signs of the B matrix give the direction of shift of the BB and HH curves when any of the exogenous variables changes. A positive b_{ij} coefficient means a downward shift of the relevant curve in figure 1.

The determinant of A, $|A|$, is positive, and the solution for $\mathrm{d}r_k$, $\mathrm{d}r_b$ is given by

$$\begin{pmatrix} \mathrm{d}r_k \\ \mathrm{d}r_b \end{pmatrix} = \frac{1}{|A|} \begin{bmatrix} \overset{-}{a_{22}} & \overset{-}{-a_{12}} \\ \overset{+}{-a_{21}} & \overset{-}{a_{11}} \end{bmatrix} \begin{bmatrix} [b_{ij}] \end{bmatrix} \begin{pmatrix} \mathrm{d}K \\ \mathrm{d}B \\ \mathrm{d}H \\ \mathrm{d}r_s \\ \mathrm{d}Y \end{pmatrix}. \tag{9}$$

The effects of changes in the exogenous variables on r_k and r_b are summarized in table 1. The K, B, H, r_s, and Y entries give the signs of the effects of changes in these variables alone; the K, B, H entries are the equivalent of "helicopter" changes in supplies of financial assets. The $\mathrm{d}K = -\mathrm{d}H$ entry gives the effect of an open-market operation in K, and the $\mathrm{d}B = -\mathrm{d}H$ entry gives the effect of an open-market operation in B, to be discussed in section 5 below. Here I will

TABLE 1
Effects of changes in K, B, H, r_s, Y on r_k, r_b.

Endogenous variables	Exogenous changes						
	K	B	H	r_s	$dK = -dH$	$dB = -dH$	Y
r_k	+	?	−	+	−	−	+
r_b	?	+	−	+	−	−	+

briefly discuss the K, B, and Y entries, leaving the others to succeeding sections of the paper.

From equation (9), the entry for $\mathrm{d}r_k/\mathrm{d}K$ is

$$\mathrm{d}r_k/\mathrm{d}K = (1/|A|)[b_{11}a_{22} + b_{21}(-a_{12})] > 0.$$

The $\mathrm{d}r_k/\mathrm{d}B$ entry is

$$\mathrm{d}r_k/\mathrm{d}B = (1/|A|)[b_{12}(a_{22}) + b_{22}(-a_{12})].$$

Filling in the a_{ij} and b_{ij} elements from equation (8) yields

$$\mathrm{d}r_k/\mathrm{d}B = (W/|A|)[(1 - F^b)(F^s_b + F^m_b) + (F^s + F^m)F^b_b].$$

The sign of the term in brackets is uncertain. Since $F^s = S/W$, etc., the sign condition for $\mathrm{d}r_k/\mathrm{d}B$ can be written as

$$\mathrm{d}r_k/\mathrm{d}B \gtreqless 0,$$

as

$$(S + M)/(K + S + M) \gtreqless -(F^s_b + F^m_b)/F^b_b.$$

Both sides of the inequality have values between zero and unity. As Tobin (1963) showed, the sign of $\mathrm{d}r_k/\mathrm{d}B$ depends on the degree of substitutability of B for K, on the one hand, and for M and S, on the other. At one extreme, if B and K are perfect substitutes, $F^k_b = -F^b_b$, and $F^s_b = F^m_b = 0$, so $\mathrm{d}r_k/\mathrm{d}B > 0$. If B is a perfect substitute for M or S, $F^b_k = 0$ and $\mathrm{d}r_k/\mathrm{d}B < 0$. Similarly, for r_b the sign of $\mathrm{d}r_b/\mathrm{d}B$ is clear from the sign patterns in equation (9), and the sign of $\mathrm{d}r_b/\mathrm{d}K$ depends on $B - K$ substitutability. The important point here, as Tobin noted, is that if the movement in r_k is the crucial variable in determining whether a monetary policy action is expansionary or contractionary, the effect of pure bond issue is unclear.

The sign of $\mathrm{d}r_b/\mathrm{d}Y$ is clear from equation (9). The expression for $\mathrm{d}r_k/\mathrm{d}Y$ is

$$\mathrm{d}r_k/\mathrm{d}Y = (W^2/|A|)[-F^b_y(F^s_b + F^m_b) - (F^s_y + F^m_y)(-F^b_b)] > 0,$$

since $F^b_b > -(F^s_b + F^m_b)$ and $F^s_y + F^m_y \geqslant -F^b_y$. One interesting point about the effect of changes in income is that if $F^s_y = -F^m_y$ and $F^b_y = F^k_y = 0$, movements in income have no effect on domestic interest rates. If, when transactions demand for money changes, asset-holders swap only between money and foreign securities S, then movements in Y will not affect r_k and r_b. This could be the case if non-traded assets were significantly less liquid than foreign securities. This is a point that might be useful to econometricians specifying models of financial markets in open economies.

As table 1 shows, in a world with both traded and non-traded assets, even with a perfectly elastic supply of traded foreign assets, the domestic interest rate structure is not fully determined by the foreign interest rate r_s. The domestic rate structure is influenced by r_s, but it is also effected by monetary policy.

4. *Effects of Changes in the Foreign Rate on Domestic Rates*

It is apparent from the signs of the A and B matrices in equations (8) and (9) that $\mathrm{d}r_b/\mathrm{d}r_s > 0$. The result for $\mathrm{d}r_k/\mathrm{d}r_s$, which is the same, is not as apparent.

The solution for $\mathrm{d}r_k/\mathrm{d}r_s$ from (8) and (9) is

$$\mathrm{d}r_k/\mathrm{d}r_s = (W^2/|A|)[(F_b^s + F_b^m)(-F_s^b) + F_b^b(F_s^s + F_s^m)]. \tag{10}$$

For $\mathrm{d}r_k/\mathrm{d}r_s \geqslant 0$, the condition on the bracketed term can be written as

$$-(F_s^s + F_s^m)/F_s^b \geqslant -(F_b^s + F_b^m)/F_b^b.$$

The value of the right-hand fraction in this inequality lies between zero and unity, since by the gross substitutes assumption $-F_b^b = F_b^k + F_b^s + F_b^m$. The left-hand fraction is at least unity for the same reason: $F_s^s + F_s^m = -(F_s^b + F_s^k)$. So the condition is met. The limiting case of $\mathrm{d}r_k/\mathrm{d}r_s = 0$ is reached when either bonds or money is a perfect substitute for foreign securities. Similarly, the limiting case of $\mathrm{d}r_b/\mathrm{d}r_s = 0$ is reached when either capital or money is a perfect substitute for foreign securities.

5. *The Effects of Monetary Policy on Domestic Rates*

There are three possible versions of monetary policy in this model. One is simple changes in H, which include wealth effects. The others are open-market operations in B or K, holding wealth constant. In the first case equation (8) can be solved for $\mathrm{d}r_k$, $\mathrm{d}r_b$, changing only H. In the cases of open-market operations equation (8) can be solved for $\mathrm{d}r_k$, $\mathrm{d}r_b$ with the condition that $\mathrm{d}B = -\mathrm{d}H$ in the bond case, and $\mathrm{d}K = -\mathrm{d}H$ in the equity case.

5.1. Simple Increases in H

From (9) and (8) the solution for $\mathrm{d}r_k$ with H changing, holding K, B, Y constant, is

$$\mathrm{d}r_k/\mathrm{d}H = (W/|A|)[-F^b(F_b^s + F_b^m) + (F^k + F^b)(-F_b^b)] \leqslant 0. \tag{11}$$

The sign of the bracketed expression is clear because $-F_b^b \leqslant F_b^s + F_b^m$ and $F^k + F^b \geqslant F^b$. The extreme case of $\mathrm{d}r_k/\mathrm{d}H = 0$ holds if there is no substitutability between K and B, so $F_b^k = 0$. Thus normally an increase in H will reduce r_k, that is, it will be expansionary.

The solution for $\mathrm{d}r_b/\mathrm{d}H$ in this case is

$$\mathrm{d}r_k/\mathrm{d}H = (W/|A|)[F^b(F_k^s + F_m^s) + (F^k + F^b)(F_k^b)] < 0. \tag{12}$$

Here both terms in brackets are negative.

5.2. Open-Market Operations in Bonds

To study the effects of an expansionary open-market swap of H for B, (8) can be solved with $\mathrm{d}B = -\mathrm{d}H$, and $\mathrm{d}K = \mathrm{d}Y = 0$. The solutions for r_k and r_b are

$$(\mathrm{d}r_k/\mathrm{d}H)|_{\mathrm{d}B=-\mathrm{d}H} = (W/|A|)[-(F_b^s + F_b^m) - F_b^b] \leqslant 0. \tag{13}$$

and

$$(\mathrm{d}r_b/\mathrm{d}H)|_{\mathrm{d}B=-\mathrm{d}H} = (W/|A|)[(F_k^s + F_k^m) + F_k^b] < 0. \tag{14}$$

Again the limiting case of $\mathrm{d}r_b/\mathrm{d}H$ is reached when $F_b^k = 0$. Thus normally open-market operations in bonds which increase H will depress both r_b and r_k, and be expansionary.

5.3. Open-Market Operations in Equities

In theory, there is no reason why the monetary authorities cannot do open-market operations on equity markets. For example, in Sweden semi-public pension funds are being invested in equities; the timing of purchases and sales by these funds could be used for monetary policy.

To study the effects of these open-market operations (8) can be solved for $\mathrm{d}r_k, \mathrm{d}r_b$ with $\mathrm{d}K = -\mathrm{d}H$ and $\mathrm{d}B = \mathrm{d}Y = 0$. The solutions are simple,

$$(\mathrm{d}r_k/\mathrm{d}H)|_{\mathrm{d}K=-\mathrm{d}H} = (W/|A|)(-F_b^b) < 0, \tag{15}$$

and

$$(\mathrm{d}r_b/\mathrm{d}H)|_{\mathrm{d}K=-\mathrm{d}H} = (W/|A|)(F_k^b) \leq 0. \tag{16}$$

6. Conclusion: Monetary Policy in an Open Economy

Comparison of (13)–(14) with (15)–(16) makes it clear that an open-market operation of a given size has a bigger effect on r_k and smaller on r_b if it is done in the K (equity) market, and vice versa if it is done in the B (bond) market. The limiting exceptional case to this result is the case of perfectly substitutable B and K, so that in (13) and (14) $F_b^s = F_b^m = F_k^s = F_k^m = 0$. Then it makes no difference in which market open-market operations are conducted.

Finally, since with r_s fixed changes in H, B, K effect r_k, r_b, it is clear that with non-traded assets there is freedom for monetary policy that either (a) swaps money for a non-traded asset or (b) simply changes the money stock, to alter financial market rates of return and thus domestic investment incentives.

Monetary policy is effective in an open economy with some non-traded assets, and it matters which non-traded assets are the subject of open-market operations. Since many "real-world" open economies do include some non-traded assets in their financial sectors, this suggests that a distinction between traded and non-traded assets might be useful in econometric models of these economies, and that monetary authorities should consider focusing open-market operations on those non-traded assets whose rates of return are most important for real activity.

References

Branson, W. H., 1972, Macroeconomic equilibrium with portfolio balance in open economies, Seminar Paper no. 22, 11/72 (Institute for International Economic Studies, University of Stockholm, Stockholm).

Branson, W. H. and J. Myhrman, 1973, Inflation in open economies: Supply-determined vs. demand-determined models, Seminar Paper no. 34, 10/73 (Institute for International Economic Studies, University of Stockholm, Stockholm).

Dornbusch, R., 1974, Capital mobility, portfolio balance and nontraded assets, manuscript.

Edgren, E., K. O. Faxén and C. E. Odhner, 1969, Wages, growth, and the distribution of income, Swedish Journal of Economics, Sept.

Girton, L. and D. Henderson, 1973, Financial capital movements and central bank behavior in a class of two country, short run portfolio balance models, manuscript presented at Econometric Society Meetings, Dec.

Mundell, R. A., 1963, Capital mobility and stabilization policy under fixed and flexible exchange rates, Canadian Journal of Economics and Political Science, April.

Tobin, J., 1963, An essay on debt management, in: Commission on Money and Credit, Fiscal and debt management policies (Prentice-Hall, Englewood Cliffs, N.J.).

Tobin, J., 1969, A general equilibrium approach to monetary theory, Journal of Money, Credit, and Banking, Feb.

Chapter 8.2

COMMENT ON BRANSON

Bertrand MUNIER

Professor William H. Branson has provided us with an ingenious and elegant model of monetary policy in an open economy. In short, what it shows is that, notwithstanding the prevailing exchange-rate system, monetary policy can be effective within the open economy of a "small" country, as soon as there are some internationally non-traded assets in the financial sector of this economy.

The result is challenging the well-known Mundell–McKinnon conclusions about the effectiveness of monetary policy under alternative exchange-rate systems. It seems however that one could raise two questions and make one suggestion about Professor Branson's present model.

1. Relevance to "Real-World" Open Economies

Professor Branson asserts in his conclusion that "many" real-world open economies do include some non-traded assets in their financial sectors: He suggests that his model is thus relevant to econometric studies of these countries. This assertion needs perhaps to be qualified in the following two ways.

(a) The open economy considered by Professor Branson is one of a "small" country in the sense that it behaves as a price-taker at least on the international financial market. This feature is important to the proof given by Professor Branson (which uses total differentiation). Such "small" countries (which can be quite large, indeed) are undoubtedly numerous. But, at the same time, it is required from the considered "open economy" to embody a financial sector developed enough as to include assets:

(i) internationally non-traded,

(ii) the market of which is nationally broad enough as to influence significantly global economic activity.

This seems to be a fairly demanding condition. Excluding the United States (which is not a "small" country), are there many countries in the world fulfilling it?

(b) Besides, the axiom of gross-substitutability is crucial to the entire proof. For, if we cannot conclude anything about the *signs* of the derivatives of the interest rates with respect to the volume of bonds or capital, we neither can assert that they are not zero, which is the relevant point. Gross-substitutability does not mean simply substitutability, but a fairly special kind of substitutability. Can this hypothesis be relevant to the kind of financial markets Professor Branson is thinking about? To answer this question, we would need either some empirical evidence or some logical justification. As for the latter, there are some arguments in favor of a *restricted degree of substitutability* between internationally traded and internationally non-traded financial assets and the gross-substitutability axiom in this case seems a fortiori to open the way to a great deal of discussion.

Thus, the relevance to real-world economies of Professor Branson's is a serious and first question to raise. We now turn to a second one.

2. Some "Forgotten" Relationships?

Professor Branson's approach is a sectoral one insofar as he is considering the financial sector alone. Besides, the concept of equilibrium put forward in this model is one of pure *stock* adjustment: it doesn't take into account any economic or financial *flow*. As a consequence, we may ask whether some relationships, important in real-world economies, have not been discounted, the significance of which could have changed or qualified the conclusions.

If we assume, for instance, full employment and fixed exchange rates in an environment of balance-of-payments equilibrium and government budget balance, it seems that an open-market purchase ($\mathrm{d}B < 0, \mathrm{d}M > 0$) would have only a *temporary* effect on the rates (r_b and r_k) of the non-traded assets. It would not be expansionary in the very sense given to the word by Professor Branson.

Assume $\mathrm{d}r_b < 0$, $\mathrm{d}r_k < 0$ following such a monetary intervention. We know $\mathrm{d}r_s = 0$ and $\mathrm{d}r_m = 0$. Thus, we end up with an excess supply of money and an excess demand for goods and bonds. The only bonds the private sector can then acquire are the foreign-issued ones (the S-type), the only goods the imported ones. Both transactions can be financed by conversion of national currency into foreign exchange. Thus, portfolio equilibrium seems to be reached.

But this cannot be the end of the story. For the quantity S^{d} of foreign-issued bonds held by nationals has now increased. Thus the income from capital account in the balance of payments has "improved" by an amount $r_s S^{\mathrm{d}}$. This means, if we are to maintain balance-of-payments equilibrium, a lesser surplus of the trade balance. Therefore, the aggregate demand is lowered, as are the equilibrium total income and, in turn, the tax income of the Government. If the latter is to maintain a budget balance, it will have to issue bonds and/or sell equities, so that r_b and r_k will rise. There will be no expansionary effect.

All this could be more precisely formulated by simply adding a small number of equations to Professor Branson's model.

The reverse conclusion holds under a regime of flexible exchange rates,[1] although at the price of some inflation.

In the underemployment cases, the issue is much more complicated and needs some further specification.

Finally it can be seen (a) that the conclusions are not as clear-cut as Professor Branson puts it, and (b) that the traditional McKinnon–Mundell conclusions about the effectiveness of monetary policy are not drastically changed when one takes into consideration non-traded financial assets.

3. Toward a More Disaggregated Model

As soon as we want to remove the hypothesis of the "small country" – as part of a response to our first question hereabove, for instance – we turn to a full general equilibrium analysis. By then, neo-classical pure and perfect competition starts to be really improper to any modeling of the international economy. We need models embodying schemes for conflicts, negotiations, etc., based on another paradigm than the Walrasian–Samuelsonian one. If it were possible to identify the key decision-centers in Professor Branson's model – which means giving up the macro-quantities – a reformulation of it within an oligopolistic framework, eventually based on game theory, would be a first step toward such a general equilibrium model.

[1]The same is true if one cannot transform national currency into foreign exchange because of the lack of reserves under a regime of pegged exchange rates and if, therefore, a devaluation is inevitable.

Chapter 8.3

COMMENT ON BRANSON

Michele FRATIANNI

Branson's world consists of two assets, capital and domestically issued bonds, which are not traded internationally, foreign securities which are traded and money. The paper tries to make two major points. First, monetary policy under fixed exchange rates can be effective (where effectiveness is taken to be the ability to alter the rate of return on capital) in the presence of non-traded assets. The mere existence of non-traded assets, however, is a necessary but not a sufficient condition for an effective monetary policy. These non-traded assets must, of course, be less than perfectly substitutable for traded assets, as Branson clearly points out in his Introduction.

The second point is that a central bank should effect open-market operations in the equity market if the maximum impact on the rate of return on capital is desired; in the bond market if the objective is to primarily alter the bond rate. Such an implication of the model is in accordance with the general principle that a market has a comparative advantage in determining and altering its "own" price.

The above conclusions, however, are not altogether new. Recently, they have been reiterated by Dornbusch (1973) who comes to the same conclusions of Branson's using a Metzleric model *cum* dynamic aspects à la Foley and Sidrauski. The basic difference between the two papers is that Dornbusch integrates the asset markets with the output (flow) market; whereas Branson deals exclusively with a pure stock-adjustment model. More on this point will be said below.

There are two characteristics of the model which require a critical assessment.

First, I am not clear about the genesis of money in the hypothesis. We know that $\mathring{M} + \mathring{B} = 0$; there is no distinction, however, between money generated via the operation of the government deficit versus that generated through an external surplus. Such a distinction would have necessitated to introduce explicitly the output market and analyze the interaction between flows and stocks as well as the steady-state conditions [which is what Branson (1972) does]. But this is the type of model which elicits the most interesting questions.

To elaborate on this point, define M^{F} as the country's foreign reserves and D as the government deficit; the time rate of change of the money stock and of the domestic (government) securities are then defined by

$$\overset{\circ}{M} = \mu D + (1-s)\overset{\circ}{M}{}^{\mathrm{F}}, \tag{1}$$

and

$$\overset{\circ}{B} = (1-\mu)D + s\overset{\circ}{M}{}^{\mathrm{F}}, \tag{2}$$

where μ and s are coefficients between zero and one, reflecting respectively the authorities' decision to finance the deficit by money creation and to sterilize balance-of-payments surpluses. Long-run full stock equilibrium require that (1) and (2) be equal to zero. The interesting point is that a steady-state equilibrium for an open economy does not necessitate that the budget be balanced. What is required is that $D = -\overset{\circ}{M}{}^{\mathrm{F}}$ and that $\mu = (1-s)$. In other words, so long as (a) budget deficits (surpluses) equal balance-of-payments deficits (surpluses) and (b) money creation and sterilization policies are appropriately coordinated, then the internal and external constraints need not be equal to zero. A special case is given by $s = 0$. Then $D = -\overset{\circ}{M}{}^{\mathrm{F}}$ and yet be non-zero if and only if $\mu = 1$. If the authorities set $\mu \neq 1$, then of necessity $D = \overset{\circ}{M}{}^{\mathrm{F}} = 0$.

Second, all asset demand schedules are specified to be independent of the price level. Even though the price level is exogenous in a framework of this kind, it does not follow that its variance is zero. Of course, one could reply with the assumption that output has an infinite supply elasticity and thus a zero price variance. Besides being an uninteresting case for a closed economy, such a vision of the world overlooks the important fact that a devaluation affects directly the price level and thus the public's demand for assets. This mechanism is presently missing in Branson's paper.

Finally, I have a comment concerning the characterization of the world in terms of traded versus non-traded goods or assets. Although intuitively appealing, this distinction, as Branson's paper shows, is not as important as general considerations about the degree of substitutability between goods or assets. Equally damaging to the concept is the a priori expectation that the evolution of market processes tends to make the distinction between traded and non-traded assets almost irrelevant for the long run. Laidler and Nobay put it quite well during the last day of the conference in saying that "the existence of a large scale tourist industry, which can take people to the point of production of any good, makes it difficult indeed to think of anything that could not be marketed at some price on a world wide basis".

References

Branson, W. H., 1972, Macroeconomic equilibrium with portfolio balance in open economies, Seminar Paper no. 22, 11/72 (Institute for International Economic Studies Seminar, University of Stockholm, Stockholm).

Dornbusch, R., 1973, A portfolio balance model of macroeconomic policies in the open economy, Paper presented at the Fourth Konstanzer Seminar on Monetary Theory and Monetary Policy, June 27–29.

Chapter 8.4

SUMMARY OF THE DISCUSSION ON BRANSON

Assar LINDBECK, *Chairman*

At the beginning of the discussion *William Branson* gave a reply to some points mentioned by the discussants. Firstly, he stressed that his model is not an adjustment model towards a full stock equilibrium in which the individuals are satisfied with their existing wealth such that the economy is in a steady state, either of a stationary or growing type. Secondly, the exogenous changes in the money supply are not initiated by the balance of payments. Thirdly, the assumption of gross substitutability among the various kinds of assets is extremely important for the conduct of monetary policy in order to know the exact effect on the rates of return. Fourthly, the lacking of an impact effect on the trade account (equally criticized by *Alexander Swoboda*) could be solved by adding the *IS* sector to the model which would also describe some effects on output.

Jacob Frenkel recognized the short-run character of the model. He considered the assumption of constant wealth as reasonable to the extent that the qualitative aspect of wealth should be held constant but that the value of wealth (in terms of prices) should be allowed for to vary. Furthermore, the assumption of a given income could be highly questionable because of the existence of traded securities and, therefore, of interest income yielded by the net ownership of foreign securities.

Ronald Jones criticized that there is no difference between bonds and capital to the extent that a change in the foreign interest rate seems to have the same effect on the rate of return of bonds as on the rate of return of capital. *Marcus Miller* noticed that Branson's model explained quite well the behaviour of the rate of return of gilt-edged securities in the UK – a fundamentally non-traded asset which is not held by any foreigner – as a function of the Euro-dollar rate.

Finally, *Ronald Jones* raised the question of what one has to understand by non-traded assets and to which extent there is a conceptional similarity or a conceptional difference with non-traded goods. One possible difference between both notions is the question of the degree of substitutability which is more asked in the case of assets than in the case of commodities. The relation of non-traded to traded goods indicates the degree of autonomy with respect to the price formation process of an economy. The degree of autonomy with respect to the interest rate of assets can be determined similarly. However, non-traded assets (like real estate) can become traded assets by the introduction of some new financial intermediaries (as the mutual fund arrangements). Consequently, the real issue of the nature of non-traded assets depends on the question of who controls their prices. If there is some substitutability among the various assets, the important feature is not the non-tradedness, but the position of the supplier within the world market determining the degree of control over their prices. *William Branson* agreed completely with Jones' proposition. He remarked that the usual assumption of a small open economy defined as a price-taker for goods and in which there are only traded assets, should be differentiated in a more sophisticated way.

Chapter 9.1

CAPITAL MOBILITY, FLEXIBLE EXCHANGE RATES AND MACROECONOMIC EQUILIBRIUM

Rudiger DORNBUSCH*

1. Introduction

This paper develops a formal two-country model with flexible exchange rates and capital mobility. The model departs from some of the recent literature, and in particular Mundell (1968), in three respects: We assume continuous full employment and price flexibility; the government's policies are subject to a budget constraint that is explicitly recognized and the effect of capital movements on asset positions and income is used to generate the equilibrium path of the economies over time.

The basic model is developed in section 2 and has as its key elements a wealth-saving relationship as well as a portfolio-balance relation. Both these elements obviously derive from Metzler (1951, 1968). In section 3, we study the equilibrium properties of the model for given policy parameters. Short-run equilibrium is defined as of a given distribution of equity in the world. Associated with the short-run equilibrium is a rate of capital movement that generates the dynamics of the system.[1] The long-run equilibrium is characterized by desired wealth and long-run demand functions for equity as well as the world supply of assets. After the study of equilibrium we turn in section 4 to some comparative static applications to determine the short- and long-run effects of various combinations of government policies. In section 5, the behavior of the exchange rate is discussed in some detail, while in section 6 the model is extended to accommodate inflationary finance and the interdependence between national inflation rates is discussed.

*I am indebted to Michael Mussa for discussions on the issues raised in this paper. I should like to acknowledge, too, helpful suggestions and comments I have received from John Pomery, Michael Schmid and Juan Urrutia.

[1]I have used a similar approach in two earlier papers [see Dornbusch (1973, 1975)].

2. The Model

In this section we lay out the structure of the model as well as the assumptions about exogenous variables and government policy. We will assume that there is a single homogeneous good the output of which is given in each country; along with the quantity of output income distribution is predetermined. The production of output, y, gives rise to income from labor y^0 and income from capital v,

$$y = y^0 + v. \tag{1}$$

With trade in assets we have to distinguish income accruing to domestic residents from the value of output; the difference arises from a net creditor or debtor position. Denoting disposable income by z, we have

$$z = y^0 + a - T, \tag{2}$$

where a denotes the number of permanent real income streams owned by domestic residents and where T denotes real lumpsum taxes.

Asset preferences between money and equities are characterized by the demand for real balances, L,

$$L = \delta(r)w, \qquad \delta_r < 0. \tag{3}$$

According to (3) the demand for real balances is a fraction δ of real wealth where the fraction is a function of the rate of interest and where real wealth is defined as the sum of real balances, m, and real equity holdings, a/r,

$$w \equiv m + a/r. \tag{4}$$

Saving is assumed proportional to the excess of target wealth, $\bar{w}$, over actual wealth,

$$S = \gamma(\bar{w} - w), \tag{5}$$

and target wealth is proportional to labor income less lumpsum taxes,

$$\bar{w} = \phi(r)(y^0 - T), \qquad \phi_r > 0. \tag{6}$$

It will be convenient to rewrite actual real wealth as a function of security holdings assuming portfolio balance equilibrium. Given the equality of the demand and supply of real balances subject to the budget constraint in (4), we have

$$m = \frac{\delta(a/r)}{1-\delta}, \tag{7}$$

and after substitution in (4), we obtain

$$w = \frac{a/r}{1-\delta}. \tag{8}$$

Substitution of (6) and (8) in the saving function (5) yields the (reduced form) rate of saving as an increasing function of the rate of interest and a decreasing function of security holdings and taxes,

$$S = \gamma\left[\phi(r)(y^0 - T) - \frac{a/r}{1-\delta}\right] = \tilde{S}(r, a, T). \tag{9}$$

The government spends at the rate G on goods and the budget is balanced. The government income derives from lumpsum taxes, T, and from the government's holdings of real income streams, g, where the latter may be negative if the government is a net issuer of debt and where it is assumed that government real consols are perfect substitutes for equities,

$$G = T + g. \tag{10}$$

Furthermore the government determines the nominal quantity of money, M. The exchange rate is flexible and links the domestic and foreign currency prices of goods in a manner familiar from purchasing-power-parity theory,

$$P = P^*e, \tag{11}$$

where P and P^* are the domestic and foreign price levels and where e is the domestic currency price of foreign exchange.[2]

We define next the trade balance and current account surplus. The trade balance surplus, B, is equal to the excess of domestic output over domestic absorption,

$$B \equiv y - (z - S) - G = (v - g - a) + S + (T + g - G). \tag{12}$$

The current account surplus, C, is equal to the trade surplus plus the service account surplus, $a + g - v$, or

$$C \equiv B + (a + g - v) = S + (T + g - G). \tag{13}$$

From (13) the current account surplus is equal to the rate of saving plus the government budget surplus which is assumed to equal zero. Noting that under flexible exchange rates the current account surplus equals the capital account deficit we appreciate that the rate of capital outflow is fully specified by the saving function and does not require an ad hoc "capital flow function".

A last point concerns the world supply of securities, Q. This is equal to the number of claims to income from capital in each country, v and v^* respec-

[2]Throughout this paper an asterisk * denotes a foreign quantity or variable.

tively, less the respective governments' holdings of claims, g and g^*, where the latter may be negative,

$$Q \equiv v + v^* - g - g^*. \tag{14}$$

Finally we will assume that the foreign country is characterized by a similar system of behavioral equations and government policies. This completes the description of the model and we can turn now to the study of the equilibrium of the system.

3. Equilibrium

In this part we study the equilibrium properties of the model. In the first section the equilibrium is studied for a given distribution of equities. Next we turn to the dynamics that describe the rate at which equities are redistributed in the world and finally in the third section we consider the steady state of the model.

3.1. Short-Run Equilibrium

At a point in time the distribution of equities between countries is given since under flexible exchange rates it is not possible for a country in the aggregate to sell money for securities.[3] This fact will permit us to use the distribution of securities as a state variable contingent upon which short-run equilibrium is defined. Over time the distribution is endogenous since saving or dissaving allows a country to add to or subtract from its holdings of securities. It is that process of redistribution that moves the system over time and connects the short run to the steady state.

The equilibrium conditions at any point in time are that the demand for money equals the real money supply in each country and that the *world* goods market clears.[4] These equilibrium conditions are stated in

[3]It is assumed that residents of neither country hold the other country's currency for speculative purposes or otherwise. Central banks are assumed not to intervene by open-market or foreign exchange market operations to stabilize the exchange rate. With these assumptions money is a non-traded asset. The counterpart is that securities can only be traded via a current account surplus so that at a point in time the existing distribution of the stocks of securities is predetermined.

[4]The *stock* budget constraint implies that the excess demand for real balances in each country is equal to the stock excess supply of securities in each country. It follows therefore that when both countries' money markets clear so will the world capital market.

$$m = \frac{\delta}{1-\delta}\,a/r, \tag{15}$$

$$m^* = \frac{\delta^*}{1-\delta^*}\,a^*/r, \tag{16}$$

$$S(r, w) + S^*(r, w^*) = 0, \tag{17}$$

where in writing (17) we have assumed given taxes and a balanced budget so that equilibrium in the world goods market implies that one country's rate of saving has to equal the other country's rate of dissaving.

Given each country's security holdings, a_0 and a_0^*, real balances by equation (7) will be a function of the number of securities and so will be wealth by equation (8) so that we can rewrite the world goods market equilibrium condition in (17) in terms of the reduced-form saving functions that embody the conditions of portfolio balance in each country as developed in (9). Deriving an equation analogous to (9) for the foreign country we have as an equilibrium condition of the system of equations (15)–(17),

$$\tilde{S}(r, a, T) + \tilde{S}^*(r, a^*, T^*) = 0. \tag{18}$$

The determination of the equilibrium interest rate and along with it the equilibrium rate of saving and the equilibrium stock of real balances is shown in figure 1.

In the left-hand figure we show the reduced-form saving rate, for a given level of a, as an increasing function of the rate of interest. The foreign rate of *dis*saving in turn is shown as a decreasing function of the rate of interest. Equilibrium in the world goods and asset markets obtains at point A, where the

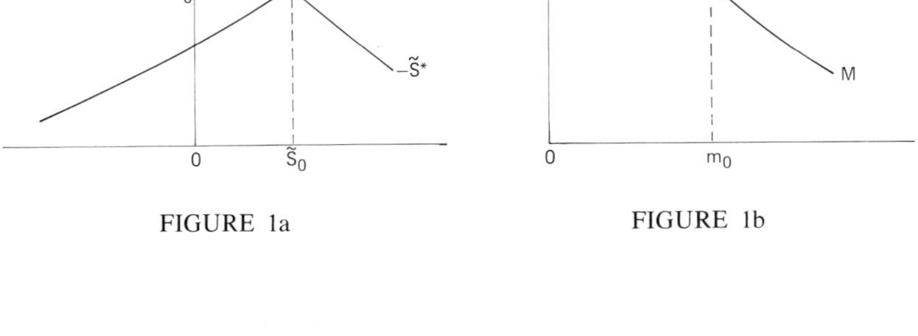

FIGURE 1a FIGURE 1b

home country's rate of saving equals the foreign country's rate of dissaving.[5] In the right-hand panel we show the home country's money market equilibrium schedule *LM*. Associated with the equilibrium interest rate, r_0, and given the number of equities, a_0, the equilibrium stock of real balances is m_0.

3.2. Dynamics

The short-run equilibrium in figure 1 is defined for a given stock of securities a and a^*. Given government holdings and in view of (14) we can take domestic holdings a to characterize the distribution of equities. Associated with the equilibrium in figure 1 is an equilibrium interest rate,

$$r = \tilde{r}(a), \tag{19}$$

and an equilibrium saving rate,

$$S = \tilde{S}(\tilde{r}(a), a). \tag{20}$$

Furthermore we note that the rate of increase in domestic holdings of equities is equal to the rate of saving times the rate of interest or the rate of saving divided by the price of equities,

$$\dot{a} = \tilde{r}(a)\tilde{S}(\tilde{r}(a), a). \tag{21}$$

Equation (21) governs the behavior of the system over time, and we will assume that a solution exists and is unique. It is important to note that the dynamics described here correspond to a continuous sequence of short-run equilibria as defined in figure 1 so that all the time markets clear and the behavioral equations are satisfied.

The dynamics may be studied in terms of figure 1. An increase in the domestic holdings of equities, a, shifts the domestic *LM* schedule to the right since it generates at the initial interest rate an excess demand for real balances. The reduced-form saving schedule, similarly, is affected and will shift to the left since at the initial interest rate target wealth is unaffected while actual wealth increases both from the increase in equity holdings and the accompanying increase in the equilibrium quantity of real balances. Abroad the opposite is true so that the foreign *dis* saving schedule shifts to the left, too. The net result is a decrease in the *equilibrium* rate of saving, S, and an increase or decrease in the rate of interest. Provided the system is stable the process of redistribution will continue shifting both saving schedules leftward until they intersect on the

[5]The asset markets clear at point A since, by construction, the reduced-form savings function embodies the conditions of equilibrium in the money markets.

vertical axis. At that time saving and hence capital flows are zero and each country has attained its steady state equilibrium.

For the stability of the process described by (21) we require that in the neighborhood of the steady-state level of domestic security holdings, $\bar{a}$, an increase in domestic security holdings causes a net capital inflow or decumulation of assets by domestic residents. It is shown in the appendix that this stability condition is satisfied at the point of long-run equilibrium.

3.3. Long-Run Equilibrium

In this section we study the properties of the long-run equilibrium. In addition to the equilibrium conditions in (15) to (17) the long-run equilibrium must satisfy the restriction that saving be zero in each country so that $w = \bar{w}$ and $w^* = \bar{w}^*$. Furthermore since in the long run the distribution of the world supply of equities is endogenous it must be true that the world demand for equities equals the world supply. That equilibrium condition is written as[6]

$$(1-\delta)\bar{w} + (1-\delta^*)\bar{w}^* = Q/r. \tag{22}$$

We note that in (22) we have, by the definition of long-run equilibrium, constrained actual wealth to equal long-run wealth. The determination of the long-run equilibrium interest rate and wealth is shown in figure 2. The

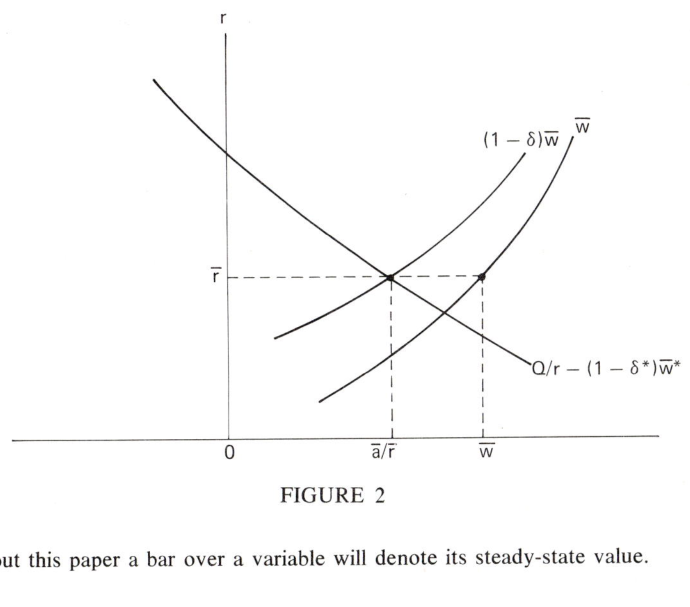

FIGURE 2

[6]Throughout this paper a bar over a variable will denote its steady-state value.

negatively sloped schedule represents the supply of equities to the home country; it is negatively sloped since a decrease in the interest rate raises the value of the stock outstanding, Q/r, and reduces the foreign demand. The domestic long-run wealth and the part of it to be held in securities are shown as upward sloping schedules. The equilibrium obtains where the domestic demand of securities equals the supply to the home country. The corresponding rate of interest is $\bar{r}$. In that equilibrium position the home country will hold $\bar{a}/\bar{r}$ of securities and $\bar{w} - \bar{a}/\bar{r}$ of real balances.

Associated with the equilibrium described in figure 2 is a composition of the trade balance that will depend on the domestic holdings of securities relative to the number of claims issued domestically. The trade balance surplus in the long run equals

$$\bar{B} = v - g - \bar{a}, \tag{23}$$

and is equal to the service account deficit.

4. Some Comparative Static Applications

In this part we consider some of the comparative static properties of the model. For that purpose we note that both the short- and long-run equilibrium are defined relative to a set of exogenous variables in particular the nominal quantity of money in each country as well as lumpsum taxes and central bank holdings of securities. Furthermore the government budget constraint implies restrictions on the independence of the parameters since changes in government expenditure have to be financed by either tax changes or changes in the government's net holdings of securities.

4.1. A Tax-Financed Increase in Government Expenditure

Consider now the effects of an increase in government spending financed by an increase in lumpsum taxes. Assuming an initial position of long-run equilibrium the impact effect is to reduce, by (6), the level of target wealth and accordingly by (5) domestic saving. It follows that at the initial equilibrium interest rate there will be a *world* excess demand for goods forcing up the equilibrium interest rate until enough "crowding out" has been generated for *world* consumption to decline by the increase in government expenditure.

Associated with that higher interest rate is a current account deficit for the home country and a lower level of real balances. Given the nominal quantity of money this implies that the domestic price level will have risen. In the foreign country the increase in the world interest rate similarly causes desired real balances to decline and the price level to increase.

Consider next the long-run effects allowing the distribution of equities to be endogenous. In terms of figure 2 the long-run effects of the increase will be reflected in a leftward shift of both the target wealth function and the long-run demand for securities function. The world excess supply schedule will be unaffected and accordingly we obtain in the long run an increase in the world interest rate, and increase in foreign wealth and security holdings and a reduction in domestic wealth and security holdings. The increase in foreign security holdings implies an increase in foreign steady state consumption and a worsening in the foreign trade balance. Domestic private consumption will be reduced by the increase in taxes and the reduction in security holdings.

4.2. *An Increase in Government Spending Financed by Income from Securities*

The government budget constraint in (10) suggests that an increase in government spending can be financed by government income from securities. Accordingly we consider now a combination of policies: A once-and-for-all open-market purchase of securities and a permanent increase in government spending so that $\mathrm{d}G = \mathrm{d}g$ and $\mathrm{d}M = (P/r)\,\mathrm{d}g$.

Consider now the short-run effect of that policy combination. The increase in the domestic nominal quantity of money and the corresponding reduction in security holdings generate at the initial interest rate and price level an excess supply of money and an excess demand for securities. In the aggregate attempt to sell money for securities the price level is bid up proportionately more than the nominal quantity of money so that real balances decline. This is shown in figure 3 by a leftward shift of the *LM* schedule. Corresponding to the reduction in real balances we have a decline in real wealth that shifts the home country's saving schedule to the right and thus generates a world excess supply of goods at the initial interest rate. The equilibrium interest rate will decline to r' and the home country will be running a current account surplus and be a net importer of securities.

The long-run equilibrium is characterized by the fact that the supply of securities to the private sector, Q, is reduced by the government's purchases. In terms of figure 2 we have a leftward shift of the excess supply schedule facing the home country and accordingly a decline in the equilibrium interest rate, in real wealth and in security holdings in both countries. The corresponding reduction in disposable income and private absorption is obviously the manner in which the government expenditure is financed.

It is interesting to note that in the long run the effect of increased government spending is to reduce private absorption in *both* countries while in the short run it lowered domestic absorption while increasing foreign absorption thereby allowing domestic residents to partially restore their security holdings.

4.3. An Increase in Government Security Holdings Accompanied by Tax Reductions

A third policy combination is a government purchase of securities accompanied by a tax reduction. The impact effect of the policy resembles that of the previous section since the open-market operation is the same. There is a difference, however, that arises from the reduction in taxes. The latter raises target wealth and therefore adds to the shift in the domestic saving function in figure 3. It follows that the impact effect is to raise the domestic equilibrium rate of saving and yield a current account surplus along with a decrease in the rate of interest.

The long-run equilibrium, viewed in terms of figure 2, is characterized by a reduction in the excess supply of debt facing the home country and an increase in the domestic target wealth function as well as in the long-run demand function for securities. The net effect of these changes is to generate a reduction in the equilibrium interest rate and a reduction in foreign wealth and security holdings. In the home country wealth may rise or decline since the

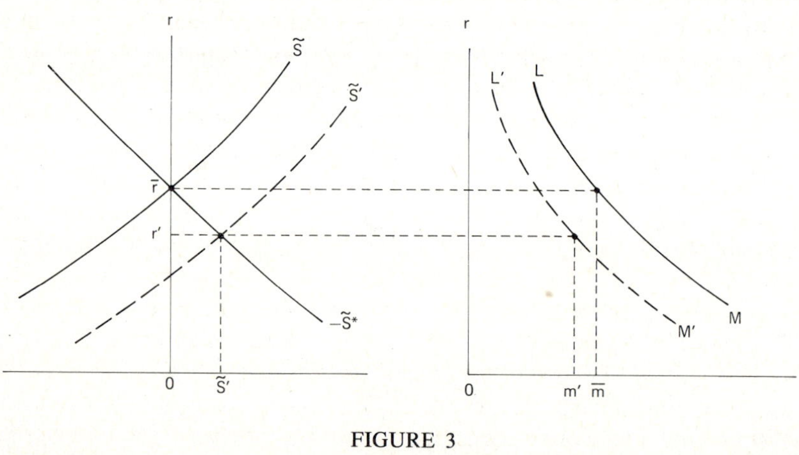

FIGURE 3

decrease in the equilibrium interest rate and the increase in target wealth operate in opposite directions.

5. The Exchange Rate

In this part we discuss in some detail the determination of the equilibrium exchange rate. For that purpose we use the relationship between price levels and the exchange rate in (11), repeated here for convenience,

$$P = P^* e.$$

To relate the exchange rate to the general equilibrium model discussed above we introduce the definition of real balances,

$$m \equiv M/P, \qquad m^* \equiv M^*/P^*, \tag{24}$$

and substitute from these definitions into (11) to obtain the following equation for the exchange rate:

$$e = (M/M^*)(m^*/m). \tag{25}$$

Equation (25) shows that the equilibrium exchange rate depends on nominal money supplies and real balances in each country. Differentiating (25) and denoting a proportional change by a ^ we have

$$\hat{e} = (\hat{M} - \hat{M}^*) + (\hat{m}^* - \hat{m}). \tag{26}$$

For a given stock of real balances in each country the rate at which the exchange rate depreciates is equal to the difference in the rates of change in nominal money supplies.[7] For given nominal money supplies the exchange rate will depend on equilibrium real balances in the two countries and is therefore related to the general equilibrium of the system. The dependence of the exchange rate on the general equilibrium of the system accounts for the ambiguity that arises in determining the effects of various policies on the exchange rate. To clarify this point we define the elasticity of real balances in (7) with respect to the interest rate as α and similarly for the foreign country.[8] Given that definition we can rewrite (26) as

$$\hat{e} = (\hat{M} - \hat{M}^*) + (\alpha^* - \alpha)\hat{r} + (\hat{a}^* - \hat{a}). \tag{27}$$

[7]The relationship between money creation, inflation and currency depreciation is further developed in section 6 below.

[8]The elasticities are defined as $\alpha \equiv [\mathrm{d} \ln \delta/(1-\delta)]/\mathrm{d} \ln r$ and $\alpha^* \equiv [\mathrm{d} \ln \delta^*/(1-\delta^*)]/\mathrm{d} \ln r$ and are both negative.

Any policy combination such as those analyzed in section 4 will affect in the short run each term in (27). Consider for example a domestic open-market purchase of securities combined with an increase in government spending. This will increase domestic nominal balances while reducing security holdings and, therefore, on both counts, will tend to depreciate the exchange rate. The decline in the equilibrium world interest rate, however, would seem to introduce some ambiguity that is captured in the second term in (27). This is not the case, however, and it can readily be shown that the exchange rate must depreciate. Considering figure 3 we note that at the lower equilibrium interest rate the foreign country is dissaving while the home country is saving. Abroad the demand for real balances increases and, therefore, the foreign price level will decline. In the home country the reduced interest rate by itself would lower target wealth and raise actual wealth and, therefore, lead to dissaving. This tendency is, however, more than outbalanced by an increase in the price level that contributes to lowering real wealth, both absolutely and relative to target wealth, and, therefore, leads to saving as shown in figure 3. Since the foreign price level declines while the domestic price level rises, there must be by (11) an unambiguous depreciation in the exchange rate. The extent of that depreciation will in turn depend on the differences in size and liquidity preference between countries as well as the responsiveness of saving to the rate of interest. These same factors will determine whether in the home country prices rise more or less than proportionately to the nominal quantity of money. Specifically, we note the "small" country case where the interest rate will remain unchanged and the exchange rate and the price level rise proportionally more than the quantity of money.

For other applications it may be convenient to assume away outright any ambiguities that may arise from differences in liquidity preference between countries. Given that these differences are neglected and that, therefore, the second term in (27) vanishes, we obtain rather strong results for the effects of parametric changes on the exchange rate. In particular, a shift out of money into securities will cause the equilibrium exchange rate to depreciate. The same result would follow from a wealth transfer from the home country to the rest of the world or an open market purchase of securities at home. More generally the country where the nominal quantity of money is increased or the demand for real balances is reduced will find its exchange rate depreciated.

The view of exchange rate determination developed here differs significantly from an approach where the exchange rate is determined by the balance between imports and exports. The present view is likely to be a much better approximation in all those circumstances where monetary disturbances or shifts in the demand for money predominate. The present approach is, however, too aggregative to cope with issues of relative prices or relative asset yields. To answer questions about the effect of shifts in relative commodity demands on the exchange rate or questions about the effect of shifts in demand between securities, a more disaggregated model is required and the present simplicity would be lost. The loss of simplicity notwithstanding, one would, however, expect such more extended models to carry the key feature of the present approach, namely, that the equilibrium exchange rate is such that asset markets clear.

6. Inflation, Deficit Financing and Interdependence

In this part we extend the earlier framework to allow for money creation as a means of financing budget deficits. To accommodate such a policy we require several alterations in our model. The government budget constraint will reflect the income from money creation, $\dot{M}/P$,

$$G - g - T = \dot{M}/P. \tag{10'}$$

To the extent that money creation by the government will, at least in the steady state, involve inflation the behavioral equations will have to reflect this element as an opportunity cost of holding money. We will make two rather strong assumptions. First, that the expected rate of inflation is equal to the equilibrium rate of inflation obtaining in the steady state. Second, that the target wealth defined in (6) is independent of the rate of inflation so that only the division of wealth between money and securities is affected.

Defining the steady-state rate of inflation as $\bar{\pi}$ we rewrite disposable income as

$$z = y^0 + a - T - \bar{\pi}m, \tag{2'}$$

the demand for real balances as

$$L = \delta(r + \bar{\pi})w, \tag{3'}$$

and the steady-state value of real balances, $\bar{m}$, as

$$\bar{m} \equiv \delta\bar{w} = \bar{m}(r, \bar{\pi}), \qquad \bar{m}_r < 0, \quad \bar{m}_\pi < 0. \tag{3''}$$

The impact effect of inflationary expectations together with increased government expenditure is to create a stock excess supply of real balances and an increase in the price level as the community attempts to shift out of money. The resulting decline in real wealth causes the saving function to shift to the right thus reducing the equilibrium rate of interest and generating a current account surplus. Thus the short-run effects are similar to those discussed in figure 3 for the case of increased expenditure accompanied by an open market operation.

In the long run, the equilibrium rate of interest and the equilibrium rate of inflation are jointly determined. The appropriate system of equations is given by the equilibrium condition in the world capital market, (22), repeated here for convenience,

$$(1-\delta)\bar{w}+(1-\delta^*)\bar{w}^*=Q/r,$$

and the government budget constraint with the long-run inflation tax base, $\bar{m}$, introduced as an argument,

$$G-g-T=\bar{\pi}\bar{m}(r,\bar{\pi}). \tag{28}$$

In figure 4 we show the determination of the long-run equilibrium interest and inflation rate. The schedule *kk* shows combinations of interest and inflation rates such that the world capital market is in equilibrium. It is negatively sloped since an increase in the rate of inflation creates, by the substitution effect, an excess demand for securities and thus has to be accompanied by a reduction in the rate of interest to maintain market equilibrium.[9] The *bb* schedule shows combinations of interest and inflation rates such that the budget remains

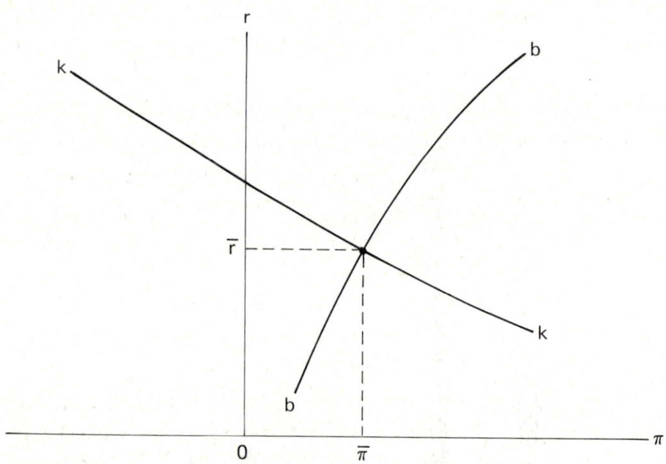

FIGURE 4

[9]In drawing figure 4 the foreign rate of inflation is assumed to equal zero. Alternatively the foreign demand for securities must be interpreted as a reduced form embodying the response of the foreign equilibrium rate of inflation to the changes in the rate of interest.

balanced. It is drawn on the assumption that an increase in the rate of inflation raises the inflation tax revenue and that an increase in the rate of interest lowers the long-run demand for real balances.

The equilibrium rate of inflation and interest are $\bar{\pi}$ and $\bar{r}$ given the remaining parameters, namely, G, g, T and the foreign policy variables.

Figure 4 can be used to enquire into the steady-state effects of changes in domestic or foreign parameters. Thus an increase in government spending, given g and T, shifts the bb schedule to the right and results in a higher equilibrium rate of inflation and a reduction in the rate of interest. An increase in government expenditure financed by increased government holdings of securities will leave the bb schedule unaffected and shift the kk schedule to the left thereby reducing both the rate of interest and the rate of inflation.

The interdependence between countries is emphasized by enquiring into the effects on the domestic rate of inflation of an increase in foreign money financed government spending. For that purpose we can parametrize the foreign equilibrium rate of inflation along the foreign b^*b^* schedule as a function of the rate of interest and the foreign budget deficit,

$$\pi^* = \pi^*(r, G^* - T^* - g^*), \qquad \pi^*_r > 0, \qquad \pi^*_{G^*} > 0, \tag{29}$$

and substitute that relation in the foreign demand for securities in (22). An increase in foreign government expenditure financed by money creation will, at a constant interest rate, increase foreign inflation, increase the foreign demand for securities and thus lead, in figure 4, to a leftward shift of the kk schedule and hence to a decrease in the domestic rate of inflation.

This interdependence between national inflation rates is well worth noting in view of the well publicized case for flexible exchange rates as a means of obtaining "monetary sovereignty". The interdependence that arises in the present analysis is due to two factors: First we assume that money creation and inflation are endogenous to the extent that a specified real budget deficit is financed by money issue. Secondly perfect capital mobility implies that each country by its choice of budget affects via the world capital market the other country's real balances or inflation tax base and thereby the equilibrium rate of inflation.

This interdependence is not surprising once it is understood that the inflation rate is a real variable and that variations in a real variable ought, in any general equilibrium model, affect all other real variables everywhere. It suggests, too, that the view of flexible exchange rates as a means of isolating a country from monetary disturbances originating abroad must be one that centers on once and for all changes in the nominal quantity of money in an environment of static expectations such as developed in the earlier parts of this paper.

7. Concluding Remarks

Rather than summarize our results here we want to draw attention to some aspects of the foregoing discussion that should generalize beyond the particulars of our model. The first is the determination and role of the exchange rate. We noted that the model determines at each point of time an equilibrium level of real balances in each country which together with a specification of nominal balances allowed us to determine national price levels and hence by (11) the exchange rate. The view of the exchange rate that emerges is accordingly that it is such that the existing quantity of nominal balances be willingly held, or, to put the same point a bit more forcefully, the exchange rate is determined on the asset market. Such a view would differ considerably from an alternative characterization of exchange-rate determination as arising in the market for foreign exchange with an emphasis on the financing of current trade flows. It is important to recognize the stock-market aspect of exchange-rate determination since what governs in the short run the equilibrium price of money is the stock demand and the stock supply.

Such a view of the determination of flexible exchange rates emerges from much of the discussion of flexible exchange rates and capital mobility in the interwar period and in particular Nurkse [League of Nations (1944)] and Kindleberger (1937, p. 106) who notes: "The fact that the French Franc is weak when the chamber of Deputies is sitting or when an unbalanced budget is announced is due to the fact that the French public fears uncontrolled inflation and begins to export capital."[10] The relationship between the budget, inflation and the exchange rate was emphasized, too, in the literature on the German hyperinflation in particular by Graham (1930) and Bresciani-Turroni (1937), while the role of capital mobility in earlier Austrian and Russian experiences is emphasized by Yeager (1969).

A second aspect that deserves emphasis is the view of capital mobility that is developed here. That view rather than specifying an ad hoc "capital flow function" derives the equilibrium rate of capital flow or the current account surplus as part of the macroeconomic equilibrium. A counterpart of that equilibrium rate of capital flow is the time path of the economy and the distinction between short-run equilibrium where the distribution of assets is given and long-run equilibrium where it is fully endogenous.[11]

[10]Kindleberger in characterizing contemporary theory notes: "The French psychological theory of the exchanges, connecting the budget with the rate of exchange can be reduced to the simple proposition that the rate of exchange can be directly affected by capital flight." See Kindleberger (1937, p. 106).

[11]A similar view is suggested in McKinnon and Oates (1966, p. 19) although their argument is presented in a Keynesian framework.

A last aspect we wish to mention concerns the interdependence between countries that arises from capital mobility and that is reflected in a common interest rate. That integration implies that all policies have repercussion effects throughout the world and that, flexible rates notwithstanding, even inflation rates are interdependent.

Appendix

This appendix shows the local stability of the linearized system. We start from the reduced form savings function,

$$S = \tilde{S}(r, a), \qquad S^* = \tilde{S}^*(r, a^*), \tag{A.1}$$

and the fact that short-run equilibrium requires that *world* saving be equal to zero,

$$\tilde{S}(r, a) + \tilde{S}^*(r, a^*) = 0. \tag{A.2}$$

Differentiating that market equilibrium condition and noting that $\mathrm{d}a = -\mathrm{d}a^*$, we have

$$\mathrm{d}r/\mathrm{d}a = -(\tilde{S}_a - \tilde{S}^*_{a^*})/(\tilde{S}_r + \tilde{S}^*_r). \tag{A.3}$$

The equilibrium rate of change in domestic security holdings equals

$$\dot{a} = \bar{r}\tilde{S}(\bar{r}, a). \tag{A.4}$$

Linearizing that equation around the equilibrium value $S = 0$, $a = \bar{a}$ yields

$$\dot{a} = (\tilde{S}_r(\mathrm{d}r/\mathrm{d}a) + \tilde{S}_a)\bar{r}(a - \bar{a}), \tag{A.5}$$

and substituting from (A.3) we obtain

$$\dot{a} = [(\tilde{S}_r\tilde{S}^*_{a^*} + \tilde{S}^*_r\tilde{S}_a)/(\tilde{S}_r + \tilde{S}^*_r)]\bar{r}(a - \bar{a}). \tag{A.6}$$

Since $\tilde{S}_r, \tilde{S}^*_r > 0$ and $\tilde{S}_a, \tilde{S}^*_{a^*} < 0$, the system is stable.

References

Bresciani-Turroni, C., 1937, The economics of inflation (Allen & Unwin, London).

Dornbusch, R., 1973, Macroeconomics in an open economy: Some comments, unpublished manuscript (University of Rochester, Rochester, N.Y.).

Dornbusch, R., 1975, A portfolio balance model of the open economy, Journal of Monetary Economics 1, Jan., pp. 3–20.

Graham, F., 1930, Exchange, prices and production in hyper-inflation: Germany, 1920–23 (Princeton University Press, Princeton, N.J.).

Kindleberger, C., 1937, International short-term capital movements (Columbia University Press, New York).

League of Nations, 1944, International currency experience (Princeton University Press, Princeton, N.J.).

McKinnon, R. and W. Oates, 1966, The implications of international financial integration for monetary, fiscal and exchange-rate policy, Princeton Studies in International Finance, no. 16 (Princeton University, Princeton, N.J.).

Metzler, L. A., 1968, The process of international adjustment under conditions of full employment: A Keynesian view, in: R. Caves and H. G. Johnson, eds., Readings in international economics (Irwin, Homewood, Ill.).

Metzler, L. A., 1951, Wealth, saving and the rate of interest, Journal of Political Economy 59, April.

Mundell, R. A., 1968, International economics (Macmillan, New York) ch. 18.

Yeager, L., 1969, Fluctuating exchange rates in the nineteenth century: The experiences of Austria and Russia, in: R. A. Mundell and A. K. Swoboda, eds., Monetary problems of the international economy (University of Chicago Press, Chicago, Ill.).

Chapter 9.2

COMMENT ON DORNBUSCH

Juan URRUTIA

Good theorizing requires the construction of models which abstract from some features which, although perhaps interesting in themselves, are not of direct concern to the problem at hand. In this respect Dornbusch's paper (1974) is a piece of excellent theorizing. I think it fair to begin this comment by emphasizing the three points to which the paper is supposed to contribute.

Firstly the paper tries to analyze the role played by the world capital market in the determination of the exchange rate. That this market should have some influence on the latter variable has been suspected for long (as Dornbusch's references illustrate), but has never been so thoroughly analyzed. In order to carry out this analysis the market for foreign exchange is eliminated from the model by means of eliminating the traditional forces underlying supply and demand in this market. The model is indeed best understood as not incorporating international trade in commodities between the two countries. It will be argued here that the resulting market structure of the model qualifies it as a neoclassical model in which the variable exchange rate is uninteresting.

Secondly, the nature of capital mobility is such that it is not based on an ad hoc "capital flow function" but emerges from macroeconomic equilibrium. Thirdly, given the nature of the exchange rate and of the capital mobility mentioned, a particular form of interdependence between the two countries emerges. Since this interdependence can not occur through the foreign exchange market (lacking in the model) it must occur through the world capital market and it is reflected in a unique rate of interest. Given this form of interdependence between the two countries a monetary measure taken in the domestic country (e.g., an open-market purchase) will, in general, affect the price level in both countries. Can we say that flexible exchange rates guarantee monetary sovereignty as Dornbusch seems to suggest?

The aspcct of the interdependence most emphasized by the author is, however, the transmission of foreign inflation to the domestic country in a modified model incorporating inflationary finance under a regime of flexible exchange rates. It is a pity that the most striking result of the paper is based on a (modified) model the local stability of which is not analyzed. The proof of it will be given here.

1. Structure of the Model

The best way of isolating the influence of the world capital market on the exchange rate is to eliminate from the outset the international trade between the two countries (and hence the foreign exchange market). This theoretically sound procedure results in a structure of markets which can be visualized as follows. In each country there is a national money market and a national goods market. In the latter full-employment equilibrium obtains since out of disposable income comes the desired rate of wealth accumulation and the remaining is consumed. The national money market is also always in equilibrium for a value of the interest rate to be determined in the world capital market. Equilibrium in the national money market means that, given real holdings of securities (i.e., given r and a), the proportion of real wealth society wants to keep in the form of real balances is always made equal to the existing quantity of real balances through movements in the price level.

The desired accumulation of wealth cannot be obtained within the country because, in the aggregate and with a flexible price level, money cannot be sold for securities. To accumulate wealth the world capital market must be used and it is in this market that the interest rate is determined. Given the new volume of real security holdings, portfolio balance requires a new price level. According to the resulting real wealth a new desired accumulation emerges and the process begins again until real wealth reaches its target value.

If this interpretation of the structure of the model is admissible there are two immediate consequences. First, the price level in each country (and hence the exchange rate) is determined by the interaction between the world capital market and the national money markets. In fact the exchange-rate variable is uninteresting because its value does not have any feed-back on the system. Second, the desired accumulation of wealth (capital outflow) is clearly the rate of saving in its reduced form. In fact the balance-of-payments terminology used is superfluous under the present interpretation.[1]

Another consequence of the interpretation given here is that the model can be classified as neoclassical. Dornbusch is implicitly saying that the model is not Keynesian, and this is correct although it could be argued that the portfolio balance relation has its roots in Keynes. The model is in fact neoclassical[2] because all markets are always in equilibrium. This is certainly true of the national goods market by construction. The national money market is in continuous equilibrium by assumption and the world capital market is instan-

[1]Under certain conditions (not so unplausible) the model could be understood as incorporating international trade in one direction with payment (in securities) in the other direction.

[2]How to classify though the wealth-saving relation?

taneously cleared because the short-run equilibrium (as defined) is assumed always to hold.

2. The Model without Inflationary Finance

Once the structure of the model has been explained and provided there is not inflationary finance, the model becomes a system for the determination of the price level in a two-country model under flexible exchange rates. The original notation and numbering of equations will be used here with minor modifications.

The system is said to be in short-run equilibrium relative to a distribution of securities (a_0, a_0^*), when

$$\tilde{S}(r, a_0, T) + \tilde{S}^*(r, a_0^*, T^*) = 0. \tag{18}$$

Equation (18) determines the rate of interest, r_0, and consequently $\tilde{S}_0$ and $\tilde{S}_0^*$. The resulting new distribution of securities, given r_0, determines the new real value of security holdings, and then the national money markets determine the price levels, P_0 and P_0^*, consistent with portfolio balance. The set of values $\{m_0, \tilde{S}_0, r_0\}$ is not a short-run equilibrium as conventionally understood but the first step in the solution of the model. It only tells us that the instantaneous rate of interest is a function of the distribution of securities,

$$r = \tilde{r}(a), \tag{19}$$

which comes from (18) for any values a_0, a_0^*. Introducing (19) into (18), we can find

$$\mathrm{d}r/\mathrm{d}a = -(\tilde{S}_a - \tilde{S}_a^*)/(\tilde{S}_r + \tilde{S}_r^*), \tag{A.3}$$

the sign of which cannot be ascertained. The distribution of securities changes according to

$$\dot{a} = \tilde{r}(a)\tilde{S}[r(a), a] \equiv \dot{a}(a), \tag{21}$$

for given T.

The two-country system is in a steady state for values of $(\tilde{r}(\bar{a}), \bar{a}) \equiv (\bar{r}, \bar{a}) > 0$ such that $\dot{a}(a) = 0$. By (21) in the steady state $\tilde{S}[\tilde{r}(\bar{a}), \bar{a}] = 0$, and hence, by (18), $\tilde{S}^*[(r, a)] = 0$. Therefore real wealth is at the desired level in each country, and the world capital market is in equilibrium at a level of r alternatively given by

$$Q/\tilde{r}(a) = \{1 - \delta[r(a)]\}\bar{w} + \{1 - \delta^*[r(a)]\}\bar{w}^*. \tag{22}$$

This equation can be interpreted to determine $\bar{a}$, and then (19) gives $\bar{r}$ and the national money markets give $\bar{m}$ and $\bar{P}$ in each country. Hence we obtain $\bar{P}/\bar{P}^* = \bar{e}$.

In order to insure existence and uniqueness of $\bar{a}$ we only would have to impose acceptable regularity conditions on $\tilde{S}$. Stability is another matter. The steady state will be globally stable if

$$\partial\dot{a}/\partial a = \tilde{S}(\mathrm{d}r/\mathrm{d}a) + \tilde{r}(a)[\tilde{S}_r(\mathrm{d}r/\mathrm{d}a) + \tilde{S}_a]$$

is negative for any value of a. Since by (A.3) the sign of $\mathrm{d}r/\mathrm{d}a$ is ambiguous, global stability cannot be insured. However, since

$$\left(\frac{\partial\dot{a}}{\partial a}\right)_{a=\bar{a}} = \tilde{r}(\bar{a})\left[\frac{\tilde{S}_r\tilde{S}^*_a + \tilde{S}^*_r\tilde{S}_a}{\tilde{S}_r + \tilde{S}^*_r}\right], \tag{A.6}$$

where use has been made of (A.3), is negative, the steady state is locally stable. Thus the model can be considered as adequate in the sense that questions of comparative statics are operationally meaningful at least in the neighborhood of the steady state.

Comments on the questions of comparative statics can briefly be made.[3] Consider the case of an increase in government spending financed by income from securities bought in the open market. Dornbusch seems to imply that the results obtained will sustain an argument for flexible exchange rates "as a means of isolating a country from monetary disturbances originating abroad". This seems not to be correct since what has actually been shown is that monetary disturbances originating in a country (open-market purchase) will generally influence the price level in both countries.

In each of the comparative statics questions considered there is a result not sufficiently emphasized. When the policy considered is such that it improves the trade balance of the domestic country we would tend to expect a depreciation of the exchange rate since both phenomena are conventionally associated. The fact that this expectation will only be realized in the special case when $\alpha = \alpha^*$ or $\beta = \beta^*$ is a salutary corrective to our thinking inertia and reminds us that the exchange rate nature, in this model, is not the conventional one.

[3]In the case of $\Delta G = \Delta T$, the effect on the exchange rate does *not* depend on the interest elasticity of L, but on the interest elasticity of $\delta = L/w = L/\bar{w}$. This explains why (24) can be used to analyze both the impact and the long-run effects. In the case of $\Delta M = \Delta g$ and $\Delta M = (P/r)\Delta g$, the long-run effect on the exchange rate *does* depend on the sign (and magnitude) of the interest elasticity, β, of the long-run demand for real balances. In fact $\bar{m}_r$ can have any sign. This ambiguity will be used later.

3. The Model with Inflationary Finance

It is important to note that once we come to the case of inflationary finance we ought to completely change the framework. Instead of having a model of the price-level determination we have a model of the rate of inflation determination. Thus the variable price level is out of the picture.[4] Existence, uniqueness and stability of the new steady state has to be examined, but this is not done by Dornbusch.

Suppose that each year there is a creation of money by the government of the domestic country, $\dot{M}$, to cover the yearly deficit $G-(g+T)$. The real income from this money creation has to suffice to cover the yearly deficit,

$$\Lambda \equiv G-g-T=\dot{M}/P. \tag{10'}$$

This continuous money creation will generate inflation in the steady state for if it does not real balances cannot be a constant. That is

$$\dot{m}=\mathrm{d}(M/P)/\mathrm{d}t=\dot{M}/P-\pi m, \tag{10''}$$

$\dot{M}/P$ being the real income generated by money creation and πm the inflation tax imposed on the public by inflation, shows clearly that $\dot{m}=0$, $m>0$, implies $\pi>0$ for $\dot{M}>0$. Moreover, since (10″) can be rewritten as

$$\dot{m}/m=\dot{M}/M-\pi \equiv \mu-\pi, \tag{10'''}$$

if the steady-state rate of inflation has to be a constant, the rate of money creation has to be a constant. When money creation and inflation proceed at a constant and identical rate, the real income generated by the initial money creation is maintained and suffices to cover Λ yearly.

Assume now that (I) the expected rate of inflation (π^e) equals the steady-state rate, and that (II) this inflationary expectation *only* affects the division of real wealth between real balances and real security holdings. Consequently we have (2′), (3′) and (3″), respectively,

$$z=y^0+a-T-\bar{\pi}m, \tag{2'}$$

$$L=\delta(r+\bar{\pi})\bar{w}, \tag{3'}$$

$$\bar{m}=\delta(r+\bar{\pi})\bar{w}\equiv \bar{m}(r,\bar{\pi}), \qquad \bar{m}_r<0, \quad \bar{m}_{\bar{\pi}}<0. \tag{3''}$$

Consider again (I). One might think that expectations are *fixed*, that is *adaptative* expectations with a coefficient of zero. If expectations are fixed we

[4] That the price level disappears as a variable is clear because a model cannot determine simultaneously the price level and the rate of inflation.

are not allowed to say later that if μ changes, and hence $\bar{\pi}$ is going to change by the same amount when steady state is reached, π^e is going to change immediately (inflationary expectations). If we want the latter to be the case, then expectations are not fixed but of a kind that might be called *perfect long-run foresight.*

That Dornbusch is actually assuming this latter type of expectation is sufficiently substantiated by his discussion of the impact effect of an increase in the money-financed budget deficit. The nature of the rate of inflation at each moment of time also emerges from this discussion. It is that rate which instantaneously equilibrates the national money market, given (I),

$$\pi = \varepsilon[m - \delta(r + \bar{\pi})w], \qquad \varepsilon = \infty. \tag{3i'''}$$

It is then clear that

$$\pi = \pi(a, m), \qquad \pi_m = \varepsilon(1 - \delta) > 0, \qquad \text{for } \delta < 1. \tag{3ii'''}$$

The workings of the system can now be represented by a couple of differential equations governing the behavior of a and m. Equation (21) still governs the behavior of a because π^e is a constant and its explicit introduction would not modify anything. Equation (10''') can be rewritten as

$$\dot{m}/m = \mu - \pi(a, m),$$

taking into account the instantaneous nature of inflation (3ii'''). Steady state, defined by $\dot{a} = \dot{m}/m = 0$, is described by

$$[1 - \delta(r + \bar{\pi})]\bar{w} + [1 - \delta^*(r)]\bar{w}^* - Q/r = k(\bar{\pi}, r) = 0, \tag{22}$$

$$\Lambda - \bar{\pi}m(r, \bar{\pi}) = b(\bar{\pi}, r) = 0. \tag{26}$$

Now, $k = 0$ is the locus of combinations of $\bar{\pi}$ and r such that the world capital market is in equilibrium and is depicted in the figure by the kk schedule. Similarly, $b = 0$ is the locus of $(\bar{\pi}, r)$ points such that the budget constraint is satisfied and it has the following slope:

$$(\partial r/\partial \bar{\pi})_b = -(\bar{m} + \pi \bar{m}_{\bar{\pi}})/\bar{\pi} m_r,$$

the sign of which depends, given the assumption $\bar{m}_r < 0$, on the sign of $(\bar{m} + \bar{\pi}\bar{m}_{\bar{\pi}})$ which is the inflation tax (marginal) revenue assumed to be positive. Lest the suspicion rises that the slope of bb in the figure[5] has something to do with stability, we now prove the local stability of the steady state. The matrix, D, of the linearized system of differential equations is

[5]Its positiveness does not guarantee existence but makes its assumption plausible.

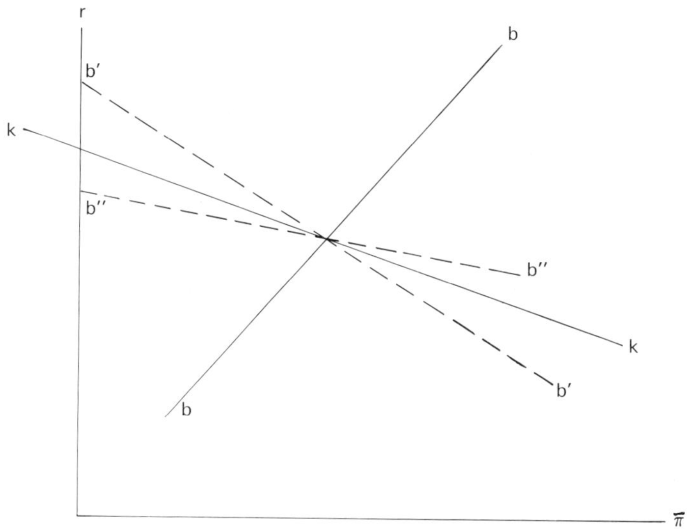

FIGURE 1

$$D = \begin{bmatrix} \partial\dot{a}/\partial a & \partial\dot{a}/\partial m \\ \partial\dot{m}/m/\partial a & \partial\dot{m}/m/\partial m \end{bmatrix} = \begin{bmatrix} - & 0 \\ -\pi_a & -\pi_m \end{bmatrix},$$

where the signs of the first row follow from (A.6). Since, by (3ii‴), $\pi_m > 0$, the tr $D < 0$ and the det $D > 0$.

It is only after local stability has been proved that questions of comparative statics can be legitimately studied. Let us concentrate on the transmission of inflation. The conclusion reached by Dornbusch has two aspects. First, inflation is actually transmitted. Second, the particular result that an increase in $\bar{\pi}^*$(resp., $\bar{\pi}$) produces a decrease in $\bar{\pi}$(resp., $\bar{\pi}^*$).

The first aspect is indeed surprising "in view of the well established case for flexible exchange rates as a means of obtaining monetary sovereignty". The surprise is not so great if we realize that "in a general equilibrium set-up, variations in a real variable ought to affect all variables everywhere".

The particular result mentioned is, according to Dornbusch, due to two factors: (i) equation (10′) and (ii) $\bar{\pi}_{\bar{m}} < 0$. Now, the first factor is the reason why there is inflation but it has nothing to do with the particular result obtained. Inflation will also result if the government creates money without a budget deficit, and it would be reasonable to ask whether it will be transmitted and how. As for the second factor the particular result is independent of $\bar{\pi}_{\bar{m}} < 0$ (i.e., of $\bar{m}_{\bar{\pi}} < 0$) because even with $\bar{\pi}_{\bar{m}} > 0$ the *bb* curve will slope positively

The real crux of the matter is the *assumption* $\bar{m}_r < 0$. If it were positive (and it can be) an increase in $\bar{\pi}^*$ will *increase* $\bar{\pi}$. Therefore the particular result seems to be rather weak.

4. Final Comments

Note that in the steady state with inflationary finance the exchange rate will be changing unless the inflation rate is equal in both countries. But, given the market structure discussed above, why should a country with all markets in equilibrium and with its target level of wealth care about the exchange rate? This reinforces our contention that the exchange rate is an unimportant variable of the model.

With reference to the case of inflationary finance it is also worth mentioning that from the point of view of a single country, the structure of the dynamic model is similar to the structure of neoclassical models of money and growth. The main difference consists in the determination of the real rate of interest in the world capital market instead of being represented by the marginal productivity of capital. Another difference is the wealth-saving relation included here but this is not crucial. Abstracting for this difference the model is similar to that of Sidrauski (1967).[6] No surprise then that the model is locally stable.

This parallelism is interesting because the confidence we might have on the results here derived is similar to the confidence we have on results based on neoclassical models of money and growth. I have argued elsewhere (1974a, b) that this latter confidence is rather slim, mainly due to the fact that these models fail to capture the role of money as a unique medium of exchange. Since the paradigm underlying any neoclassical model of any degree of aggregation is a Walrasian tâtonnement process, all goods are media of exchange.

References

Dornbusch, R., 1974, Capital mobility, flexible exchange rates and macroeconomic equilibrium, Discussion Paper 74-6 (University of Rochester, Rochester, N.Y.).

Sidrauski, M., 1967, Inflation and economic growth, Journal of Political Economy 75, pp. 796–810.

Urrutia, J., 1974a, Money, growth and unemployment in a properly characterized economy (University of Bilbao, Bilbao).

Urrutia, J., 1974b, An alternative equilibrium model of money and growth (University of Bilbao, Bilbao).

[6]In Sidrauski's model, however, (3‴) would read $L = \delta(r + \pi^e)$, $\pi^e = f(\pi)$ because expectations are really adaptive. In his model the money market is always in equilibrium through adjustments in the demand side while in the present model it is the supply side which adjusts.

Chapter 9.3

SUMMARY OF THE DISCUSSION ON DORNBUSCH

Assar LINDBECK, *Chairman*

To the request of *Jacob Frenkel* and *Robert Mundell, Rudiger Dornbusch* explained in more detail on which market of his model the exchange rate is determined. It is not determined by a flow view in terms of the demand for imports and of the supply of exports, but it results from a general equilibrium model in which price levels, interest rates and the exchange rates are determined simultaneously and in which the market for assets has a dominating effect on the prices of assets (including money). This stock view of the determination of the exchange rate is consistent with other statements on the nature of the exchange rate as it is described by the purchasing power parity or by the monetary approach according to which the rate of change in the exchange rate over time is equal to the difference between the rate of monetary expansion and the rate of change in the demand for real cash balances.

Ronald Jones remarked that the results of Dornbusch's paper with respect to the effects of an increase in government spending financed by higher taxes depend crucially on the treatment of private wealth. One can have an asymmetrical view on wealth as in the paper by Dornbusch in which any transfer of wealth from the private to the public sector involves a reduction in private wealth with the consequences on the behaviour functions to restore the desired level of wealth. However, the impact of an increased government spending on the economy will be completely different, if government expenditures and taxes are properly discounted by the private sector. *Rudiger Dornbusch* agreed that his model is extremely sensitive to what one assumes about the government.

Marcus Miller pointed out the insufficient specification of the formation of exchange-rate expectations. If Dornbusch's model allows for volatile movements in the exchange rate, the assumption of steady expectations of the exchange rate (in the non-inflationary part of the model) should be replaced by a proper function of the expectation formation or/and by the introduction of a forward market of foreign exchange. Furthermore, in this same case of flexible exchange rates, money becomes a non-tradable asset such that foreigners cannot switch between securities and (domestic) money. *Milton Friedman* emphasized another aspect of the point raised by Marcus Miller which concerned the question of exchange-rate expectations, now in the context of inflationary economies. He made the difference between people who expect the equilibrium rate of inflation (as in Dornbusch's model) and people who expect the actual rate of inflation – this latter case could result in an unstable system. *Dornbusch* agreed that other specifications on the expectations of the exchange rate would give rise to a different model. However, the fact that only real assets are tradable assets is only important for the contention of unique real world rate of interest; foreigners could hold domestic money which would not change the results of his model.

PART IV

International Aspects of Inflation

Chapter 10.1

INTERNATIONAL ASPECTS OF INFLATION: A SURVEY*

David LAIDLER and A. R. NOBAY

1. Introduction

The recent worldwide inflation is not altogether without historical precedent. There have been previous periods in which the price levels of many countries have moved together, and not always in an upward direction: witness the price decline in the latter years of the 19th century that at one time was known as "the Great Depression". One salient difference between the present episode and previous ones lies in the relative lack of agreement among economists as to its causes. Though there were always dissenting voices in the past, the dominant view was that the behaviour of prices was largely to be explained in terms of the time path of the supply of money, which in its turn was to be explained by the behaviour of the output of the precious metals.

The current inflation certainly may be, and indeed by some economists is, explained in monetary terms, but it is far from clear that this is a majority viewpoint.[1] Indeed, far more influence upon policy has been accorded to alternative explanations that invoke such sociological concepts as "relative deprivation" and postulate that inflation is the outcome of a struggle between social groups (perhaps, but not necessarily, the traditional Marxist socio-economic classes) for increasing shares of real income. Within this framework the international aspect of inflation is explained in terms of demonstration effects which lead to real income aspirations becoming coordinated across national boundaries.

*We are extremely grateful to George Zis for most helpful comments on an earlier draft.

[1]But notice that a monetary explanation of inflation requires an explanation of why it is that the money supply is increasing. Since this cannot now, as it was in earlier times, be attributed to specie discoveries, there is ample scope for those who wish to argue that there are important differences between the current inflation and any of its predecessors. The fact that the behaviour of the world's money supply is now open to political influence is clearly an important factor in understanding what has happened in recent years. Both Serge-Christophe Kolm and Robert Mundell stressed this point when this paper was presented.

The two views to which we have alluded here were captured in the contributions of Johnson and Marris to the 1971 Dauphine conference, and the vigour with which the debate continues is reflected in the programme for this year's conference.[2] In this paper we will outline the economic analysis whose failure has forced so many economists to adopt a non-economic explanation of inflation and contrast this analysis with a framework which, because it accords a much more prominent role to money in the economic system, does seem capable of providing an economic explanation of inflation. Then we shall proceed to bring out and discuss what seems to us to be some important unresolved issues concerning the international transmission of inflationary impulses that are present in the monetary explanation of the phenomenon. In this way we hope to strike a useful compromise between providing a survey of previous literature and making some contribution to moving the debate, or at least one side of it, a little further forward.

2. The Keynesian Approach

The events of the 1920's and 1930's, and the developments in economic analysis that accompanied them, seemed to overturn (but we shall argue in some ways merely interrupted) an intellectual tradition that had been dominant for a century and a half. That tradition can be summed up in the two phrases "quantity theory of money" and "price specie flow mechanism"; its dominant analytic property was to link the behaviour of the domestic price level of any country through the balance of payments to events in the rest of the world. In retrospect it seems incredible that a worldwide monetary contraction and an associated worldwide deflation should have been regarded as providing a definitive refutation of this point of view, but that is what happened. The inability of the quantity theory to provide an explanation of output fluctuations distracted attention from the other things that it could explain and a new body of doctrine grew up to replace it.

The quantity of money was replaced by the level of autonomous expenditure as the central variable in this new analysis, and it emphasized the determination, not of prices, but of the level of income and employment. The price level was not ignored altogether however. The level of money wages was usually taken as an exogenous variable and the price level was either, in simpler versions, treated as determined by a markup on money wages, or in more complex versions of the model, as a result of the profit maximizing pricing behaviour of perfectly competitive firms each experiencing diminishing returns to labour. The quantity of money only influenced the price level as one of the

[2] Cf., Claassen and Salin (1972).

several variables that might influence aggregate demand and hence output and thus was accorded no key role in determining prices.[3]

As to the balance of payments, its monetary aspects were totally ignored by the new approach, for it was assumed, more often implicitly than explicitly, that the monetary authorities could always completely sterilize these by appropriate open market operations. Exports came into the picture as an injection of real expenditure and imports as a leakage. The levels of real exports and imports were both characterized (though not necessarily exclusively so) as depending upon relative prices, and those relative prices in turn were regarded as being open to influence by exchange rate changes. The "elasticities approach" to the balance of payments thus was a natural complement to the income expenditure approach to domestic income determination.

Whatever the virtues of this body of doctrine as a means of dealing with the policy problems of the 1930's, it would be hard to devise a framework less well suited to those which emerged in the 1950's and have been dominant ever since. If the principal determinant of prices in a model is an exogenous money wage rate, that model is not going to be much help in explaining inflation; if the principal consequence of a devaluation in a model is to produce a net injection of aggregate demand into the system, an injection which has to be met with an output change if the balance of payments is to be improved, then it is not going to be much help in dealing with the balance of payments problems of a country which finds itself operating at full employment. That the "absorption approach" to the balance of payments represents an attempt to remedy the latter defect is well known; this body of analysis needs not retain us here because our main concern is with the economics of inflation. The Phillips curve was the analytic device introduced to cope with inflation and for nearly a decade it seemed capable of doing so.[4]

The Phillips curve hypothesis in its original and simplest form stated that the rate of money wage inflation varies inversely with the level of unemployment, the latter variable being a proxy for the level of excess demand for labour. When one's basic economic model postulates that the principal determinant of

[3]But this is not to say that, within the broad framework of post-Keynesian economic theory, it was not possible to build models which did accord an important role to money; within that framework, the importance of money depends very much upon the interest sensitivity of both expenditure and the demand for money. The quantitative judgements of the majority of economists on these matters, however, seems to have been such as to accord money a relatively unimportant role. This is particularly the case in Britain where the views expressed in the Radcliffe Report (1959) dominated professional and official thinking on these matters in the 1950's and 1960's.

[4]Phillips' celebrated paper appeared in 1958. The Phillips curve had already been invented by Irving Fisher in the 1920's, but the relevant paper was published in a sufficiently obscure source as to make it understandable that this work was overlooked. Less understandable is the fact that A. J. Brown's (1955) discovery of the same relationship should have been ignored, particularly by British economists.

price level changes is money wage variation, a simple hypothesis about what changes money wages is obviously very attractive, particularly when it has as much empirical support as the Phillips curve appeared to command.[5] These factors alone explain the, at first sight, curious phenomenon that, though price inflation was always the policy problem, it was wage inflation that had most analytic and empirical attention paid to it in the orthodox macroeconomics of the 1960's. Understand wage inflation, control it and price inflation is automatically under control in a world of simple markup or competitive pricing.

In policy discussions, the excess demand for labour quickly became regarded as a variable susceptible to control through demand management policy. Thus, it seemed as though the rate of wage and hence price inflation could be brought under the control of the domestic authorities by using such a policy. The introduction of import price inflation alongside wage inflation as a determinant of domestic price inflation did introduce a variable not under the direct control of the domestic authorities, but one whose effects could nevertheless still be offset by appropriate domestic demand management.[6]

Evidence generated in the late 1960's and 1970's has, of course, thoroughly undermined this view of the world. In all countries, whatever semblance of a stable smooth inverse relationship between unemployment and wage inflation there might have been in the past, it has completely vanished over the last five or six years. This evidence is widely regarded as demonstrating that the economics of a competitive market economy no longer apply to the world in which we are living: hence the search for sociological and socio-psychological explanations of inflation and policy prescriptions of wage–price controls.[7] Another important matter is the international character of the current inflation. For want of an economic explanation of inflation, its international character must be attributed to demonstration effects. Hence the call, heard particularly from OECD, not just for wage and price controls, but for international coordination of wage and price controls as the appropriate means of countering inflation.

Now if it was indeed the case that recent experience showed that economics was incapable of explaining inflation, one might have to go along with all this. However, this evidence shows no more than that a particular body of economic doctrine–albeit widely accepted–is incapable of dealing with the problem. If we look to see what the salient characteristics of this failed body of doctrine are, one factor above all stands out. It is permeated by the view that economic

[5]But the major support for the curve came from British evidence. Samuelson and Solow (1960), for example, showed clearly that the relationship got much less support from United States data, but nevertheless went on to policy towards inflation as if the relationship's existence was reasonably firmly established.

[6]Phillips was careful in his 1958 paper to refer to the effects of fluctuations in import prices.

[7]The inter-relationship between non-economic explanations of inflation and the case for wage price controls is discussed in Ward and Zis (1974).

agents are incapable of distinguishing between real and nominal values of economic variables. Inflation, of course, would not worry anyone if they could not make this distinction; indeed they would be unaware of it! What has broken down is a body of doctrine that tried to explain inflation while simultaneously assuming that economic agents were incapable of noticing it. When a theory contains as massive an internal inconsistency as this, it is hardly surprising that it is found wanting in the face of evidence.

It would be as well to point out the places where money illusion plays a vital role in the analysis we have been describing, for the removal of that assumption whenever it occurs is an important ingredient of the recent work in the so-called "monetarist" tradition that is attempting to build up a coherent *economic* analysis of the inflationary process. This is not the only distinguishing feature of monetarist analysis, of course, but it is a vital one.

The most obvious place in which the macroeconomics of the 1960's rested on money illusion was in the Phillips curve itself. Elementary market economics say that the rate of change of *real* wage reacts to changes in the excess demand for labour.[8] The Phillips curve is concerned with the behaviour of money wages and hence either rests on the implicit assumption that prices are constant or that their behaviour is irrelevant. Since an explanation of wage inflation is required as a prelude to an explanation of price inflation it must be the latter, and the presence of the rate of price inflation as an extra variable in some formulations of the Phillips curve does not detract from this point: it invariably entered with a fractional coefficient in the relevant empirical work.

However, it is not just in the Phillips curve itself that money illusion turns up. An analysis of inflation which has causation running uni-directionally from demand management policy to unemployment and wage inflation and thence to price inflation, also rests implicitly on this premise. A given demand management policy must involve picking a given time path either for the nominal money supply or for nominal interest rates. Given such time paths, what happens to prices influences the real money supply and real interest rates. Hence there is a two-way interaction between price inflation and aggregate demand. This interaction was widely ignored in discussions of inflation in the 1960's and this must mean that one of two implicit assumptions was being made. Either it was assumed that the time path of money and interest rates had no effect on aggregate demand, or that it was the nominal magnitudes of these variables that were important.[9]

[8]This elementary proposition is of course one of the bases of the expectations augmented Phillips curve of Phelps (1967) and Friedman (1968).

[9]Of course, there is nothing inherent in post-Keynesian macro theory that compels its adherents to assume money illusion. However, in discussing inflation they seem to have done so. Cf., for example, Samuelson and Solow (1960), where there is no trace in the discussion that the authors recognize the two-way nature of the interaction of aggregate demand and inflation.

The elasticities approach to balance-of-payments theory similarly rests on a form of money illusion. If it is possible to make a permanent difference to the volume of imports and exports by devaluation – a fundamental postulate of this doctrine (and of the absorption approach) – then the value productivity of resources employed in export industries in terms of foreign goods must rise more than payments to them measured in the same terms; real factor incomes measured in terms of world prices are thus lowered by devaluation. Only if this is not noticed by resource owners would one expect no further repercussions. In short the effect of devaluation on the domestic price level and hence on domestic money wage bargaining, to say nothing of its effects on the real value of the domestic stock of nominal balances, are ignored. Again, we have an implicit assumption of money illusion, and of a type that is not obviously consistent with that alluded to in our discussion of the Phillips curve.

Now none of this necessarily means that the late 1960's did not see a major change in the social forces operating to determine wages and prices in the developed world. All it means is that a body of economics that accorded the quantity of money a minor role and that rested heavily on the assumption that economic agents were unable to distinguish between real and nominal values proved, not surprisingly, incapable of explaining the relevant evidence. It remains to show that a theory that puts money in the centre of matters and does not rely on money illusion is capable of so doing, and it is to that task which we now turn.

3. *The Revival of the Monetary Approach*

The revival of interest in monetary economics began, of course, in the mid-1960's, long before orthodox macro theory was widely regarded as having been discredited by events. Though Friedman himself restated the Quantity Theory not as a theory of income determination or price level determination, but as a theory of the demand for money, it is nevertheless true that much of his early empirical work, and that of his associates, dealt with the determination of the time path either of prices or money income.[10] To this extent however much Friedman's theoretical work might owe to the *General Theory* of Keynes, a good deal of the related empirical work harked back to an earlier tradition which had apparently disappeared with the 1930's.[11]

[10]Cf., for example Friedman and Meiselman (1963), Friedman and Schwartz (1963), or indeed Cagan (1956).

[11]On the extent of Friedman's debt to Keynes and the relationship of his monetary theory to a pre-Keynesian tradition, cf., Patinkin (1969) and Friedman (1972).

The focal point of the quantity theory regarded as a theory of the level of prices or the rate of inflation is the interaction of a demand for real balances function with a nominal stock of money. The determinants of the demand for real balances are regarded as some sort of real income variable and an opportunity cost of holding money variable. With these two given, the price level adjusts to ensure that, whatever the stock of nominal money, the volume of real money is equal to the amount demanded. Thus if the nominal money supply is exogenously given, it determines the price level. With the exception of the relatively minor complication of the inclusion of an opportunity cost variable in the demand for money function, this is, of course, pure David Hume.

A major contribution of modern monetary literature is the demonstration that the stable demand for money function postulated by Hume and his successors (though not in these terms) does indeed exist for a wide variety of different countries and historical periods, and that its characteristics are independent of the means whereby the nominal money supply is generated.[12] Given a stable demand for money function, the time path of prices is determined by the time path of the nominal money supply, provided that the other arguments in the demand for money function are constant. As is well known, to consider the determinants of the money supply in an open economy operating in a world of fixed exchange rates involves us in looking at the balance of payments. Hence the rest of the world, rather than being tacked on to an essentially closed economy model as it was in orthodox post-Keynesian macroeconomics, is accorded a potentially central role in the monetary approach to inflation theory. In terms of the monetary approach, the international character of inflation in a world of fixed exchange rates between convertible currencies is not a puzzle to be explained; it is something to be taken for granted as following naturally from the analysis. A puzzle would arise for the exponent of monetary theory if inflation turned out not to be international in nature in such a world. Let us now see why this is so.

The nominal money supply in any country is equal, by accounting identity, to the sum of the foreign exchange holdings of, and the domestic credit extended by, the banking system (including the Central Bank). An appropriate definition of the phrase "balance of payments" will ensure that the change in a country's foreign exchange reserves is identical to it and thus, unless domestic credit outstanding always varies systematically to offset changes in reserves, the balance of payments will affect the nominal money supply.

[12]Much of the relevant evidence is surveyed in Laidler (1969). An important source of extra evidence on these matters is Meiselman (1971).

This, of course, is not to say very much. The balance of payments is just one factor that influences the nominal money supply. Moreover, what happens to prices when the money supply changes depends on what happens to the other arguments in the demand for money function. At this level, the monetary approach provides not an hypothesis about the international transmission mechanism for inflation but a framework in terms of which more detailed discussion can now proceed. It is helpful here to distinguish between theories of the long-run equilibrium characteristics of economies and those that have to do with the way in which economies behave when out of equilibrium – even though some of the literature with which we are here dealing is not always careful about this distinction.

The following would seem to be what modern monetary theory postulates to be the characteristics of the long-run equilibrium of a set of small open economies operating in a world of fixed exchange rates.[13] First, whatever might be the case in the short run, in the long run each economy's output is determined at full employment level by the application of given technology to available productive resources, the level of which is independent of the behaviour of the nominal money supply. The real interest rate is also given to each economy, for, whatever barriers there might be to the international mobility of capital in the short run, these are of no importance in the long run. Thus the forces of "productivity and thrift" on a world-wide basis determine the real rate of interest and our small open economy takes this variable as exogenously given to it.

A similar, though more complex, argument is advanced to deal with the determination of the price level. Whatever scope is available for individual countries to indulge in product differentiation in the short run, in the long run every country is a price-taker in the world market for every good. With fixed exchange rates operating, the world money supply is simply equal to the sum of domestic money supplies, and its rate of change is the rate of change of this sum.

In each country, and hence in the world, we have a given level of real income, while a determinate rate of inflation in the world price level is implied by the rate of expansion of the world money supply. In long-run equilibrium this inflation rate is fully anticipated. Thus the world demand for real balances is determined and hence, given the world money supply, the equilibrium level of world prices at any moment.

Each individual country then takes this price level as its own and also takes

[13]The following passage draws heavily on the work of Mundell e.g. (1971), Johnson e.g. (1972), and Swoboda e.g. (1974).

its rate of inflation as that ruling in the world market. If the rate of domestic credit expansion changes in one country, in the long run this affects the country's inflation rate only to the extent that it influences the rate of expansion of the world money supply and hence the world inflation rate. Its principal effect on the individual country is to change the balance of payments, for this is the route whereby a change in domestic credit expansion in one country finds its way into world markets.

Now we have presented here an account of the long-run equilibrium relationships between variables. We have said nothing about the transmission mechanism whereby a change in the domestic credit expansion rate of one country alters that country's balance of payments and raises the world inflation rate. All we have done is to assert that, in the long run, these things must happen. It is in the answers to the questions about short-run behaviour implicit here that the analysis of most relevance to the conduct of economic policy might lie; but it is also the case that, within the tradition of monetary analysis, there is ample room for disagreement about what factors are important here. There is room for disagreement not only because more than one model of short-run behaviour is compatible with the same long-run equilibrium, but also because as yet we have no fully articulated and satisfactory short-run model.

The description of long-run equilibrium which we have just given would, with suitably amended institutional detail to allow for the role of gold as an international and national money, and suitable changes in vocabulary, be recognizable to David Hume, or indeed to any other writers who contributed to the international aspects of the Quantity Theory tradition. An economy with full employment and an interest rate determined by real as opposed to monetary forces does after all lie at the background of all their work. However, from the French revolutionary wars onwards, monetary economics always developed in the context of the discussion of current policy problems; hence the relevant literature had a good deal to say about short-run adjustment processes as well. The dominant viewpoint, at least in British discussions, evolved as a development of Hume's price specie flow mechanism, and its essentials may be set out as follows.[14]

The level of prices in any country at a particular moment is determined solely by the quantity of money in circulation in that country. In turn, the country's balance of trade, which dominates the balance of payments, depends upon the relationship between domestic prices and those ruling abroad. Thus, a country whose money stock is higher than that required for long-run equilibrium will

[14]The present essay is not concerned with the History of Economic Thought for its own sake. The development of British monetary theory in the 19th century is admirably dealt with by Fetter (1965).

also have too high a price level, an adverse trade balance, a contracting money stock and hence a falling price level. The chain of causation here, as far as the transmission of price level changes between countries is concerned, is clear. An increase, for whatever reason, in the domestic money stock of one country bids up prices there, and not until domestic prices have risen does the balance of trade change and money begin to flow out to bid up prices elsewhere. It is the flows of money that are the central factor in the transmission of price changes between countries and these are triggered by relative price level discrepancies.

More complicated versions of this analysis bring international capital flows into the picture, but do not alter its fundamentals. At that point in the process at which too high a price level is leading to an outflow of money on the trade account, an increase in interest rates can produce an offsetting capital inflow. This will slow down and hence smooth out the consequences of monetary stringency, thus turning a potential crisis into an orderly contraction. However this does not alter the basic, trade-dominated interaction of prices, the balance of payments and the money supply.

The mechanism just described, though a priori plausible, does not square with the facts even of the late 19th and early 20th centuries, let alone with those of more recent history. It would lead one to expect that, if a particular country experienced an increase in the rate of expansion of the domestically generated portion of its money supply, this would result in an increase in the rate of growth of the money supply itself, an increase in the rate of inflation, eventually a growing balance of payments deficit and hence, again eventually, a slowdown in the rate of monetary expansion. Then there would be a deceleration of the inflation rate as domestic prices returned towards a level compatible with long-run equilibrium. This is not what seems to have happened in such circumstances. Payments deficits followed increases in domestic credit expansion rates, to be sure, but apparently without the intervention of important changes in relative price levels; in particular the sensitivity of capital flows to small changes in international interest differentials seems to have played an important role here. In short, it is hard to find evidence of the relative price level changes that are so central to the price specie flow theory of short-run international monetary disequilibrium so that the empirical validity of this particular approach to the problems under discussion becomes hard indeed to defend.

Now there was, of course, always a strong body of thought that dissented from the dominant orthodoxy albeit within the monetary tradition. This is worth mentioning if only to show how deeply rooted in past work is much modern thought on the subject at hand. When the national currency of a country is convertible on demand into specie at a fixed price, and the specie price of commodities is determined on world markets, it is hard indeed to see how the price of commodities in terms of any national currency could get very far out of line. This point lay at the root of the Banking School's insistence that, even in the short run, it made more sense to think of the price level as determining the quantity of money in circulation in a particular country than vice versa, for, unlike their anti-bullionist predecessors, they were extremely careful to confine this proposition to the case of money convertible into specie and hence to a case where the arbitrage necessary to preserve the relevant price structure was possible.[15] Wicksell's analysis of monetary disequilibrium and inflation drew heavily on the Banking School work, and centred upon the behaviour of interest rates. He always took a high degree of international capital mobility for granted and regarded his "cumulative process" as something that would work out in a world economy with the time period over which interest rates could differ between countries as being relatively short. Hence there is no suggestion in his work that prices in individual countries would ever move in anything but close harmony.[16]

This dissenting viewpoint underlies much recent work and amounts to saying that the long-run equilibrium situation, whose properties we described earlier, is one from which the world does not deviate very far even in the short run, and one that is quickly reached after any disturbance. Thus, it may actually be a better approximation to reality to treat the world as if it was always in long-run equilibrium than to treat it as if the specie flow mechanism was operative in the short run. Thus, this alternative viewpoint has the domestic inflation rate of any country determined on the world market even in the short run. Flows of money between countries therefore are looked upon not as the vital link that transmits price level fluctuations between countries but simply as the means whereby the consequences of domestic credit expansion are adjusted to the rate of change in the quantity of money demanded in each country, the determinants of the demand for money being given independently of any domestic monetary policy (except to the extent that domestic credit expansion in an individual country contributes to inflation on a world-wide basis).

However, we cannot stop at this point. If inflation rates do not differ between countries in the short run in a manner compatible with the price specie flow mechanism, they do nevertheless differ for significant time periods, and probably by more than can be explained simply by measurement problems.

[15]This matter is discussed in detail in Laidler (1971).

[16]The Currency School, whose views came to dominate British monetary thought, never achieved so dominant a position on the Continent. There the Banking School position retained a respectable place for itself. For Wicksell's views on the Banking School, cf., Wicksell (1935).

Moreover, in the long run the world may be at full employment but a major policy problem as far as the control of inflation is concerned involves the interaction of inflation and unemployment rates.

If inflation rates do indeed differ between countries, then it cannot be the case that the prices of all goods always are given by the equilibrium properties of world markets. Recent efforts to deal with discrepancies between national inflation rates take this observation as their starting point and postulate the existence of two types of goods: "tradeables" and "non-tradeables". Tradeables are simply goods for which there exists a world-wide market and non-tradeables those which are confined to national markets. The world market determines the time path of the price level of tradeables which must always be the same for every country. Persistent discrepancies between national inflation rates are explained in terms of different productivity growth rates in the two sectors, while shorter-term discrepancies are explained by delays in the transmission of inflationary impulses from the tradeables sector in any economy to its non-tradeable sector.[17] We will concentrate on the latter point here.

Two, by no means mutually exclusive, routes whereby changes in the inflation rate in world markets can be transmitted to non-tradeables may be identified. First, an increase in the rate of inflation in world markets ought to result in an increase in the rate of change of money wages in the tradeable sector. Given labour mobility between the tradeable and non-tradeable sectors, money wage inflation, and hence price inflation, in the non-tradeable sector could also be expected to increase. Second, an increase in the rate of price inflation in the tradeables sector will initially lead to a changing structure of relative prices and a switch of demand towards non-tradeables, and hence will generate pressure towards an increase in the inflation rate there.

In the long run one would expect a given relative price structure to be consistent with equilibrium in the two sectors (or a given time path of relative prices if productivity is growing at different rates in the two sectors), so that marked discrepancies in inflation rates between one country and that ruling in the rest of the world are to be explained in terms of lags in the mechanism whereby inflation is transmitted from one sector of the economy to the other. Thus, in this view, the transmission of inflation goes directly from world prices into the domestic prices of tradeables and thence, through either the labour market or through a tendency to substitution between goods, to the prices of non-tradeables. In the meanwhile the balance of payments provides whatever

[17]The distinction between tradeables and non-tradeables bears a close relationship to that between the exposed and sheltered sectors of an economy in the so-called Nordic model of inflation. Here differences in productivity growth rates between sectors play a key role.

change in reserves is needed, given domestic monetary policy, to generate the rate of monetary expansion that will support the rate of inflation thus determined.[18]

Such analysis as this does not tell us anything about the determinants of real income fluctuations. It simply assumes that these will not take place; but of course they do. It is here that monetary analysis borrows from the now discredited orthodoxy, for a version of the Phillips curve, free of the assumption of money illusion, provides a vital link in the argument at this point. The development in question is the so-called "expectations augmented" or "sophisticated" Phillips curve of Friedman and Phelps. In essence, this analysis has wage and price inflation rates being determined not "by markets" but by the price-setting activities of firms, each one of which sets its rate of wage and price change equal to the rate it expects its competitors to choose, these expectations being largely extrapolated from past experience. Firms then modify their initial price and wage decisions in response to market excess demand. Variations in excess demand manifest themselves in output changes so that fluctuations in income and employment become an integral part of the mechanism whereby the inflation rates of both prices and wages can be changed.

Though developed in the context of a closed economy model, this type of analysis is readily transferable to the open economy case when a non-tradeable sector which does not take its prices directly from the outside world is postulated. Fluctuations in output and employment may be accorded a role in the transmission of changes in the world inflation rate from the tradeable sector to the rest of the economy. Though analytically possible, the introduction of the expectations augmented Phillips curve into the monetary analysis of international inflation in this way is nevertheless theoretically awkward. The device belongs to the "new microeconomics" while the postulate that firms in the tradeable sector take their prices from world markets comes from the "old microeconomics".[19]

The coexistence of the two theories of price formation, one for the tradeable sector and one for the non-tradeable sector, in one model is not easy to justify, but then nor is the distinction between tradeable and non-tradeable goods. One might think that the distinction could roughly correspond to one between goods

[18]The model presented by Parkin (1972) deals with these matters concentrating in particular on the labour market as a vehicle for the transmission of inflationary impulses.

[19]The model dealt with in Laidler (1973) uses the expectations augmented Phillips curve in the manner outlined here in order to produce output fluctuations as an integral part of the mechanism whereby an open economy's inflation rate changes either as a result of domestic or outside impulses. This model is vulnerable to the criticisms levelled here.

which can physically be transported from their place of production to other locations before being consumed, and those which must be consumed as they are produced, at the point of production. However, the existence of a large-scale tourist industry, which can take people to the point of production of any good makes it difficult indeed to think of anything that could not be marketed at some price on a world-wide basis.

Instead of having one sector of the economy for which world market conditions are all important and another on which world market conditions have no direct influence it seems more reasonable to postulate a spectrum of goods lying across the entire range between these two extremes.[20] Moreover, there is no reason to persist with two theories of pricing behaviour. One will do. The whole spirit of the monetary approach is to treat the world as if it was a single closed economy, and there is no reason why we cannot have world-wide fluctuations in income and employment as a necessary accompaniment to changes in the world-wide inflation rate. Fluctuations in the output of all industries, and not just those operating in isolation from world markets then become part of the mechanism whereby changes in the world inflation rate are brought into any one economy.

To make this argument more precise would carry us beyond the bounds of the current state of knowledge of the economics of inflation in open economies, and it is the current state of knowledge that is the main focus of this paper. We will therefore not carry this argument any further here but rather will turn to summarizing the analysis developed above, and argue that it accords well with the broad outlines of recent economic history, and then raise questions about the extent to which changes in the exchange-rate regime affect its relevance for the future.

4. Conclusions

The monetary theory of inflation which we discussed in the last section of this paper is not, of course, a radically new departure. Rather, as we have stressed, it represents a continuation of an analytic tradition that goes back to Hume, though it has more in common with the dissenting Banking School–Wicksellian branch of that tradition than with its predominating orthodoxy. Moreover, it

[20]But of course one may regard the tradeable – non-tradeable dichotomy as being a very simple special case of such a spectrum with only two extreme categories. Thus its use may still be defended as a means of achieving analytic simplicity despite the arguments advanced here. We are indebted to Alexander Swoboda for making this point during the discussion following the presentation of this paper.

draws on the new microeconomics in order to integrate the analysis of output fluctuations with that of inflation.

In essence, it treats the world as a large highly integrated closed economy in which there is no sharp product differentiation between individual countries. This lack of product differentiation is essential to the proposition that each country takes its price level from the world economy and to the accompanying emphasis on monetary aspects of the balance of payments. Thus, the model seems a priori better adapted to deal with a world in which international trade is dominated by trade among industrial countries than to a world in which exchange is predominantly between, say, agricultural and industrial economies, where outputs are more sharply differentiated. But this also means that it is a model well adapted to deal with the international economy of the 1960's which was indeed dominated by trade between industrial countries.

Just as world goods markets are viewed as being highly integrated so too are world capital markets, and again, the 1960's saw an enormous increase in the international mobility of capital and in the volume of internationally mobile capital. Thus, the preconditions for a monetary view of international inflation to have empirical content would seem to have been approximately met until recently, for a regime of fixed exchange rates between convertible currencies also underlies the foregoing analysis, and such a regime existed, approximately, among major Western nations until 1971 or thereabouts.

The theory would then tell us to look for one factor to explain an increase in the international inflation rate: a marked increase in the world wide rate of monetary expansion. This did indeed take place, originating in the United States, whose monetary authorities essentially played the role accorded to gold miners in 19th century monetary theory. The increase in the rate of monetary expansion originated as is well known, in the budget deficits that resulted from the attempt to finance the Vietnam war without tax increases – indeed alongside tax cuts – and was accentuated on a world-wide basis by the once-and-for-all phenomenon of the development of the Eurodollar market where the United States' balance of payments deficit provided a reserve base for the creation of further additions to the world money supply.

At the same time, the theory would tell us to expect world-wide variations in the inflation rate to be associated with world-wide fluctuations in real income and employment. Again, the stylized facts fit the theory, for one of the most striking features of the last few years has been the way in which real output fluctuations have moved together on a world-wide basis. The sharp United States monetary contraction of 1969 was felt throughout the Western world and produced real output contractions and slowdowns in the inflation rate elsewhere over the following three years, while the subsequent expansion preceded the world-wide recovery of real output and inflation rates.[21]

The result of all this, as we know, has been for individual countries to try to cut themselves free of the international monetary system in an attempt to gain control over their own employment and inflation rates.[22] The length of the time lags involved in the transmission of inflationary impulses are almost certainly too long for us to have any idea of whether these attempts have been successful or not, for it can only have been in 1973 that the effects of relatively independent domestic policies taken since 1971 began to dominate the trends inherited from the past. Nor indeed do we know whether the attempts at achieving independence have been successful.

It is true that greater exchange-rate flexibility should lead to greater scope for independent national monetary policies, but all our received theories on the way in which flexible exchange rates work seem premissed on a world where international transactions are dominated by the trade account rather than the capital account. The growth in importance of capital movements forced a higher degree of monetary integration on countries than they were willing to live with under the Bretton–Woods system. It is not clear what its effects are on the way in which a system of flexible rates will operate.

Be that as it may, one thing above all should be stressed at the close of the paper. We began by showing how a body of economic theory reasonably well adapted to dealing with the special circumstances of the 1930's broke down when applied to the 1960's. We then went on to show how, suitably adapted, an older theoretical tradition did seem better able to cope with recent economic history. However, the breakdown of the fixed exchange-rate system has already removed an essential pre-condition for that body of theory to be applicable. We must be careful, therefore, not to apply it blindly, and without modification, to current and future policy discussions.

References

Bell, G., 1973, The Eurodollar market and the international financial system (Macmillan, London).

Brown, A. J., 1955, The great inflation, 1939–1951 (Oxford University Press, London).

Cagan, P., 1956, The monetary dynamics of hyperinflation, in: M. Friedman, ed., Studies in the quantity theory of money (University of Chicago Press, Chicago, Ill.).

[21]When countries' outputs are differentiated, the elasticities approach to the balance of payments takes on relevance, as does the price specie flow mechanism as an account of the monetary side of balance of payments disequilibrium. We are indebted to Milton Friedman for making this point during the discussion that followed the presentation of this paper.

[22]Cf., Bell (1973) for a lucid account of many of the matters raised in the last few paragraphs.

Claassen, E. and P. Salin, 1972, Stabilisation policies in interdependent economics (North-Holland, Amsterdam).
Fetter, F. W., 1965, The development of British monetary orthodoxy, 1797–1875 (Harvard University Press, Cambridge, Mass.).
Friedman, M., 1968, The role of monetary policy, American Economic Review 58, March, pp. 1–17.
Friedman, M., 1972, Comments on the critics, JPE, Sept.–Oct., pp. 906–950.
Friedman, M. and D. Meiselman, 1963, The relative stability of monetary velocity and the investment multiplier in the United States, 1898–1958, in: Commission on Money and Credit, Stabilization policies (Prentice-Hall, Englewood Cliffs, N.J.).
Friedman, M. and A. J. Schwartz, 1963, Money and business cycles, Review of Economics and Statistics 45, Feb., Suppl. pp. 32–64.
Johnson, H. G., 1972, Inflation and the monetarist controversy, De Vries Lectures 1971 (North-Holland, Amsterdam).
Laidler, D. E. W., 1969, The demand for money – Theories and evidence (International Textbook Co., Scranton, Penn.).
Laidler, D., 1972, Thomas Tooke on monetary reform, in: M. Peston and B. Corry, eds., Essays in honour of Lord Robbins (Weidenfeld & Nicholson, London).
Laidler, D., 1973, Price and output fluctuations in open economies, mimeo. (University of Manchester, Manchester).
Meiselman, D., ed., 1971, The varieties of monetary experiences (University of Chicago Press, Chicago, Ill.).
Mundell, R. A., 1971, Monetary theory: Inflation, interest and growth in the world economy (Goodyear, Pacific Palisades, Calif.).
Parkin, J. M., 1972, Inflation, the balance of payments, domestic credit expansion and exchange rate adjustment, mimeo. (University of Manchester, Manchester).
Patinkin, D., 1969, The Chicago tradition, the quantity theory and Friedman, Journal of Money, Credit and Banking 1, Feb., pp. 46–70.
Phelps, E., 1967, Phillips curve, expectations of inflation and optimal unemployment over time, Economica NS 34, Aug., pp. 254–281.
Phillips, A. W., 1958, The relation between unemployment and the rate of change of money wage rates in the United Kingdom, Economica NS 25, Nov., pp. 283–299.
Radcliffe Committee (Committee on the Working of the Monetary System) Report, 1959 (HMSO, London).
Samuelson, P. A. and R. Solow, 1960, Analytic aspects of anti-inflation policy, American Economic Review 50, May, pp. 177–194.
Swoboda, A. K., 1974, Monetary policy under fixed exchange rates: Effectiveness, the speed of adjustment and proper use, in: H. G. Johnson and A. R. Nobay, eds., Issues in monetary economics (Oxford University Press, London).
Ward, R. and G. Zis, 1974, Trade union militancy as an explanation of inflation: An international comparison, Manchester School 52, March, pp. 46–65.
Wicksell, K., 1935, Lectures on political economy (London); first published in 1905.

Chapter 10.2

COMMENT ON LAIDLER AND NOBAY

Manfred WILLMS

The paper of Laidler and Nobay (L&N) is a well developed survey of the national and the international aspects of the economics of inflation. It begins with a critical analysis of theories of inflation in which the quantity of money plays no role or a minor role like the wage markup inflation or the Phillips curve relationship. L&N show convincingly that these theories are neither able to explain the increase in national prices nor the world-wide increase in the price level. The wage markup inflation rests on the assumption that prices are determined by an exogenous money wage rate. As there is no economic explanation of money wages the door is open to all kinds of sociological and psychological explanations of the wage rate and thus the rate of inflation. In the Phillips curve relationship the wage rate and the rate of inflation is explained by the dynamics of the labour markets.

L&N make it very clear why these theories were incapable of dealing with the problem of inflation: They neglect the importance of money and they do not distinguish between nominal and real values, i.e., they assume money illusion of the various economic agents. If economic policy is based on an inconsistent theory it must fail. Therefore income policy and demand management are inadequate and insufficient instruments to fight inflation. L&N's criticism of broadly accepted but impractical doctrines can only be supported.

In order to explain national and international inflation of the 1960's L&N draw heavily on the new monetary approach of the determination of the price level. This approach rests on the assumption of a system of fixed exchange rates, highly integrated world markets for commodities and capital, and the possibility of severe balance-of-payments deficits of at least one international dominating country and corresponding surpluses of other countries. According to the monetary approach the rate of inflation in the world economy is determined by the rate of the world monetary expansion relative to the world rate of real economic growth. Excessive money creation of one or more countries spreads through the world commodity and capital markets and establishes one world price level and one world level of interest rates. National price levels and national levels of interest rates must conform to the international levels. There is no possibility for small open economies to escape the international rate of inflation.

L&N make it very clear that these results are only valid for the long-run equilibrium situation. Only in the long run every country has the same rate of inflation. However, in the short run inflation rates can differ from country to country. Why?

L&N argue that the difference is often explained by the existence of traded and non-traded goods. The transmission of inflation goes directly from world prices to the domestic prices of tradables and from there through the labour market or through substitution effects to the prices of non-tradables. Time is involved in this adjustment process and thus a deviation of national prices from world prices is possible.

L&N are aware of the fact that the segmentation of the economy into two different sectors implies the application of two different theories of price formation, one for the tradable sector and one for the non-tradable sector. They argue that the two markets may be interrelated not by the labour market but by the demand of tourists for non-tradable goods.

This approach is not very convincing. More important for international price adjustments seem to be the activity of multi-national companies and the reduction of transport costs which reduces the relative importance of non-tradables.

What one is missing in the paper of L&N is a convincing explanation of existing international price differences. It seems to me that, besides different methods to measure price levels in the different countries, differences in the rates of inflation between countries are due to the following facts:

(1) different monetary policies,
(2) different fiscal policies,
(3) different importance of tradable and non-tradable goods.

Particularly the policy implications are obviously of great importance. The consideration of different economic policies do not have to stay in the centre of a theoretical survey. However, they are of tremendous practical and empirical importance.

Chapter 10.3

SUMMARY OF THE DISCUSSION ON LAIDLER AND NOBAY

Anthony B. ATKINSON, *Chairman*

Milton Friedman suggested that the distinction between the price–specie mechanism and the monetary theory of the balance of payments was not as important as it could appear in the Laidler–Nobay paper. The fundamental issue is really one of the speeds of adjustment of various variables in the adjustment process. It is alleged that both theories mainly differ in that, when a country experiences a more rapid real income growth, a balance-of-payments deficit would be predicted by the price–specie mechanism and a surplus by the monetary theory of the balance of payments. In fact, a deficit is implied by the Keynesian variety of the price–specie mechanism, where imports are assumed to be linked to income and exports to be autonomous. However, it can be assumed that a country with a higher productivity growth increases its supply of exports and reduces its dependence on imports, whereas capital flows are attracted by this higher rate of growth. Therefore, there is a balance-of-payments surplus.

The phenomena described by the price–specie mechanism have some role to play in explaining reality, since the price–arbitrage mechanism does not work perfectly and instantaneously. In fact, there is a different exchange rate for each good and the distinction between tradables and nontradables only replace a whole frequency distribution by a border line between two categories of goods.

Manfred Willms recalled the distinction made by the "Scandinavian" models between sheltered and exposed sectors. It may happen that tradable goods are produced by sheltered sectors, which is important insofar as the price determination mechanisms may be different in both sectors.

Robert Mundell underlined that the purchasing-power parity theory à la Cassell worked perfectly well in the past years of high inflation rates and the differences in inflation rates between countries, under fixed rates, are only minor and depend upon what indices are used (since there are real forces and terms of trade factors). In a world of flexible rates, the countries which devalue are going to be more inflationary and the countries which appreciate are going to be more deflationary. Therefore, a temporary depreciation of the exchange rate can have lasting inflationary effects, since it increases inventory prices, decreases real wages and, therefore, calls for higher wage pressures.

Assar Lindbeck recalled the 1971 debate[1] on world inflation, where he defended an "eclectic" position and reaffirmed it. A lot of factors (income freezes, price freezes, elections, aggressiveness of labour unions, etc.) introduce noises in equations which try to explain inflation through a limited number of factors, and the weight of these noises are different according to the length of time one considers. That may also explain why for instance, the distinction between tradables and non-tradables, which seemed very fruitful a priori, has not a better explanatory power than, for instance, the Phillips curve as shown by Branson and Myhrman. The "eclectic" position also leads to the view that there are now a lot of non-market information processes: for instance, wage claims by trade unions are modified by what they happen to know about wage increases in other countries or their concern about a risk of unemployment when wages rise too much.

Michael Parkin challenged the eclectic view of Assar Lindbeck by recalling that, when properly formulated, the models stemming from the expectation-augmented excess demand hypothesis did amazingly well. Therefore, while it is a good thing to be eclectic – open-minded – when formulating assumptions, it is intellectually criminal to remain eclectic in the face of empirical evidence. Thus, economists must stop saying that all inflation explanations are equal since certain models explain remarkably well quarterly variations in the rate of change of money wages and money prices.

According to *Alexander Swoboda*, there is a risk with eclecticism, namely to end up describing reality and to explain only divergencies, while forgetting the central phenomenon.

David Laidler stated that he was not in favour of eclecticism because good science implies the simplest explanation. Eclecticism prevents from looking for the simplest explanation.

Jacques Melitz said that, in his opinion, the main difference in the explanations of inflation was between those who believe that money – or the money base – is

[1]E. M. Claassen and P. Salin, eds., 1972, Stabilization policies in interdependent economies (North-Holland, Amsterdam).

endogenous and those who believe it is exogenous. In the first case, the quantity of money is simply determined by the behaviour of households and firms.

Serge-Christophe Kolm doubted that, contrary to Laidler and Nobay's opinion, there was any historical precedent to the present situation of world-wide high inflation.

Wolfgang Stützel expressed the view that the observed very large fluctuations of the exchange rate under a system of floating rates may be a proof that in such a regime exchange rates do not reflect the purchasing power parity.

William Branson regretted that the paper under discussion was mostly concerned with demand sources of inflation, although, for instance, agricultural shortages can be a source of inflation; at present time, commodity prices have doubled in one year, but money stocks have not doubled in one year.

Michael Parkin underlined that, in a fixed rates world, measured international differences in inflation rates are not really differences in inflation rates, but relative price movements which have been measured. If, for instance, starting from equilibrium in a one-commodity world, you disturb it, during the disequilibrium adjustment process there will be a price distribution rather than a point price, since people react differently, as was shown by the new microeconomics. Now, there is nothing at all in this analysis about the geographical, national or political location of the temporary excess demands, so that international differences are not explained by any systematic national factor.

David Laidler agreed with the distinction made by Michael Parkin between systematic and random deviations in national inflation rates; but, in the short run, even random deviations may seem large.

Assar Lindbeck expressed scepticism about the validity of simple models explaining inflation in terms of past inflation.

Milton Friedman declared himself in agreement both with Michael Parkin and Assar Lindbeck. In fact, it is irrational for people to maintain the same expectation function in the light of changing phenomena. If we assume that people are forming expectations in some rational way, they ought to take into account what they know about the economic theory of the formation of prices; therefore, modifications in the behaviour of monetary authorities and changing behaviours in price level formation will imply changes in the expectation functions. Models allowing for changes in the expectation function–as did Robert Lucas and Tom Sargent–are thus better than models assuming stable expectation functions.

To elaborate on William Branson's reference to a doubling of commodity prices, *Robert Mundell* underlined that the present world has some very powerful sources of inflation, for instance the fact that central banks can revaluate the value of their gold reserves or the fact that the Eurodollar market is unconstrained and can create huge amounts of liquidity.

Chapter 11.1

A NOTE ON INTERNATIONAL CURRENCY AND WORLD INFLATION

Pascal SALIN

The present paper tries to evaluate the desirable rate of creation of an international currency (IC), issued by an international organization and held by central banks only, as is the case for the Special Drawing Rights of the International Monetary Fund. We further discuss its effects on the rate of world inflation and the distribution of seigniorage attached to the creation of international reserves.

The decision to create the SDR system can be interpreted as having had two justifications: (i) to regulate the quantity of international liquidity or the level of public reserves; (ii) to introduce more symmetry in the international monetary system, so that the dollar would loose a part of its role as an international reserve asset, and the amount of seigniorage paid to the United States would decrease.

In the sixties, it seemed that there was a "shortage of international liquidity", so that SDR's were supposed to "supplement"[1] existing reserves, whenever they appeared to be insufficient. Such a doctrine implies that, for a given rate of world inflation, the rate of creation of SDR's ought to be higher the lower the rate of growth of other reserve assets is. In fact, the demand for international reserves must be analyzed as a demand for real balances. Therefore, there cannot be a long-run shortage (excess) of international reserves, except in that sense that the rate of growth of international reserves is lower (higher) than the sum of the real rate of growth of world production and of the rate of world inflation. In other words, as world inflation is determined by the rate of growth of the sum of all national quantities of money, the supposed existence of a shortage (excess) of international reserves would imply that central banks

[1]The IMF Articles of Agreement state that "To meet the need, as and when it arises, for a supplement to existing reserve assets, the Fund is authorized to allocate special drawing rights to members that are participants in the Special Drawing Account" (article XXI, section 1). The question is at times put in a somewhat different way: in order to ensure the desired quantity of international money should one create SDR's in order to supplement other forms of liquidity or to "control" the growth of other forms?

accumulate international reserves at a rate lower (higher) than the rate at which they create their national currencies. Such a situation may happen in some exchange systems. For instance, in the former gold standard, gold was the only component of public reserves and its price was fixed in terms of any national currency. As, collectively, central banks issued money at a rate higher than the rate of gold accumulation, it finally seemed that there was a shortage of reserves, given the (too high) level of world prices. In fact, the problem was one of excess-creation of money by central banks.

Throughout the paper, we assume perfectly fixed exchange rates. The world is supposed to be composed of two countries, America and Europe, issuing, respectively, the dollar and the franc. There is no real growth, so that the rate of world inflation is equal to the rate of money creation in the world.

The international currency is held by central banks only, so that commodity prices cannot be set in terms of IC. World inflation means an increase in the absolute level of prices in terms of one or the other currency. Therefore, the creation of units of IC can be inflationary inasmuch as it induces an additional creation of national currencies. The relation between IC creation and national currency creation depends on the exchange rate system, as we see later. In the present paper we limit ourselves to three possible systems of fixed rates: a dollar standard, and two possible reformed international systems supposed to be symmetrical. We conclude that the possible inflationary effects of IC creation are not the same in all three systems and the rules for creating an IC are, therefore, different. These discussions may throw some light on the afore-mentioned controversial problem concerning the creation of SDR's and the relevance of the "supplementation doctrine".

1. The Dollar Standard

Under a dollar-standard system, the dollar is the only intervention currency and it can be considered as the monetary base of the world quantity of money. In our simplified two-country world, the dollar is used by the Europe central bank to stabilize the exchange rate between the franc and the dollar. More generally, in an n-country and n-currency world, only $n-1$ exchange rates exist and, while $n-1$ central banks have to intervene on the market, the nth country is "chosen" as the country which does not have to hold reserves, i.e., which can have a zero ratio of reserves to its monetary base. This country determines the world rate of inflation in a system of fixed parities, as can be easily shown.

Let us assume that, before the introduction of the IC, the rate of dollar creation is λ_a, and the rate of credit expansion in Europe – i.e., the rate of growth of the non-reserve component of the monetary base – is λ_e. As the quantity of money is growing in the world and there is no real growth, an excess demand for commodities appears and there is a world inflation. The increase in the world quantity of money is a weighted average of λ_a and λ_e. If the international monetary system was not asymmetrical – i.e., no currency had the unique role of being the intervention currency – the rate of world inflation would be equal to this weighted average of national money growth rates. Meanwhile, the country with the higher rate of money creation would have a permanent balance-of-payments deficit and would get a major part of the inflation tax. However, in an asymmetrical system as the dollar standard, the Europe central bank is the only intervening central bank and it continuously accumulates dollars at a rate higher than its rate of credit expansion if $\lambda_e < \lambda_a$, Therefore, the rate of creation of francs becomes higher than the rate of credit expansion. Only two long-run solutions are possible:

(i) The ratio of dollar reserves to the monetary base is steadily growing. Ultimately, the rate of money creation in Europe tends to be equal to the rate of growth of dollar reserves and the world rate of inflation is determined by the rate of dollar creation in the long run.

(ii) More probably, the Europe central bank will not accept to accumulate dollars without limits, and it will more or less rapidly adopt a more expansionare monetary policy, if it does not want to change the exchange rate, so that, finally, the rate of credit expansion becomes equal to the rate of dollar creation. In this case too, the world rate of inflation is determined by the rate of dollar creation.

Similarly, if the Europe central bank expands credit at a rate higher than the rate of dollar creation, there is a European deficit, which can not be maintained in the long run, since the Europe central bank would loose its dollar reserves.

Let us assume now that an IC is created, but we first assume that units of IC are given to the Europe central bank only and not to the America central bank. IC's and dollars are supposed to be perfect substitutes in Europe official reserves, but IC's cannot be used directly for intervention so that they can be considered as a mere right given to Europe to get additional dollars for intervention without having to pay the corresponding seigniorage[2] to America in the form of a balance-of-payments surplus. In other words, they mean an

[2]Strictly speaking the transfer from Europe to America is rather an inflation tax than a seigniorage. However, if – contrary to our assumptions – there was a positive real rate of growth in Europe, the transfer would be composed both of a seigniorage and an inflation tax. The IC would have the same effects on both.

obligation for America to deliver dollars to Europe at a zero price whenever it is asked to do so.[3]

Let us further assume that $\lambda_e < \lambda_a$. As before, the rate of world inflation is a weighted average of both rates. The allocation of IC's to the Europe central bank is of no help to the European private sector in its desire to increase its money balances because of a world inflation which occurs at a rate higher than λ_e.

IC's are not at the origin of the creation of an additional quantity of national currency, since they are created via the exchange of *ad hoc* created public bonds.[4] Therefore, the only possibility for the private sector to get additional balances is still to sell more goods to America and to cause a balance-of-payments surplus.

Under such circumstances, what can be the impact of IC creation? Given the rate of credit expansion in Europe and the rate of dollar creation, the amount of reserves held by the Europe central bank is increased by the existence of IC's. Therefore, the ratio of international reserves to the monetary base is increased, which may induce the central bank to decide upon a more expansionary monetary policy at some earlier date.

In other words, the only process by which IC creation can be a cause of national money creation is an indirect way, i.e., the reaction of the central bank to the level of its reserves. In that sense it could be said that IC's are inflationary, since they are at the origin of a monetary creation. In fact, even in the absence of an IC, the central bank would have had to adopt a more expansionary monetary policy. The existence of an IC is only a means of exerting a pressure on a central bank to adopt an equilibrating policy, i.e., a monetary policy parallel to that of the rest of the world in a system of fixed rates. World inflation is not caused by the creation of IC's, but by the creation of dollars.

Meanwhile, the existence of an international currency has international distribution effects. Let us assume that, initially, the ratio of international reserves to the monetary base in Europe is R_0/B_0. Then dollar creation becomes more rapid than credit expansion in Europe. Let us further assume that there is a maximum reserve ratio $(R/B)_m$, at which the Europe central bank

[3]In fact, if some interest is paid by a country which holds less IC's than its cumulative allocations and is received by a country which holds more IC's than its cumulative allocations – as is the case for SDR's – the latter country receives a seigniorage. If the rate of interest on IC's is lower than the rate of interest on dollars, the amount of seigniorage transferred to the dollar-issuing country is lower than it would have been in the absence of the IC.

[4]However, it may happen that the IC is created as a counterpart of a Treasury bond and, when the Treasury sells the new units of IC to the central bank, the cash balances of the Treasury are increased. IC creation is then a direct cause of national currency creation.

decides a monetary policy in line with that of America. In a pure dollar system (without IC) the shift from R_0/B_0 to $(R/B)_m$ corresponds to a payment of seigniorage by Europe to America. Let us call R_t and B_t these "final" values of R and B, i.e., the values of R and B when the Europe central bank embarks on a more expansionary policy – $(R/B)_m$ is then reached.

Similarly, let us call R_v and B_v the values of R and B when the IC exists and the ratio $(R/B)_m$ is reached. As the allocation of units of IC increases the rate of accumulation of reserves by Europe, period v is reached before period t and $R_v < R_t$. Therefore, the quantity of dollars bought by Europe from America, before a more expansionary policy is decided upon in Europe, is smaller in a system with an IC than in a system without an IC. The cumulative value of European balance-of-payments surpluses is decreased by the existence of the IC.

Therefore, the role of the IC is twofold: (a) It allows a different distribution of seigniorage or inflation tax, the country issuing the intervention currency – the dollar – receiving a smaller real transfer. (b) It is inflationary in that very limited sense that it induces the central bank of a country, which does not issue an internationally used currency, to adopt more rapidly an expansionary monetary policy, in line with that of the rest of the world. In any respect this policy would have had to be adopted in a system of fixed rates. In other words, IC creation does not modify the long-run rate of world inflation.[5] This conclusion stems from the fact that in a system where the IC cannot be held by the private sector, the level of prices is determined by the quantity of national currencies in the world, and more precisely by the rate of growth of dollars under a dollar standard.

If dollar reserves increase more rapidly in a country than the national components of the monetary base, American monetary policy being more inflationary than that of the country concerned, the "supplementation doctrine" would imply that IC creation is then decreased, since Europe appears to have *too many* reserves. In fact, we know that IC creation must parallel dollar creation, both because it allows Europe not to pay an excessive inflation tax and it favors the adoption of the desirable monetary policy by Europe.

Had we supposed that the rate of credit expansion was initially lower in Europe than in America, a similar conclusion would have been reached, namely that the long-run world rate of inflation is determined by America. However, in this case, the existence of an IC would have lengthened the period during which the European monetary monetary policy was too expansionary.

[5]However, for a given rate of dollar creation, less dollars are absorbed by Europe. It could then be assumed that dollar prices increase more rapidly, unless the American monetary policy be adjusted to a given target of inflation.

The above conclusions would no more be modified if one assumed that units of IC are also allocated to America, inasmuch as the allocation of IC does not modify the monetary base, as has been explained earlier. It can also be recalled that, under a dollar system, America can always finance possible balance-of-payments deficits with dollars, so that it has no need for IC in the long run. Therefore, even if IC allocation meant an additional credit of the America central bank to the Treasury, the over-all monetary policy of America might not be more expansionary, since its role as an issuer of the international intervention currency allows it to have a perfectly independent monetary policy: additional credits to the Treasury can be compensated by less credits to the private sector without any external disequilibrium. However, a higher rate of inflation could be considered as an instrument of retaliation for America, since the IC deprives it of a part of the seigniorage it previously obtained. Accelerating the rate of IC creation could be the answer of Europe. In such a sequence, as in any war of retaliation, the world as a whole would lose.

2. An International Currency in a Symmetrical Exchange System

We examine two such systems: (i) a system where all currencies have the same role as intervention currencies; (ii) a system where the IC plays a role in world monetary management.

(i) We know that the asymmetry in the dollar system comes from the $n-1$ problem: for the system to work, it is necessary that one central bank does not intervene and, in a system where the dollar is the currency must commonly used by the private sector, it is quite natural that the dollar should be chosen as the intervention currency. However, the $n-1$ problem does not necessarily exist in an international monetary system with n currencies: for instance, the intervention of all central banks cannot be at cross-purposes when exchange margins do not exist or when the central banks are not allowed to intervene inside the flexibility band.[6] Let us assume then that the world is under such a system, i.e., both the America and Europe central banks intervene to stabilize the dollar–franc exchange rate. Let us further assume that the rate of credit expansion is higher in America than in Europe. The world rate of inflation is a weighted average of both rates and there is an American deficit (a European surplus): both central banks sell francs and buy dollars; America is losing reserves and

[6]We discuss these problems in an unpublished paper: "The Problem of Symmetry in the Process of Adjustment and the Reform of the International Monetary System".

Europe is getting reserves. Depending on which country is the first one to adapt its rate of credit expansion to the rate of the other country, the long-run world rate of inflation will converge towards one or the other rate.

In such a case, an IC is certainly inflationary in the long run, since it makes possible larger and longer deficits in the most inflating countries. Units of IC – as we have defined it and as SDR's are defined – just represent a right given to deficit countries to get credits in national currencies from other countries. Whenever they use these credits, i.e., they exchange units of IC against the currencies of other countries, a new creation of these currencies occurs and they are sold on the market via the intervention of deficit countries.

In a symmetrical system, all currencies can potentially be intervention currencies, so that the distribution of seigniorage is more equal. Thus, the IC loses one of its justifications (a fairer distribution of seigniorage from international money creation). The other justification is also debatable: there cannot be a world shortage of international liquidity since all currencies are used as international currencies. An international shortage of liquidity would mean that the world quantity of money is insufficient for the level of world prices, which cannot obviously be true in the long run.

The only possible problem is a problem of distribution: for a given rate of world inflation, some countries – deficit countries – have a shortage of international liquidity and an excess of national liquidity (which implies that their currencies are not accepted without limits as international reserves), other countries – surplus countries – having an excess of international liquidity and a shortage of national liquidity. This problem is an adjustment problem and not a liquidity problem. Therefore, if the international monetary system was to be reformed in such a way, the mere existence of an IC, similar to SDR's, could be questioned. Moreover, an international fiat currency would be inflationary by shifting the pressure to adjust to surplus countries.

(ii) Another symmetrical system would be a system where all countries would be obliged to hold a given proportion of their reserves (or their monetary base) in the form of an IC, and all central banks would intervene on the exchange markets. The long-run average rate of money creation would thus depend on the rate of IC creation. A deficit country would have to limit its rate of credit expansion, a surplus country would have to increase its rate of credit expansion. There would be a centralized world monetary management, insofar as all countries would be able to maintain fixity of their exchange rates. The creation of units of IC would be inflationary if their rate of growth exceeded the world rate of growth. But there is no *a priori* reason to believe that this system would be more or less inflationary than any alternative system.

To summarize, an IC is not inflationary, in the long run, under a system such as the dollar standard. It is only a means to redistribute seigniorage and, in that respect, the desirable rate of growth of the IC must be equal to the rate of dollar creation. In a reformed, more symmetrical, international monetary system, an IC would be less justified (case of a "multi-currency system"), except if it constitutes the world money base.

Chapter 11.2

COMMENT ON SALIN*

Friedrich A. LUTZ

Professor Salin begins with the following assumptions:

(1) Perfectly flexible wages and prices.
(2) Fixed exchange rates.
(3) The money supply is a constant multiple of the monetary base.
(4) Two "countries" only: America and Europe.
(5) America provides the key currency.
(6) The dollar balances held by Europe are the monetary base for Europe.

The unknown is the rate of inflation in Europe.

On these assumptions Professor Salin obtains the result that the rate of inflation in Europe is determined by the rate of inflation in America. In this model the key currency country, America, obtains what the author calls a seigniorage equal to the American deficit in the balance of payments, because America obtains this import surplus in exchange for dollars which cost America nothing. However, if the dollars accumulating in the hands of the European monetary authorities are invested in American earning assets, the seigniorage will be returned to Europe since the discounted value of the interest received by Europe will equal the American deficit.

This basic model depicts a case in which the European inflation is entirely imported.

I have no quarrel with the logic of the argument. It is hardly worth mentioning – Professor Salin is fully aware of it – that the model is far from depicting the real world, even before August 1971 when the exchange rates were fixed. None of the assumptions I mentioned are realistic.

In dealing with the problem of the creation of SDRs, Professor Salin first assumes that SDRs are only given to Europe and then investigates the long-run working of the system without caring much about the short term. I shall reverse the order. The process of creation of SDRs during the transition to a situation

*This comment is a much abridged version of the original one, Pascal Salin's paper having been modified so that some remarks made by Friedrich Lutz were no more relevant.

in which the desired[1] ratio of the two components in Europe's reserves is finally reached can then be depicted as follows (I am not absolutely certain that Professor Salin would subscribe to my description in every detail):

In a first period during the transition an arbitrarily chosen amount of SDRs are given to Europe. They enter the monetary base in Europe and cause inflation or a higher rate of inflation than prevailed before. Europe's trade surplus declines; the central bank accumulates fewer dollars and the ratio of SDRs to dollars rises. It must be assumed that the higher rate of inflation in Europe tends to be transferred to a certain extent to America. Thus, in the transition period, America imports inflation from Europe. If we postulate the same rate of monetary expansion in America as existed before the SDRs were introduced, this increase in the rate of inflation in America must come about because fewer dollars are transferred to Europe and therefore stay in the American circulation. However that may be, we cannot, it seems to me, assume that the rate of inflation in America is exogenously given. In a second period during the transition the process is repeated with a somewhat greater dose of SDRs being injected. (I think it can be shown that the dose must increase if the desired ratio of the two components in the European reserves is finally to be reached.) This process of injecting SDRs goes on until the desired ratio establishes itself. Once this point is reached, SDRs are added at the rate at which dollars accrue to Europe. We then can again consider the American rate of inflation as given and equal to the rate that existed before the SDRs were introduced. The American inflation again sets the pace for the European inflation. SDRs are therefore in the long run not inflationary. The main effect of their introduction is, in the long run, that Europe does no longer have to buy dollars to the same extent as was the case under the pure dollar standard because it gets part of its reserves free of charge. The real value of Europe's trade surplus, and therefore the seigniorage Europe has to pay to America, has decreased in the ratio of the SDR component to the dollar component.

[1]The "desired" ratio is the one which gives Europe a "fair" part of the seigniorage.

Chapter 11.3

SUMMARY OF THE DISCUSSION ON SALIN

Anthony B. ATKINSON, *Chairman*

Alexander Swoboda raised two points. The first one is: how could inflation rates differ in the long term? There is only one possibility, namely that there exist two goods, an import good and an export good, without any substitution effect, so that the terms of trade can have any value. The second puzzle is concerned with the fact that SDR creation does not affect the rate of world inflation. It seems that this result stems from the fact that, dollar creation being endogenous, there is only one rate of SDR creation which is compatible with portfolio equilibrium in the model, namely the same rate as for dollars.

Assar Lindbeck gave comment on a point previously raised by William Branson and said that it is not certain that the inter-country variability of inflation has fallen. In fact, it fell in relative terms (in relation to the mean rate of inflation, which has increased), but the absolute differences between country inflation rates and the mean value has been about constant.

Milton Friedman, referring to Assar Lindbeck's comments, underlined that, to evaluate the variability of inflation rates, it would be necessary for recent years, to eliminate the effect of exchange rate changes on the rates of inflation. He also believed that the amount of seigniorage retransferred from the United States to Europe by paying interest on reserves was even higher than the seigniorage received by the United States by selling reserves to Europe.

Pascal Salin accepted the points raised by Alexander Swoboda. As regards the effect of SDR creation, things could be put somewhat differently: if the target of the international community, and more precisely of Europe, is to get a given distribution of seigniorage, then there is only one possible rule, which is to link the rate of SDR creation to the rate of dollar creation. In that case, there is no long-term effect of SDR creation.

Chapter 12.1

MONETARY AND FISCAL POLICY IN OPEN, INTERDEPENDENT ECONOMIES WITH FIXED EXCHANGE RATES

Karl BRUNNER and Allan H. MELTZER*

1. Introduction

Analysis of open economies has been restricted in several important ways. One is the assumption, common also in much of the macro-economic analysis of a closed economy, that total output is fixed and invariant. A second restriction arises from treatment of the representative country as a small unit in a large market. All prices are set in competitive world markets, and exchange rates adjust to equate domestic and foreign prices. Three, asset portfolios are restricted to money and real capital, the latter is generally fixed or grows at a steady rate. Bonds and real capital are perfect substitutes, as in the Metzler model (1951) or Mundell's several extensions of that model (1968).

Lending and borrowing is the most common means by which countries with fixed exchange rates adjust short-term imbalances in trade or payments. Short- or long-term capital movements have long been recognized as a means of adjusting or disturbing the equilibrium of open economies with fixed or floating exchange rates. Recent work by Dornbusch (1973), McKinnon (1969) and Myhrman (1976) attempts to analyze stock-flow interaction in open economies. However, there is no analysis linking short-term movements of output and prices to the long-run analysis that is the standard fare of international economics.

In this paper, we analyze economies with markets for assets and output. Countries and their citizens borrow and lend at home and abroad. Governments have budget deficits or surpluses and issue or retire bonds or money. All of these decisions affect interest rates, output, and the prices of assets and output in the home country and abroad. They affect, also, the balance-of-payments position in a system with fixed exchange rates.

*We have had helpful discussions with Rudiger Dornbusch, Michael Hamburger, Pieter Korteweg and Michael Mussa. We are indebted to the National Science Foundation for continued support of our work.

We begin with a closed economy. Changes in fiscal and monetary policy alter the short- and long-run position of the economy and the prices of assets and output. We show the adjustments as a sequence of equilibria, from short- to long-run equilibrium. Then we open the economy to trade and capital movements and, using the closed economy short- and longer-run equilibria as building blocks, we show the interaction of the home country and the rest of the world. Throughout capital stocks generally remain fixed. Changes in anticipations of future prices and in technology are neglected throughout.

2. A Model of a Closed Economy

The closed economy from which we start has three main sectors described by markets for assets and output and a government budget equation. In the background is a labor market, important for long-run but not short-run adjustment. Four processes of adjustment occur: (1) a short-run flow adjustment to given stocks represented by the response of the output market to changes in the position of the asset markets; (2) an intermediate-run adjustment of the asset markets determined by the interaction of the asset markets, the output market and the government's budget position; (3) a longer-run adjustment of employment and the labor and output markets; and (4) long-run adjustment of capital stock and wealth. This section presents the model.

Equilibrium on the output market occurs when the output of the private sector, y, equals the real expenditure of the private sector, d, and of the government, g,

$$y = d(i - \pi, p, P, W_n, W_h, e) + g, \qquad d_1, d_2 < 0, \quad d_3, \ldots, d_6 > 0. \tag{1a}$$

Private decisions to purchase depend on the market rate of interest, net of any inflation premium, $i - \pi$, the price level of current output, p, the price of outstanding assets (or the market value of a unit of real capital), P, the market value of wealth both human, W_h, and non-human, W_n, and the anticipated return to real capital, e. W_h and e depend on tax rates, τ, and income or anticipated income if the two are distinguished. W_h also depends on money wages, w, and the absorption of labor by the government, lg,

$$W_h = W(y, w, p, lg, \tau), \qquad W_1, W_2, W_3, W_4 > 0, \quad W_5 < 0, \tag{1b}$$

$$e = e(y, K, \tau), \qquad e_1 > 0, \quad e_2, e_3 < 0. \tag{1c}$$

Non-human wealth consists of base money, B, government securities, S, and real capital, K,

$$W_n = PK + v(i, \tau)S + (1+\omega)B, \qquad v_1, v_2 < 0. \tag{1d}$$

Securities are issued at par and valued at market prices with valuation, v, dependent on market interest rates and tax rates. The parameter ω is the net worth multiplier of the banking system including the Pesek–Saving effect of non-competitive banking arrangements.

A price-setting function completes the description of the output market. For given anticipations output prices, p, depend on money wages (per efficiency unit), the capital stock, and output,

$$p = p(y, K, w), \qquad p_1, p_3 > 0, \quad p_2 < 0. \tag{1e}$$

There are two asset markets. On the credit market, the public supplies earning assets to banks, and the banks make loans and purchase securities. The stock of outstanding securities is distributed between banks and the public. On the money market the banks produce and the public absorbs the nominal stock of money. Together, the asset markets determine i and P for given conditions on the output and labor markets.

Two equilibrium conditions summarize the interaction of the banks and the public. The banks' portfolio – the product of an earning asset multiplier, a, and the monetary base, B – equals the public's supply of earning assets to banks, σ. The latter is the sum of loans from banks and the public's excess supply of securities, $S - Sp$, with Sp the stock of securities held by non-banks,

$$a(i, P, W_n, W_h, e\ldots)B = \sigma(i - \pi, p, P, W_n, W_h, e, S), \tag{2}$$

$$a_1, a_2, a_3 > 0, \quad a_4, a_5 < 0,$$
$$\sigma_1, \sigma_3 < 0, \quad \sigma_2, \sigma_6, \sigma_7 > 0.$$

The stock of money is the product of a money multiplier, m, and the monetary base. The money market is assumed to proximately determine P, and the bank credit market proximately determines i. The force of these assumptions is that, whenever the credit market and money market response differ, interest rates change in the direction implied by the credit market equation and asset prices change in the direction implied by the money market equation,[1]

[1]Without this restriction, the signs of some of the responses below would be indeterminate. The point is developed in greater detail in Brunner and Meltzer (1972). The missing items in equations (2) and (3), represented by dots, include policy variables such as reserve requirement ratios and the rediscount rate and variables reflecting the institutional arrangements applicable to particular countries.

$$m(i, P, W_n, W_h, e\ldots)B = L(i, e, p, P, W_n, W_h), \tag{3}$$

$$m_1, m_4, m_5 > 0,\quad m_2, m_3 < 0,$$
$$L_1, L_2 < 0,\quad L_3, \ldots, L_6 > 0.$$

The government's budget equation describes the budget position and the financing of deficits or surpluses. Expenditure consists of purchases of goods, pg, purchases of labor services, wlg, and interest payments, $I(i)S$. The government hires labor at the market wage rate without regard to productivity in governmental activities. Interest payments depend on the maturity structure of the debt and increase with market rates; $I_i > 0$. Tax collections rise and fall proportionally as prices and output change. Tax rates are fixed.[2] Base money and securities,

$$pg + wlg + I(i)S - t(p, y, wlg; \tau) = \mathring{B} + \mathring{S}, \tag{4}$$

are issued to finance deficits and withdrawn in the event of a surplus.

Equation (5) is a summary description of the labor market in the form of a generalized Phillips curve. The acceleration or deceleration of money wages depends on changes in the rate of inflation and on the deviations of current output from the output that prevails in long-run equilibrium.[3] With

$$d(\mathrm{d}w/w) = h(y - y_0) + \mathrm{d}\pi, \qquad h_1 > 0, \tag{5}$$

efficient use of resources, all profitable opportunities realized, unchanging policies and a given stock of capital, $y = y_0$. Increases in capital and labor force raise y_0; increased absorption of labor by the government lowers y_0.[4]

[2]Proportional tax rates could be replaced by progressive tax rates and the assumptions that households expect either (1) tax reduction or (2) a rising share of output to be absorbed by government as prices and output rise and conversely when prices and output fall.

[3]If technology were permitted to change, money wages would not be required to fall at times of excess supply. Deceleration of wages often would be sufficient to restore equilibrium. Equation (5) would be rewritten as a relation between the acceleration or deceleration of money wages per efficiency unit and the acceleration or deceleration of prices.

[4]Long-run output, y_0, also depends on K, but K is fixed. Extension of the analysis to a world of changing capital can be made by letting the sum of net investment, $\mathring{K}$, plus depreciation, δK, be proportional to total private expenditure, d. The derivatives of the d-function are then weighted averages of the response of consumer expenditure and investment expenditure, and the distribution of output between investment and consumption depends on relative prices. The current capital stock is the sum of prior net investment. Specifically, $(\mathring{K} + \delta K)/d = k(i - \pi, p, P, e)$ and $K = \int \mathring{K}$.

3. Solution Procedure

The system of equations yields solutions for prices and output once the values of the policy variables – g, lg, τ, and either $\mathring{B}$ or $\mathring{S}$ – and the capital stock and labor force are given or fixed. Our procedure distinguishes short-, intermediate- and longer-run solutions by first imposing and later relaxing restrictions on adjustment. In this section, we discuss the sequential procedure and the solution to the closed economy model at various runs. In the following section, we analyze monetary and fiscal changes and determine the signs of the principal responses on the markets for assets and output.

There are four types of variables. One is policy variables; the current values of these variables are set by the decision of government. These include g, lg, τ, and either $\mathring{B}$ or $\mathring{S}$ or some combination of $\mathring{B}$ and $\mathring{S}$, for example, the portion of the deficit or surplus financed by issuing or withdrawing base money and securities. Such other policy variables as reserve requirement ratios, the rediscount rate, borrowing quotas and the like can be included in the asset market equations. In the open economy model with fixed exchange rates, the exchange rate is an additional policy variable. Two, in a closed economy current values of B and S represent the history of deficit finance and open market operations. In an open economy, B includes the cumulated balance-of-payments deficit or surplus. We treat B and S as determined relative to the current market process. Three, w, K, y_0 and π are neither controlled by policy-makers nor affected by short-run changes on the markets for assets and output. Money wages adjust gradually to market conditions, as shown by equation (5), and our longer-run equilibrium recognizes the effects of changes in w on prices and output. Additional equations would be required to analyze the adjustment of K and π and the effect of their adjustment on the markets for assets and output. Four, all remaining variables are determined by the system of equations. Our stylized procedure treats the solution as a series of runs to recognize differences in the adjustment process on the markets for assets, output and labor.

The notation attempts to make explicit the variables held constant in a particular adjustment. The short-run response of the asset markets to changes in policy variables is an adjustment of the prices, P and i, at which nominal stocks are willingly held. The solutions are obtained from equations (2) and (3) holding constant the position of flow equilibrium but recognizing the dependence of W_h and e on y. The solutions for P and i can be written as

$$P = P(y, p, B, S; K, w, \pi), \tag{6a}$$

and

$$i = i(y, p, B, S; K, w, \pi). \tag{6b}$$

Partial elasticities are obtained from these solution equations by differentiating and expressing the results as elasticities. The partial elasticities describe the response of P and i to current values of B, S, p and y holding constant the position of the output market and the government budget equation. We use the symbol AM, for example, $\varepsilon(P, B|AM)$, to denote the elasticities obtained from the asset market equations.

The solutions for P and i that satisfy the two-asset market equations also determine the nominal stocks of money and credit. The equilibrium stocks of money and bank credit, $\hat{M}$ and $\hat{\sigma}$, depend on P and i and on the variable in equations (6a) and (6b).

To find the short-run equilibrium position of the output market, we substitute the solutions for P and i, denoted $\hat{P}$ and $\hat{i}$, obtained from the asset market equations in equation (1a). The $d+g$ curve of figure 1 is an equilibrium

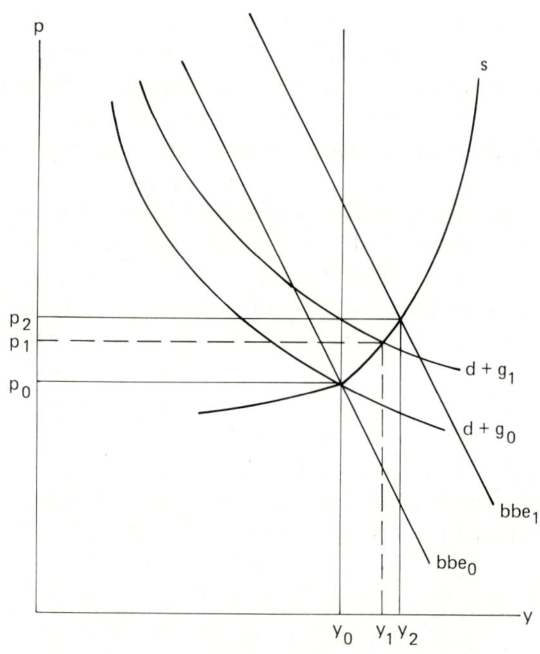

FIGURE 1

relation, equation (7), drawn in the p, y plane. K, w and π are held constant, and as before, the dependence of W_h and e on y and p is recognized,

$$y = d[\hat{i}(B, S, y, p|AM), \hat{P}(B, S, y, p|AM), p, y, B, S; K, w, \pi] + g. \tag{7}$$

The $d+g$ line is the locus of all p, y combinations satisfying simultaneously the markets for output and assets for given values of all stock variables and anticipations. Equation (7) implicitly defines p as a function of y for any values of the remaining variables. We can derive a measure of the slope of the $d+g$ line by differentiating (7) with respect to y and expressing the result as an elasticity. We use the notation $\varepsilon(p, y|d+g)$ to denote this slope, and we use $\varepsilon(p, B|d+g)$, $\varepsilon(p, g|d+g)$, or $\varepsilon(p, S|d+g)$ to denote the change in p, holding output constant, induced by monetary and fiscal policies. These elasticities are shown as vertical shifts of $d+g$ in figure 1. The vertical shift $p_2 - p_0$, with $y = y_0$, shows the response to an expansive policy action obtained from equation (7).

The short-run equilibrium position of the output market is at $p_1 y_1$, not at $p_2 y_0$. Short-run changes in output are described by the s-curve of figure 1, equation (1e) with K and w held constant. The short-run equilibrium reached after a change in fiscal or monetary policy is obtained by solving equations (7) and (1e), given the values of B, S, K, w and π and the position of the budget equation. We use the notation O, AM to show that the short-run position includes the response of the output market (O) and the asset market (AM).

Short-run equilibrium is a flow equilibrium. Asset prices and interest rates change, and the stocks of money and credit change, but the stock equilibrium position at the intersection of the budget equation and $y = y_0$ remains unchanged. The stocks of financial assets have not adjusted to an equilibrium position consistent with the prevailing budget position, and p and y are not fully adjusted to the values of asset stocks that must obtain in a stock-flow equilibrium.

A balanced budget is a necessary and sufficient condition for stock equilibrium in a closed economy with fixed capital stock. From equation (4), we see that when $\mathring{B} = \mathring{S} = 0$, the budget is balanced, asset stocks are constant, and total nominal government expenditure, G, equals tax collections t. After substituting for i in equation (4), we can write the stock equilibrium as

$$G[\hat{i}(p, y, B, S|AM), S; g, w, lg] = t(p, y; \tau). \tag{8}$$

Equation (8) is shown in figure 1 as the *bbe* line. The line shows positions of budget balance. To the right of the line, the budget has a surplus; to the left, the budget has a deficit. In both cases, the stocks of financial assets change. The slope of the line, expressed as a partial elasticity, is denoted $\varepsilon(p, y|bbe)$. The position of the line depends on the values of current policy. Changes in policy change the position of the *bbe* line. The response to the base is denoted $\varepsilon(p, B|bbe)$ and similarly for other variables.

An intermediate-run equilibrium is a position of stock-flow equilibrium at the intersection of the *bbe* line and the flow equilibrium. The budget is balanced, and P, i, p and y have adjusted to the values of B, S, g and τ consistent with budget balance. There is no change in K, w or π, so the position of the s-curve remains unchanged. In figure 1, the intersection of a $d+g$ curve, s, and *bbe* at p_2y_2 is a position of intermediate-run equilibrium.

Gradual adjustment of money wages, as shown by equation (5), moves the economy from an intermediate-run to a longer-run equilibrium. Capital stock is held constant in the longer-run equilibrium, but output and prices change in response to a change in w. Changes in w alter the government's budget and the position of the *bbe* line and, by changing W_h, change expenditure. Output prices rise and fall with w, and the equilibrium position moves in the direction of full equilibrium at $y = y_0$. To identify the longer-run equilibrium response of p and y to g, we use $\varepsilon(y, g|O, AM, s)$ and $\varepsilon(p, g|O, AM, s)$ and similarly for B, S, or other policy variables.

A return to full steady-state equilibrium following policy changes, particularly fiscal changes, requires adjustment of K and y_0. We do not analyze changes in the composition of output between consumption and investment here, and we do not take into account the effects on output and prices of the adjustment of the capital stock.

4. Responses to Fiscal and Monetary Policy

The general procedure we have just described provides the framework within which we analyze the response of the closed economy to fiscal and monetary change. The framework becomes applicable to an open economy after adjustment to permit interaction of home country markets with markets in other countries and to recognize the influence of the balance of payments. In this section, we develop the closed economy framework more fully and show the determinants of the size and direction of responses on the markets for assets and output.

We begin with the output market. The $d+g$ curve, equation (7), relates aggregate real expenditures to market prices, to existing stocks and to policy variables. The slope of the curve in the p, y plane can be expressed as an elasticity,

$$\varepsilon(p, y|d+g) = \frac{1-(1-\gamma)\bar{\varepsilon}(d, y)}{(1-\gamma)\bar{\varepsilon}(d, p)} < 0.$$

The parameter γ is the proportion of output absorbed by the government, g/y. The numerator and denominator contain total elasticities (shown by a bar over ε) of the output market, including the response of P and i on the asset market. Signs of components appear beneath the components,

$$\bar{\varepsilon}(d, p) = \underset{-}{\varepsilon(d, p)} + \underset{-}{\bar{\varepsilon}(d, i)}\underset{+}{\varepsilon(i, p|AM)} + \underset{+}{\bar{\varepsilon}(d, P)}\underset{-}{\varepsilon(P, p|AM)} + \underset{+}{\varepsilon(d, W_h)}\underset{+}{\varepsilon(W_h, p)} < 0,$$

and

$$\bar{\varepsilon}(d, y) = \underset{-}{\bar{\varepsilon}(d, i)}\underset{+}{\varepsilon(i, y|AM)} + \underset{+}{\bar{\varepsilon}(d, P)}\underset{-}{\varepsilon(P, y|AM)} + \underset{+}{\varepsilon(d, W_h)}\underset{+}{\varepsilon(W_h, y)} + \underset{+}{\varepsilon(d, e)}\underset{+}{\varepsilon(e, y)} > 0.$$

The elasticities of i and P are the responses of interest rates and asset prices to any variable taken as predetermined when solving for P and i on the asset markets. We use $\bar{\varepsilon}(d, i)$ and $\bar{\varepsilon}(d, P)$ to note that these elasticities include the change in wealth induced by changing i and P.

The total price elasticity of expenditure, $\bar{\varepsilon}(d, p)$, is negative despite the positive term at the end. Homogeneity of degree zero of the d-function in prices and nominal wealth assures that $\varepsilon(d, p)$ is much larger than $\varepsilon(d, W_h)$. The positive sign of the numerator requires that the last two terms in $\bar{\varepsilon}(d, y)$ dominate the elasticity. We constrain $\bar{\varepsilon}(d, y)$ to positive values.

The short-run response of the flow equilibrium to changes in B, S and g depends on the slope of the $d+g$ curve, $\varepsilon(p, y|d+g)$, the slope of the price setting function, $\varepsilon(p, y|s) > 0$, and on the shift in $d+g$ resulting from the policy change. Expansive policies shift the $d+g$ curve of figure 1 upward, and contractive policies shift the curve downward. The vertical shift of $d+g$ induced by a change in the base, government expenditure or debt is shown in equations (9); signs of components are shown below the components,

$$\varepsilon(p, g|d+g) = \frac{-1}{\bar{\varepsilon}(d, p)}\frac{\gamma}{1-\gamma} > 0, \tag{9a}$$

$$\varepsilon(p, B|d+g) = -\frac{\bar{\varepsilon}(d, B)}{\bar{\varepsilon}(d, p)} > 0, \tag{9b}$$

with

$$\bar{\varepsilon}(d,B)=\underset{-}{\bar{\varepsilon}(d,i)}\underset{-}{\varepsilon(i,B|AM)}+\underset{+}{\bar{\varepsilon}(d,P)}\underset{+}{\varepsilon(P,B|AM)}+\underset{+}{\bar{\varepsilon}(d,W_n)}\frac{(1+\omega)B}{W_n}>0;$$

$$\varepsilon(p,S|d+g)=-\frac{\bar{\varepsilon}(d,S)}{\bar{\varepsilon}(d,p)}>0, \tag{9c}$$

with

$$\bar{\varepsilon}(d,S)=\underset{-}{\bar{\varepsilon}(d,i)}\underset{+}{\varepsilon(i,S|AM)}+\underset{+}{\bar{\varepsilon}(d,P)}\underset{+}{(P,S|AM)}+\underset{+}{\varepsilon(d,W_n)}\frac{vS}{W_n}>0.$$

The size of the responses of $d+g$ to B, S, and g depends on $\bar{\varepsilon}(d,p)$. A large price elasticity of expenditure lowers the response to fiscal and monetary changes. The response to government expenditure increases as the relative size of government, γ, increases. The response to a change in the base is larger than the response to a change in S, and both are positive. The stability of the system requires that $\bar{\varepsilon}(d,S)$ be positive, so $\bar{\varepsilon}(d,i)\varepsilon(i,S|AM)$ must be smaller than other terms of $\bar{\varepsilon}(d,S)$.[5]

The elasticities in equation (9) describe the change in expenditure induced by changing B, S or g, holding output constant. They are the vertical shifts of the $d+g$ line in figure 1. The short-run flow equilibrium depends on these responses and on the slopes of the expenditure and price-setting functions. Equation (10) shows the short-run responses of prices and output to a change in g allowing as before the interaction with the asset market. The denominator contains the slopes of the expenditure and price-setting functions, expressed as elasticities. Similar responses for B and S can be obtained by substituting $\varepsilon(p, B|d+g)$ or $\varepsilon(p, S|d+g)$ in the numerator of equations (10),

$$\varepsilon(p,g|O,AM)=\frac{-\varepsilon(p,g|d+g)/\varepsilon(p,y|d+g)}{-1/\varepsilon(p,y|d+g)+1/\varepsilon(p,y|s)}$$

$$=\frac{-\varepsilon(p,g|d+g)\varepsilon(p,y|s)}{\varepsilon(p,y|d+g)-\varepsilon(p,y|s)}>0, \tag{10a}$$

[5] Our hypothesis also contains the restriction $\varepsilon(P,B)>0$. This requires the money market response to dominate the response of P and the credit market response to dominate the response of i. See footnote 1 and the accompanying text.

and

$$\varepsilon(y, g|O, AM) = \frac{-\varepsilon(p, g|d+g)}{\varepsilon(p, y|d+g) - \varepsilon(p, y|s)} > 0. \quad (10b)$$

Monetary and fiscal policies also change the budget position. The budget position depends on price and output and, therefore on g, B and S. With given tax rates and government purchases of goods and labor services, the outstanding stocks of financial assets, B and S, increase or decrease until output and prices reach a level at which the budget is balanced.

Equation (8) above defines budget balance in terms of p, y, B and S. The slope of the budget equation in figure 1 depends on fiscal policies, particularly the decision to use g (rather than pg) as a policy variable and on the progressivity of taxes. We use $\varepsilon(p, y|bbe; g)$ to denote the slope of the line obtained on the assumption that g (rather than pg) is held constant,

$$\varepsilon(p, y|bbe; g) = \frac{\varepsilon(t, y) - \varepsilon(I, i)\varepsilon(i, y|AM)\, IS/t}{(pg/t) - \varepsilon(t, p) + \varepsilon(I, i)\varepsilon(i, p|AM)\, IS/t} < 0. \quad (11)$$

Proportional tax rates are assumed throughout.

The position of the bbe line also depends on fiscal and monetary policy. The elasticities in equation (12) show the shift in the position of the line for changes in g, lg, B or S. The response to a change in w (not shown) is identical to the response to lg.[6] Increases in g, lg, w and S raise the bbe line and increase the deficit or reduce the budget surplus; increases in the base reduce the deficit or increase the surplus,

$$\varepsilon(p, g|bbe; g) = \frac{-pg/t}{\Delta bbe; g} > 0, \quad (12a)$$

$$\varepsilon(p, lg|bbe; g) = \frac{\varepsilon(t, wlg) - wlg/t}{\Delta bbe; g} > 0, \quad (12b)$$

$$\varepsilon(p, B|bbe; g) = \frac{-\varepsilon(I, i)\varepsilon(i, B|AM)\, IS/t}{\Delta bbe; g} < 0, \quad (12c)$$

[6] If the government pays competitive wage rates, the government's wage bill rises with money wages during periods of economic expansion, and falls if money wages fall during recession. With a constant level (lg) of employment in the government sector, the government's wage bill has a pro-cyclical effect on the budget even if the private sector maintains constant money wages per efficiency unit. If money wages are slow to decline in recession, wage changes have an inflationary bias even if unit labor costs in the private sector remain constant.

$$\varepsilon(p, S|bbe; g) = \frac{-[1 + \varepsilon(I, i)\varepsilon(i, S|AM)]IS/t}{\Delta bbe; g} > 0, \tag{12d}$$

with

$$\Delta bbe; g = (pg/t) + \varepsilon(I, i)\varepsilon(i, p|AM)\, IS/t - \varepsilon(t, p) < 0,$$

The elasticities in equation (12) determine the direction in which prices change to reach stock equilibrium. Open market purchases *reduce*, and open market sales *raise*, the price level at the new stock equilibrium. Expansive fiscal policies induce a larger increase in the price level at which the economy reaches stock equilibrium if budget deficits are financed primarily by issuing debt or if budget surpluses are used to retire base money. Since the position of the *bbe* line divides the plane into deficits and surpluses, the financing of deficits and surpluses influences the size of subsequent deficits or surpluses and, given both stock and flow adjustments induced by changes in B and S, affects the speed of adjustment to a new stock-flow equilibrium.[7]

Return to figure 1. An expansive fiscal policy has shifted the *bbe* line to bbe_1. Comparison of equations (10a) and (12a) shows that the *bbe* line shifts much more than the $d+g$ curve. The new *bbe* line is to the right of the short-run flow equilibrium at p_1, y_1. There is a budget deficit. B and S increase; the $d+g$ curve moves to the right; output and prices rise. The new short-run flow equilibrium lies to the right of the old, the distance depending on the method of financing the deficit. In figure 1, deficit finance leaves the *bbe* line at bbe_1, so the $d+g$ curve converges to the intersection of s and bbe_1.

If wages, capital and anticipations remain fixed, an intermediate-run equilibrium is reached where the $d+g$, s and *bbe* lines intersect. The budget is balanced at the values p_2 and y_2 that clear the output market. The output market equilibrium is defined relative to the asset prices and interest rates determined by the asset market equilibrium. The two conditions – budget

[7] With proportional tax rates, constant population and a fixed capital stock, the long-run position depends on the ratio of S to B. The long-run flow equilibrium, y_0, can be solved for B/P and i in terms of S/B and the fiscal variables. The budget constraint is then

$$\frac{p}{B}g + I\left[i\left(\frac{S}{B}, y_0 \ldots\right)\right]\frac{S}{B} = t(p, y_0)\frac{1}{B}.$$

With a linear, homogenous tax revenue function,

$$t(p, y; \tau)\frac{1}{B} = t\left(\frac{p}{B}, y; \tau\right).$$

The budget equation determines the ratio of S to B and, for given fiscal policy, is independent of the levels of S and B.

balance and flow equilibrium – assure that asset stocks are constant and willingly held at prevailing prices.

To prove that the economy reaches intermediate-run equilibrium, we substitute in the budget equation until the equation contains only variables taken as predetermined in reaching flow equilibrium. The price level, p, is replaced by the price-setting function, equation (1e). Then all values of i and y are replaced by their flow equilibrium solutions. The solutions depend on B, S, g, wlg, τ and, of course, on K and w, so the revised budget equation can be written as

$$\mathring{B} + \mathring{S} = F(B, S; g, wlg, \tau). \tag{13}$$

In a closed economy, the stocks of B and S tell the history of past budgets and open market operations. Let D be the cumulated deficit and μ the (average) share of the deficit or surplus financed by issuing or withdrawing base money. B_0 and S_0 are the nominal stocks of B and S that were produced independently of deficit finance, for example the result of open market operations with a balanced budget,

$$B = B_0 + \mu D \quad \text{and} \quad S = S_0 + (1-\mu)D, \qquad 0 \leq \mu \leq 1. \tag{14}$$

After replacement of B and S by the values in (14), equation (13) relates the current deficit, $\mathring{D}$, to the cumulated deficit, D, to μ and to the fiscal policy variables. The budget converges to an intermediate-run equilibrium if the budget deficit or surplus reaches zero at the flow equilibrium values of p and y. Convergence is assured if $\partial F/\partial D$ is negative for any admissible value of μ,

$$\frac{\partial F}{\partial D} = \mu \frac{\partial F}{\partial B} + (1-\mu)\frac{\partial F}{\partial S}, \tag{15}$$

where

$$\frac{\partial F}{\partial B} = \frac{pg}{B}\left(\varepsilon(y, B|O, AM)\left[\varepsilon(p, y|s)\left\{1 - \varepsilon(t, p)\frac{t}{pg}\right\} - \varepsilon(t, y)\frac{t}{pg}\right]\right.$$
$$\left. + \varepsilon(I, i)\bar{\varepsilon}(i, B|O, AM)\frac{IS}{pg}\right) < 0,$$

and

$$\frac{\partial F}{\partial S} = \frac{pg}{S}\left(\varepsilon(y, S|O, AM)\left[\varepsilon(p, y|s)\left\{1 - \varepsilon(t, p)\frac{t}{pg}\right\} - \varepsilon(t, y)\frac{t}{pg}\right]\right.$$
$$\left. + \left[\varepsilon(I, i)\bar{\varepsilon}(i, S|O, AM) + 1\right]\frac{IS}{pg}\right).$$

The elasticities denoted O, AM are short-run flow equilibrium responses similar to the elasticities in equation (10). The negative sign of $\partial F/\partial B$ follows from: (1) the positive value[8] of $\varepsilon(y, B|O, AM)$, (2) proportional taxes, and (3) the relatively small negative values of the interest payments effect in the last term. A negative value of $\partial F/\partial S$, however, is less certain. With $\varepsilon(y, S|O, AM)$ positive, the first term is negative but much smaller than the corresponding term in $\partial F/\partial B$. The interest payments effect is positive and (numerically) larger than the corresponding term in $\partial F/\partial B$. However, the weight on the first component, t/pg, is much larger than IS/pg, so $\partial F/\partial S$ is rather small, and $\partial F/\partial D$ is negative for all values of μ.[9] The system converges to intermediate-run equilibrium.

Equations (13) and (15) permit the response of the financial stocks to fiscal policy variables to be expressed as derivatives or elasticities of the F-function. The elasticity of D with respect to g is

$$\varepsilon(D, g) = \frac{-\varepsilon(F, g)}{\varepsilon(F, D)} > 0,$$

where

$$\varepsilon(F, g) = \frac{pg}{F}\left[1 + \varepsilon(y, g|O, AM)\left\{\varepsilon(p, y|s)\left[1 - \varepsilon(t, p)\frac{t}{pg}\right] - \varepsilon(t, y)\frac{t}{pg}\right\} + \varepsilon(I, i)\,\varepsilon(i, g|O, AM)\frac{IS}{pg}\right],$$

and the denominator is the elasticity corresponding to $\partial F/\partial D$ in equation (15). Similarly, we obtain the response of the cumulated deficit and the stocks of financial assets to w/g and to τ.

Our analysis implies that fiscal policy has a powerful influence on the equilibrium position the economy reaches in the intermediate run. This influence differs from the influence of fiscal variables in Keynesian analysis or in the familiar *IS–LM* model. There, changes in government expenditure and tax rates affect mainly flow variables via "the multiplier" mechanism. Our analysis implies that the dominant effect of fiscal policy is on the stock equilibrium position and is transmitted mainly by changes in the stocks of debt and base money. In a closed economy, the behavior of financial stocks is governed by fiscal policy and, to a lesser extent, by open market operations that

[8]The sign of $\varepsilon(y, B|O, AM)$ can be checked by substituting $\varepsilon(p, B|d+g)$ for $\varepsilon(p, g|d+g)$ in equation (10b).

[9]A slight positive value of $\partial F/\partial D$ would not require any important change in our analysis. Slightly progressive tax rates or a minimum value of μ would replace proportional tax rates or an unrestricted value of μ.

proceed independently of fiscal policy. The stock disequilibrium generated by changes in g, wlg or τ has a much greater effect on the price level than the initial flow adjustment resulting from the increase in expenditure.

An increase in the size of the government or a reduction in tax rates raises the price level in intermediate-run equilibrium. Money wages are unchanged, so real wages are lower. Open market sales also raise the price level and reduce real wages in intermediate-run equilibrium. Open market purchases and reductions in the relative size of government lower the price level in intermediate-run equilibrium. With money wages fixed, real wages rise.

The adjustment of money wages occurs slowly in our analysis. With the passage of time, however, the gradual acceleration or deceleration of money wages cumulates as a rate of change, $\mathrm{d}w/w$, and the cumulated rate of change shifts the supply curve of output, raising or lowering prices and changing the equilibrium position of the output market.

Let $\varepsilon(p, w|s)h(t)$ denote the shift in the price-setting function induced by a change in the money wage rate. An increase in money wages raises prices and reduces output, and a reduction in money wages lowers prices and raises output. The flow equilibrium moves from the intermediate-run equilibrium in the direction of y_0. Equation (16) shows the longer-run response of prices and output to a change in g, $\varepsilon(p, g|O, AM, s)$ and $\varepsilon(y, g|O, AM, s)$. Similar expressions for B and S can be written by replacing g with B or S and making appropriate adjustments on the right-hand side of the elasticities,

$$\varepsilon(p, g|O, AM, s) = \frac{-\varepsilon(p, g|d+g)\varepsilon(p, y|s) + \varepsilon(p, y|d+g)\varepsilon(p, w|s)h(t)}{\varepsilon(p, y|d+g) - \varepsilon(p, y|s)} > 0, \tag{16a}$$

and

$$\varepsilon(y, g|O, AM, s) = \frac{-\varepsilon(p, g|d+g) + \varepsilon(p, w|s)h(t)}{\varepsilon(p, y|d+g) - \varepsilon(p, y|s)}. \tag{16b}$$

The adjustment of money wages also affects the stock equilibrium position. The reason is that the government's budget equation includes wage payments, wlg. Changes in money wages change the size of the deficit, per unit of $\mathrm{d}w/w$, by $\varepsilon(p, w|bbe) = \varepsilon(p, lg|bbe)$, shown above as equation (12b). The stock equilibrium position changes in the same direction as the flow equilibrium but by a smaller amount. The adjustment of money wages reinforces the effect of monetary and fiscal policies on prices. If prices were higher in the intermediate-run equilibrium than at the initial position, prices rise more; if prices fall to reach the intermediate-run equilibrium, prices fall more to reach the longer-run equilibrium.

The adjustment of money wages returns the system to the neighborhood of full employment but does not assure the return to full employment at y_0. The choice of fiscal policies, g, lg, and τ, affects the position of full-employment output, y_0, by changing the composition of output and by absorbing or releasing labor from the government sector. Moreover, the method of financing deficits or surpluses, and open market operations, change the composition of financial assets and the relative prices of assets and output. For full, long-run, stock-flow equilibrium, we must have $p = P$. The full response to monetary and fiscal policy involves adjustment of the capital stock if these conditions for full equilibrium are not met. In general, the capital stock must adjust to restore full equilibrium following monetary and fiscal changes.

The sequential adjustment from short-run to longer-run equilibrium is a highly stylized representation of the adjustment process in a closed economy. Actual adjustment is, of course, more of a continuous process and less a sequence of steps than our procedure suggests. The interaction of stocks, flows and the government budget in a closed economy is more clearly revealed, however by the sequential process. Of importance for present purposes is that the framework permits extension to an open economy in which output changes and in which foreigners respond to relative prices by purchasing and selling assets and output on the home country markets.

5. Extension to an Open Economy

The responses obtained for the closed economy form the base for our analysis of interdependent, open economies. Changes modify the descriptions of the markets for credit and output and the definition of non-human wealth. Foreigners buy and sell on the home country markets for output and in the credit market; citizens of the home country buy and sell goods and securities in foreign markets for output and assets. The balance of payments constrains the world economy and acts as an additional link between the home country and the rest of the world.

In this section we make adjustments to open the model to trade in goods, services and securities. The description of the "rest of the world" is the same as our description of the home country. Asterisks are used to denote rest of the world variables. Technology and capital stocks are fixed, and population is constant. There is no migration of labor force or population. All countries have proportional tax rates.

Real expenditure now has an additional component, the real value of exports, denoted X. Exports depend on economic activity abroad, on relative prices and on the exchange rate, ρ. Domestic expenditure, d, depends on the prices at home and abroad and on the exchange rate. Government expenditure is, as before, set in real terms. The equilibrium condition for the output market is now

$$y = d + g + X, \tag{17a}$$

$$d = d(i - \pi, p, P, W_n, W_h, e, \rho p^*), \qquad d_1, d_2 < 0, \quad d_3, \ldots, d_7 > 0, \tag{17b}$$

$$X = X(i^* - \pi^*, p^*, P^*, W_n^*, W_h^*, e^*, p/\rho),$$

$$X_1, X_7 < 0, \quad X_2, \ldots, X_6 > 0.$$

The price-setting function is adjusted to permit substitution of imports for domestic production. The price-setting function becomes

$$p = p(y, K, w, \rho p^*), \qquad p_1, p_3, p_4 > 0, \quad p_2 < 0. \tag{17c}$$

Domestic non-human wealth now includes foreign assets owned by domestic residents and excludes liabilities to foreigners,

$$W_n = PK + v(i)(S - S_f) + v^*(i^*)S_f^*\rho + (1 + \omega)B, \tag{18a}$$

with liabilities to foreigners, S_f, and foreign assets owned by domestic residents, S_f^*, valued at market prices. The definition is more useful for our analysis if wealth is restated in terms of the net monetary base, B_n. The definition of the net foreign liability position $B - B_n$, can be obtained from equation (18c). The base includes, and the net base excludes, the net foreign liabilities of the banks and the public,

$$W_n = PK + v(i)S + (1 + \omega)B_n + \omega[v(i)S_f - v^*(i^*)\rho S_f^*], \tag{18b}$$

$$B_n = B - \bar{v}(i)S_f + \bar{v}^*(i^*)\rho S_f^* = B_0 + \mu D + B_2. \tag{18c}$$

B_2 is the stock of base money resulting from surpluses or deficit on current account, the accumulated current account balance, and B_0 now includes any initial reserve of commodities used as money. Securities are valued in equation (18c) at weighted average values, $\bar{v}$ and $\bar{v}^*$, and at market value in equation (18b).[10] The last term of equation (18b) measures the contribution of the net foreign position to the net worth of the financial system and is set at zero.

The open economy imposes an additional constraint on asset stocks. The

[10]The difference in valuation between (18b) and (18c) arises because wealth is valued at current market prices but international reserves and base money are valued at the time they are received. Initially, wealth and international reserves change by the same amount, the market value of the change in the public's net foreign position. Later, wealth and the market value of securities change with interest rates, and the capital gain or loss is included in wealth. The value of international reserves and the base are not affected by capital gains and losses. The average values $\bar{v}$ and $\bar{v}^*$ reflect the convenient assumption that over time changes in the public's net foreign position and changes in international reserves occur at the average market value of securities.

current account balance each period is the sum of the trade balance and interest payments,

$$pX - p^*X^*\rho^* + i^*v^*(i^*)S_f^*\rho - iv(i)S_f = \mathring{B}_2. \tag{19}$$

Devaluation raises the exchange rate, ρ. With fixed exchange rates, ρ is constant and the equation proximately determines the balance on current account and the related change in the base, $\mathring{B}_2$. The net base, B_n, is taken as predetermined relative to the current market process. Net foreign liabilities, $B - B_n$, are determined by relative prices.

The credit market distributes the stock of domestic securities between banks, S_b, the domestic non-bank public, S_p, and foreigners, S_f. The total stock, S, depends on the cumulated budget deficit, D, as in the closed economy. The distribution of S now depends on the decisions of domestic and foreign residents,

$$S = S_0 + (1 - \mu)D = S_p + S_b + S_f.$$

In open economies, asset markets are interdependent. The public's supply of earning assets to banks, σ, now excludes absorption of domestic debt by foreigners, S_{f_1}, and includes absorption of foreign debt by the domestic market, S_f^*. Changes in relative interest rates induce lenders or borrowers to shift from one country to another. Adjustment of interest rates and the value of net foreign liabilities affects the model in three ways. One, with fixed exchange rates, changes in the net foreign position change the base, B, and changes in the base induce changes in the stocks of money and credit. We formalize the effects of relative prices on the net foreign liability position in an equation for the net foreign position,

$$(B - B_n) = b(i - \pi, P, p, e, i^* - \pi^*, P^*, p^*, e^*, \rho), \qquad b_1, b_4, b_6, b_7, b_9 > 0, \quad b_2, b_3, b_5, b_8 < 0.$$

Two, foreign purchases and sales of securities (S_f) on the home credit market have the same effect on the supply of earning assets (σ) as purchases or sales by the domestic public. Increases in domestic rates increase S_f and lower the volume of outstanding securities offered to banks; domestic liabilities to foreigners rise. Increases in rates abroad induce sales by foreigners. S_f declines and the net foreign position is reduced,

$$S_f = \varphi(i^* - \pi^*, i - \pi, P^*, p^*, y^*, \rho), \qquad \varphi_1, \varphi_5 < 0, \quad \varphi_2, \varphi_3, \varphi_4, \varphi_6 > 0.$$

There is a similar equation for S_f^*. Since S_f depends on foreign prices and output, foreign holdings of domestic securities introduce the exchange rate, foreign prices and output into the σ-function. Three, capital gains and losses and changes in the net foreign liability position change the value of domestic wealth and, therefore, change spending and money holding.

As before, $a()B = \sigma$ is the equilibrium condition for the credit market. In an open economy, the credit market distributes the stocks of foreign and domestic securities. Loans by banks can be cancelled on both sides of the equilibrium condition. Domestic securities and the net foreign position remain. The securities are distributed between banks and non-banks by the adjustment of interest rates and prices,

$$vS_b + v^*S^*_b = v(S - S_p - S_f) + v^*(S^*_f - S^*_p).$$

Domestic and foreign securities are substitutes in the portfolios of wealth owners, but money and real capital are, by hypothesis, owned only by domestic residents. Achieving equilibrium values of domestic and foreign asset prices requires internal adjustment, as in closed economies, and adjustment of interest rates on domestic and foreign markets. The equilibrium conditions for the bank credit and money markets show the interdependence of domestic and foreign asset markets,[11]

$$a(i, P, \ldots)B = \sigma(i - \pi, P, p, W_n, W_h, e, S - S_f, S^*_f\rho) \qquad (20a)$$
$$a_1, a_2 > 0, \quad \sigma_1, \sigma_2 < 0, \quad \sigma_3, \ldots, \sigma_8 > 0,$$

$$m(i, P, \ldots)B = L(i, P, p, W_n, W_h, e), \quad m_1 > 0, \quad m_2 < 0, \qquad (20b)$$
$$L_1, L_6 < 0, \quad L_2, \ldots, L_5 > 0.$$

Other equations of the closed economy model remain as before. Opening the economy to trade and capital movements affects the government budget position and the value of human wealth by changing the prices of assets and output and speeds of response. In the following sections, we develop the interaction of the asset and output markets, the government budget equation and the balance on current account for open economies with fixed exchange rates.

6. Flow Equilibrium in Open Economies with Fixed Exchange Rates

Solutions for the asset and output market equations of the open economy modify the responses of the closed economy. At each step of our stylized procedure, moving from short-run through intermediate- to longer-run solu-

[11]If we disregard the effects of devaluation on wealth, changes in exchange rates affect the money market only through the adjustment of asset prices and interest rates, and ρ does not enter equation (20b).

tions, the open economy responses differ. The differences depend on the choice of monetary arrangements. In this paper, we consider only economies with fixed exchange rates. This section develops the response of the output market to changes in policy variables. We allow for the interdependence of world markets for assets and output and the effects of interdependence on p, y, p^* and y^*. In the following section, we discuss the adjustment of asset stocks in the two countries and the simultaneous solutions on the asset and output markets in a world with fixed capital stock.

We begin with the asset markets. There are now four interacting asset market equations that simultaneously determine i, i^*, P, P^* for given stocks of assets and given economic activity and output prices at home and abroad. As in the closed economy, first, we hold output and output prices constant and determine the set of asset prices and interest rates at which the stocks are willingly held. The stocks of money and bank credit are determined in this process for the given price levels and outputs at home and abroad. The net foreign liability position $B - B_n$ depends on the relative prices and is determined at the asset market equilibrium. The notation A, A^* identifies the short-run asset market equilibrium as a world equilibrium.

Next we analyze the response of the output market allowing for the change in the equilibrium position of the asset markets. The initial response of expenditure and output to any policy change does not include the effect of interaction between domestic and foreign output markets. We use $\varepsilon(y, B_n|OA, A^*)$ to denote the response to the base and similarly for other elasticities. Then, we permit interaction between the output markets and determine the short-run equilibrium position of the open economy, denoted OAO^*A^*. Output responds to price changes as in the short-run equilibrium of the closed economy, and exports and imports respond to relative prices. At the short-run equilibrium position, stocks of financial assets are not fully adjusted to policy (or other) changes and K, w, π, K^*, w^* and π^* are held constant.

The longer-run adjustment of output and prices involves gradual changes in money wages. In an open economy, wage adjustments affect prices and output at home and abroad. The response, obtained from the price-setting functions, include these interactions. In our notation, these responses are $\bar{\varepsilon}(p, y|s, s^*)$.

The solution of the asset market equations for a closed economy shows that the relative change in i is

$$\frac{\mathrm{d}i}{i} = -\bar{\varepsilon}(i, B|AM)\frac{\mathrm{d}B}{B} + \bar{\varepsilon}(i, S|AM)\frac{\mathrm{d}S}{S} + \varepsilon(i, y|AM)\frac{\mathrm{d}y}{y} + \varepsilon(i, p|AM)\frac{\mathrm{d}p}{p}.$$

A similar equation determines the short-run response of P. The elasticities in the equations for i and P are ratios expressing the responses of the excess supply functions of the credit and money markets to changes in the proximate determinants (including any induced response of wealth). With interacting credit and money markets, changes in net liabilities to foreigners modify the response of interest rates and asset prices. The solutions for i and P now have the general form of equation (21),

$$i = i(B_n, S, i^*, P^*, y, y^*, p, p^*). \tag{21}$$

If i^* and P^* are now replaced by the solutions of the equations for the foreign asset market, analogous to equations (20a) and (20b) we can obtain the total response of i and P (and of i^* and P^*) to changes in the proximate determinants. Some elasticities obtained from equation (21), after replacing i^* and P^* by their solutions, are shown in table 1.

The response of i or P to B_n in an open economy is a weighted average of the closed economy responses with weights expressing the interaction of the asset markets. Similar responses to S, p, and y are shown by $\varepsilon(i, y|A, A^*)$ and $\varepsilon(P, y|A, A^*)$. P and i also depend on B_n^*, S^*, y^* and p^* in an open economy; $\varepsilon(i, B_n^*|A, A^*)$ shows a typical elasticity.

The size of the elasticities in table 1 depends on the relative size of the home country. For a relatively small or a relatively large country, the response to B, S, y and p are approximately the same in an open economy as in the corresponding closed economy. The reason is that a_{11}, a_{22} and the denominator approach unity for both large and small countries, and a_{12} and a_{21} approach zero. The reasons differ. In large countries, the effect of foreign asset prices on domestic prices is relatively small; all elasticities of i and P with respect to i^*

TABLE 1

$$\varepsilon(i, B|A, A^*) = \frac{\varepsilon(i, B|AM)a_{22} + \varepsilon(P, B|AM)a_{12}}{a_{11}a_{22} - a_{12}a_{21}} < 0$$

$$\varepsilon(P, B|A, A^*) = \frac{\varepsilon(P, B|AM)a_{11} + \varepsilon(i, B|AM)a_{21}}{a_{11}a_{22} - a_{12}a_{21}} > 0$$

$$1 > a_{11} = 1 - \varepsilon(i, i^*|AM)\varepsilon(i^*, i|AM^*) - \varepsilon(i, P^*|AM)\varepsilon(P^*, i|AM^*) > 0$$

$$a_{12} = \varepsilon(i, i^*|AM)\varepsilon(i^*, P|AM^*) + \varepsilon(i, P^*|AM)\varepsilon(P^*, P|AM^*) < 0$$

$$a_{21} = \varepsilon(P, i^*|AM)\varepsilon(i^*, i|AM^*) + \varepsilon(P, P^*|AM)\varepsilon(P^*, i|AM^*) > 0$$

$$1 > a_{22} = 1 - \varepsilon(P, P^*|AM)\varepsilon(P^*, P|AM^*) - \varepsilon(P, i^*|AM)\varepsilon(i^*, P|AM^*) > 0$$

$$\varepsilon(i, y|A, A^*) = \frac{\varepsilon(i, y|AM)a_{22} + \varepsilon(P, y|AM)a_{12}}{a_{11}a_{22} - a_{12}a_{21}} > 0$$

$$\varepsilon(P, y|A, A^*) = \frac{\varepsilon(P, y|AM)a_{11} + \varepsilon(i, y|AM)a_{21}}{a_{11}a_{22} - a_{12}a_{21}}$$

$$\varepsilon(i, B_n^*|A, A^*) = \frac{\begin{array}{l}[\varepsilon(i, i^*)\varepsilon(i^*, B_n^*|AM^*) + \varepsilon(i, P^*)\varepsilon(P^*, B_n^*|AM^*)]a_{22} \\ + [\varepsilon(P, i^*)\varepsilon(i^*, B_n^*|AM^*) + \varepsilon(P, P^*)\varepsilon(P^*, B_n^*|AM^*)]a_{12}\end{array}}{a_{11}a_{22} - a_{12}a_{21}} < 0$$

and P^* approach zero. In a small country, the responses of i^* and P^* to i and P are small. Since home country and foreign responses always appear as a product, the product approaches zero whenever there is substantial difference in relative size.

Interdependence of the asset markets is most important if countries or currency areas are of approximately equal size. In small countries, the effect of interdependence can be approximated by the response to foreign variables. As shown by $\varepsilon(i, B_n^*|A, A^*)$, the influence of foreign variables does not vanish. In a large country, all influences from abroad are of small order of magnitude and can be neglected. The responses on the asset markets of a large open economy can be approximated by the elasticities obtained from the model of a closed economy.

Opening the economy to trade and capital movements modifies our analysis of the output market in four ways. First, output and prices become subject to influences from both domestic and foreign asset markets. The elasticities denoted A, A^* replace the AM elasticities. Second, the dependence of d on p^* and the inclusion of exports in expenditure provide channels for interaction between foreign and domestic expenditure. These interactions modify the slope of the expenditure function and the response of real expenditure to changes in B, S, and g. Third, the price setting function now includes p^*. Interaction between p and p^* affects output and the slope of the price setting function. Fourth, both output and asset market equations show that changes in y^* affect the home country. Interaction between y and y^* alters the equilibrium positions of the two output markets and the two asset markets through W_h, e, W_h^* and e^*. The partial derivatives of d and X with respect to y and y^* are combinations of the derivatives with respect to W_h and e or W_h^* and e^*.

From equations (17a) and (17b) we obtain the slope of the expenditure function in the p, y plane – the counterpart of $\varepsilon(p, y|d+g)$ for the closed economy – and the shifts induced by changes in g, B and S. The responses recognize interaction on the asset markets and the response of the price level to asset prices holding output constant and neglecting interaction between y, p, y^* and p^*. The slope is denoted $\varepsilon(p, y|d+X+g)$ and the shifts in position are now $\varepsilon(p, g|d+X+g)$, $\varepsilon(p, B|d+X+g)$, etc. These elasticities are defined for given values of g, B_n, S, B_n^*, S^*, and y^*. Table 2 shows typical responses to domestic and foreign variables.

Opening the economy to exchanges of goods and securities lowers the slope of the expenditure function in small and large economies, but the change in slope is relatively small. The total price elasticity of domestic expenditure, $\bar{\varepsilon}(d, p)$ contains $\varepsilon(p^*, p)$ and $\varepsilon(p, p^*)$. One of the two vanishes in large and small countries. We have shown that the AA^* components differ little from the AM components so that $\bar{\varepsilon}(d, y)$ and $\bar{\varepsilon}(d, p)$ in table 2 are similar to the

TABLE 2

$$\varepsilon(p, y|d+X+g) = \frac{1-[(1-\beta-\gamma)\bar{\varepsilon}(d, y)+\beta\bar{\varepsilon}(X, y)]}{(1-\beta-\gamma)\bar{\varepsilon}(d, p)+\beta\varepsilon(X, p)} < 0$$

$$\varepsilon(p, g|d+X+g) = \frac{-\gamma}{\Delta OM} > 0$$

$$\varepsilon(p, B_n|d+X+g) = \frac{-[(1-\beta-\gamma)\bar{\varepsilon}(d, B_n)+\beta\varepsilon(X, B_n)]}{\Delta OM} > 0$$

$$\varepsilon(p, B_n^*|d+X+g) = \frac{-[(1-\beta-\gamma)\bar{\varepsilon}(d, B_n^*)+\beta\varepsilon(X, B_n^*)]}{\Delta OM} > 0$$

with $\beta = X/y$, $\gamma = g/y$, and ΔOM = the denominator of $\varepsilon(p, y|d+X+g)$.

Typical components and signs are

$$\bar{\varepsilon}(d, y) = \overset{+}{\varepsilon(d, y)} + \overset{-}{\bar{\varepsilon}(d, i)}\overset{+}{\varepsilon(i, y|A, A^*)} + \overset{+}{\bar{\varepsilon}(d, P)}\overset{\pm}{\varepsilon(P, y|A, A^*)} > 0$$

$$\varepsilon(X, y) = \overset{-}{\varepsilon(X, i^*)}\overset{\pm}{\varepsilon(i^*, y|A, A^*)} + \overset{+}{\varepsilon(X, P^*)}\overset{\pm}{\varepsilon(P^*, y|A, A^*)} \sim 0$$

$$\bar{\varepsilon}(d, p) = \overset{-}{\varepsilon(d, p)} + \overset{-}{\bar{\varepsilon}(d, i)}\overset{+}{\varepsilon(i, p|A, A^*)} + \overset{+}{\bar{\varepsilon}(d, P)}\overset{+}{\varepsilon(P, p|A, A^*)} +$$
$$\overset{+}{\varepsilon(p^*, p)}[\overset{-}{\varepsilon(d, i)}\overset{+}{\varepsilon(i, p^*|A, A^*)} + \overset{+}{\varepsilon(d, P)}\overset{-}{\varepsilon(P, p^*|A, A^*)} + \overset{+}{\varepsilon(p, p^*)}]$$

$$\varepsilon(d, B_n) = \overset{-}{\bar{\varepsilon}(d, i)}\overset{-}{\varepsilon(i, B_n|A, A^*)} + \overset{+}{\bar{\varepsilon}(d, P)}\overset{+}{\varepsilon(P, B_n|A, A^*)} > 0$$

$$\varepsilon(X, B_n) = \overset{-}{\varepsilon(X, i^*)}\overset{-}{\varepsilon(i^*, B_n|A, A^*)} + \overset{+}{\varepsilon(X, P^*)}\overset{+}{\varepsilon(P^*, B_n)} > 0$$

$$\varepsilon(d, B_n^*) = \varepsilon(d, i)\varepsilon(i, B_n^*|A, A^*) + \varepsilon(d, P)\varepsilon(P, B_n^*|A, A^*) > 0$$

corresponding elasticities in a small or large closed economy.

The slope of the open economy expenditure function in table 2 differs in two main ways from the slope in a closed economy. One is the presence of $\varepsilon(X, p)$, the partial price elasticity of exports. The other is β, the ratio of exports to domestic output. Differences in the response of open and closed economies are reduced by the relatively small size of β in large economies and increased by the relatively large value of β in small countries.

The conclusion about the slope $\varepsilon(p, y|d+X+g)$ carries over to the responses to policy variables. For large economies, the responses to policy variables shown in table 2 differ little from the closed economy responses. For small countries, the effects of B_n^*, y^*, p^* and possibly S^* cannot be neglected.

The supply response of the open economy can be obtained directly from equation (17c). We recognize the interdependence of p^*, p, y^*, and y by rewriting the equation as

$$p = p[y, K, w, \rho p^*(y^*, K^*, w^*, p/\rho)].$$

The slope of the supply curve in the p–y plane, neglecting interaction between

y and y^* (as in the elasticities of the expenditure function), is[12]

$$\bar{\varepsilon}(p, y|s) = \frac{\varepsilon(p, y|s)}{1 - \varepsilon(p^*, p)\varepsilon(p, p^*)}.$$

Opening the economy to trade increases the slope of the supply function. The change is small, however, in small or large countries. In these cases, either $\varepsilon(p, p^*)$ or $\varepsilon(p^*, p)$ vanishes. For a country approximately the same size as its trading partners, the interaction between domestic and foreign prices cannot be neglected.

The short-run response of output and prices in the home country to changes in g, B_n, S, B_n^*, S^*, or y^* is completely determined by the slopes and shifts. The response abroad is the mirror image of the home country response. For each country, we have determined a position of short-run flow equilibrium that is an exact analogue of the short-run flow equilibrium of the closed economy shown in figure 1 and equation (10). All variables held constant when determining the slopes of the expenditure and price-setting functions are treated similarly, and the response in the rest of the world is again a mirror image of the home country response.

Our analysis of the interaction of the flow markets with fixed money wages and fixed capital stock requires one additional step. The responses just described are obtained holding y^* constant at home and y constant abroad. Changes in y and y^* and their interaction affect the position of flow equilibrium in two ways, by changing the equilibrium values of P, i, P^* and i^* determined on the four-asset markets and by the interaction of the output market variables. To avoid additional, cumbersome notation, we rewrite the flow equilibrium condition for the home country and the rest of the world in terms of the existing stocks and the variables y and y^*,

$$y = d(B_n, B_n^*, S, S^*, y, y^*) + X(B_n, B_n^*, S, S^*, y, y^*) + g, \tag{22a}$$

and

$$y^* = d^*(\qquad\qquad) + X^*(\qquad\qquad) + g^*. \tag{22b}$$

The two equations express the full effect on expenditure of the interaction of asset markets and output markets in the two countries. The effects on d, X, d^*, and X^* of i, P, i^* and P^* are now implicit in the elasticities with respect to the variables in equations (22). Table 3 shows some principal responses obtained

[12]An additional effect occurs if domestic money wages depend on foreign prices or on foreign wages. We neglect any direct effect of this kind. Below, we recognize an effect on wages from excess supply or demand as in the closed economy.

TABLE 3

$$\varepsilon(y, B_n|OA, A^*) = \frac{(1-\beta-\gamma)\bar{\varepsilon}(d, B_n) + \beta\bar{\varepsilon}(X, B_n)}{1-(1-\beta-\gamma)\bar{\varepsilon}(d, y) - \beta\bar{\varepsilon}(X, y)} > 0$$

$$\varepsilon(y, B_n|OAO^*A^*) = \frac{(1-\beta-\gamma)[\bar{\varepsilon}(d, B_n) + \bar{\varepsilon}(d, y^*)\varepsilon(y^*, B_n)] + \beta[\bar{\varepsilon}(X, B_n) + \bar{\varepsilon}(X, y^*)\varepsilon(y^*, B_n)]}{1-(1-\beta-\gamma)[\bar{\varepsilon}(d, y) + \bar{\varepsilon}(d, y^*)\varepsilon(y^*, y)] - \beta[\bar{\varepsilon}(X, y) + \bar{\varepsilon}(X, y^*)\varepsilon(y^*, y)]} > 0$$

$$\varepsilon(y, g|OAO^*A^*) = \frac{\gamma}{\Delta} > 0$$

$$\varepsilon(y, g^*|OAO^*A^*) = \frac{\gamma^*[(1-\beta-\gamma)\bar{\varepsilon}(d, y^*) + \beta\varepsilon(X, y^*)]}{\Delta} > 0$$

$$\varepsilon(y, B_n^*|OAO^*A^*) = \frac{(1-\beta-\gamma)[\bar{\varepsilon}(d, B_n^*) + \varepsilon(d, y^*)\varepsilon(y^*, B_n^*)] + \beta[\varepsilon(X, B_n^*) + \varepsilon(X, y^*)\varepsilon(y^*, B_n^*)]}{\Delta} > 0$$

from the two equations. The responses in the rest of the world are, again, mirror images of the home country responses.

The first elasticity in table 3, $\varepsilon(y, B_n|OA, A^*)$, is obtained from equation (22a) ignoring interaction with the output markets in the rest of the world, equation (22b). The components of $\varepsilon(y, B_n|OA, A^*)$ are described more fully in table 2 where the numerator appears as the numerator of $\varepsilon(p, B_n|d+X+g)$, and the denominator is the numerator of $\varepsilon(p, y|d+X+g)$.

The full response of output to a change in the base and other policy variables includes the interaction with output markets abroad, equation (22b). All remaining elasticities in table 3 recognize the interaction and are denoted OAO^*A^*. The pattern is recognizable. The two terms in the numerator of $\varepsilon(y, B_n|OAO^*A^*)$ contain the total response of domestic expenditure and exports to B_n on the output and asset market. Each has two components. The first, $\bar{\varepsilon}(d, B_n)$ and $\bar{\varepsilon}(X, B_n)$ are the same terms appearing in the numerator of $\varepsilon(y, B_n|OA, A^*)$. The second component of each term allows for a response of y^* to B_n taking account of the full interaction of the markets for assets and output. The denominator contains $\bar{\varepsilon}(d, y)$ and $\bar{\varepsilon}(X, y)$ from table 2, modified by the interaction of the asset and output markets expressed by $\bar{\varepsilon}(d, y^*)$ and $\bar{\varepsilon}(X, y^*)$. If the export response is the larger of the two, interaction lowers the denominator. The numerator increases, so allowing for interaction raises the response. The responses to S and S^* are obtained by substituting S and S^* for B and B^*.

As before, the values of the elasticities depend on the relative size of the two markets. For small countries $\varepsilon(y^*, y)$ is small, and for large countries, $\varepsilon(d, y^*)$ and $\varepsilon(X, y^*)$ are small. The total response over output and asset markets at home and abroad differs little from the domestic response. For a large country the effects of g^*, B_n^* and S^* are small also, so the closed economy results remain valid. For a small country, the closed economy results are approximate measures of the effect of B_n, g, and S, but output in the open economy depends heavily on B_n^*, g^* and S^*.

Determining the longer-run equilibrium price response requires one additional step. Each response of y is multiplied by the response of p to y obtained from the price-setting function allowing for the full interaction of domestic and foreign markets. The adjustment of p induced by changes in B_n, B_h^*, S or other variables in table 3 is the product of the response of real output to the particular variable shown in table 3 multiplied by $\bar{\varepsilon}(p, y|s, s^*)$.

$$\bar{\varepsilon}(p, y|s, s^*) = \frac{\varepsilon(p, y|s) + \varepsilon(p, p^*)[\varepsilon(p^*, y^*)\varepsilon(y^*, y)] + \varepsilon(p, w)h(t)}{1 - \varepsilon(p, p^*)\varepsilon(p^*, p)} > 0. \tag{23}$$

The term $\varepsilon(p, w)h(t)$ shows that elasticity includes the longer-run adjustment of money wages implicit in equation (5).

The response of prices in a small or large open economy is similar to the response in a closed economy. Again, the symmetry of the results for large and small countries depends on different terms that appear multiplicatively. And again, the terms expressing the interaction of the home country with the rest of the world increase the slope of the price-setting function in countries of moderate size.[13]

7. Stock-flow Equilibrium with Fixed Exchange Rates

The longer-run flow equilibrium position in each country depends on the stocks of debt and base money outstanding at home and abroad. The extent of dependence on foreign stocks varies with the relative size of the country and is largest for countries approximately equal in size to their trading partners. With fixed exchange rates, no country is entirely isolated from foreign influence, but a relatively large country with a relatively small foreign sector experiences relatively little short-run feedback from its own policies and is not much affected by the policies of foreign governments. A relatively small country also receives very little feedback from its policies but is affected much more by

[13]Since capital stocks remain fixed throughout this analysis, the longer-run equilibrium position generally is not a full equilibrium. For full equilibrium the relative prices of assets and output must adjust until $p = P$. In open as in closed economies, full adjustment generally requires changes in the composition of output and changes in the capital stock.

influence from abroad. The determination of equilibrium stocks and flows differs with the size of the country.

The stocks of base money and debt in each open economy are a consequence of current and past domestic and international monetary and fiscal policies. In this section, we discuss mainly the longer-run stock-flow equilibrium position, the determination of the stocks of assets consistent with the longer-run flow equilibrium of the previous section.

Determination of equilibrium stocks of financial assets – B, B^*_n, S and S^* – involves three equations introduced earlier, the government budget equations for the two countries and the common current account balance. Table 3 and equation (23) show that the longer-run equilibrium values of p, y and i depend on financial asset stocks and policy variables. By substituting the solutions for i, p, and y in the budget equations of each country, we can express the current budget deficit or surplus as a function of outstanding asset stocks and policy variables. The resulting equations, equations (24a) and (24b), are the analogues in an open economy of equation (13) of the closed economy. F and F^* determine the deficit or surplus in the budget of the home country and the consolidated budget of the rest of the world.

Equation (24c) is obtained in a similar way. All flow variables in the current account balance, equation (19), are replaced by their solution in terms of financial asset stocks and policy variables. The stocks of domestic assets are combined as D and D^*; the cumulated current account balance is B_2,

$$\mathring{D} = F(\overset{-}{D}, \overset{-}{D^*}, \overset{-}{B_2};\quad \overset{+}{g}, \overset{-}{g^*}, \overset{+}{wlg}, \overset{-}{wlg^*}, \overset{-}{\tau}, \overset{+}{\tau^*}, \overset{-}{\mu}, \overset{-}{\mu^*}, \overset{-}{\rho}), \tag{24a}$$

$$\mathring{D}^* = F^*(\overset{-}{D}, \overset{-}{D^*}, \overset{+}{B_2};\quad \overset{-}{g}, \overset{+}{g^*}, \overset{-}{wlg}, \overset{+}{wlg^*}, \overset{+}{\tau}, \overset{-}{\tau^*}, \overset{-}{\mu}, \overset{-}{\mu^*}, \overset{+}{\rho}), \tag{24b}$$

$$\mathring{B}_2 = C(\overset{-}{D}, \overset{+}{D^*}, \overset{-}{B_2};\quad \overset{-}{g}, \overset{+}{g^*}, \overset{-}{wlg}, \overset{+}{wlg^*}, \overset{+}{\tau}, \overset{-}{\tau^*}, \overset{-}{\mu}, \overset{+}{\mu^*}, \overset{+}{\rho}). \tag{24c}$$

The signs above the variables show the direction of change in $\mathring{D}$, $\mathring{D}^*$ and $\mathring{B}_2$ for positive changes in the stocks and policy variables. As in the closed economy [equation (15)] the response of F to D may require some restriction on the size of $\partial F/\partial S$. The same is true of $\partial F/\partial D^*$ because of the presence of $\partial F/\partial S^*$, but to a lesser degree because $\partial F/\partial S^*$ is small. A small minimum value of μ may be required for a negative derivative in open as in closed economies. Similar comments apply to the F^* equation, and to a minimum μ^*, by the symmetry built into our solution. The signs of C require some restrictions on the response of exports and imports to domestic and foreign prices. These are the usual restrictions on the size of direct responses relative to feedback from abroad.

8. The Scope for Independent Policies in Interdependent Economies

Inspection of the dynamic system, equations (24a) to (24c), shows that the adjustments of the two economies are determined by fiscal variables – $g, g^*, \tau, \tau^*, wlg, wlg^*$ – and by monetary policy expressed by the financial parameters μ and μ^* and by exchange rate arrangements. Some questions about the properties of the system arise. How many independent policy choices can be made without endangering the stability of the system? Can all countries maintain independent fiscal policies and fixed exchange rates? What is the required policy in countries that seek to harmonize fiscal and monetary policies? This section attempts to answer these questions by examining the stability of the system and the conditions for stability. A diagram summarizes the discussion.

In principle, every policy change affects the net foreign positions, the balances on current account and the budget positions of the rest of the world, but our analysis has shown that the size of any effects on the rest of the world and from the rest of the world depends on the size of the country. Small countries have little influence on large countries but are greatly influenced by the policies of large countries.

The stability of the fixed exchange rate system depends on the properties of the differential equation describing the adjustment of financial assets in the interdependent world economy. If the differential equation has only negative real roots, the fixed exchange rate system is stable. The homogenous differential equation formed from equations (24a) to (24c) has the general form[14]

$$a_0\lambda^3 + a_1\lambda^2 + a_2\lambda + a_3 = 0.$$

The Routh–Hurwitz conditions imply that a sufficient condition for instability of the system is $a_3 < 0$. The sign of a_3 can be found from

$$a_3 = F_D(F^*_{B_2}C_{D^*} - F^*_{D^*}C_{B_2}) + F^*_D(F_{D^*}C_{B_2} - F_{B_2}C_{D^*}) + C_D(F^*_{D^*}F_{B^2} - F_{D^*}F^*_{B_2}).$$

The sign of the first term of a_3 depends on relative orders of magnitude, but is probably positive. All other terms are negative, so $a_3 < 0$ and the fixed exchange rate is unstable under a wide variety of conditions. Moreover, conditions that assure a positive value of the first term, large $F^*_{D^*}$ and C_{B_2}, also raise the absolute value of the other terms.

[14]The coefficient $a_0 > 0$. All other coefficients are obtained from the matrix of partial derivatives used to form the characteristic equation

$$\begin{vmatrix} \lambda - F_D & -F_{D^*} & -F_{B_2} \\ -F^*_D & \lambda - F^*_{D^*} & -F^*_{B_2} \\ -C_D & -C_{D^*} & \lambda - C_{B_2} \end{vmatrix} = 0.$$

Instability of the system means that once the world economy leaves an equilibrium position, there is no mechanism that restores equilibrium at the fixed rates. One reason is that governments engage in independent policy operations. Financial assets are created and destroyed to finance budget policies and the balance of payments. The world stock of money changes with μD, $\mu^* D^*$ and B_2. There is no mechanism assuring that the rates of change of money and the stocks of financial assets remain consistent with prevailing exchange rates once the analysis incorporates independent budget processes.

Suppose a country disturbs equilibrium by expansive fiscal policy, increasing g, keeping tax rates and financial policy (μ) unchanged. The budget deficit rises ($\mathring{D} > 0$) and the outstanding stock of financial assets, D, increases. Prices rise in the expanding country and in the rest of the world. There is a deficit on current account ($\mathring{B}_2 < 0$) and a budget surplus in the rest of the world ($\mathring{D}^* < 0$), shown in equations (24b) and (24c) by the responses to g and D. The budget surplus abroad reduces D^*, reducing the stocks of foreign financial assets and slowing the rate of increase of money and securities in the world. The reduction of B_2 works to equilibrate prices in the expanding country and the rest of the world. The familiar price–specie flow mechanism decelerates prices in the expanding country and accelerates prices in the rest of the world. In addition, the changes induced by the movements of international reserves raise the budget deficit in the expanding country and the budget surplus in the rest of the world. These responses are shown by the effects of B_2 on $\mathring{D}$ and $\mathring{D}^*$ in equations (24a) and (24b). The rate of increase in assets slows if fiscal policy and financial policy remain unchanged.

The damping of the response to a change in g (or other expansive policy action) depends not only on the price–specie flow mechanism but on the budget policy mechanism. The rest of the world must absorb some of the assets created to finance the home country budget and must run a budget surplus to reduce their outstanding stocks of base money and securities.

If foreigners choose to maintain fixed exchange rates, they cannot select an independent fiscal policy. Every choice of g^* and τ^* imposes restrictions on the policy choices available to the home country.

Maintenance of equilibrium with fixed exchange rates imposes restrictions on fiscal and financial policies. For a time, a country can offset some of the effect on prices, output and asset stocks by changing current (marginal) μ^* relative to average μ^*. Opportunities of this kind are limited and decline with the length of run. In the longer-run equilibrium at fixed exchange rates persists if and only if wealth owners treat domestic and foreign assets as perfect substitutes at the prevailing exchange rates and commodities sell at equivalent prices.

A diagram brings out some implications of our analysis. In figure 2, equations

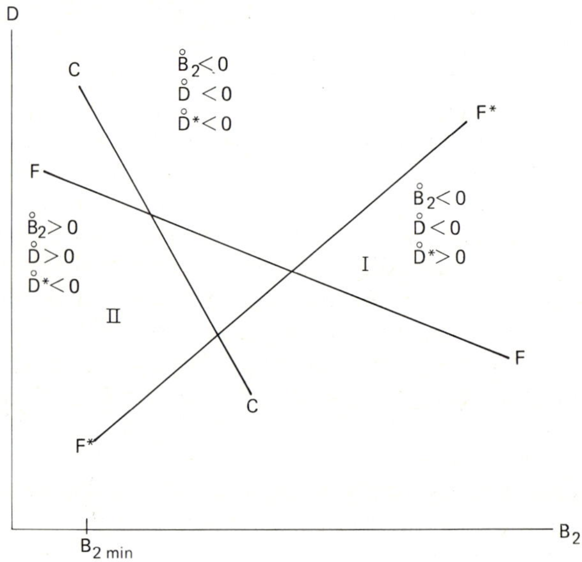

FIGURE 2

(24a) to (24c) are shown as equilibrium relations. Each differential equation is set equal to zero and solved for D as a function of B_2. The position of each line depends on D^* and on the policy variables. The FF line defines a balance in the home country budget, $\overset{\circ}{D} = 0$. The F^*F^* line defines a balanced budget in the rest of the world, $\overset{\circ}{D}^* = 0$. The CC line defines a current account balance for both countries, $\overset{\circ}{B}_2 = 0$.

The intersection of the three lines is a position of world equilibrium. At all other positions at least one market is not in equilibrium. At values of B_2 to the right of CC, FF and F^*F^*, $\overset{\circ}{B}_2$ and $\overset{\circ}{D}$ are negative and $\overset{\circ}{D}^*$ is positive. The home country has a deficit on current account and a surplus in the government budget. B_2 and D decline, so B_n and S decline. The rest of the world has a surplus on current account, equal to the home country deficit, and a deficit in the budget. Domestic assets of foreign countries increase, and B_n^* and S^* rise. The point, or area, labelled I has these properties.

The opposite set of circumstances is found at values of B_2 to the left of CC, FF, and F^*F^*. The point labelled II has the properties $\overset{\circ}{B}_2 > 0$, $\overset{\circ}{D} > 0$ and $\overset{\circ}{D}^* < 0$. The home country has a surplus on current account and a deficit in the government budget; the rest of the world has a deficit on current account and a budget surplus. In the home country, stocks of base money and securities rise; in the rest of the world, assets stocks fall.

From point *II*, the home country moves toward the *CC* and *FF* lines under the impact of rising asset stocks. The movement is in the direction of stock equilibrium for the home country but may be away from the F^*F^* curve. The budget surplus abroad, however, complicates the adjustment. The effect of falling B^*_n and S^* is to raise the *FF* and F^*F^* lines and lower the *CC* line. F^*F^* and *CC* move toward point *II* and *FF* moves away.

Whether the total effect is a convergence toward equilibrium stocks or a movement away from equilibrium depends on the choice of policies in the two countries. There are sets of policies that move the system toward equilibrium. However, fixed policies – constant $g, g^*, \mu, \mu^*, \tau, \tau^*$ – are inconsistent with world equilibrium at fixed exchange rates as shown earlier.

An example brings out the problem of holding exchange rates fixed while choosing independent monetary and fiscal policies in open, interdependent economies. Suppose, as before, that the home country increases g thereby putting the world economy inside the triangle formed by the *CC*, *FF* and F^*F^* lines of figure 2. At every point in the triangle, $\mathring{B}_2 < 0$, $\mathring{D} > 0$ and $\mathring{D}^* < 0$. The home country has a deficit in the current account balance and a budget deficit. The rest of the world has a surplus on current account and a budget surplus. With $\mathring{B}_2 < 0$ and $\mathring{D} > 0$, B_2 falls and D rises in the home country, moving the world economy toward the intersection of *CC* and *FF*. The surplus in the foreign budget, however, lowers *CC* (shifts *CC* to the left) and raises *FF* and F^*F^*. The *FF* and *CC* lines move away from equilibrium. Instability implies that these movements are large relative to the adjustment toward equilibrium in the home country. Stocks of foreign exchange move toward a minimum, critical level, $B_{2\,\mathrm{min}}$ in figure 2, before the payments imbalance is corrected. At the minimum level of B_2, devaluation is a likely solution.

Devaluation is not the only solution. Before reaching the minimum level of B_2 a reduction in g or an increase in τ helps to restore equilibrium. An increase in g^* or a reduction in τ^* also moves the system toward equilibrium. As we emphasized earlier, there are sets of policies that help to maintain fixed exchange rates, but the system is unstable with independent fiscal policies. If policy changes in a country of moderate or larger size disturb world equilibrium the world economy does not return to the previous equilibrium. The diagram demonstrates the point we have emphasized. In open, interdependent economies with fixed exchange rates, countries cannot maintain independent fiscal and monetary policies.

9. Conclusion

The main policy conclusion reached in our analysis is that the fixed exchange-rate system is likely to be unstable. Departures from stock-flow equilibrium do not set off a process that restores equilibrium. There are too many sources of money and debt creation in open economies to assure that the system returns to equilibrium at unchanged exchange rates. The many devaluations and revaluations under the Bretton–Woods system support this implication.

Our conclusions are derived from a model that differs in several ways from recent analyses [Mundell (1968)]. Output is variable; prices of assets and output change; the conditions of world equilibrium do not hold at every instant but are a consequence of the behavior of economic agents responding to policy and other changes. Countries are not all "small". They differ in size, and the effects of policy and other changes depend on size.

Decisions of large countries have considerable influence on prices and output in small countries, but the reverse is not true. Large countries bent upon an independent policy course find their influence on world prices and output magnified by the fixed exchange-rate system. Countries approximately equal in size to their trading partners are in an intermediate position. Interdependence increases with the size of a country's trading partners.

For small and large countries, the effects of domestic policy actions is very similar in open and closed economies. Opening the economy to trade in assets and current output does little to enhance or weaken the effects of monetary and fiscal policies in these countries.

In open and closed economies, fiscal policy has a powerful influence on the stock-flow equilibrium position. The influence comes from the effect of fiscal policy on the outstanding stocks of financial assets, money and bonds. The effect on asset stocks is considerably larger and more durable than the effect of fiscal policy on flows, so much emphasized in the past. Fiscal policy is the major determinant of asset stocks in a closed economy, and the level and composition of assets has a dominant effect on equilibrium prices and output. In an open economy, stocks of financial assets depend on fiscal policy and on the balance of payments.

The dependence of assets stocks on domestic and foreign fiscal policy and on the balance of payments is the primary reason for instability of the system. The Bretton–Woods system did not restrict fiscal policy or establish rules limiting the size of budget deficits or the power of central banks to finance budget deficits. Whenever rates of fiscal and monetary expansion in a particular country remained above or below the rates in the rest of the world, devaluation or revaluation followed. In the absence of restrictions on the use of fiscal policy and the financing of budget deficits, there is no reason to expect any future system of fixed exchange rates to be durable or stable.

References

Dornbusch, R., 1973, Capital mobility, portfolio balances and nontraded assets, multilithed.
McKinnon, R., 1969, Portfolio balance and international payments adjustment, in: R. Mundell and A. Swoboda, eds., Monetary problems of the international economy (Aldine, Chicago).
Metzler, L., 1951, Wealth, saving and the rate of interest, Journal of Political Economy.
Mundell, R., 1968, International economics (Macmillan, London).
Myhrman, J., 1976, A macroeconomic model with asset equilibrium for an open economy, Journal of Monetary Economics.

Chapter 12.2

COMMENT ON BRUNNER AND MELTZER

Helmut FRISCH

The paper "Monetary and Fiscal Policy in Open, Interdependent Economies with Fixed Exchange Rates" by K. Brunner and A. Meltzer consists of two parts: a model of a closed economy and a model of an open economy, which is a further development of the closed model. A commodity market, two financial markets (a market for bankloans and a money market) and a labor market (Phillips curve) are formulated. Using the implicit differentiation rule the model is formulated in terms of elasticities. The technic of analysis – if I understand this correctly – is a refined version of the *IS–LM* model. The main procedure is to change the exogenous variables and to study the adjustment of the system. The two authors use a stepwise procedure, and consider four adjustment procedures: (1) *short-term adjustment* defined as the commodity market reaction to changes in the asset market; (2) *intermediate adjustment* of the asset market determined by the interaction of the asset market, the commodity market and the government budget; (3) *a longer-run adjustment* of employment and labor and the output market; and (4) *a long-run adjustment* of capital stock and wealth.

Let us consider one of the main ideas of the closed model, which is represented in figure 1. The initial equilibrium is (y_0, p_0), the intersection of the "desired" demand function $d + g_0$ and the "desired" supply function $s(w_0)$ and the "capacity limit" y_0, the maximum production for a given stock of capital and the given amount of labor. If this situation is changed by an exogenous shift of desired demand to $d + g_1$, then the new equilibrium position (p_1, y_1) is only *notional* (the intersection of the "desired" supply and the "desired" demand function).[1] Reading horizontally the distance AB measures the excess demand in the commodity market. A Walrasian price adjustment for the commodity market

[1]It is important for the argument to stress the point that the supply and demand functions are "planned" or "desired" supply and demand functions and not actual demand and supply [Hicks (1965, p. 76 ff.)]. Arrow and Hahn (1971, p. 363) work with the difference between "target" and "active" supply and demand function.

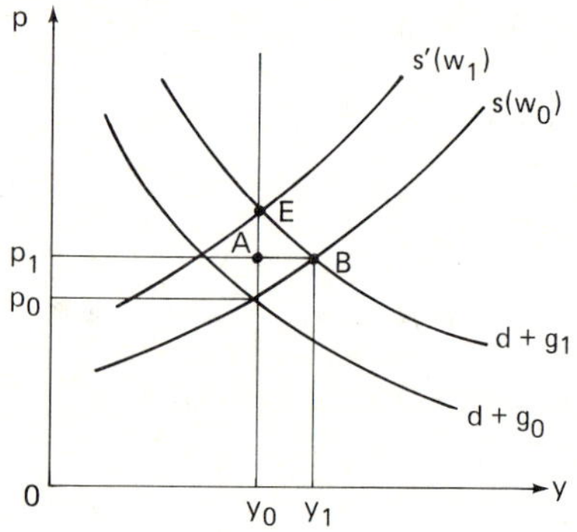

FIGURE 1

would fit into the spirit of this model,

$$dp/dt = f(d + g_1 - y_0).$$

The distance AB can also be considered as an index of excess demand in the labor market (factor gap); because "desired" production, y_1 (at price p_1) is larger than the full-employment output y_0. The difference $y_1 - y_0$ measures the demand pressure in the labor market, a modified Phillips curve for wage adjustment,

$$dw/dt = h(y - y_0) + dp/dt,$$

will express this pressure.

The increase in nominal wage moves the supply curve north-west, because the fixed nominal wage rate w is a parameter of function $s(w)$. The curve will move towards s', where at E a new short-run equilibrium position is obtained. In this interpretation the increase of the expenditure to $d + g_1$ sets in motion a price–wage spiral, without causing any real effects.[2] The statement of B&M: "An increase in money wages raises prices and reduces output and a reduction in money wages lowers prices and raises output" can not be true under these conditions.

To show that a monetary impulse will produce also a real effect (i.e., will change real production), a more careful development of the labor market and some assumptions about disequilibrium behavior seem necessary. For example, Solow and Stiglitz (1968) consider the following model. If the system is out

[2]The argument is of course a variant of Bent Hansen's famous model of an open inflation (1951, ch. VII); see also Lindbeck (1967, p. 59 ff).

of equilibrium (A) the (representative) firm needs a hypothesis what actual production would be (figure 2). It seems reasonable to assume that "actual" (realized) production is limited by the smaller of the two quantities (d, s); actual production $y = \min(s, d)$. A (ultra) short-run equilibrium will be found for example at E. If the production function is $y = F(N)$, the labor demand function (actual demand) would be $N^D = F^{-1}(y)$. The commodity gap $d - y_0$ (distance EB) will increase the price level, say to p_1. At point C desired production is y_1 and labor demand $N^D = F^{-1}(y_1)$ is larger than $N^D(y_0)$. Solow and Stiglitz introduce a labor accumulation function,

$$\mathrm{d}N/\mathrm{d}t = g[F^{-1}\min(s, d) - N^D(y_0)] > 0.$$

In this model prices *and* employment ($\mathrm{d}N/\mathrm{d}t > 0$) will increase and as a consequence the real production will go up from $y_0 \rightarrow y_1$. This kind of adjustment produces "real effects" and would fit into the longer-run adjustment process of the model; perhaps Brunner and Meltzer had a similar adjustment process in mind.

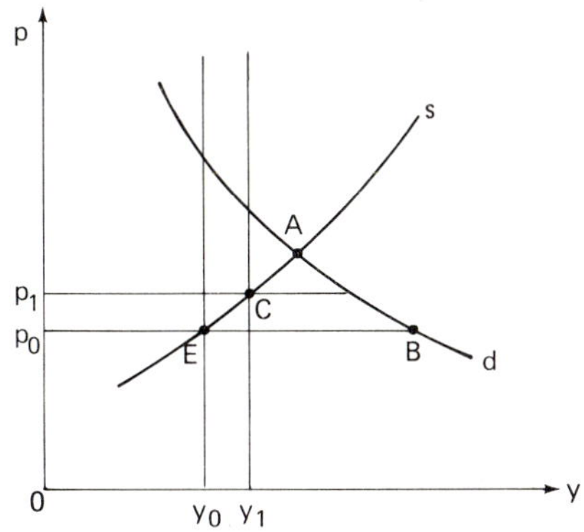

FIGURE 2

In the second part, the model is extended to an open economy. By contrast to the results for the closed economy the elasticities show now also the influence from abroad. In this model the elasticities usually appear pairwise and multiplicative, for example, $\varepsilon(i, i^*) \cdot \varepsilon(i^*, i)$ means the response of the domestic rate of interest, i, to a change of the foreign rate of interest, i^*, times the response of the foreign interest rate, i^*, to a change of the domestic rate. The multiplication of these two elasticities serves as a measure of the interdependence of the domestic and the foreign economy. One of the final results is the formula for $\bar{\varepsilon}(p, y/s, s^*)$; the slope of the domestic demand function (in the price–quantity space), including the total response of commodity and asset-markets at home and abroad, is

$$\bar{\varepsilon}(p, y/s, s^*) = \frac{\varepsilon(p, y/s) + \varepsilon(p, p^*)[\varepsilon(p^*, y^*)\varepsilon(y^*, y)]\varepsilon(p, q)h(t)}{1 - \varepsilon(p, p^*)\varepsilon(p^*, p)}.$$

Take a small European country like Austria, Belgium or the Netherlands: $\varepsilon(p, p^*)$ will be positive and possibly large, expressing "imported" inflation, while $\varepsilon(p^*, p)$ the response of the foreign price level to a domestic price change may be very small or zero, just as $\varepsilon(y^*, y)$. Therefore we have to conclude that $\varepsilon(p, y/s, s^*) = \varepsilon(p, y/s)$.[3] This means that a change in the foreign variables would not have an impact on the domestic price elasticity of demand. With the elasticities appearing multiplicative, the authors are forced to conclude that "the response of prices in a small or a large open economy is similar to the response in a closed economy".

The corollary seems plausible for the relation of a large economy to a small one, but is counter-intuitive vice versa. Here the limitations of this model are apparent. To study the problem of price and interdependencies in open economies, other concepts of modeling seem necessary. Some recent work done by Scandinavian economists appear more promising to me. There the domestic price increase is explained by productivity differences in different sectors of the economy and by the international inflation, which determines the development of nominal profits and wages in the "exposed" sector of the economy.[4]

The last more or less sketchy part is concerned with monetary and fiscal policy and the long-run stock equilibrium of the economy. A system of three differential equations (21a–c) is formulated and solved for the variables D (accumulated base money and security) and B_2 (international reserves). It is difficult to understand why the solution of these three equations should be linear as pictured in figure 2 of the paper. For such a result more restrictive assumptions are necessary than mentioned in the paper. If the set of the solutions *CC*, *FF*, F^*F^* are nonlinear, all kinds of situations are possible; for example, that the three functions will never intersect so no (full) equilibrium will exist or that more than one equilibrium will exist. But even if one would accept the linear solution the actual position of these three functions depends on

[3]Both formulas differ only with respect to the money wage term $\varepsilon(p, w)h(t)$.

[4]Edgren et al. (1969), Branson and Myhrman (1973).

the size of 10 different parameters so that an infinite set of alternative positions of these three equations are possible. To develop the economic argument it seems reasonable to start with a full equilibrium, a position where the FF, F^*F^* and CC lines intersect, to introduce separate exogenous shifts of each of these lines and to consider the dynamic forces of that experiment, particularly the problem of a stable or unstable equilibrium. There seems to be a conjecture that this system is (globally?) unstable. The connection of this analysis to the commodity and asset market (the first part of the paper) should be made more explicit.

References

Arrow, K. J. and F. H. Hahn, 1971, General competitive analysis (Holden-Day, San Francisco, Calif.).

Branson, W. and J. Myhrman, 1973, Inflation in open economies: Supply-determined vs. demand-determined models, Seminar Paper no. 34, 10/73 (Institute for International Economic Studies, University of Stockholm, Stockholm).

Edgren, E., K. O. Faxen and C. E. Ohdner, 1969, Wages, growth and the distribution of income, Swedish Journal of Economics, Sept.

Hansen, B., 1951, A study in the theory of inflation (Kelley, Clifton, N.J.).

Hicks, J., 1965, Capital and growth (Oxford University Press, London).

Lindbeck, A., 1967, Monetary–fiscal analysis and general equilibrium (Helsinki).

Solow, R. M. and J. E. Stiglitz, 1968, Output, employment and wages in the short run, Quarterly Journal of Economics 82.

Chapter 12.3

SUMMARY OF THE DISCUSSION ON BRUNNER AND MELTZER

Anthony B. ATKINSON, *Chairman*

Following Helmut Frisch's comments, *Allan Meltzer* corrected a false impression, which could come from his paper. The inflation effects come through the expenditure side (imports and exports) and not through the slope of the supply curve, which is the same for all sorts of economies, small or large, open or closed. There is an interaction between the home country prices and foreign prices, and the interaction effect is expressed in the same way for all countries; but small countries are more dependent than large countries on effects coming through the balance of payments.

Jacques Melitz: To adapt Meltzer's work to continental European cases, one must not forget that most of these countries have not a huge national debt. Moreover, the government is very often a large supplier of credit so that it can finance itself by reducing the supply it provides to the public. This is important since in the Brunner–Meltzer model there is a distinction between the security market and the credit market, but also, from a more conceptual point of view, because financing through a reduction of credit supply to the public may involve a stronger financial constraint on the private sector than issuing securities. In other terms, it resembles more the case of balanced budget financing with increased taxes than that of financing by increased national debt.

Chapter 13.1

INFLATION, CAPACITY CHANGE AND THE BALANCE OF PAYMENTS: A DISEQUILIBRIUM MODEL*

Sven W. ARNDT

1. Introduction

One important class of problems in macroeconomic theory deals with the functioning of automatic adjustment mechanisms when aggregate demand and supply fail to match at prevailing prices. Another concerns the proper role of governmental stabilization policies in cases in which the economy's automatic responses cannot be relied upon to return the system to equilibrium with acceptable speed.

This paper investigates the first problem by means of a disequilibrium model in which households and firms fail to realize their planned sales and purchases at prevailing prices. This calls for distinction between situations in which realized transactions do and in those in which they do not appear as arguments in the excess demand functions.[1] Individual behavior is altered in a fundamental sense by the existence of such market constraints.

It is argued that the path and speed of disequilibrium adjustment are governed not by conventional constraint-free excess demands, but by their constraint-inclusive counterparts. The distinction, which tends to dissolve as the system approaches general equilibrium, is of special interest to the analysis of open economies in disequilibrium; it implies that in such economies there exist three measures of the balance of payments.

A related question concerning the speed and direction of adjustment and the range of policy options arises in connection with the conventional assumption that an economy's productive capacity is invariable over the policy horizon.

*Earlier versions of this paper were presented at the annual meeting of the Econometric Society in 1972, at the University of California, Berkeley, and at Duke and Stanford Universities. Professors E. Ray Canterbery and Donald J. Mathieson deserve special thanks for their helpful comments on earlier drafts.

[1]The work of Clower and of Grossman (1971) and Barro and Grossman (1971) is relevant here.

This approach, which has dominated the literature on macroeconomic adjustment, has the weakness of relying on autonomous and policy-induced variations in investment as an important vehicle of adjustment, while considering its expenditure but not its capacity effects. The cyclical consequences of variations in the level of investment expenditure are thus seriously misrepresented. The approach tends, moreover, to generate excessive preoccupation with aggregate demand management as a counter-cyclical tool to the exclusion of supply management. Such a perspective is defensible for economies plagued with underemployed resources and excess capacity, but it is inadequate for economies in which the dominant problem is one of excess demand and of supply shortages.

The framework to be developed in the following pages incorporates the capacity effects of investment and examines the forces of adjustment when aggregate demand and aggregate capacity are both variable. As an immediate consequence, the *composition* as well as the *level* of aggregate expenditure matters for stabilization purposes and a government's counter-cyclical policies need to be evaluated with respect both to their effects on the level of total demand and to their impact on its composition. Policies which leave the level of aggregate demand unchanged can nevertheless alter the time-path of the system's response to disturbances if they change the composition of expenditure between capacity-generating and capacity-using outlays.

The basic framework is presented in section 2 in which the several concepts of the balance of payments are also examined. Section 3 then outlines the mechanism on the basis of which prevailing prices change in response to constraint-inclusive excess demands. A brief concluding section completes the discussion.

2. Trade and Payments in Disequilibrium

This section examines the nature of disequilibrium adjustment in an inflationary open economy. The focus is on excess demand and on the economy's self-regulatory properties; little will be said about excess supply disequilibria.

Unlike models which employ tâtonnement, recontracting or other processes, the proposed approach permits trading at false prices. In disequilibrium, transactions occur at prices which are not market-clearing prices. Consequently, the plans of some transactors go unfulfilled, an outcome which violates one of the conditions on the basis of which conventional demand and supply equations are derived. These equations are constructed on the condition that individuals expect to be able to realize their plans; they do not perceive themselves as constrained by shortages and by associated rationing schemes in any of the markets in which they conduct their business.

Individual demand and supply functions and market excess demands may thus be constructed under two sets of conditions characterized by important differences in available choice patterns. The approach in what follows is to derive, for given price vectors and other initial conditions, a set of excess demand functions which does and a set which does not contain realized transactions as an argument.

We begin by defining a *decision frame* for which constraint-free and constraint-inclusive excess demand functions are specified. These ex ante magnitudes are then compared with realized quantities and divergencies between them set the stage for a new round of decisions. The discussion then proceeds to several alternative concepts of trade and payments imbalances. The economy is composed of markets for goods, bonds and money and of a market for labor which, however, plays a subsidiary role in the analysis. Decision-makers are firms who purchase inputs and sell output and bonds, and households who sell labor services and purchase goods and bonds and who hold money balances.

2.1. The Decision Frame

In examining the disequilibrium properties of an economy faced with excess demand it is necessary to specify the behavior of firms and households operating at microeconomic decision-making levels. For an economy in general equilibrium planned and realized transactions are identical; at the prevailing price vector firms are able to obtain inputs and sell outputs which are consistent with profit maximization and households are able to sell labor services and purchase goods and assets which are consistent with utility maximization. Budget constraints and production functions constitute the only relevant constraining factors.

In disequilibrium this is not the case. Decisions are made which turn out to be realizable only in part or not at all. Divergence of realization from plans leads to a new round of decisions and the process continues until a consistent set of plans has been established. Suppose that the following describes the process by which the system through its many individual decision-makers gropes towards a set of consistent plans and its associated market-clearing price vector.

Suppose that decisions to purchase and sell are made, exercised and reviewed during a time interval which we shall call a decision frame. Each frame opens with a certain configuration of prices, wages, interest rates, and endowments, all inherited from the preceding frame. Inherited information and endowment form the basis for profit- and utility-maximizing decisions by firms and households during the current frame. When the price vector is a market-clearing vector, planned transactions will be realized and the decision frame is an equilibrium frame which will be reproduced in future frames for as long as underlying conditions do not change.

When the price vector is not a market-clearing vector, some plans remain partly or entirely unrealized. The frame ends with establishment of new prices on the basis of which decisions will be made in the next frame. In this stylized representation of the decision process prices are altered "between frames" so that each frame is viewed as identifying a set of consumption, saving, production and investment plans based on a temporarily frozen price vector.

2.2. Prior and Posterior Demand and Realized Magnitudes

When a firm or household perceives itself as able to bring its plans to realization, when it expects to be able to purchase and sell planned quantities of factors, goods and assets, its behavior is different than when it perceives its capacity to realize plans as constrained in one or more markets. The market constraint operates in addition to production or budget constraints and is incorporated into the maximization process along with price vectors, production functions and budget constraints.

When a household perceives itself as unencumbered by external constraints in factor, goods and asset markets, it will supply labor services and demand goods and assets in accordance with conventional utility maximization based on the price vector and on its budget constraints. The relevant demand and supply functions contain prices, expectation variables and initial stocks of wealth, but not income as such because the latter is a choice variable which is maximized out.

Where a firm perceives itself as able to purchase and sell without constraint, the relevant demand and supply functions incorporate the prevailing price vector and the firm's internal production constraint. Where the firm can obtain whatever quantities of productive factors it requires and sell whatever output it determines to bring to market at current prices, profit maximization is constrained only by the production function.

We shall call these demand and supply functions the household's and the firm's *prior demand* and *prior supply*. They are *prior* in the sense of being formulated without consideration of external constraints. They are to be distinguished from another set of functions which does take external constraints into account.

The second set of functions is constructed on the perception that some planned transactions will not be completed. Such functions are relevant to firms and households who enter a decision frame confronting not only the prevailing price vector and given internal constraints but also an external constraint which arises from supply or demand shortages in one or more markets. Specifically, we suppose that the individual's perception of his ability to complete transactions is some function of his past successes and failures. If a household, for example, failed to complete its spending plans because of market supply constraints, it will take this experience into account in formulating its current spending and saving plans. If a firm failed to obtain all the capital goods it required in order to carry out investment plans in the preceding frame, the experience will be reflected in its current plans.

Where the household perceives itself as constrained in any one of the markets in which it trades, its behavior in all markets will be affected. The relevant demand and supply functions governing its behavior under constraint incorporate the constraint(s). Suppose, for example, that in an underemployed economy excess supply in the labor market prevents households from selling all the labor services they would offer at prevailing prices. Since the actual quantity of labor services the household is able to sell falls short of the prior quantity, the household's income from labor services is no longer a choice variable to be maximized out in the process of utility maximization. It is a variable bound by exogenous constraints and thus enters explicitly into the utility-maximizing calculus. By implication the shortfall of realized labor income relative to prior income constrains the household's ability to trade in goods and asset markets, and the relevant goods and asset and leisure demand functions must reflect this constraint.

Where the firm perceives itself as unable to obtain all the input it desires or to sell all the output it planned to produce, such a constraint perceived in any one market alters its demand and supply in all markets.

These functions, inclusive of external constraints, are the firm's and household's *posterior demand* and *posterior supply*. They are posterior in the sense of containing further or additional information as an argument.[2]

While government is ignored in the present section, the analysis suggests an analogous distinction between government policies which are unconstrained or prior and those which are constrained or posterior.

[2]The concepts of prior and posterior demand and supply are closely related to Clower's "notional" and "effective" demand and supply, which have been further developed in two important papers by Barro and Grossman (1971) and Grossman (1971). The role of information and search costs in disequilibrium behavior has been treated in Barro (1972) and in Phelps et al.

The proposition that transactors may be unable to complete their planned sales or purchases at prevailing prices, raises the issue of the compatibility of perfect competition with disequilibrium.[3] We shall not develop a detailed argument, but the following observations appear appropriate. We assert that firms and households, who are perfect competitors and thus price-takers when equilibrium conditions prevail, acquire monopoly powers in disequilibrium. Disequilibrium creates the conditions under which every transactor possesses actual or potential monopoly power, but this is a transient state of affairs which tends to disappear as equilibrium is reestablished.[4] The slower the process of convergence toward equilibrium, the more extensive the opportunities afforded the individual household or firm for exploiting inherent price-making powers. Monopoly power flows partly from our assumption that trading at false prices does in fact take place.[5] Households and firms may be satisfied in factor, goods, and asset markets on a first-come, first-served basis with their positions in the queuing or rationing scheme determined by a random process. Alternative rationing schemes may be utilized, however, where sellers of scarce factors and commodities sell to regular customers, or to large customers, or where they require tie-in purchases. Where governmental rationing programs create black markets, the resulting need for secrecy and information control generates inherent monopoly powers.

In disequilibrium, uncertainty and lack of information about future prices place a premium on an individual's ability to evaluate the size of existing market imbalances, to predict the future movement of prices and to act on these considerations before his competitors act. Individual responses will vary with the degree of uncertainty, with the duration and past history of market imbalance, with the costs of search, information and transactions and with risk preferences. As equilibrium and a market-clearing price vector are reestablished, monopolistic elements in individual market positions tend to be dissipated.

If adjustment to a situation of excess demand takes time, the dimension of any one individual supplier's monopoly power is a function of the rate and effectiveness of his responses relative to the average response of all suppliers in the given market. If, for example, he can come up with additional quantities faster than they, he may temporarily charge monopoly prices for such quantities. His monopoly power flows from his having the only available

[3]Arrow has treated this problem. See also Barro (1972).

[4]This leaves open the possibility that a prolonged state of disequilibrium may permanently alter market structure, permitting one or more firms to emerge with monopoly powers which persist indefinitely.

[5]Compare this assumption with those associated with recontracting or tâtonnement processes.

supplies; one of the conditions which makes him a perfect competitor and thus a price-taker in equilibrium, namely, that alternative sources of supply are available at known prices, is held in temporary suspension during disequilibrium.

2.3. The Disequilibrium Frame: Prior Demand and Supply

Consider an open economy characterized by markets for goods, bonds and money.[6] Bonds are issued by firms in the process of capital formation and are held by households and passively by foreigners. Following Patinkin all variables are expressed in terms of quantities which accrue over a given frame and thus assume the dimension of stocks. This convenient disposition of the stock-flow dichotomy appears appropriate for the purposes at hand and does not affect the main thrust of the analysis.

In figure 1 the economy is presented in a typical disequilibrium frame.[7] Vector OZ in quadrant 1, located to the right of the 45°-line, OE_d, gives the excess of real prior absorption (A) over real prior capacity output (Q).[8] In accordance with the argument presented above, these are ex ante levels of capacity output and of absorption generated under the assumption that in making their decisions firms and households perceive themselves as capable of completing all plans. Prior absorption is the sum of prior consumption and prior investment demand; prior output capacity is determined by the level of capacity inherited from the preceding frame ($\bar{Q}_0$) plus whatever new capacity firms plan to bring on stream during the current frame as a consequence of ongoing prior capital formation and labor force growth.

In quadrant 2, function X_g is the prior export supply function which makes the level of prior exports an increasing function of prior capacity. For a given level of prior absorption, any increase in prior capacity either generates a

[6]For present purposes we need not consider explicitly the consequences of excess demand in the labor market. The implications of sustained disequilibrium in labor markets are examined in Arndt (1974a, 1974c). See also Barro and Grossman (1971). The main purpose of the analysis, which is to outline a framework for disequilibrium adjustment, is unaffected by the aggregative character of the goods market, although a number of interesting problems cannot be treated. For a discussion of disequilibrium in a multi-sector economy see Arndt (1974b).

[7]In the text, prior demand and prior supply and the prior imbalances associated with them are given without special markings, posterior functions and imbalances carry a tilde; and realized magnitudes, constraints and ex post imbalances carry a bar.

[8]We assume throughout that the quantity of output which firms currently plan to produce is always equal to the quantity the economy's capacity enables them to produce. For a discussion of the implications of shortfalls between capacity and actual output and the associated problem of "unemployment", see Arndt (1974a).

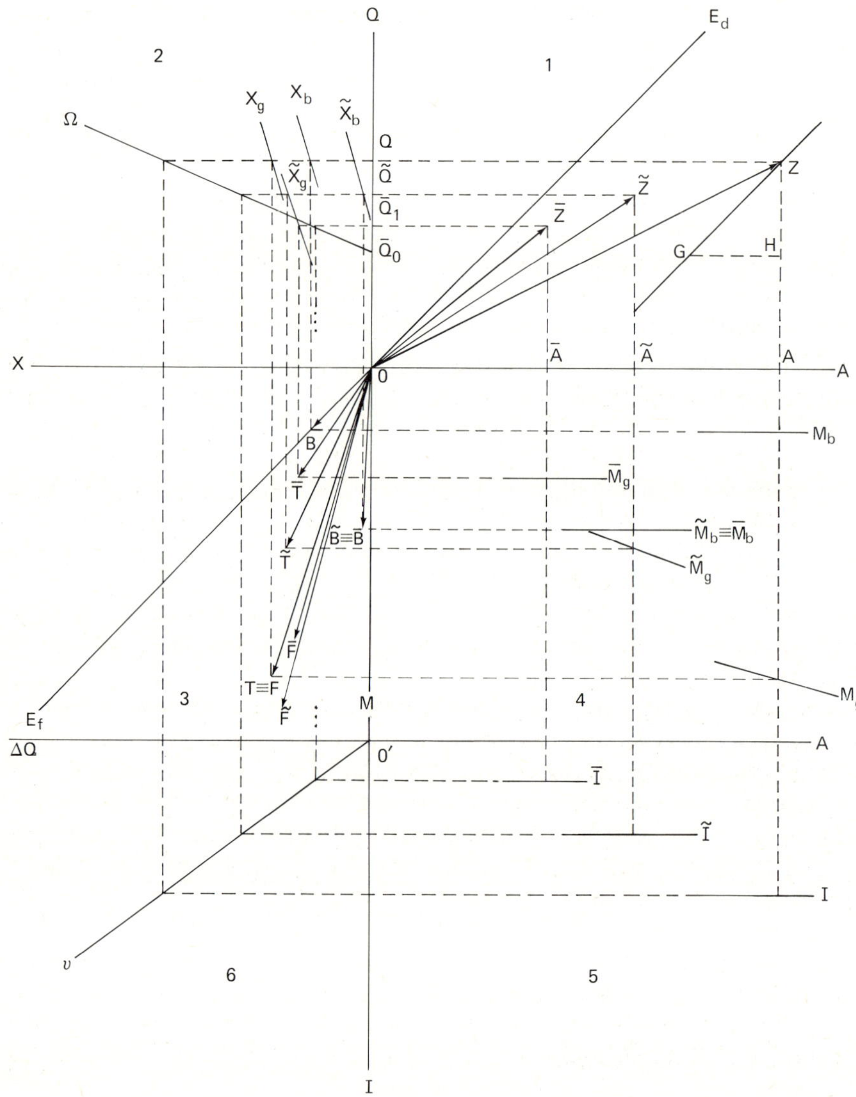

FIGURE 1

higher volume of prior exports or a reduced volume of prior imports or both. For a given level of prior capacity, a decrease in prior absorption with prior imports constant shifts the prior export supply function outward. In quadrant 4, the M_g-function is a prior import demand function which makes prior imports an increasing function of prior absorption. For a given level of prior output, an increase in prior absorption implies an increase in prior imports (and/or a reduction in prior exports as represented by a rightward shift in X_g). For a given level of prior absorption and of prior exports, an increase in prior output implies an upward shift in the prior import demand function.

Movements along and shifts of prior import demand and export supply functions are, therefore, interdependent and related to (rotation of) vector OZ. An increase in prior absorption with prior output constant implies a movement along M_g, an inward shift of X_g, or both. An increase in prior capacity with prior absorption constant implies a movement along X_g, an upward shift in M_g, or both.[9] As a rule, prior absorption and prior capacity will change simultaneously, so that variations in prior export supply and prior import demand reflect a series of complex interrelationships. The country's prior balance of trade, which is directly related to excess prior demand in the goods market, is given by vector OT in quadrant 3.

Current prior investment is represented by the I-function in quadrant 5. Investment has expenditure as well as capacity effects. An increase in prior investment demand which takes the form of a downward shift of the I-function is also reflected in changes in vector OZ. Vector OZ extends and rotates in accordance with the effect of new investment on prior capacity and with its effect on prior absorption.

The capacity effect of prior investment is traced in quadrants 6 and 2. The function v in quadrant 6 is an incremental investment/output ratio which relates the quantity of additional output to the level of ongoing investment. New output destined to come on stream during the current frame is added to existing output by means of translator function Ω. The intersection of the Ω-function with the Q-axis indicates the level of productive capacity inherited from the preceding frame. Even where capital formation is zero, however, the Ω-function shifts upward if the net effect on capacity of capital stock depreciation and labor force growth is positive. Investment expenditure is financed by bonds which are sold to domestic households or to foreigners.

Any prior disequilibrium in the market for bonds will be reflected in the prior balance on capital account. Functions X_b and M_b indicate prior bond export

[9]In general, the slope of X_g which gives the prior marginal propensity to export output will be less than unity. Analogously, the slope of M_g with respect to the A-axis will be less than unity, implying that even at constant levels of prior capacity only a fraction of new prior absorption will spill over into new prior imports, the remainder being accommodated by reductions in prior exports. This postulated response of exports to domestic demand and supply conditions represents an important departure from the usual assumption that exports are exogenously determined.

supply and import demand; the resulting prior balance of payments on capital account is given by vector OB in quadrant 3. It is for convenience assumed to be in exact balance. The prior bond import function is drawn independent of prior absorption, though certain types of absorption changes might have a direct effect on bond import demand, in which case the function might even be negatively sloped. The function will shift in response to changes in a variety of variables, including the relative price of bonds, rates of return on physical capital, expected rates of inflation and changes in the stock of real balances.

The X_b-function in quadrant 2 shows prior bond export supply as an increasing function of prior capacity and so reflects the fact that bonds are issued by firms in order to finance investment.

Bond import and exports functions are clearly interdependent. An increase in prior output, for example, which flows from ongoing prior capital formation implies that new bonds must be issued. Consequently prior bond exports must increase, prior bond imports must decrease or both.

A separate money market is not shown in the figure, but it is evident that a net excess prior demand for bonds and goods implies an equal excess prior supply of real balances. That excess supply is shown by vector OF, the overall prior balance of payments.

2.4. Posterior Demand and Supply

At the vector of prices governing decisions in the current frame prior absorption thus exceeds prior output and the prior trade balance is in deficit. Let us suppose that their experience during preceding frames leads individuals to perceive themselves as unable to obtain all the domestic goods and imports indicated by their prior functions. Individual perceptions of current market positions are some function of past experience and current information. An individual who failed to realize his plans in preceding frames is more likely to be pessimistic about his ability to realize current plans than is one who succeeded in the past. Past experience augmented by current information thus determines individuals' views of their current market positions.

Under conditions of uncertainty and incomplete information individuals hold such views with less than complete conviction. Consequently, perceptions are described by probability distributions and their parameters, where the parameters reflect each individual's experience over a sequence of recent frames with the influence of past history decaying according to some appropriate weighting scheme.

Suppose that in aggregate terms the constraint manifests itself as an expected shortage of domestic and imported goods. According to the previous discussion a constraint in one market necessitates reevaluation of demand and supply in all other markets. Unlike prior functions, the emerging posterior functions contain the constraint as an argument. Households and firms respond to shortages in the market for domestic goods by increasing their posterior demand for imported goods, for bonds and for money.[10] Similarly, perceived shortages in the market for imported goods must be reflected in all other market functions including those in the market for domestic goods.

Functions $\tilde{X}_g$, $\tilde{M}_g$, $\tilde{X}_b$, $\tilde{M}_b$ and $\tilde{I}$ represent the relevant posterior demand and supply schedules. Vectors $O\tilde{Z}$, $O\tilde{T}$, $O\tilde{B}$ and $O\tilde{F}$ indicate the associated posterior imbalances. Levels $\tilde{Q}$ and $\tilde{A}$ are the posterior output and absorption levels, respectively. Posterior functions have been drawn relative to their prior counterparts on the basis of plausible but not exclusive hypotheses concerning responses of the representative firm and household to perceived constraints.

Thus, the position of $\tilde{X}_g$ to the right of X_g reflects the hypothesis that a perceived shortage of domestic goods reduces the availability of exportables. Location of $\tilde{X}_b$ to the right of X_b and of $\tilde{M}_b$ below M_b reflects the argument that firms respond to the goods market constraint by reducing investment plans, which explains the location of $\tilde{I}$ above I, and the reduced size of $\tilde{Q}$ relative to Q.[11] Reduced investment plans require smaller bond issue which tends to reduce the supply of exportable bonds. In addition, household posterior demand for bonds has increased as a consequence of the goods shortage, creating pressures for $\tilde{M}_b$ to shift down relative to M_b and for $\tilde{X}_b$ to move further inward. Finally, location of $\tilde{M}_g$ above M_g reflects the interaction of constraints in the markets for domestic and imported goods. Overall posterior absorption is down relative to its prior counterpart and with cuts in exports bridging some of the excess demand, posterior import demand is also down.

In addition to direct responses by firms and households to goods shortages, indirect effects are likely to operate. Such effects may become particularly

[10]In a general model containing a labor market it can be shown that the constraint increases the demand for leisure, thus producing a reduction in labor supply as a consequence of excess demand for goods. See Arndt (1974a, 1974c) and Barro and Grossman (1971).

[11]Posterior investment may under plausible alternative assumptions rise rather than decline relative to prior investment. If firms were unable in past frames to make desired additions to capacity, they may attempt in the current frame to make up for that failure by adding the unfulfilled portion of past investment plans to normal investment plans for the current frame. In that event $\tilde{I}$ lies below I.

In a multiple-country framework multi-national corporations respond to constraints by cutting posterior investment plans in one country while increasing plans in others. Such responses also play a role when labor market constraints differ among countries. See Arndt (1974c).

important if shortages are widespread and persist over many frames, so that price and profit expectations are altered. These indirect consequences, however, will change *both* prior and posterior demand and supply.

Posterior absorption ($\tilde{A}$) is shown as smaller than its prior counterpart. This is consistent with a smaller $\tilde{I}$ relative to I, with assumed smaller consumption[12] (not shown separately in figure 1), and with imperfect substitutability of imports for domestic goods. Posterior output ($\tilde{Q}$) is below its prior counterpart due to the gap between posterior and prior investment demand.[13] Posterior excess demand is indicated by vector $O\tilde{Z}$.

The posterior trade balance deficit is the external counterpart of excess demand in the goods market. The deficit, given by vector $O\tilde{T}$, is smaller than the prior trade deficit, though the gap could go the other way under appropriate assumptions about the reactions of households and firms. The posterior capital account ($\tilde{B}$) is in deficit as a result of smaller posterior bond exports and larger posterior bond import demand. The capital imbalance reflects the emergence of posterior excess demand in the bond market occasioned by supply shortages in the markets for domestic and imported goods.

The overall posterior balance of payments has deteriorated (vector $O\tilde{F}$). The worsening is consistent with a greater posterior demand for cash balances.

2.5. Ex Post Magnitudes

Inasmuch as prior and posterior functions are ex ante concepts, the question finally turns to actual quantities traded during the current decision frame. While planned and realized magnitudes are identical in equilibrium, they must by definition diverge in at least some markets for an economy in disequilibrium. Suppose that the ex post shortage of domestic and imported goods during the current frame is indicated by functions $\bar{M}_g$ and $\bar{I}$ and by vector $O\bar{Z}$.[14] Realized goods imports, that is, the quantity of imports available at import price levels

[12]The relationship between current posterior consumption and experiences of past supply shortages is not necessarily unambiguous. Persistent shortages may create expectations of further shortages (as distinct from expectations of higher future prices which affect *both* prior and posterior functions), in which case current posterior consumption demand will rise as households attempt to hoard goods.

[13]This leaves aside the possibility that substitution of imported capital goods for unavailable domestic goods diminishes the productivity of investment. Such an outcome would be reflected in counter-clockwise rotation of the v-ratio. See Arndt (1974c).

[14]The ex post shortage of goods may, but need not, be identical to the perceived or predicted shortage which entered into posterior demand and supply functions. The current frame's ex post magnitudes become part of the succeeding frame's decision process.

governing decisions for the current frame, are thus limited to level $\bar{M}_g$, which is smaller than M_g and $\tilde{M}_g$.[15]

Realized investment is down (at $\bar{I}$), reflecting the discrepancy between posterior demand for goods and realized supply; the precise burden of the shortage falling on investment is a function of firms' positions in the prevailing rationing scheme. The smaller level of actual investment during the frame necessarily generates a smaller level of realized overall capacity ($\bar{Q}_1$).

Divergencies between planned and realized magnitudes imply that in addition to prior and posterior balances of payments there exists an ex post measure of the balance of payments and of its components. It follows from $\bar{M}_g$ and $O\bar{Z}$ that the ex post trade balance deficit ($O\bar{T}$) is smaller than the posterior and prior deficits. On the assumption that households can obtain all the bond imports they demand without pushing up world bond prices, the ex post capital account deficit ($O\bar{B}$) coincides with its posterior counterpart ($O\tilde{B}$), so that the overall ex post payments deficit is given by vector $O\bar{F}$.

2.6. *Fixed versus Flexible Exchange Rates*

Interpretation of the current import shortage depends on whether the world is on a fixed or flexible exchange standard. This may be briefly illustrated with the aid of two examples.[16]

The first example assumes that figure 1 describes the case of a fixed exchange rate regime. $\bar{M}_g$ is then the maximum quantity of imports to be had without raising world import prices provided, of course, that the monetary authority's holdings of foreign exchange are sufficient to finance the implied payments deficit. The loss of official reserves during the current frame is therefore determined by the size of the ex post payments imbalance ($O\bar{F}$).

The second example stipulates a flexible exchange rate and the associated condition that overall ex post payments must be in balance at the governing exchange rate.[17] The implication is that if the posterior trade balance deficit is to be realized, the ex post capital account must show an imbalance equal in magnitude but opposite in sign. Under flexible exchange rates the problem is one of allocating a given quantity of foreign exchange between goods and bond

[15]The import constraint is thus interpreted as the supply available at the governing price of imports, not as an absolute limit regardless of price. As we shall see, the excess of $\tilde{M}_g$ over $\bar{M}_g$ tends to drive up import prices which govern decisions in the next frame; the price increase tends to produce an upward shift in M_g and $\tilde{M}_g$ and a downward shift in $\bar{M}_g$.

[16]For a more complete analysis in the context of a multi-country framework, see Arndt (1974c).

[17]This excludes the possibility of trading on credit.

importers. Hence the nature and bias of the existing foreign exchange rationing scheme have important implications for the ability of households and firms to realize their respective posterior plans.

To take an extreme case, suppose that bond importers are able under the existing allocation scheme to fully realize their posterior import demand so that realized and posterior capital account deficits are identical as they were in the previous example of fixed rates. It follows that the ex post trade balance must show a surplus of equal magnitude to assure ex post balance in overall payments. This implies a goods import constraint far more severe than that indicated by $\bar{M}_g$ and thus lower levels of ex post absorption, investment and output.

This is an extreme bias in foreign exchange allocation; some bond import demand as well as some goods import demand is likely to remain unrealized. It nevertheless dramatizes the potential effect on ex post capital formation and output growth of foreign exchange rationing. The future path of prices and of output growth are critically affected by the process of disequilibrium exchange allocation. By influencing this process government policy-makers can shape the pattern of the economy's adjustment and the extent to which it encompasses cyclical changes in output as opposed to cyclical variation in price levels.

2.7. Three Concepts of the Balance of Payments

The preceding analysis has produced three measures of the balance of payments. Two of these are ex ante measures, one is ex post.[18] It is a trichotomy intimately associated with disequilibrium and one which is suspended for economies in equilibrium.

This trichotomy is of some interest, for it raises a question concerning which of the three concepts is to guide policy-makers in their stabilization decisions. Governments typically have direct information only on ex post imbalances, though it is often possible to estimate the underlying ex ante disequilibrium. But what if the ex ante imbalance is a posterior imbalance different from its prior counterpart? Will not policies designed to eliminate posterior excess demand adjust the system by too little or too much? Or in the wrong direction?

The trichotomy sheds light on the debate over the effectiveness of price changes in trade and payments adjustment. Suppose that trade is the only foreign activity of a country and that a trade deficit in the current frame increases import prices directly under a fixed rate and indirectly through

[18]For discussion of another trichotomy, see Machlup (1964).

exchange rate variations under a flexible regime. In response to rising prices, and assuming other things unchanged, function $\tilde{M}_g$ will tend to shift up and $\bar{M}_g$ down. For as long, however, as posterior import demand exceeds the constrained supply forthcoming, that is, so long as $\tilde{M}_g$ lies below $\bar{M}_g$, the level of imports increases as a consequence of import price increases. In supply-constrained disequilibrium the observed level of imports is a constrained quantity implying a reservoir of unrealized demand; only when price increases have removed that excess demand, will further price increases begin to reduce the observed level of imports.

Analogous considerations apply to divergences between posterior and realized exports; and the analysis is readily extended to other subaccounts of the balance of payments.[19]

3. Disequilibrium Adjustment

In the preceding section the role of market constraints in the formulation of posterior demand and supply functions was examined. In this section we discuss the effect of posterior excess demands on prices, interest rates and exchange rates. Transition from one decision frame to the next involves establishment of a new vector of prices, interest rates and exchange rates and a new round of decisions about consumption, saving, investment and production. Price adjustment in the goods market is discussed in some detail, and brief sketches of adjustment of interest rates and exchange rates are presented.

3.1. Price Variation in Disequilibrium

The proposed model of price adjustment rests on the hypothesis that representative individuals are price-makers in disequilibrium. In a situation of excess demand this means in particular that suppliers of goods, and, by extension, of labor services hold monopoly powers which affect their behavior. In disequilibrium "established" prices do not exist and price-makers have no knowledge of

[19]This offers a possible explanation for the insensitivity or perverse response of imports and exports to price changes which have been reported in many econometric studies, including those by Adams, Eguchi and Meyer-zu-Schlochtern (1969) and by Arndt (1970). What is being fitted in such instances is neither a conventional demand or supply function nor a conventional demand–supply intersection, but rather a supply-constrained market situation characterized by trading at false prices.

market-clearing prices; the view is one of a system groping its way toward such prices.

Consider the typical firm in an excess demand situation. At the start of the frame it perceived its marginal cost to be given by MC in figure 2. That function is drawn on the assumption that the firm perceived itself as unconstrained in factor, capital goods and materials markets; the curve is a prior marginal cost curve. The marginal revenue (MR) and demand (D) curves are likewise prior functions in that they exclude consideration of constraints in the firm's own or any other markets. For the current frame the firm's prior price–output combination is (p, q).

Suppose that past excess demand in its own and/or in other markets leads the firm to conclude that it could at price p have sold a larger quantity of its product, say, $\overline{pR}$ ($= \overline{Oq'}$). The firm may consider this disparity as spurious and ignore it; or it may conclude that the actual demand curve for its product lies to the right of D and that R is a point on it. In order to be able to reevaluate its price–output combination, the firm must estimate at least the relevant range of the new demand curve of which it thus far "knows" but a single point. Suppose

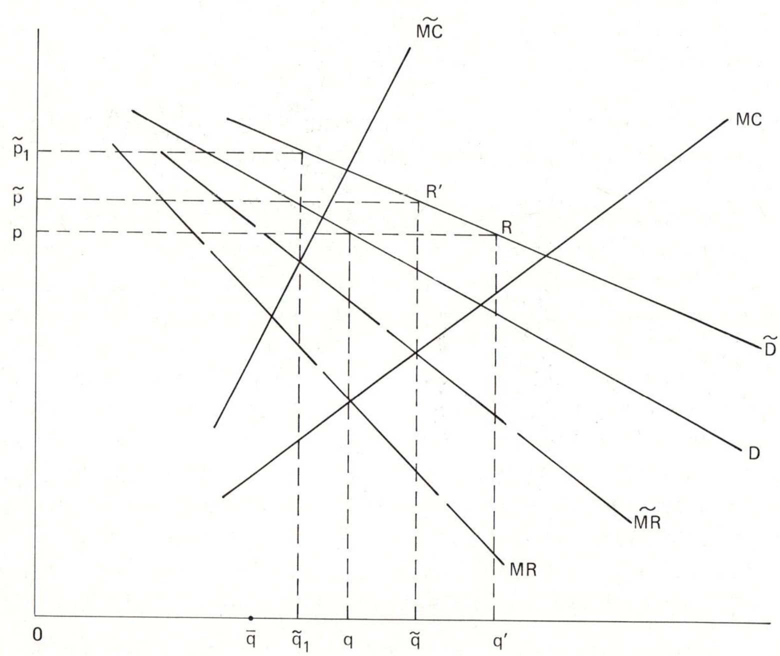

FIGURE 2

that $\tilde{D}$ and $\tilde{MR}$ are the firm's estimates of the new functions, so that $(\tilde{p}, \tilde{q})$ is its posterior price–output combination. It will be this posterior set of functions which will guide the firm's behavior during the current frame.

The representative firm thus enters each disequilibrium frame with two sets of demand and marginal revenue functions. The set of prior functions represents price–quantity combinations which are consistent with general equilibrium.[20] Where the firm is a perfect competitor in equilibrium, prior marginal revenue and demand curves are horizontal and coincident at p. The posterior set of curves, on the other hand, takes into consideration experiences of excess demand. For the "competitive" firm whose prior functions are horizontal in equilibrium, the posterior functions will slope downward to reflect the monopoly powers inherent in market disequilibrium.

In making its price–output decisions, the firm has up to now considered itself unconstrained in its factor markets so that the prior marginal cost curve (MC) was the relevant cost schedule. When excess demand in one or more of its input markets has in the previous frame or frames prevented the firm from procuring desired inputs, its current decisions will reflect such past constraints. The new schedule, of which $\tilde{MC}$ is an example, will be located above the prior MC curve and may be substantially different in character; indeed, we cannot rule out the possibility that it may be kinked or possessed of other forms of discontinuity.

The relevant posterior price–output combination is now given by $(\tilde{p}_1, \tilde{q}_1)$, with output smaller and price higher than before introduction of the input constraint.

Inasmuch as these are ex ante decisions, the firm will in due course discover whether and to what degree its posterior plans are to be realized. If it predicted its own market situation correctly, realized magnitudes will equal posterior plans. If, on the other hand, the firm underestimated the extent of excess demand in output markets, it will find once more that it could have sold more at price $\tilde{p}_1$. If, alternatively, it overestimated its capabilities in procuring inputs so that the realized quantity of inputs falls short of desired levels, a smaller amount of output, such as $\bar{q}$, may be the firm's maximum currently realizable output. This quantity is the microeconomic counterpart of the macroeconomic $\bar{Q}$ of preceding sections, while $\tilde{q}_1$ and q correspond to $\tilde{Q}$ and Q, respectively.

In disequilibrium buyers and sellers grope for market-clearing prices. Unlike the "established" prices of equilibrium, the situation is characterized by a distribution of prices in each market and by general search activities on the part

[20]In the microeconomic context unrealized demand in the market for one good does not imply increased posterior demand in the markets for all other goods. In markets of complementary goods, the constraint has the effect of shifting demand down relative to its prior counterpart.

of transactors. Thus, analysis over a number of frames of such price distributions and their parameters emerges as a possible approach to the study of the equilibrating mechanism and of the vitality of the system's self-correcting capabilities.

Firms continue to adjust their contemporary price–output combinations in response to continuing imbalances. While our attention has focused on the behavior of prices and quantities in spot markets, inconsistent spot and futures prices are likely to prevail in many markets in disequilibrium, thus providing broad opportunities for arbitrage. The preceding discussion, moreover, sidesteps the issue of inventories and buffer stocks and their role in the system's response to disturbances. In practice, firms bridge the gap between current output and current demand by running down inventories. When buffer stocks are large, especially in the early phases of an excess demand situation, upward adjustment of prices probably plays a much less prominent role than during the later stages of persistent excess demand situations when buffer stocks are likely to have been exhausted. The relative importance in the adjustment process of price and quantity variations should thus be expected to change over the cycle and to depend on the size of the disturbance (as measured by the location of vectors OZ and $O\tilde{Z}$ relative to E_fOE_d) and by its duration. Variability in the system's automatic responses to given shocks implies that policy measures need to be manipulated to reflect non-uniformity of responses. It follows that the probable importance of output-expanding relative to demand-controlling policies is correlated with the size of buffer stocks.

3.2. *Disequilibrium Variation in Interest and Exchange Rates*

The disequilibrium behavior of price–quantity combinations in bond markets, and in asset markets in general, may be supposed to be determined by analogous decision processes. Over a series of frames, bond prices rise in proportion to unsatisfied posterior demand. Since firms are the sole issuers of bonds in this model, they will price bonds in response to perceived demand; their price–quantity decisions will be influenced by the presence of monopoly elements in their market positions. The disequilibrium situation is characterized by distributions of prices in bond markets; the shape and time path of adjustment may be studied from the perspective of the evolution of those distributions over a succession of frames.

Where the exchange rate is flexible we may imagine that exchange rates are fixed by traders in proportion to unsatisfied posterior demand. Apart from the process of exchange-rate adjustment itself, we are interested in the speed of adjustment relative to speeds in other markets. It is to be expected that adjustment speeds will be higher in this market, implying that the time path of exchange-rate adjustment will affect time paths elsewhere through its impact on the domestic currency values of goods and bond imports.

4. Concluding Remarks

Unlike conventional models of the cyclical behavior of open economies, the proposed framework incorporates a capacity effect. This transforms policy-making from its one-dimensional concern with demand management into one involving both supply and demand management.[21] In economies suffering from excess aggregate demand, what happens to output is important in determining the time path along which general equilibrium is reestablished.

The pure expenditure and the output–expenditure approaches may be compared with the aid of figure 1. When the effect of investment on current capacity is ignored, the output–absorption combination for the frame in question would be indicated by a vector terminating at *H* rather than *Z*. At *H* the expenditure effect of prior investment (*I* in quadrant 5) is accounted for in aggregate absorption, but the capacity effect is ignored so that output remains unchanged from its initial level (on the assumption of a zero rate of depreciation and labor growth). Consequently, goods market excess prior demand is overstated by the proportion *GH* and the corresponding magnitudes of trade and payments imbalances are equally upward-biased.

These biases carry over into analysis of *changes* in economic activity because autonomous and policy-induced variations in investment are permitted to alter aggregate expenditure but not aggregate output. Moreover, exclusion of capacity effects permits analyst and policy-maker alike to be indifferent as to the effects of expenditure-reducing and expenditure-switching policies on the *composition* of aggregate demand between investment and consumption. Unlike the proposed output–expenditure model, conventional pure expenditure approaches are concerned with the composition of aggregate demand only to the extent that components are not equally sensitive to policy instruments, as when investment and consumption exhibit different sensitivities to variations in interest rates.

When the capacity effect is taken into account, an aggregate deflationary policy which aims at reducing investment generates a different time path of

[21]For discussion of various aspects of policy mixes involving supply management, see Arndt (1972, 1973).

adjustment than one which is keyed on consumption, because the two policies have different effects on the creation of productive capacity. The output–expenditure approach acknowledges the importance of a policy's impact on the composition of aggregate activity as well as on its level. Consequently, broad fiscal and monetary policies may in fact be too broad and aggregative. Even a policy which leaves the level of total expenditure unchanged, affects the system's time path of adjustment to the extent that it alters the composition of private expenditure between investment and consumption and of public expenditure between capacity-generating and capacity-using outlays.[22]

In addition, the proposed model develops a distinction between prior and posterior demand and supply schedules and in turn differentiates these from realized transactions. We have seen how this trichotomy affects the analysis of international trade and payments, but it also illuminates the disequilibrium behavior of broad activity categories like investment.

Consider the likely response of investment to a policy-induced increase in interest rates. Assuming that investment demand is inversely related to the market rate of interest, an increase in that rate shifts the prior and posterior investment schedules up. This movement, however, will have no effect on the observed magnitude of realized investment so long as market constraints place $\bar{I}$ (which is shifted itself) above its ex ante counterparts. Interest-rate policy will appear to have been ineffective in curbing the level of investment expenditure. After posterior investment has shifted to a position inside the constraint, however, investment will appear to be relatively sensitive to variations in interest rates.

Analogous remarks apply to household consumption and saving. In disequilibrium, goods market constraints impose upon households' actual levels of saving in excess of desired magnitudes. Under these circumstances, policy-induced increases in interest rates will have little effect on observed household saving until the posterior saving schedule comes to dominate the constraint, that is, until shifts in the posterior function and the constraint have brought ex ante saving inside the constraint. While price variations affect plans and thus alter the size of excess demand, their initial impact on the observed magnitudes of disequilibrium trading may not only be small or absent, but may run in "perverse" directions.

This argument is readily extended to bond and other asset markets. An increase in one country's interest rates relative to foreign rates will under broad categories of market constraints fail to improve the *observed* capital account

[22]Such a policy may combine consumption taxes (which could be scheduled for rebate at another point in the cycle) and investment credits.

even where ex ante demand and supply schedules of international capital are sensitive to variations in interest-rate differentials.[23]

References

Adams, F. G., H. Eguchi and F. Meyer-zu-Schlochtern, 1969, An econometric analysis of international trade (OECD, Paris).

Arndt, S.W., 1970, Income and price adjustment and France's basic balance of payments, 1961–66, Rivista Internazionale di Scienze Economiche e Commerciali, May. [See also: Prix et revenus dans l'ajustement de la balance des paiements en France de 1961 à 1966, Revue d'Economie Politique, Jan./Feb.

Arndt, S. W., 1972, Macroeconomic policy planning in an open economy, in: E. Claassen and P. Salin, eds., Stabilization policies in interdependent economies (North-Holland, Amsterdam).

Arndt, S. W., 1973, The role of world trade policy: The view from the advanced countries, in: R. Thorp and V. Urquidi, eds., Latin America in the international economy (Macmillan, London).

Arndt, S. W., 1974a, A disequilibrium model of income, employment and the balance of payments, unpublished manuscript.

Arndt, S. W., 1974b, Disequilibrium in an open economy with two sectors, unpublished manuscript.

Arndt, S. W., 1974c, An international economic system in general disequilibrium, unpublished manuscript.

Arrow, K. J., 1959, Toward a theory of price adjustment, in: M. Abramowitz, ed., The allocation of economic resources (Stanford University Press, Stanford, Calif.).

Barro, R. J., 1972, A theory of monopolistic price adjustment, Review of Economic Studies XXXIX, Jan.

Barro, R. J. and H. I. Grossman, 1971, A general disequilibrium model of income and employment, American Economic Review LXI, March.

Clower, R. W., 1965, The Keynesian counter-revolution: A theoretical appraisal, in: F. H. Hahn and F. Brechling, eds., The theory of interest rates (Macmillan, London).

Grossman, H. I., 1971, Money, interest and prices in market disequilibrium, Journal of Political Economy 79, Sept./Oct.

Machlup, F., 1964, International payments, debts, and gold (Scribner's, New York) ch. 3.

Patinkin, D., 1965, Money, interest and prices, 2nd ed. (Harper and Row, New York).

Phelps, E. S. et al., 1970, Microeconomic foundations of employment and inflation theory (Norton, New York).

[23]The effect of changes in interest-rate differentials on international capital flows in disequilibrium is examined in Arndt (1974c).

Chapter 13.2

COMMENT ON ARNDT

J. C. PATTISON

This is a useful paper insofar as its theoretical core concerns two current and important problems in economics. The first is the role of supply factors in economic stabilization; the second is the microeconomics of employment and income theory. It is probably true that the accepted economic theory, as passed on in text-books and government policy-making, is concerned with the insufficiency of aggregate demand which denigrates supply aspects and renders unnecessary a proper consideration of price and wage determination.

In many respects, it is not surprising that Keynesian economics have been associated with the insufficiency of aggregate demand insofar as "The General Theory" was written during a period of vast unemployment and an overvalued exchange rate. On the other hand, Keynes was intelligent enough to cast his theoretical structure in a more flexible framework that would take financial and expectational variables explicitly into account. In a sense, this is where recent disequilibrium models enter the scene. The Arndt paper follows on the work of Barro and Grossman (1971, p. 82), who have noted that "the natural focus of Keynesian analysis is on the implications for behaviour in one market of the existence of . . . a divergence (between actual quantities transacted and quantities demanded or supplied) in another market". The usefulness of such disequilibrium models is obviously great in times of inflation as text-book Keynesian models assume market equilibrium which abstracts from reality and present economic problems. In addition, it is probably fair to say that until the 1960's the text-book model did not contain the price level, or alternatively the workings of the model were discussed with a fixed price level. Inflation is clearly a disequilibrium phenomenon and creates distortions in labour and commodity markets when unanticipated. The treatment of supply constraints is obviously a useful addition to such a model as our current inflation has been partly fuelled by supply bottlenecks.

The model itself provides a useful analytical framework to consider the implications of a constraint in any one market on demand and supply in those remaining. This seems to me to characterize the macroeconomic problems one actually runs into, yet equilibrium models do not allow an easy interpretation of such problems. On the other hand, the analytical framework does not readily lend itself to qualitative solutions. By treating the effects of constraints in various markets on remaining markets, virtually any economic situation can arise. Arndt applies the theoretical model to certain questions such as flexible versus fixed rates, foreign exchange control schemes, etc., yet in reality we need a good deal of information about the structure of the equations of the model in order to reach concrete results in such a framework. In an econometric format the implementation of the model would seem to pose substantial problems, for example in determining the posterior demand and supply functions. The author notes that "we suppose that the individual's perception of his ability to complete transactions is some function of his past success or failure to do so". This would accord with distributed lag formulations of the equations since, under certain assumptions, optimal forecasts can be generated in this way.[1] Yet this would itself lead to many econometric difficulties. These, however, are not Arndt's problems as the paper is meant to be theoretical.

I profess to having two minds about the microeconomic framework of the paper. I personally find that the general sketch given by Arndt rubs my intuition the right way, but not my prejudices. Yet this field of market behaviour with imperfect information is a relatively new one, where no firm results have been established. I think Arndt and his microeconomic precursors are correct in stating that one important aspect of behaviour out of equilibrium is that price-takers in equilibrium states become monopolists out of equilibrium insofar as knowledge about alternative supplies, their quantity and price is monopolized or at least only found after a costly search. The so-called new microeconomics that suggests that firms and labour continue to raise prices because of uniformly-held expectations about future prices, does not seem realistic in an atomistic economy with the usual competitive axioms.

Fortunately for those interested in these questions, Michael Rothschild (1973) has just written a survey of developments in models of markets with imperfect information. He noted in his conclusions that (1973, p. 1303):

> "...it is almost too easy. The number and variety of different models make it hard to draw any firm conclusions about the consequences of different types of market failure... Results are likely to come from... systematic taxonomy and analysis of restraints imposed by equilibrium."

These models are essentially microeconomic and the relevance for macro systems in disequilibrium is not immediately obvious. I would suspect that the

[1]See, for example, Muth (1960).

relevance of individual theories would differ by market. For example, in bond markets information is readily accessible to all of a large number of market participants at relatively low costs, whereas in labour markets not only is information less easy to obtain but price-setting is not determined in a competitive manner but probably in a model that would correspond more closely to bilateral monopoly. We do not know much about this area of economic behaviour and my main point is that the reader should be aware that the micro foundations of such macro models are tenuous.

The strength of the Arndt paper lies in the recognition of an obvious but unexploited economic truth: that market participants often meet constraints. Unfortunately for economists, reactions to such constraints in an uncertain world can take place in a variety of ways, either optimal or sub-optimal. There are other attempts to link market imperfections to macro models and papers such as Arndt's, Barro and Grossman (1971), Eichner's (1973), as well as those of micro theorists will hopefully lead to some convergence of ideas.

One of the main uses of these theories will be in formulating policy. Yet we have a wide variety of competing theories ranging from excessive market power to U.S. balance-of-payments deficits, government fiscal policies and excessive world money creation. These phenomena would all seem to be disequilibria that could be incorporated into an Arndt-type model. The viability of policy prescriptions will depend upon the underlying micro behaviour which is poorly understood.

References

Barro, R. J. and H. I. Grossman, 1971, A general disequilibrium model of income and employment, American Economic Review LXI, pp. 82–93.

Eichner, A., 1973, A theory of the determination of mark-up under oligopoly, Economic Journal 83, pp. 1184–1200.

Muth, J., 1960, Optimal properties of exponentially weighted forecasts, Journal of the American Statistical Association 55, pp. 299–306.

Rothschild, M., 1973, Models of markets with imperfect information: A survey, Journal of Political Economy 81, pp. 1283–1308.

Chapter 13.3

SUMMARY OF THE DISCUSSION ON ARNDT

Anthony B. ATKINSON, *Chairman*

Serge-Christophe Kolm underlined that monetarist models assume implicitly classical general equilibrium theory à la Walras and neglect more recent developments (with very few exceptions, among which Sven Arndt's paper). Mathematical economists, among which several Frenchmen, have shown that there can be no equilibrium at all, or a multiplicity of equilibria. If, for instance, there is an accumulation point and if we get a disturbance from a present equilibrium, all chances are that we are going to another equilibrium. For instance, in that case, the quantity theory would be wrong if one takes it as meaning that, after a change in the quantity of money, the prices will adjust proportionately.

According to *Helmut Frisch* there is an important distinction in Sven Arndt's paper between notional variables and actual variables. For instance, in a Walrasian system, the tâtonnement process implies that there is no trade until price equilibrium is reached. However, we do know that trade takes place in disequilibrium. The equilibrium theory is very important from an intellectual point of view, but theory must move towards a clearer distinction between what is notional and what is actual.

Marcus Miller indicated that the U.K. Treasury model for national income forecasting includes the possibility of a disequilibrium between supply and demand curves; if, for instance, given export elasticity, total demand exceeds total supply, there is a constrained solution where the demand curve is not satisfied.

PART V

Floating Exchange Rates

Chapter 14.1

SUMMARY OF THE DISCUSSION ON FLOATING EXCHANGE RATES

Jacques RUEFF, *Chairman*

A panel discussion on "floating exchange rates", under the chairmanship of Mr. J. Rueff, Chancelier de l'Institut de France, took place on March 28, 1974, at the Eiffel Tower restaurant in Paris, on the occasion of an international conference at the University Paris–Dauphine. The debaters were Professors Milton Friedman (University of Chicago), Robert Mundell (University of Waterloo), Fritz Machlup (Princeton University and University of New York), Assar Lindbeck (University of Stockholm), and Harry G. Johnson (University of Chicago and London School of Economics and Political Science).

Due to a technical failure, the discussion has not been recorded; however, Professors Machlup, Lindbeck and Johnson have written papers giving the main lines of their statements. We are pleased to be able to publish them, and we want to thank them.

Milton Friedman gave a vigorous plea in favor of floating exchange rates, which are the only ones to be able to allow really independent economic policies. In fact, most countries desire an economic autonomy, which is in contradiction with the growing internationalization of the world economy.

A very stimulating debate took place in this respect between Milton Friedman and Jacques Rueff. Each of them favors different solutions for the international monetary system, but would share part of the underlying analysis. Both are sceptical about the capacities of authorities to succeed on a fine tuning of economic policies. But, from this, Jacques Rueff concludes that it is necessary to constrain the authorities with such a system as the gold standard in order that their monetary policies become consistent, while Milton Friedman concludes that the desire of the authorities to run independent policies must be taken as a fact of life so that it is necessary to compensate for possible divergencies between monetary policies via floating exchange rates.

Thus, Milton Friedman views floating exchange rates not as the best possible solution in an ideal world, but as a second-best solution, allowing for the freedom of exchange for goods and capital, particularly in a world of high and variable rates of inflation. A system of floating exchange rates "makes adjustments easier and makes possible to adapt to crises situations". Milton

Friedman declared that he preferred imperfect floating exchange rates than fixed but irrealistic exchange rates. On an other hand, the large fluctuations in the price of gold contributed to demonetize gold. The decision – which, at that time, could only be considered as likely – by the American administration to authorize American citizens to buy gold can only contribute to the demonetization of gold.

Robert Mundell was the only one – apart from Jacques Rueff – to favor a system of fixed rates. In his opinion, floating exchange rates are responsible for the international transmission of inflation, more than fixed rates were. In fact, floating exchange rates would favor unwise economic policies and would not be able to isolate national economies from external inflationary influences.

Jacques Rueff concluded by wishing a revaluation of the price of gold and a "vigorous effort towards more orderly public finance and credit conditions".

Chapter 14.2

RECENT EXPERIENCES WITH FLOATING CURRENCIES

Fritz MACHLUP

When a professor of economics is asked "How is your wife?" he answers with a counterquestion "Compared with what?" He knows too well that it makes little sense to judge a state of affairs without a standard of comparison. The question "How well or how badly has the system of floating currencies worked" cannot be answered before one makes clear with what alternative system or practice it is to be compared.

Once we comprehend this, we can immediately understand why the Governors of the International Monetary Fund at the Annual Meeting in Nairobi (September 1973) gave so conspicuously contradictory reports about the "experience" with floating currencies. Not that they had observed a different world or had differently interpreted the same observations. They merely compared the results of floating with different hypothetical courses of events and failed to state what alternatives they had in mind. Most of them compared the results of floating with those of hypothetical fixed parities and stable exchange rates and did not realize that this was not a real alternative. The system in which monetary authorities could maintain fixed rates had become impossible; it was not voluntarily given up by acts of free choice, say, on the basis of some ministers' convictions or in execution of the recommendations of wise economic advisors. Fixed exchange rates could no longer be maintained, because it was patently too costly to maintain them and any re-fixing at new levels would not work either. Most ministers and governors loved the system of rigid rates, but this love was not requited, the rates refused to be rigidly fixed and the system deserted its faithful admirers. These jilted admirers were disconsolate and continued to tell the public how beautiful the beloved system was and how nice it would be to have it back.

To answer the question "How has the system of floating currencies worked" we would have to compare it with genuine alternatives. For example, we could compare the system of managed floating with a hypothetical system of clean floating or with a hypothetical system of parities adjusted every few weeks – or with anything that might conceivably work.

Some people believe that we have given the system of clean floating a fair chance to prove its workability and that we went over to managed floating only after we saw that the free foreign-exchange market had led to excessive fluctuations of exchange rates. I could quote some Governors of the Fund making such statements about the bad experiences with "the free floating system". Let us examine whether we had "free" floating in the period in question, that is, from March to July 1973. Free or clean floating means the absence both of official interventions (sales and purchases) in the foreign-exchange market and of governmental interferences (prohibitions, restrictions, direct controls) with private foreign-exchange transactions and foreign payments. It is well known that many countries maintained or even reinforced such interferences, but it is not so well known that several monetary authorities are rather active as purchasers and sellers of foreign exchange in the second quarter of 1973.

Let us first look at the total official holdings of foreign exchange by the countries listed in the statistical tables of the IMF. The size of their total foreign-exchange reserves increased from the end of March to the end of June 1973 by 4 billion dollars, but the liquid liabilities of the United States decreased by 630 million dollars. The difference between the foreign-exchange reserves of the world and the liquid liabilities of the United States and the United Kingdom increased by 4 billion dollars. One may conclude that the whole increase must have been either in Eurodollars or in non-dollar currencies. Now, it is public knowledge – see, for example, the Annual Report of the German Bundesbank – that several central banks were busy diversifying their exchange reserves by exchanging dollars and dollar assets against other currencies. These official sales of dollars may not be regarded as "typical" interventions in the exchange market, because they were not motivated by attempts to influence the external values of the currencies issued by the countries in question. Nevertheless these official sales undoubtedly must have depressed the market value of the dollar, no less than any offers of dollars by private speculators. The exchange reserves of "Industrial Europe" as a whole and of the individual ten countries in this group changed only a little during the three months. During the same time, however, Japan reduced its exchange reserves by 3 billion dollars and in subsequent months went on reducing them by another 4 billion dollars.

That the total amount of dollar holdings of the monetary authorities did not reflect the sales of dollars by Japan and by the countries selling dollars against other currencies does not indicate that this selling spree did not affect the price of the dollar. The central banks that absorbed the dollars which other central banks offered for sale had stopped paying fixed prices for the dollar and took them in at constantly declining prices. What is strange about the period in question is that so many officials described the events as the dirty work of speculators. They complained about the "speculative attack" against the dollar under a system of "freely floating currencies". It should now be clear that the currencies were not "freely floating" and that only by including several monetary authorities among the "speculators" could we reasonably attribute the fall of the dollar in the spring and early summer of 1973 to destabilizing speculation.

Contributing to the weakness of the dollar in the period in question may have been another factor, to which a report by the economists of the Morgan Guaranty Trust Company called our attention: the "jointness" of some European currencies within the "floating snake" tended to exaggerate the decline of the dollar rate. The major force in the exchange markets of the time was the heavy demand for D-Mark by private as well as official money managers. This demand might drive up the rate of the DM by a certain percentage, if the DM were floating all by itself; if, however, the DM is bundled up tightly with several other currencies within a slender snake, so that it cannot appreciate in terms of the other inmates, the currencies outside the snake, especially the dollar, have to depreciate by a larger percentage. In other words, exchange-rate rigidity within a block of currencies increases volatility of the rates of currencies outside the block.

The amplitude of the fluctuations of the exchange rate between dollar and D-mark since March 1973 has worried several half-hearted advocates of greater flexibility and has elicited from several fixed-rate worshippers a proud "I told you so". Using December 1972 as a base, the DM had appreciated vis-à-vis the dollar by 13.5% as of March 30, 1973, and by 40.1% as of July 6; the jump in the last week of this period, that is, from the 29th of June to the 6th of July was from 32.9% to 40.1%, which is a substantial jump. The turnaround from the DM peak or dollar trough was quite drastic; by January 25, 1974 the DM was down to an appreciation of 13.2%, that is, lower than it had been in March 1973. Since the end of January 1974 the dollar has moved down again – within four weeks the appreciation of the DM increased from 13.2% to 21.7% against the December 1972 benchmark.

How did the German foreign-exchange reserves behave during these ups and downs? You will remember that after early July 1973 *controlled* floating, and therefore accumulations and decumulations of reserves, had become the order of the day. (Charlie Coombs, in his latest report, claims that "the speculative wave was abruptly broken on July 9 as reports circulated of an imminent resumption of exchange operations by the Federal Reserve". The Fed in fact supported the dollar in five instances but, subsequently, with the dollar rising in the markets, both the Fed and the Treasury purchased foreign currencies to repay debts to other countries and to the I.M.F.) The German Bundesbank increased its exchange holdings from $25 billion at the end of June to 28 billion at the end of September 1973 but then reduced them in November, December, and January; its holdings at the end of January 1974 were only $24 billion, or less than at any time during the preceding ten months. Official sales of foreign exchange, presumably dollars, by the ten industrial countries of Europe during the month of January amounted to $3.8 billion, evidently enough to stop the recovery of the dollar and reverse the movement. I wonder whether in the face of these official sales we have to resort to the hypothesis that a renewed loss of confidence in the dollar on the part of private speculators has caused the renewed weakening of the dollar in the markets.

The steep roller-coaster of the dollar may be the major spectacle in the story of floating currencies, but there were other surprising happenings. In the minds of many observers, the Swiss franc and the German mark are linked as the two strongest currencies, and the common belief has been that they have usually moved in step with each other. What have been the facts? On May 25, 1973, the German mark was down by 5% against the Swiss franc, taking the end of 1972 as our base. Subsequently the mark rose, and by the end of September 1973 it was 5% above the franc; on November 2 this appreciation reached 5.7%. From this peak the mark fell rather quickly and all through December and January the relation between the two currencies was within 1% of the rates of December 1972. In February 1974, the Swiss franc started to rise, and on February 22, the German mark was again down to a depreciation of 3.2%. Thus, to repeat, over a period of twelve months the mark went down to minus 5%, then up to plus 5.7%, and down again to minus 3.2% against the Swiss franc. I do not know to what extent these fluctuations were accompanied by official interventions in the foreign-exchange market.

I am not going to go into the stories of the French franc and Japanese yen; they have been told on recent occasions, especially when their exchange rates exhibited unexpected large degrees of flexibility. But we must now ask whether all the allegedly disruptive fluctuations on the exchange markets disrupted foreign trade or reduced the volume of trade, as it had been predicted by large numbers of practitioners and also a few economists. The answer is: "definitely not". The volume of world trade increased during the first half of 1973 at an annual rate of 9.5%, which compares with an average growth rate of 8.3% over the ten years 1960 to 1970.[1] The figures for the full year 1973 will probably be similar. The increase, admittedly, was partly due to higher prices, but, in any case, the rise in world trade exceeded by far the rise in world production.

The continued growth of world trade does not mean that individual exporters

[1]The International Monetary Fund, Annual Report, September 1973.

have not suffered losses or reductions of profits; indeed, with large fluctuations in exchange rates we should expect the exporters of different countries to take turns in faring well and faring badly. Since businessmen have a habit of complaining when business is bad but remaining silent when business is good, we must take it for granted that only the complaints are recorded. Even when the volume of world trade expands at record rates, we shall hear how the fluctuations in the foreign-exchange market are killing the export business.

One complaint of the people in foreign trade is probably justified: the spreads between the buying and selling prices of foreign exchange become wider during periods of wider fluctuations. These are risk premiums which bankers collect from their customers. Of course, unless bankers take wrong positions, these risk premiums swell the banks' profits from their foreign-exchange operations. We have heard of some banks which suffered heavy losses from poor speculations, but the large majority of banks have made record profits from their foreign-exchange business. Since many bankers had predicted chaos and collapse to result from a system of flexible exchange rates, they will now dramatize the heavy risks they have to take and will say little or nothing about the fine profits they are making.

A wise central banker – yes, Harry, there are a few – has recently said that one cannot come to a sensible appraisal of the experience with floating currencies on the basis of talks with individual businessmen and individual bankers. Individual experiences have been different from firm to firm, bank to bank, country to country. Only an analysis of the total picture can give us useful clues. Why only clues and not answers? Because the analysis of what has actually happened will allow us no judgment if we have not a comparative analysis of what would have happened under alternative systems. And since this is the point where I came in, and you would hardly want to sit through another reel of my talking picture, I had better recognize that the time has come for me to yield the floor to the next member of this panel.

Chapter 14.3

EXPERIENCES WITH FLOATING RATES

Assar LINDBECK

I would like to discuss four aspects of the recent experiences with a quasi-floating exchange-rate system: (1) the frequency and size of the fluctuations of exchange rates; (2) the consequences for foreign trade; (3) the implications for stabilization policy; and (4) the effects on economic integration and policy harmonization among countries. On the last point, I will concentrate on aspects relevant mainly for the West European scene.

(1) It would seem that the experiences during the past year support *neither* those who believed that a shift away from fixed rates would result in wild fluctuations of the rates *nor* those who argued that a system with floating rates would create a world with very small and continuous changes in exchange rates. As we know, "effective rates" have during the past year changed by some 10–15 percent up and down for various countries. And the movements have in several cases been cyclical (with temporary "over-shootings") rather than monotonic. Thus, perhaps the experiences have been somewhat disappointing as compared to conditions in Heaven, where all relative prices presumably are constant in a stationary state, but not necessarily as compared to the realistic alternative, which during the past year of turmoil in the international economy had been a continuous balance-of-payments crisis, temporary closing-downs of official foreign exchange markets, sudden discretionary changes in exchange rates, and drastic shifts in domestic economic policies for balance-of-payments reasons. It is, however, an open question to what extent the fluctuations in exchange rates in recent times reflect temporary conditions when we *move* from one exchange-rate system to another, or to what extent we would also expect such fluctuations when *having permanently* a system without fixed pegs.

(2) The choice of exchange-rate systems has, in the general discussion, often been tied to the issue of which system is supposed to be more favorable for international trade. On this issue, I think we have to draw the conclusion from past and present experience that *both* the previous system of fixed rates *and* the contemporary system of quasi-floating rates are quite consistent with a

rapid expansion of international trade. In fact, we have during the period of quasi-floating rates experienced one of the most rapid expansions in international trade ever – both for the volume and for the value of trade. Perhaps this suggests that both the academic and the practical discussions have overemphasized the importance for trade of uncertainty about the exchange rate. It is possible that the main importance of the exchange-rate system for trade is *not* the "direct" effect on trade due to uncertainty about exchange rates, but rather the indirect effect by way of the influence on the behavior of politicians.

More specifically, it is possible that the system which results in the smallest degree of policy intervention in foreign trade – by way of tariffs, import controls, capital controls, and internal demand management designed to influence trade – is also the most favorable system for international trade. As a system of floating rates provides an automatic equilibrating mechanism for the balance of payments, perhaps we are entitled to assume that the closer we are to floating rates the smaller are the political interventions in trade, and the more rapidly is international trade likely to expand.

(3) In the field of stabilization policy, the basic argument for floating (or flexible) exchange rates has been that such a system gives the individual country a considerable freedom to choose its own trade-off between inflation and unemployment, rather than being forced by balance-of-payments restrictions to accept a certain "non-desired" combination. More specifically, the argument is, as we know, that a country with stronger domestic inflationary tendencies than the outside world in a system with *fixed* rates has to create more unemployment than it really likes – to prevent balance-of-payments deficits. And a country with smaller inflationary tendencies than the outside world would be forced to "import" inflation from other countries if the exchange rate is not allowed to change.

In other words, whereas a fixed rate system, from time to time, tends to punish "the inflationary sinners" with unemployment, floating rates give "the inflationary sinners" the rate of inflation they "deserve", without forcing them to accept unemployment for balance-of-payments reasons. Thus, floating rates would be expected to give such countries a *more rapid* inflation than fixed rates, whereas countries with relatively small domestic inflationary tendencies would be expected to get a *slower* rate of inflation at floating rates than at fixed rates.

It is also quite likely that exchange-rate flexibility is getting increasingly effective as a means of influencing the domestic price level, relative to its effect on the balance of payments. The reason is that domestic wages and prices perhaps tend to adjust more rapidly than earlier to exchange-rate changes –

both discretionary and automatic. This could make exchange-rate policy more and more a "domestic" policy instrument, and less and less an instrument for the "external balance" only – except in a rather short (perhaps a one-to-two year) perspective.

These simple observations suggest a simple "policy-norm" for countries which tend to have stronger domestic inflationary tendencies than the outside world: The more we are in favor of full employment, the more we should be in favor of floating rates, and the more we are in favor of price stability, the more we should be in favor of fixed rates.

For countries with weaker domestic inflationary tendencies than the outside world, floating (or at least "flexible") rates are consistent with both full employment and a high degree of price stability.

It is interesting to notice that the two main "early" proponents of floating rates among professional economists, James Meade and Milton Friedman, seem to have been thinking about two quite different countries when recommending floating rates. Meade obviously wanted to help the "inflationary sinner" to avoid unemployment for balance-of-payments reasons, whereas Milton Friedman probably wanted to help countries with relatively weak domestic inflationary tendencies to avoid importing inflation from abroad.

If we look at recent experiences, it would indeed seem that both types of countries have tried to exploit the increased autonomy for national stabilization policy. The U.K. pursued an expansionary unemployment-reducing policy during 1972–73, and thus avoided the earlier stop–go policy for a while – until inflation became so great that the authorities for *domestic* reasons wanted to reduce inflation (in 1974). It is also clear that a number of countries have tried – in some cases with certain success, such as West Germany – to shield their domestic economies from international inflation by revaluation of the currency, i.e., by "bottling up" to some extent the inflation in the outside world; in 1974 West Germany seemed to get 4–5 percent less inflation than other OECD-countries.

This increased national autonomy for stabilization policy during the period of quasi-floating rates is probably a reason why the *variability* among countries in the rate of inflation has recently increased again, after a long period of falling variability during the system of fixed exchange rates.

(4) As I have just argued that floating rates probably are favorable both for free trade and for national autonomy in stabilization policy, I am led also to the conclusion that floating rates are the obvious choice for those who argue for integration of *markets* but not for *harmonization or stabilization policies.* This means, of course, that the kind of Europe that is likely to develop is a rather

different one in a system with floating rates than in a system with fixed rates. In a floating rate system, we are likely to get a system of customs unions, or of free-trade areas, with integrated markets and possibly some harmonization of other policies than stabilization policy, whereas a system of fixed rates, or even more currency unions, would make another Europe. However, it is not clear that this "other" Europe would be characterized by harmonized stabilization policy. It is possible that it would instead be a rather protectionist and mercantilist Europe, where the various countries try to guard themselves against the international forces, for instance to protect their balance of payments, by nationalist actions, as there is in such a world no automatic equilibrating price mechanism in the exchange market.

Is a Return to Fixed Rates Likely?

My final questing is whether a return to a fixed rate regime is likely. Let's first look briefly at the U.S.–European relations.

One way to approach this issue is to ask why a fixed rate system could function so relatively well for such a long time after the War. The explanation is, I believe, to be found in a number of *specific* historical circumstances. I would here like to emphasize just one: the disequilibrium situation, which was created by the fixed rate system, was a very special one. There was a permanent balance-of-payments deficit for the reserve currency country, i.e., the U.S., and this deficit happened to "fit" well with the wishes of the outside world, at that time, to increase their dollar reserve. Thus, we had a "flow disequilibrium" in the balance of payments between the U.S. and Europe, which happened to fit the "stock disequilibrium" for the reserve holdings of the outside world (wanting to accumulate dollar assets).

As long as the rest of the world wanted to accumulate dollar reserves, a deficit for the U.S. balance of payments was exactly what was required for the international monetary system. However, when the outside world had accumulated enough reserves, a situation emerged where international balance required that the U.S. balance of payments be returned to equilibrium. As instead the deficit *increased*, a crisis was bound to occur.

As the earlier historical circumstances, which were rather favorable for a fixed rate system, are not likely to occur again, the conclusion is, it seems to me, that a fixed rate system between the U.S. and Europe is not likely to reemerge.

The next question, then, is if Europe itself is a "viable" fixed rate area. I am inclined to answer "no" on this question too, as factor mobility within Europe is hardly much higher than factor mobility between the U.S. and Europe, and as it does not seem much easier to harmonize stabilization policy within Europe than it is between the U.S. and Europe. Moreover, there seems to be no good reason to expect prevailing comparative advantages, and the relative competitiveness of nations, to change less in the future than in the past. The conclusion is, I believe, that Europe is not a viable fixed rate area. Moreover, it is hardly possible to force the European countries to coordinate their policies by keeping fixed rates. It is more likely that a fixed rate system would break down than that the countries would give up their national autonomy in stabilization policy. Or to quote Harry Johnson in a somewhat similar context: "it will be the dam rather than the river that has to yield".

Sometimes a currency union for Europe is motivated by the existence of a common currency system within the United States. However, it should be noticed that the adjustments to a common currency within the United States during the eighteenth and nineteenth centuries took place in a period when the policy ambitions concerning full employment were exceedingly modest. The Common Market in Europe, by contrast, is contemplating a system of fixed exchange rates, or even a common currency area, in a period of high ambitions concerning the employment level. It is therefore exceedingly difficult to believe that fixed rates can be forced upon these countries before a fundamental similarity in preferences and trade-off opportunities have emerged within Europe.

The conclusion of all this is, I believe, that the major European countries are not, as a group, much closer to a "viable" fixed exchange area than is North America and Western Europe taken together. Thus, a rather high flexibility of exchange rates among the major nations in the West is the most likely development for the future.

Intervention

Mr. Kolm has asked the following question: "Is not your assertion that managed floats is the only feasible system a tautology since both fixed rates and purely floating rates are specific cases of it?"

It is true, of course, that we may visualize a more or less "continuous" spectrum between complete rigidity and complete flexibility of the exchange rates; on that ground we could perhaps say that fixed and floating rates are just specific cases of a managed float. However, the present system of managed float is, I believe, different enough both from the previous system of fixed rates and from a system of "freely" floating rates that it nevertheless makes sense to talk about a "managed float" as a specific system, different from both fixed rates and freely floating rates. From that point of view, I don't see why it would be a "tautology" to say that a managed float, rather than fixed rates and freely floating rates, is the "only feasible" system in the world where we live today.

Chapter 14.4

THE FUTURE OF FLOATING RATES

Harry G. JOHNSON

Discussions of floating exchange rates are in many respects like floating exchange rates themselves. Participants affirm that they would much prefer to sit rigidly in their accustomed seats, and that when they are obliged to float in front of the audience they will hold forth only for the minimum possible time and resume their seats in passive rigidity as soon as possible. But once they begin to float the discussion, they find it very difficult to stop: there are always incidents of interest that need to be dealt with, or new difficulties that need to be surmounted, before it is safe to sit down in confidence that one has found the proper point at which to return to immobility. One is tempted to continue indefinitely; and only overt indications that the audience is getting bored eventually force one to terminate the euphoric experience.

Discussions of floating rates by their proponents have a natural tendency to become protracted, through the natural propensity of Cassandras to say "I told you so" with chapter and verse of detail. In the course of one's life as a floating rate proponent – a career that itself requires great intestinal fortitude – one soon acquires a long checklist of cases in point illustrating the foolishness of sticking inappropriately to fixed rates – and the thick skin required to take a suffering audience through the list once again. On the other side, one acquires a checklist of the reasons why in individual cases the authorities were right to stick by their guns so long as they had any ammunition, or even credible-looking packing cases marked "Ammunition", at their command, and why the resort to floating rates was either a Pyrrhic victory or a subtle defeat for the floating-rate cause. The debate thus becomes a war of attrition in the marshalling of cases in point.

My assignment on this occasion, to discuss the future of floating exchange rates, fortunately for the audience, debars me from presenting yet another review of the troop of veterans of past international monetary debates. The future provides no case-studies to differ in interpreting. Consequently I can be fairly brief in impeding the audience from asking its questions of my learned colleagues.

To begin with, I think it fair to say that the experience of floating exchange rates since March 1973 has already shown that most of the standard objections to floating rates have not held water. Earlier modern experiences could be dismissed as special cases, in terms either of the countries involved – e.g., Canada, or Germany in 1969 – or of the nature *and* duration of the experience, e.g., the brief interval of "dirty floating" in the autumn of 1971 between the "New Economic Policy" and the Smithsonian Agreement. The period of general floating since March 1973 has not been one of temporary transition; and despite the dire predictions, interpretations, and policy projections of the spring and early summer of 1973, the system has worked broadly as it should have. To be specific, predictions of a sharp trend towards proliferation of capital market controls have not materialized; it has become clear that the alleged pressure for such controls was associated with the desire of some of the European countries to maintain fixity of their rates with each other, and not a consequence of floating as such; and in the event instead of a proliferation of controls there has been abandonment of the objective of a common European currency.

The success of the floating rate system, and the need for continuing with it rather than hastily moving back towards a fixed rate regime, had already become clear by the time of the Nairobi meetings of the International Monetary Fund, well before the oil crisis began. What the proceedings of the Committee of Twenty demonstrated, in brief, and to quote Lewis Carroll, was that "all the King's horses and all the King's men couldn't put Humpty Dumpty together again". In more academic language, one might say that, like the gold standard before it, the I.M.F. system rested on a foundation of mythological belief and conventional assumptions, conceptions, and responses that, once shaken by severe crisis, resolved into the underlying conflicting national interests whose basic inconsistencies they had previously served to disguise, interests that it is inevitably difficult to envisage re-harmonizing by intelligent reconstruction of a rational and logical international monetary system.

The subsequent oil crisis, and the disintegration of concern for regional and international cooperation in a scramble for national self-protection against general scarcity induced by political as well as economic considerations, has led governments and international monetary institutions and officials to resign themselves to postponing a return to a fixed rates system until such indefinite time as the energy crisis has blown over, or the new high-oil-price world economy has settled down. Thus floating exchange rates as a world monetary system seem established for an indefinite period ahead. This, or so those of us who have more or less consistently advocated flexible rates firmly believe, should be good for the world economy, the cause of international peace and goodwill, the inculcation of proper humility among the central banking fraternity, and in general the brotherhood of man. Whether it is or not, it will undoubtedly be good for ourselves as professional experts on the international monetary system, whether oriented towards pure theory, empirical research, or policy discussion and prescription, since for the most part all we need do to present the world with fresh exhibitions of our artistic talents is to turn the pictures in our academic galleries upside down, and, in Sir John Hick's terminology for demand theory, convert our balance-of-payments models and analysis from "p-theory" to "q-theory" (i.e., from the effects of prices on quantities to the effects of quantities on prices).

It is worth noting in passing that the recent willingness to live for the time with floating exchange rates itself rests largely on basic misunderstandings of balance-of-payments theory on the part of national government and I.M.F. officials. There is, in standard monetary theory, absolutely no presumption that a rise in the price of a particular commodity achieved through the establishment of a monopoly or cartel will lead the rest of the community to run down its cash balances or the monopolist to run his up (apart from secondary influences of redistributions of real income on desired holdings of real balances, which raise some tricky conceptual questions about the relation between nominal and real balances when relative prices change). But the short official argument for delaying international monetary reform is that nothing can be done until it becomes clearer which countries will have the deficits and which the surpluses – a proposition which raises another question of logic, namely, why do you have to know the names of the saints and the sinners before you can devise a system that deals out justice impartially to everyone?

The more interesting question is whether, assuming that the disturbances due to the recent oil crisis, and in a more fundamental sense to the emergence of world inflation at erratically differing national rates, that led to the breakdown of the fixed exchange-rate system initially, settle down into a more stable pattern of international economic relations in a few years, the world will continue with a floating rate system or will proceed to restore some sort of fixed exchange-rate system, presumably on the lines that have been emerging from the official and academic thinking of past few years.

My colleagues in the floating exchange-rate camp, so far as I can safely summarize their opinions in a common view, seem to me to be unjustifiably optimistic in this regard. Specifically, they tend to appear to be convinced that experience of floating rates, and the explosion of past myths about them by prolonged present experience, will win the day for economic logic and good sense. I am much more pessimistic. In general, there seems to me little reason to hope that fixed rate adherents previously impervious to rational argument will be any more persuaded by the test of empirical evidence and experience on which rational argument ultimately relies. It is at least as likely that they will continue to base their policy beliefs and preferences on magical and imaginal thinking and select and interpret experience to lend apparent practicality to courageous wishfulness.

I have two reasons for my pessimism. The first is my reading of the lessons of economic history in the relevant historical period. One has, in particular, the decision of the British to return to the pre-war gold value of the pound after the Napoleonic Wars and, much more painfully, after the First World War. This established an important reference point for thinking on what may be called the tradition of Western economic culture, due to the importance of Britain in the world monetary system until the 1967 devaluation of the sterling, and of the British literature in the formation of current-day international monetary economic theory. Again, the United State's historical experiences with floating rates prior to 1971 and 1973 – the post-civil-war period 1862–79 much cited by contemporary American "monetarists", and the brief transition period of revaluing the dollar in 1934–35 – were dominated by the ultimate objective of return to a fixed rate system; and that has been true of American ideas of the reform of the international system since 1971 (and earlier, before floating was thinkable). And even a Canadian exchange-rate policy chauvinist has to admit both that Canadian officialdom and the Canadian public have typically been somewhat ashamed of the country's propensity to resort to floating rates, and on the other side that despite the utter stupidity of the return to a fixed rate in 1962 there was a grain of misplaced common sense in it, inasmuch as fixed rates would have reduced the damage done under floating rates by a perverse monetary policy.

There is therefore good reason, though reason based on economic sociology and "institutionalism" rather than economic theory, for expecting a return to fixed exchange rates eventually. And there is also a second good reason, flowing somewhat more directly from theory, for the same expectation. Theorists of floating rates have taken great care to emphasize, correctly, that floating rate *systems* do not necessarily mean violent fluctuations or trends in *actual* exchange rates. Instead, they emphasize that floating rates will tend to be stable if the economic conjuncture and economic policies are stable (with the corollary that fixed rates would get into equal or greater trouble under circumstances that would generate violent movements of floating rates). But the implication is that, normally, there will be little observable difference between a fixed and a floating rate system, inasmuch as both will result in stable rates with small random fluctuations that will either fall within the permissible band of fluctuation of a fixed rate around its parity or occasion so little official stabilization activity that the latter will be indistinguishable from private stabilizing speculation. Under these circumstances, it will obviously seem a small and unimportant step to refurbish and restore to use the paraphernalia of official fixity; indeed, as the British experience before the restoration of the gold standard in 1925 showed, the step may appear to be trivial even if it is not, since private speculation can be enlisted in the short run to produce the apparent fulfillment of the requirements for official fixing of the exchange rate even when the rate chosen is unsustainable in the longer run.

Given an emotional desire for exchange-rate fixity, and the strong likelihood that sooner or later the situation will arise in which the emotion will appear to be gratifiable at no real cost, one can, I think fairly confidently, predict that a fixed exchange-rate system of some kind will be restored, and the histories of the decline and fall of the gold standard and the I.M.F. system will be repeated in broad outline – though one hopes that next time the breaking point will be geared to occur at a lower threshold level of pain and strain.

Questions and Answers

(1) Mr. Bray: Do you think that the floating system is only valid for times of crises?

Certainly not. On the contrary, I would put the point the other way. Any exchange-rate system will work in times when there is no crisis – unless government is mad enough to create a crisis when none is necessary otherwise. But a fixed rate system by its very nature – at least under contemporary circumstances of governmental assumption of responsibility for maintaining full employment, stimulating economic growth, securing a just distribution of income, and promoting "high-technology" industries – generates crises which its managers cannot solve, eventually, without resorting to floating exchange rates. Fixed rates produce the times of crisis, and floating rates resolve them. One can go further, if one likes, and regard the question as a nonsense question to begin with. Times of crisis are created by fixed exchange rates; a floating rate system will never generate a balance-of-payments crisis, though problems of economic change or mistaken economic policy may well show up in a different form. Hence the proposition becomes: a floating system is a valid alternative only when you have a fixed rate system and the crisis that eventually destroys it. Obviously, a floating system cannot logically be regarded as an alternative to itself. In short, the right answer is that a fixed rate system is valid only for times of non-crisis, when a floating rate system would work just as well and prevent a crisis from ever arising.

(2) Mr. Maass: If the speakers were present at the C-20 meeting in Washington what recommendations would they make for a world system of floating rates, particularly for gold?

This is really two questions. If I were present at the C-20 meeting, I would recommend a floating rate system. That would automatically rule out the need for recommendations on a wide range of other issues, e.g., the need for indicators to signalize the desirability of exchange-rate changes, the desire of the less developed countries to impose a nuisance tax on the creation of paper international reserves, and the development of further stand-by credit facilities for countries in balance-of-payments difficulties. About the only subject that might call for more specific recommendations concerns devices for co-ordinating exchange-market interventions by central banks and exchange equalization account authorities to prevent their working at cross purposes, if, as is unfortunately only too likely, it is thought that such interventions are called for by the superior ability of officials using the public's money, as compared with private traders using their own money, to speculate profitability on the exchange markets.

The problem of gold in this context would be not an integral part of world monetary reform, but a question of regularizing the liquidation of a commodity formerly used as money, which has come to have a book value wildly different from its market value. The central problem is to enable monetary authorities to buy and sell gold without returning to a situation in which the price of gold is set by the monetary authorities and private speculators gamble on whether that price can be held at the agreed artificial level. It seems to me that the easiest system would be to allow the world's central banks to deal in gold at any price that suited them – the existence of the private market would then automatically become a reference point for the official price without the latter fixing the former – though probably subject to "surveillance" by an official committee representative of the chief official holders of gold.

(3) Mr. Jacques Rueff: I was surprised to hear several of our eminent debaters favor floating exchange rates without saying that they paralleled inflation rates of 10 to 12% and interest rates of 12 to 14%. Do they really think that such a system is really viable?

I am sometimes surprised by the capacity of our French colleagues to be surprised by phenomena that we, English-speaking people, consider pragmatically as normal facts of present life. It is quite normal to expect interest rates of 12 to 14% with inflation rates of 10 to 12%. In fact, this would imply a real return of 2% and perhaps even negative real interest rates if one takes account of income taxes. Therefore, nominal interest rates ("money interest rates") may be too low.

If present inflation was not viable, the governments and the public opinions would have stopped it. They are in a position to do it and economists have the required theory. Thus, inflation is "viable", in that sense that public opinions have a "revealed preference" for it.

The larger question which is asked by Mr. Rueff, is to know if a community can survive nowadays *as a society* when its government accepts an erratic inflation rate higher than 10%, after about two-hundred years of a slight tendency towards a decrease in prices, certainly broken at times by inflations clearly caused by large-scale wars, but during which social institutions have been founded on expectations of price stability and the assumption that nominal interest rates are identical to real interest rates. I agree with him, I do believe, if one considers his question as a question which transcends traditional borders of formal economic analysis.

INDEX OF NAMES

INDEX OF SUBJECTS